THE ULTIMATE
SCENE & MONOLOGUE
SOURCEBOOK

UPDATED AND EXPANDED EDITON

THE ULTIMATE
SCENE & MONOLOGUE
SOURCEBOOK

**AN ACTOR'S GUIDE TO OVER
1,000 MONOLOGUES AND SCENES FROM
MORE THAN 300 CONTEMPORARY PLAYS**

ED HOOKS

BACK STAGE BOOKS
An Imprint of Watson-Guptill Publications • New York

Senior Acquisitions Editor: Bob Nirkind
Editor: Cathy Hennessy
Designer: Meryl Levavi
Production Manager: Alyn Evans

First published in 2007 by Back Stage Books,
an imprint of Watson-Guptill Publications
The Crown Publishing Group, a division of
Random House, Inc., New York
www.crownpublishing.com

ISBN-10: 0-8230-9949-0
ISBN-13: 978-0-8230-9949-8

Library of Congress Cataloging-in-Publication Data

Hooks, Ed.
    The ultimate scene and monologue sourcebook : an actor's guide to over
1,000 monologues and scenes from more than 300 contemporary plays / by
Ed Hooks. — Updated and expanded ed.
        p. cm.
    Includes indexes.
    ISBN-13: 978-0-8230-9949-8 (alk. paper)
    ISBN-10: 0-8230-9949-0 (alk. paper)
    1. Acting—Bibliography. 2. Monologues—Bibliography. 3. Drama—20th
century—Bibliography. 4. Drama—21st century—Bibliography. I. Title.
    Z5784.A27H66 2007
    [PN2080]
    016.808.8245—dc22

                                        2007016896

Printed in the United States of America

First printing, 2007

    4 5 6 7 8 9 / 15 14 13 12 11

"I had a friend once said, 'Norman, I don't care if there are only three people out front, or if the audience laugh when they shouldn't, or don't when they should; one person, just one person is certain to know and understand. And I act for him.' That's what my friend said."

The Dresser BY RONALD HARWOOD

FOR DAGNY

"…into that good night."

DYLAN THOMAS

ACKNOWLEDGMENTS

First, thanks must go to Mark Glubke and Robert Nirkind, senior editors at Back Stage Books. I was late—very late—with this final manuscript owing to unforeseen developments in my personal life, and these people could not have been more compassionate or patient. I am deeply appreciative to them both and to the publisher at Watson-Guptill.

Second, I want to thank Matthew Love and his top-notch team at Drama Book Shop in New York City. As has been the case for many years, Drama Book Shop is the best of the best if you are looking for stage material, and I am fortunate that Matthew allowed me limitless access to the plays on the store shelves when I was working on this revision. Without his assistance, I would not have been able to consider the many hundreds of plays I ultimately used.

Talented friends have offered suggestions of plays and scenes, and I am grateful to them. In particular, thanks to Alice Elliott, Russell Treyz, Jean Schiffman, and Le Anne Rumbel.

And, as always, my best editor and cheerleader is my wife, Cally. She keeps the wind gently at my back with her encouragement and support.

CONTENTS

INTRODUCTION

The first edition of *The Ultimate Scene and Monologue Sourcebook* was published in 1994. Many of the plays referenced in that first edition are classics or standards, and so I have left them in this new edition. But there are many revisions: I deleted approximately 15 percent of the plays from the first edition because, after reconsidering them, they felt out-of-date to me, topically irrelevant, or perhaps had gone out of print. And I replaced them with as many new ones. The overall text of this new handbook is actually longer than that of the first edition.

As before, the standard I applied to inclusion was whether or not a play or monologue would work in an acting class or audition. As all professional actors know, conflicts and/or obstacles provide essential elements of a scene or monologue, and I have paid particular attention to where they arise. It is not interesting or theatrically satisfying for an audience to watch two characters on stage simply talking about something. There must be negotiation, either with oneself, with the other character, and/or with the situation. One can be certain that the scenes and monologues from the plays referenced in this book are well structured and playable.

I personally learned a lot about acting while performing in original plays off-Broadway and off-off-Broadway. The challenge with original plays is that while the work itself may be flawed, the actor must nevertheless make it work. It is a different creative process from working on, say, *The Glass Menagerie* by Tennessee Williams. You know from the start that a Williams play will work. It is up to you, the actor, to find a key that opens it. You don't have to wonder whether the play itself is weak. Everything in this volume has been kitchen-tested in front of paying audiences at one time or another. In short, the plays themselves work. That doesn't mean they are all the modern-day equivalent of Shakespeare, but it does mean that actors and acting teachers can trust them.

HOW TO USE THIS BOOK

The Ultimate Scene and Monologue Sourcebook is a reference tool. It is not like most monologue or scene books. In it, you will find a synopsis of each play, descriptions of scenes, first and last lines, plus notes that I consider pertinent. I may, for example, suggest that a particular play is best for experienced actors rather than for beginners. Pinter, for instance, is usually not the best playwright to start with during initial training (as opposed, say, to Sam Shepard or Arthur Miller) because so much of the conflict is under the surface. When you find something in the book that you want to work on, you will still have to go out and find the complete play. I have not printed entire excerpted scenes or monologues, which is the case in most scene and monologue books. I think it essential that an actor read the whole play.

The book contains seven parts, which you can cross-reference. Part One lists the plays alphabetically and includes a synopsis and analysis of each. If you read through the synopses beginning to end, you likely will find descriptions of plays you want to work on. At the end of each synopsis entry is a reference as to what sort of scenes from the play you will find to work on. There are parts in the book for Male/Female Scenes, Female/Female Scenes, Male/Male Scenes, Female Monologues—and so on. When you find something you like in the synopses, you can easily flip to the appropriate cross-referenced section for further descriptions of individual scenes or monologues.

In the last pages of the book, you will find multiple indexes. You can search the material by playwright, scene type, age, gender, or ethnicity. If you are specifically looking for a play by Eugene O'Neill to work on, then go first to the Playwright index and look under O'Neill. That will tell you on which pages to look for the material.

Finally, as you use *The Ultimate Scene and Monologue Sourcebook,* please keep the following provisos in mind. Just because I reference only one or two scenes from a given play does not mean the play does not contain other suitable material. I have tried to list only what I consider to be the strongest material, but it is entirely possible that, when you read the entire play, you will find something you like better.

Whenever possible, I use acting editions as source material. Acting editions are often different from library editions and can lead to a bit of confusion if you are not careful. Take, for instance, the work of Tennessee Williams. He originally wrote many of his plays in a three-act format, but the works also appear in two-act versions because he continued to fiddle with them long after he "finished" them. To a lesser degree, I encountered the same kind of problem with the works of Lillian Hellman and William Inge. As a result, if you select a scene or monologue that is referenced here but then can't find the material in the compilation from your local library, don't despair. It is probably in the text somewhere; you just need to do a little more investigating. If, however, you are unable to locate the scene or monologue in question, you might wind up having to order an acting edition of the play. For this reason, and because many of the referenced plays can't be found in libraries, I included contact information for a few major theatrical retailers.

Ed Hooks
Chicago
July 2007

PART ONE

PLAY SYNOPSES/ANALYSES

ABSENT FRIENDS
by Alan Ayckbourn (Samuel French)

SYNOPSIS: Colin's fiancée recently drowned, and a group of former friends have invited him to a tea party to lift his spirits. The problem is that his friends have marital and other personal problems of their own, and Colin is quite happy with his sentimental memories. The more they try to take his mind off his deceased lover, the more he insists on talking about her, which depresses everyone. He then good-naturedly tries to solve their problems, which makes the get-together even more disastrous.

ANALYSIS: This play is one of Alan Ayckbourn's less-often performed comedies, significant for its lack of physical action. For the most part, the characters sit around a table talking, so the humor comes from what the audience members discover about their lives. All levels.

SCENES/MONOLOGUES: Male Monologues (1), Female Monologues (1), Female/Female Scenes (1)

ABSURD PERSON SINGULAR
by Alan Ayckbourn (Samuel French)

SYNOPSIS: Three couples gather on three consecutive Christmas Eves, and the action takes place in their respective kitchens. In the course of these three years, the characters go through reversals of fortune. The struggling couple in Act I become real-estate moguls in Act III, while the bank manager who lends them money in Act I watches his marriage and business fall apart at the same time. The third couple, an architect and his wife, go from blue skies to attempted suicide.

ANALYSIS: This 1972 comedy starts out with humor, leans toward farce in Act II, and by the end, turns dark. With Alan Ayckbourn, the structure is frequently the thing. All levels.

SCENES/MONOLOGUES: Male Monologues (2), Three-Person Scenes (1)

AFTER THE FALL
by Arthur Miller (Dramatists Play Service)

SYNOPSIS: The action takes place in Quentin's mind and memory as he tries desperately to find meaningful connections in his life. There is no plot per se; the scenes jump around like the workings of his mind, involving confrontations with former wives, as well as his parents, brother, and business associates.

ANALYSIS: Difficult, intellectually challenging material appropriate for advanced actors.

SCENES/MONOLOGUES: Male Monologues (1), Male/Female Scenes (3)

AGNES OF GOD
by John Pielmeier (Samuel French)

SYNOPSIS: A troubled young nun with practically no exposure to the outside world surprises everyone by having a baby at the convent. At birth, the infant is killed and stuffed into a wastebasket. Who is the father? Who killed the baby? Was Agnes alone in the room when the baby was born? She claims not to remember anything about the event and refuses to name the father, even under hypnosis. The core of the drama focuses on the efforts of a court-appointed psychiatrist to determine whether Agnes is sane and the psychiatrist's conflict with Catholicism and Agnes's Mother Superior.

ANALYSIS: This marvelously theatrical drama, which is played out on a bare stage, is chock-full of tense scenes that address universal issues. Each of the characters is strongly defined. Amanda Plummer won a Tony for playing Agnes in the 1982 production. All levels.

SCENES/MONOLOGUES: Female Monologues (2), Female/Female Scenes (3)

AH, WILDERNESS!
by Eugene O'Neill (Samuel French)

SYNOPSIS: An innocent coming-of-age story set on the Connecticut shore, July 4, 1906. Exploding fireworks provide the backdrop for exploding passions, both romantic and political, for sixteen-year-old Richard Miller, fresh out of high school and already a confirmed individualist. When he presents his lady love with verses of purple poetry from the pages of Algernon Charles Swinburne, all hell breaks loose. Everyone gets upset for a while but in the end, the young lovers are together once again—and probably forever.

ANALYSIS: Completed in 1942, this is Eugene O'Neill's only full-length comedy. It draws on his memories of a boyhood love for one Maibelle Scott. The famous George M. Cohan played Nat Miller in the first production. All levels.

SCENES/MONOLOGUES: Male Monologues (2), Male/Female Scenes (2)

ALL MY SONS
by Arthur Miller (Dramatists Play Service)

SYNOPSIS: The background: Joe Keller and Steve Deever were neighbors and business partners until their company sold defective airplane-engine parts during World War II, a crime for which Steve went to prison. Joe maintained his innocence, served a very short prison sentence, and continued to build a prosperous business alone. But he was actually more at fault than Steve. The defective parts resulted in twenty-one plane crashes, and when Steve's Army-officer son, Larry, learned the truth about his father's complicity, he was so deeply ashamed, he committed suicide in combat.

During the play, Joe's youngest son, Chris, becomes engaged to Larry's former fiancée, Ann, and everyone in the family finally has to confront the facts of Joe's crime. Unable to live with the guilt of his actions once they are out in the open, Joe commits suicide.

ANALYSIS: A classic from 1947 about the decisions people make in life and their consequences. Elia Kazan won the very first Tony Award for directing the play. All levels.

SCENES/MONOLOGUES: Male Monologues (1), Female/Female Scenes (1), Male/Female Scenes (1)

AMADEUS
by Peter Shaffer (Samuel French)

SYNOPSIS: The story of Mozart's life and early death as told by Antonio Salieri, a less-talented, fatally jealous composer and court favorite. The premise of the play is that Salieri himself orchestrated Mozart's tragic demise.

ANALYSIS: Brilliant in concept and presentation, *Amadeus* unfortunately provides little opportunity for scenework. It won Tony Awards for Best Play and Best Director in 1980. All levels.

SCENES/MONOLOGUES: Male Monologues (1), Male/Female Scenes (1)

AMEN CORNER, THE
by James Baldwin (Samuel French)

SYNOPSIS: Sister Margaret Alexander is the pastor of a small Harlem church located above the apartment where she lives with her son, David, and her older sister. To all appearances, Margaret is a passionate, committed spokeswoman for the Lord. But her entire life starts to crumble when her former husband, Luke, shows up, clearly nearing the end of his life. His presence in the home rivets the couple's eighteen-year-old son, who has been trying to decide whether or not to follow in the footsteps of his musician father, a life that his mother claims is sinful. Luke also affects Margaret, reminding her of the pleasures of marriage she left behind ten years ago when she walked out with son David.

Meanwhile, the church elders are watching this family drama play out and have come to question Margaret's sanctity. They conspire to have her removed as a pastor. In the final moments of the play, David leaves home for good, determined to be a professional musician, and Margaret acknowledges her love for Luke as he dies in her arms. Although she'll no longer lead the small church, she has found a more profound peace in human love and acceptance.

ANALYSIS: A lovely 1961 drama by a major American writer, full of insight and poetry. The entire cast is African-American. All levels.

SCENES/MONOLOGUES: Male Monologues (3), Female Monologues (1), Male/Male Scenes (1), Male/Female Scenes (2)

AMERI/CAIN GOTHIC
by Paul Carter Harrison (*Totem Voices: Plays from the Black World Repertory*, edited by Paul Carter Harrison, Grove Press)

SYNOPSIS: Harper, a private investigator responsible for reconnoitering a Memphis motel before Martin Luther King's arrival, is distracted from his job when he comes across Cass. She is a recluse living in the rooming house from which the fatal bullet is ultimately fired. Cass is suffering from a grave sense of imminent violence and solicits Harper's help.

ANALYSIS: Difficult two-character play requiring strong, intelligent, trusting actors. A continual air of danger and sexual attraction permeates the drama.

SCENES/MONOLOGUES: Male Monologues (1), Female Monologues (1), Male/Female Scenes (1)

AMERICAN BUFFALO
by David Mamet (Samuel French)

SYNOPSIS: Three small-time crooks plot to steal a coin collection. Don Dubrow, the owner of the junk shop where they hang out, is calling the shots. Teach maneuvers to cut Bob, his rather slow-witted gofer, out of the job and the money. In the end, violence erupts, and the robbery doesn't take place.

ANALYSIS: This play, David Mamet's first to reach Broadway, won the Drama Critics' Circle Award for Best American Play in 1977. All levels.

SCENES/MONOLOGUES: Male/Male Scenes (3)

AMERICAN PLAN, THE
by Richard Greenberg (Dramatists Play Service)

SYNOPSIS: Eva Adler, her daughter, Lili, and their maid, Olivia, are spending another summer in the Catskills. Lili meets, falls in love with, and becomes engaged to a nice young man staying in the hotel across the lake. Then everything unravels as the audience learns that the young man is gay. Lili is emotionally frail, and Eva is haunted by memories of Nazi Germany. The play covers a twenty-year span from the 1950s through the 1970s.

ANALYSIS: Very complex characters populate this finely imagined 1991 play. At first it appears almost like a romantic comedy but then turns quite dark. Most individual scenes are fairly straightforward, but the subtext takes them to a different level. This makes for some interesting acting challenges. For sophisticated actors.

SCENES/MONOLOGUES: Male Monologues (1), Male/Male Scenes (1), Male/Female Scenes (3)

ANASTASIA
by Marcelle Maurette (adapted by Guy Bolton, Samuel French)

SYNOPSIS: Bounine, former aide-de-camp to the late Russian tsar Nicholas II and more recently a cab driver in Berlin, discovers a young woman who has confessed to a hospital nurse that she is the Tsar's only-surviving daughter, Anastasia. When Bounine confronts her with this rumor, she denies it, claiming that she just made up the story for something to do. However, he is aware that if the real Anastasia were ever to surface, she would inherit the huge fortune left behind when all the other members of her family were assassinated in 1918. So Bounine and some unscrupulous cohorts conspire to pass the woman off as the real Anastasia with the intention of gaining access to the money.

The trouble with the men's scheme is that the woman is inconsistent; sometimes she cooperates and sometimes she doesn't. She may, in fact, be brain-damaged from a violent factory explosion. Nonetheless, the men persist until they finally persuade the woman to go alone with their plan. Then, at the very moment she is to be presented to the public and the press, she walks out the back door and disappears into the streets. The play ends with a strong implication that the woman may indeed be the real Anastasia, but life has become too complicated for her to handle.

ANALYSIS: This 1954 play deals with a large subject. There are several good scenes. All levels.

SCENES/MONOLOGUES: Female/Female Scenes (1), Male/Female Scenes (3)

ANDERSONVILLE TRIAL, THE
by Saul Levitt (Dramatists Play Service)

SYNOPSIS: Based on the actual 1865 trial of Confederate officer Henry Wirz, who was in charge of the infamous Andersonville Prison in Georgia during the Civil War. Approximately 14,000 Union soldiers died there, most of whom fell prey to bad food and water, insufficient clothing, and disease. Wirz was found guilty of conspiracy to kill the soldiers and was executed.

ANALYSIS: Courtroom dramas can be fun because they frequently address moral issues head-on. On the other hand, the plays provide few two-person scenes. Young George C. Scott played Colonel Chipman in the 1959 premiere. All levels.

SCENES/MONOLOGUES: Male/Male Scenes (1), Male Monologues (1)

AND MISS REARDON DRINKS A LITTLE
by Paul Zindel (Dramatists Play Service)

SYNOPSIS: The ultimate dysfunctional family, full of religious guilt and plenty of dirty little secrets. Probably set in Queens, New York, although the location isn't specified. Three sisters work in the educational system: Anna is a high-school chemistry teacher, Catherine is an assistant principal, and Ceil is a member of the school board. After their mother's recent death, Anna had a nervous breakdown and was sexually involved with a high-school student. His parents are now threatening to sue the school unless Anna is sent to a hospital for psychological treatment. The action of the play revolves around Ceil and Catherine's struggle to decide whether to have Anna committed. Ultimately, they do put her in the hospital.

ANALYSIS: Well-written, caustic. Played Broadway in 1971. Estelle Parsons was nominated for a Tony, and Rae Allen won one. All levels.

SCENES/MONOLOGUES: Female/Female Scenes (1), Three-Person Scenes (1)

ANGELS IN AMERICA: A GAY FANTASIA ON NATIONAL THEMES, PART I: MILLENNIUM APPROACHES
by Tony Kushner (Theatre Communications Group)

SYNOPSIS: A simple description of the characters and plot is not only impossible but also can't begin to do justice to this remarkable play, which blends reality with fantasy, humans with angels, and the past with the present—and then asks the audience to look at the meaning of it all through the rosy prism of Ronald Reagan's vision of America. The vast canvas of this challenging work is anchored by two couples, one gay and one heterosexual, whose respective relationships dissolve and recombine in unexpected ways.

ANALYSIS: *Angels in America: A Gay Fantasia on National Themes* is presented in two parts, the first of which is *Millennium Approaches,* and the second of which is *Perestroika*. Graphic and frequently disturbing as the play wrestles with erotic and political themes, scenework is appropriate for experienced actors. The play won the 1993 Pulitzer Prize as well as four Tony Awards, including Best Play.

SCENES/MONOLOGUES: Male/Female Scenes (3), Male/Male Scenes (2)

ANNA CHRISTIE
by Eugene O'Neill (*Anna Christie, The Emperor Jones, The Hairy Ape;* Vintage Books)

SYNOPSIS: Anna has traveled from middle-America to New York City for a reunion with her father, whom she hasn't seen for fifteen years. She moves in with him on the coal barge he captains and is happy in the fresh sea air and crisp fog. A few days later, a group of shipwrecked sailors are brought on board, and Anna immediately falls in love with one of them, an Irishman named Mat Burke. He proposes marriage but, strangely, Anna won't accept. Then, in a tumultuous confession, she tells Mat and her father that she isn't the innocent farm girl they presume her to be, and that she was abused by her foster family and had turned to prostitution. The men react not with compassion and understanding, but with horror and anger. Both feel betrayed by Anna's sordid past. When they stumble off on a drunken binge, Anna concludes that all men are despicable and that reform is futile.

But as Anna prepares to return to the street, the men come back, full of remorse. Mat still wants to marry her after all, and her father has made arrangements for her financial security while he is away at sea. Ironically, the two men are going to ship out on the same boat to Cape Town. Anna accepts Mat's proposal and, as the men depart, she promises to make a nice home for them to return to.

ANALYSIS: Eugene O'Neill took a great deal of heat for—and was defensive about—putting a too-pat happy ending on *Anna Christie*. Still, this 1921 drama popularized O'Neill's name once and for all and won him a second Pulitzer Prize. Greta Garbo's first "talking" film was the 1930 version of *Anna Christie*. All levels.

SCENES/MONOLOGUES: Male/Female Scenes (3), Female Monologues (1)

ANOTHER ANTIGONE
by A. R. Gurney, Jr. (Dramatists Play Service)

SYNOPSIS: Henry Harper is an intellectually aloof teacher of Greek drama at a Boston college. One of his senior students, Judy Miller, hands in a new version of the Greek classic *Antigone*, readapting it so that it now reads as an antinuclear-arms statement. Unimpressed by Judy's efforts, Henry considers the rewrite to be "another *Antigone*," lacking in discipline and ignorant of the meaning of tragedy, just like similar efforts made by previous students; he refuses to give her a passing grade. When Judy decides to follow through with her play, to see it produced at the college, teacher and student divide into warring camps. In the spirit of Greek tragedy, these opposing forces cause each other grief.

ANALYSIS: This is a relatively unknown gem from A. R. Gurney, Jr.; intellectually challenging, full of excellent scenes and monologues, beautifully written and conceived. All levels.

SCENES/MONOLOGUES: Male/Female Scenes (4), Male Monologues (1), Female Monologues (1)

APPROACHING ZANZIBAR
by Tina Howe (Samuel French)

SYNOPSIS: The Blossom family drives 2,000 miles from Hastings, New York, to Taos, New Mexico, in order to visit Aunt Olivia, a famous artist, before she dies. On the way they frolic, argue, meet strangers, have nightmares, play jokes, sleep in tents, and learn about life.

ANALYSIS: The sole reason I am including this play is because it contains an excellent monologue for an older actress. All levels.

SCENES/MONOLOGUES: Female Monologues (1)

ART
by Yasmina Reza (Faber and Faber)

SYNOPSIS: Serge buys a white-on-white modern painting for a small fortune. His long-time friend Marc cannot understand how someone he thinks he knows so well could do something so stupid. The purchase calls into question the values held by each man.

ANALYSIS: This is wonderful material for acting class. Written in the British vernacular, you may have to adapt it a bit if you want to do it American style.

SCENES/MONOLOGUES: Male/Male Scenes (2)

AUTUMN GARDEN, THE
by Lillian Hellman (Dramatists Play Service)

SYNOPSIS: Constance Tuckerman hosts the same visitors each year at her summer boardinghouse near the Gulf of Mexico, about one hundred miles from New Orleans. Most of the people are middle-aged or older, facing the autumn of their lives, and the play, which takes place during September 1949, provides a platform for them to take stock of their personal values and prospects.

ANALYSIS: Lillian Hellman must have been influenced by Anton Chekhov's manner of probing the human character when she wrote *The Autumn Garden*. She and producer Kermit Bloomgarden even hired Harold Clurman of Group Theatre fame to direct this character-driven 1951 work on Broadway. It received mixed notices and closed after 102 performances. It is excellent fodder for scene study, however. All levels.

SCENES/MONOLOGUES: Male Monologues (1), Female/Female Scenes (1), Male/Female Scenes (3)

BABY DANCE, THE
by Jane Anderson (Samuel French)

SYNOPSIS: Rachel and Richard are a childless, upwardly mobile, educated Hollywood showbiz couple who advertise for, and then decide to purchase, the as-yet-unborn child of Wanda and Al, a dirt-poor Louisiana couple. Act I takes place in Wanda and Al's trailer home, and Act II is set in the hospital on the day the baby is born. As the play evolves, the baby suffers oxygen deprivation, and the Hollywood couple back out of the deal on account of the possibility that they might be purchasing "damaged goods."

ANALYSIS: This play forces the audience to confront some volatile modern-day issues. *The Baby Dance* is billed as a drama, a good point to keep in mind since there is considerable opportunity for comedy. All levels.

SCENES/MONOLOGUES: Male/Male Scenes (1), Female/Female Scenes (1), Three-Person Scenes (3)

BABY WITH THE BATHWATER
by Christopher Durang (Dramatists Play Service)

SYNOPSIS: The story follows the mostly irrational events in the life of a male child named Daisy. That's right, Daisy. The boy has a girl's name, and most people think he is in fact a girl.

ANALYSIS: An outlandish 1984 comedy that is full of unexplained leaps and acting transitions. Actors who work on the piece should carefully read Christopher Durang's notes (in the back of the Dramatists Play Service acting edition pp. 55–62).

SCENES/MONOLOGUES: Female/Female Scenes (1), Three-Person Scenes (1)

BAD HABITS
by Terrence McNally (1990 revised edition, Dramatists Play Service)

SYNOPSIS: On either side of a tranquil lake somewhere near New York City are two sanitariums where people come to be cured of their bad habits. At Dunelawn the patients are encouraged to revel in self-indulgence. They can, for example, smoke, drink, and eat high-cholesterol diets on the premise that it is best to be happy and that, if you are, the habits are not bad. The regimen at Ravenswood, on the other hand, calls for extreme self-denial and injections of serum that transform all the patients into identical automatons. There are no plots per se in these back-to-back one-act plays, just a crazy-quilt assembly line of neurotic characters trying to work out their problems.

ANALYSIS: Actors love to work on this material because it is broad and wacky. Remember, however, that underneath the comedy, each character is serious. All levels.

SCENES/MONOLOGUES: Female/Female Scenes (1), Male/Female Scenes (3), Female Monologues (1)

BAREFOOT IN THE PARK
by Neil Simon (Samuel French)

SYNOPSIS: Corie and Paul are newlyweds who have moved into their very first apartment, a fifth-floor walk-up on New York's Lower East Side. Visitors one encounters during the play include Corie's widowed mother, a telephone repairman, a deliveryman and the colorful upstairs neighbor, Victor Velasco. The primary action involves Corie's attempt to set up her mom on a blind date with Mr. Velasco. Also, Corie and Paul have their first big marital argument, which is, of course, way overplayed because they are newlyweds.

ANALYSIS: *Barefoot in the Park* was first produced in New York in 1963. It is the play that made Robert Redford a star. Its joy derives from its total innocence and goodwill.

SCENES/MONOLOGUES: Male/Female Scenes (1), Female/Female Scenes (1)

BEAR, THE
by Anton Chekhov (*The Sneeze: Plays and Stories by Anton Chekhov*, translated and adapted by Michael Frayn, Samuel French)

SYNOPSIS: Widow Popova's late husband owes Smirnov 1,200 rubles. When she can't pay the debt, Smirnov flies into a rage, refusing to leave her home until she comes up with the money. They argue and bicker until they agree to a pistol duel. But as Smirnov teaches the widow how to use the weapon, he realizes that he has fallen in love with her. So he proposes marriage. After some resistance, she accepts. **ANALYSIS:** Delightful short comedy, truly funny. Michael Frayn does with Anton Chekhov what Richard Wilbur does with Molière. All levels.

SCENES/MONOLOGUES: Male/Female Scenes (1), Male Monologues (1)

BEAU JEST
by James Sherman (Samuel French)

SYNOPSIS: Sarah Goldman is a nice Jewish girl whose parents won't leave her alone about marriage. The truth is that she is happy being single. Furthermore, her current boyfriend, Chris, is not Jewish. To get her parents off her back, Sarah invents—out of thin air—a "proper" boyfriend, a Jewish doctor. Her parents of course insist on meeting him, and so Sarah arranges for a small dinner party. To complicate things, she contacts an escort service and hires a man who will pretend to be the Jewish doctor. The escort, Bob Schroeder, arrives and plays his part perfectly, completely winning over Sarah's parents. Later, Sarah and Bob fall for each other for real. Amid much comic confusion, Sarah and Bob look forward to the future together.

ANALYSIS: Good-natured, often very funny comedy. All levels.

SCENES/MONOLOGUES: Male/Female Scenes (1)

BEAUTY QUEEN OF LEENANE, THE
by Martin McDonagh (Dramatists Play Service)

SYNOPSIS: Maureen, a forty-year-old, mentally fragile virgin, is locked into terminal codependency with her continually complaining seventy-year-old mother, Mag. The two of them live in a sad little cottage in County Galway, Ireland, continually abusing one another. At times their exchanges are wildly funny and, at others, downright dangerous. Like an iceberg in which only a small fraction of the ice shows above the waterline, this complex mother/daughter relationship runs deep and, in the end, gives way to violence. The catalyst for the final resolution is a failed romantic courtship between Maureen and a local man named Pato Dooley. Mag is of course threatened by the prospect of Maureen abandoning her for a husband, and Maureen sees Pato as perhaps her only way out.

ANALYSIS: This rich material is appropriate for advanced actors. Don't try it unless you are comfortable portraying an Irish accent and Irish ways.

SCENES/MONOLOGUES: Male/Female Scenes (1)

BEDROOOMS: FIVE COMEDIES
by Renée Taylor and Joseph Bologna (Samuel French)

SYNOPSIS: My favorite of these comedies is *Bill and Laura*, in which a recently separated couple accidentally turns up as guests at the same dinner party. The entire confrontation takes place in the bedroom where the guests put their coats on a bed. It is wild and wooly physical comedy that ends with the two of them back in one another's arms.

There is also a charming monologue in *David and Nancy*. David is the nervous father of the bride-to-be. He wakes his daughter, Nancy, in the middle of the night to tell her that he has changed his mind about allowing her to get married. The scene ends with a tender embrace and, naturally, the wedding is on.

ANALYSIS: Renée Taylor and Joseph Bologna are top-notch comedy writers, always fun. All levels.

SCENES/MONOLOGUES: Male/Female Scenes (1), Male Monologues (1)

BELL, BOOK AND CANDLE
by John Van Druten (Samuel French)

SYNOPSIS: Gillian Holroyd is an honest-to-goodness witch who lives in the Murray Hill section of New York City among her relatives. She becomes smitten with Sheperd Henderson, the handsome publisher who lives in her building, so she casts a spell on him to guarantee his affections. When Sheperd finds out what Gillian did, he storms out. By then, however, she is truly in love, an emotion that causes her to lose her magical powers. (Witches can't fall in love, you see.) But in the end, Gillian and Sheperd get back together anyway and proceed down the yellow brick road.

ANALYSIS: Silly stuff, but this 1951 comedy holds up surprisingly well. It ran for 200 performances on Broadway and then was made into a 1958 movie starring Jimmy Stewart and Kim Novak. It is also part of the material upon which the hit TV series *Bewitched* was based. All levels.

SCENES/MONOLOGUES: Female/Female Scenes (1), Male/Female Scenes (3)

BENT
by Martin Sherman (Samuel French)

SYNOPSIS: One of the few classes of people considered lower than Jews in Nazi Germany were homosexuals. Jews were required to wear yellow stars, and homosexuals forced to wear pink ones. Here, Max and Rudy must flee Berlin after a high-ranking homosexual Nazi officer is murdered. They are caught, and while being transported to Dachau, the guards kill Rudy. In the camp, Max begins a relationship with another gay prisoner, Horst, an act of love that sustains them even though they can't touch one another physically. In the end, both men die in the camp.

ANALYSIS: Powerful, sexually graphic, beautifully written. Absolutely inappropriate for novice actors.

SCENES/MONOLOGUES: Male/Male Scenes (4)

BETRAYAL
by Harold Pinter (Dramatists Play Service)

SYNOPSIS: This one-act play begins two years after the end of Jerry and Emma's seven-year affair and moves progressively backward in time, ending with the day they decided to begin their relationship. Along the way, the consequences of their choices are sifted and exposed.

ANALYSIS: Wonderful adult material, complex relationships, brilliantly written by one of the twentieth century's greatest playwrights. Harold Pinter was awarded the Nobel Prize for Literature in 2005. *Betrayal* was turned into a superb 1983 movie starring Jeremy Irons, Ben Kingsley, and Patricia Hodge. All levels.

SCENES/MONOLOGUES: Male/Male Scenes (1), Male/Female Scenes (4)

BETWEEN DAYLIGHT AND BOONVILLE
by Matt Williams (Samuel French)

SYNOPSIS: Set against a background of the strip-mining coal industry in southern Indiana, the story focuses on the relationships between three miners' wives:

Carla, Marlene, and Lorette. Carla longs to take her child and escape her dreary trailer park existence and a husband who has let himself go to pot. Marlene, pregnant and already the mother of two, thinks she should stand by her man no matter how tough things get. Lorette has seen it all in her sixty years and thinks the other two women are plain silly. Then, suddenly, Marlene's husband is killed in a mining accident, and the issues the women face take on deeper implications.

ANALYSIS: There is a nice feeling of authenticity about this 1979 comedy-drama. The playwright captures the dialogue of small-town America. Maybe the play gets a bit corny at times, but it is definitely worth the effort. Good material. All levels.

SCENES/MONOLOGUES: Female/Female Scenes (1), Male/Female Scenes (1), Female Monologues (1)

BEYOND THERAPY
by Christopher Durang (Samuel French)

SYNOPSIS: Bruce and Prudence meet through a personal ad, but they don't click right away. It turns out that Bruce is living with his male lover, Bob, and Prudence is sleeping with her psychiatrist. Soon, both their therapists and Bob are mixed up in a bizarre quest for romance and happiness. There doesn't seem to be a sane character in the play. But then, what is sanity?

ANALYSIS: Wild, wonderfully improbable comedy. Actors love to play this stuff. All levels.

SCENES/MONOLOGUES: Male/Female Scenes (5), Three-Person Scenes (1)

BIRDBATH
by Leonard Melfi (*Encounters: Six One-Act Plays by Leonard Melfi*, Samuel French)

SYNOPSIS: Velma and Frankie work at a New York cafeteria, she as a waitress, he as a cashier. Tonight, for the first time, they speak to one another, and Velma winds up going to Frankie's apartment for some tea. Once there, he drinks premixed martinis until he is stoned and, after a while, she joins him. As the alcohol takes effect and as Frankie pushes Velma gently but insistently toward the bed, the audience learns how deeply troubled and strange Velma really is. She becomes increasingly agitated until, finally, in an outburst, she pulls a blood-encrusted knife from her purse, threatening to stab Frankie. Then she confesses that she killed her mother that very morning. Exhausted by hysteria and fear, Velma falls asleep on the bed as Frankie writes a poem about her.

ANALYSIS: This is vintage 1960s off-off Broadway material, intensely emotional. A classic of its kind, it is still produced in regional theaters today.

SCENES/MONOLOGUES: Male/Female Scenes (2)

BIRDY
by Naomi Wallace (adapted from the William Wharton novel, Broadway Play Publishing)

SYNOPSIS: Birdy got his curious nickname back in high school because of his obsession with—and even identification with—birds. He used to actually attempt flight by donning feathers and jumping off high places; he also collected many pigeons, canaries, and parakeets in his bedroom. By the time we meet him in his early 20s in a military psychiatric hospital after World War II, he has totally withdrawn into a bird world. He squats on his bunk, will not talk, and must be hand-fed by hospital orderlies. His lifelong friend, Al, who also has psychological problems—though nothing approaching schizophrenia—winds up in the same hospital. Al tries to penetrate the mental fog that surrounds Birdy in order to pull him back into the real world.

ANALYSIS: This is challenging and fascinating material. Unfortunately, most of the scenes in Ms. Wallace's adaptation are not useful for workshop because they bounce back and forth in time and involve three or four actors. I have selected one that will work (if you eliminate a character), plus three monologues. Naomi Wallace is, by the way, a MacArthur "Genius" Award winner.

SCENES/MONOLOGUES: Male/Male Scenes (1), Male Monologues (3)

BITTER SAUCE
by Eric Bogosian (*Love's Fire—Seven New Plays Inspired by Seven Shakespearean Sonnets,* William Morrow)

SYNOPSIS: Rengin is a pie-faced drunk when we first meet her. And she is sloppily wearing the wedding gown she is supposed to don tomorrow when she gets married to Herman. Soon we discover that Rengin has a secret: She has been carrying on a sex-only relationship with a biker named Red, who is scheduled to arrive shortly for a little pre-wedding nookie. Herman, her good hearted and totally unsuspecting fiancé, arrives first and sets about sobering her up. During all of this he finds out about Red and is, of course, astonished. Before he can really resolve that issue with Rengin, Red arrives and there is a confrontation between the two men. Herman outwits Red, sending him packing into the night. Rengin and Herman will probably live happily ever after.

ANALYSIS: Actors love to do this one-act comedy because they get to "chew the scenery." The given circumstances are outrageously funny, and it is always fun to portray a comic character that is drunk. Also, Rengin has all of this sexual hanky-panky going on. In short, this is a wonderful workout.

SCENES/MONOLOGUES: Male/Female Scenes (1), Male/Male Scenes (1)

BLUE WINDOW
by Craig Lucas (Samuel French)

SYNOPSIS: Libby was seriously injured and her husband killed in a freak fall from their New York apartment building balcony. The action of *Blue Window* revolves around a dinner party—her first attempt to socialize since the accident. It follows the goings-on in three different apartments as the party guests prepare for and then attend Libby's party. The blue window of the title refers to a wished-for window into people's emotions.

ANALYSIS: It can be a little difficult to read this play because of the unusual way it is laid out on the printed page. It works wonderfully on stage, however. All levels.

SCENES/MONOLOGUES: Male/Female Scenes (1), Female Monologues (1)

BORN YESTERDAY
by Garson Kanin (Dramatists Play Service)

SYNOPSIS: Harry Brock, a self-made millionaire and brash con man, is worried that his beautiful but dumb girlfriend, Billie Dawn, is going to be an embarrassment to him as he wines and dines the movers and shakers in Washington, DC. He is intent on "purchasing" self-serving legislation. So, as he continues along his path of corruption, he arranges for a serious-minded journalist to tutor Billie Dawn, to "show her the ropes" in Washington. Naturally, the tutor and his charge fall in love and, as she becomes better educated, Billie develops a social conscience. In the end, the new lovers exit together, managing to thwart Harry's dastardly scheme.

ANALYSIS: A delightful 1946 Broadway comedy that ran for 1,642 performances. Judy Holliday became a star playing the ex-chorine, Billie Dawn. All levels.

SCENES/MONOLOGUES: Male/Male Scenes (1), Male/Female Scenes (3)

BOSOMS AND NEGLECT
by John Guare (revised edition, Dramatists Play Service)

SYNOPSIS: Deirdre and Scooper have sat across from one another in their psychiatrist's New York waiting room for years but have never spoken until today. The event that motivates them to talk is their shrink's imminent, always-anxiety-provoking yearly August vacation. For serious and committed psychotherapy patients, this means they will be on their own for a few weeks. And so Deirdre and Scooper meet and wind up at her apartment telling one another about their respective lives. Scooper's blind octogenarian mother, Henny, is suffering from advanced cancer, and he has been having a long-term affair with his best friend's wife. Deirdre exposes her violent side when she describes the time she hit a lover in the head with a glass ashtray. It was that confrontation, in fact, that brought her into psychotherapy. Clearly Deirdre and Scooper both have troubled and questing souls, and their unresolved issues and tensions are what comprise the bulk of *Bosoms and Neglect*. Often clever, always literary, and at times surprisingly violent and erotic, their relationship is fascinating and complex.

ANALYSIS: John Guare (*House of Blue Leaves, Marco Polo Sings a Solo*) can be an intellectual playwright when he wants to be, and here he is truly strutting his stuff. Page after page of *Bosoms and Neglect* contains literary references and, speaking just for myself, I felt sort of stupid from time to time because I was unfamiliar with some of the books. But I stuck with it. In the end, you don't really need to be an avid reader to grasp the dynamic and mutually needy relationship that develops between Deirdre and Scooper.

SCENES/MONOLOGUES: Female Monologues (2), Male/Female Scenes (1)

BOYS' LIFE
by Howard Korder (Dramatists Play Service)

SYNOPSIS: Jack, Don, and Phil navigate the dating/marriage scene during the disjointed, upwardly mobile, spiritually empty, sexually threatening 1980s.

ANALYSIS: This one-act play, which was nominated for a Pulitzer Prize in 1988, captures the undercurrent of anxiety in respect to dating and hints at a major confusion about male/female relationships. All levels.

SCENES/MONOLOGUES: Male/Female Scenes (1), Male Monologues (2), Three-Person Scenes (1)

BREAKING THE CODE
by Hugh Whitemore (Samuel French)

SYNOPSIS: Based on the true story of Alan Turing, a gay British mathematician who broke an important secret German code during World War II. Homosexuality was a crime in England during the 1940s, and Turing's government trial caused him acute public embarrassment and humiliation. Ultimately, Turing committed suicide.

ANALYSIS: Derek Jacobi and Michael Gough received Tony nominations in 1988 for their work in this play. Written in the British vernacular. All levels.

SCENES/MONOLOGUES: Male/Male Scenes (2), Male/Female Scenes (2), Male Monologues (1)

BROOKLYN BOY
by Donald Margulies (Theatre Communications Group)

SYNOPSIS: Eric Weiss, now in his mid-forties and stumbling into a divorce, has achieved overnight success as a novelist. His book, *Brooklyn Boy,* is number eleven on the *NY Times* best seller list, and he's making money at last. Theoretically, Eric has moved up a notch in social status, but it's not enough to overcome his Brooklynite middle-class background: Can you ever actually escape your roots?

ANALYSIS: Donald Margulies won a Pulitzer Prize for Drama in 2000 for *Dinner with Friends*. He is an immensely talented writer with a knack for creating characters that are instantly recognizable. *Brooklyn Boy* is maybe a bit more personal for him because, as he explains in an introduction, it was inspired by his personal relationship with the late playwright Herb Gardner (*A Thousand Clowns*). Gardner suggested to Margulies that he write something about his Brooklyn roots.

SCENES/MONOLOGUES: Male/Female Scenes (2)

BURN THIS
by Lanford Wilson (Dramatists Play Service)

SYNOPSIS: This play deals with the people who come together after a freak boating accident during which Robbie, Anna's gay roommate, is killed. Pale, Robbie's erratic and volatile brother, comes to collect Robbie's belongings and immediately begins a tempestuous romance with Anna, who has become bored by the sterile relationship she has with Burton, a Hollywood screenwriter. Anna, however, is frightened by Pale's powerful personality, his unpredictability, and her own needs. When Larry, Anna's other gay roommate, realizes that she should be with Pale and not Burton, he choreographs a situation that brings them together by the final curtain.

ANALYSIS: Hip and well written. The character of Pale, played first by John Malkovich, is particularly colorful and challenging. Appropriate for mature actors of all levels.

SCENES/MONOLOGUES: Male/Female Scenes (1), Male Monologues (1), Female Monologues (1)

BUTLEY
by Simon Gray (Samuel French)

SYNOPSIS: Ben Butley is a bisexual English professor at the College of London University, a man burnt out on teaching and love. The play follows him through a single day during which he learns that his estranged wife plans to remarry, and that his male lover—and former student—is going to move in with another man. All the action takes place in Butley's cluttered office.

ANALYSIS: Alan Bates successfully nailed the title role in the London production, which was directed by Harold Pinter, and again on Broadway in 1972. Written in the British vernacular.

SCENES/MONOLOGUES: Male/Male Scenes (3)

CANDIDA
by George Bernard Shaw (Signet)

SYNOPSIS: In 1894, Candida Morell and her minister husband, James, befriend a sensitive and rather helpless young poet, Eugene Marchbanks. Subsequently, she has to choose between the men, who have radically different notions about love and marriage. In the surprising final moments of the play, she chooses "the weaker of the two," namely, her strong, manly, vigorous husband. By doing this, she benevolently rejects the romantic premises of each man, establishing her own turf as an independent woman.

ANALYSIS: George Bernard Shaw's fifth play, frequently revived. Actors who appreciate the lush use of language will enjoy working on this most. All levels.

SCENES/MONOLOGUES: Male/Male Scenes (1), Male/Female Scenes (1), Female Monologues (1)

CAT ON A HOT TIN ROOF
by Tennessee Williams (Dramatists Play Service)

SYNOPSIS: Big Daddy, a millionaire southern landowner with an estate that includes some 28,000 acres, is dying and doesn't have a will. The central event of this play revolves around a family celebration for Big Daddy's sixty-fifth birthday. While he does not yet realize that his illness is terminal, everybody else does, so that there is a great deal of jostling for favor in the will they all hope he'll write.

Big Daddy's greedy older son, Gooper, is in a nasty contest of one-upmanship with Maggie, his brother Brick's wife. If anyone is a sentimental favorite to be named prominently in the will, however, it is Brick, the alcoholic son who is indifferent to the prospect of great wealth. He is also bored by the spectacle of everybody kissing up to Big Daddy. Brick is depressed by the death of his longtime friend, Skipper. A constant background question in *Cat on a Hot Tin Roof* is whether or not Brick and Skipper were lovers. What is certain is that Brick no longer is intimate with Margaret, and everybody knows it.

ANALYSIS: This great American classic won the 1955 Pulitzer Prize. Tennessee Williams was criticized in some quarters for not resolving the question of Brick's sexuality. All levels.

SCENES/MONOLOGUES: Male/Male Scenes (1), Male/Female Scenes (1)

CHAPTER TWO
by Neil Simon (Samuel French)

SYNOPSIS: Novelist George Schneider is recovering from the death of his wife. Actress Jennie Malone is rebounding from a divorce. So George's brother arranges a blind-date introduction. After an ecstatic two-week courtship, George and Jennie marry and leave on their honeymoon. But memories of George's deceased wife haunt him, and he is unable to commit to this new union. When Jennie realizes that she can't successfully compete with a memory, the newlyweds split up. Within weeks, however, George undergoes a catharsis and reunites with Jennie, presumably to live happily ever after.

ANALYSIS: This semiautobiographical 1977 play is dedicated to actress Marsha Mason, whom Neil Simon married shortly after the death of his first wife. Witty and moving. All levels.

SCENES/MONOLOGUES: Male/Male Scenes (1), Male/Female Scenes (3), Female Monologues (1)

CHASE, THE
by Horton Foote (Dramatists Play Service)

Synopsis: Law-abiding citizens in the tranquil Texas town of Richmond are terrorized by "Bubber" Reeves, a homegrown escaped murderer who is bent on revenge against the local sheriff. One by one, frightened business leaders turn against Sheriff Hawes when he is frustrated in his search for the killer and won't provide each of them with individual guard service. They remind him who pays his salary, threaten to see him defeated in the next election, and promise to deny him the farm loan he wants badly. By the time Hawes finally shoots down Bubber in a shack outside of town, the citizens have shown their true colors. They have proven themselves to be the moral and ethical equals of the man they've been hunting.

Analysis: Shades of *High Noon*. This 1952 play was the basis for the 1966 movie of the same name, starring Marlon Brando and Robert Redford. All levels.

Scenes/Monologues: Male/Male Scenes (2), Male/Female Scenes (1)

CHEATERS
by Michael Jacobs (Samuel French)

Synopsis: Michelle walks out on Allen because he won't seriously commit to their relationship. She thinks that eighteen months is long enough to have been living together, and she wants to get married. The breakup leads to the involvement of their respective parents who, it turns out, are having affairs with one another. In the end, Michelle and Allen set a wedding date.

Analysis: This 1972 comedy has a thoroughly convoluted plot, but the opening scene between Michelle and Allen is hysterically funny and very well written. All levels.

Scenes/Monologues: Male/Female Scenes (1), Female Monologues (1)

CHERRY ORCHARD, THE
by Anton Chekhov (*Chekhov, The Major Plays;* translated by Ann Dunnigan, Signet Books)

Synopsis: Unable to pay taxes on the family estate, Lyuboff Ranevskaya and her brother wind up losing the property in a public auction, rather than allowing their beloved cherry orchard to be sold to a developer.

Analysis: Anton Chekhov's last play, arguably his best. It doesn't provide many opportunities for workshop scenework, however, because the stage is almost always full of characters. The few possibilities that exist are, in my opinion, too short. All levels.

Scenes/Monologues: Male Monologues (1)

CHILDREN OF A LESSER GOD
by Mark Medoff (Dramatists Play Service)

Synopsis: James Leeds is a teacher at a state school for the deaf, and his new student, Sarah Norman, is a deaf woman who adamantly refuses to speak; she prefers to sign. The teacher/student relationship evolves into a love affair that by Act II results in their marriage. Their union isn't a perfect one, however, because Sarah suffers on account of her deep shame. Before long, her attempts to turn away from her deaf friends and to merge completely with the hearing world force Sarah and James to reassess the basis of their relationship and, indeed, the basis of all communication.

ANALYSIS: Written in 1980 as a vehicle for deaf actress Phyllis Frelich, *Children of a Lesser God* won a Tony for Best Play. Frelich won for Best Actress, and John Rubinstein won for Best Actor. The role of Sarah requires expert use of signed English.

SCENES/MONOLOGUES: Male/Female Scenes (5), Male Monologues (1)

CHILDREN'S HOUR, THE
by Lillian Hellman (Dramatists Play Service)

SYNOPSIS: Karen and Martha saved their money for eight long years to purchase a farm and start a girls' school, and the place is just starting to pay for itself when their world falls apart. A fourteen-year-old student accuses the women of being lesbians, and the resulting public furor destroys their reputation and business. When Dr. Joseph Cardin, their only ally and Karen's fiancé, admits that he, too, suspects that the allegations are true, the women are thrown into utter desperation. Martha, in a moment of deep introspection, wonders aloud if perhaps she does love Karen in an "unnatural" way. When Karen responds to this insight with hostility, Martha walks into the next room and kills herself. Then, in an anticlimax, it comes to light that the charges were false, the construction of a maladjusted child.

ANALYSIS: On one level, *The Children's Hour* is the story of a devilish child running amok; on a more serious level, it is an examination of the relationship between two women. Ultimately, playwright Lillian Hellman doesn't resolve this bigger issue about their sexuality, and the ending is therefore something of a letdown. Still, this was Hellman's first produced play and her biggest hit, running 691 performances on Broadway. In 1934, lesbianism was a controversial subject, and the play was widely banned, most notably in London and Boston.

SCENES/MONOLOGUES: Female/Female Scenes (2), Male/Female Scenes (1)

CLOSER
by Patrick Marber (Dramatists Play Service)

SYNOPSIS: The action of the play takes place in London over a four-and-a-half-year period, during which two contemporary couples repeatedly arrange themselves into varying romantic configurations. The situations they encounter are frankly sexual and totally adult in nature. The words they speak are alternately biting, caressing, and stinging. Given all of that, *Closer* is still not a vulgar or cheap play. The playwright was striving to see how much anger and fury could be shoved into a formal, even classic framework. (It is fascinating how much the form resembles that of Noel Coward's *Private Lives*.)

ANALYSIS: Mike Nichols adapted *Closer* for the big screen in 2004, and the movie was rated R for strong language and sexual situations. Many actors in professional-level workshop will love to work on this material precisely because it cuts so deeply and requires mutual trust. There is no physical nudity involved, but there is plenty of "emotional nudity." I recommend this play for experienced adult actors only.

SCENES/MONOLOGUES: Male/Female Scenes (6), Female/Female Scenes (1), Male/Male Scenes (1)

COASTAL DISTURBANCES
by Tina Howe (Samuel French)

SYNOPSIS: The play is set in an upscale beach community on Massachusetts's North Shore during the last two weeks of August. Leo and Holly are both rebounding from troubled relationships when they encounter one another.

ANALYSIS: A light treatment of contemporary relationships. All levels.

SCENES/MONOLOGUES: Male/Female Scenes (2), Male Monologues (1), Female Monologues (1)

COLORED MUSEUM, THE
by George C. Wolfe (Grove Press)

SYNOPSIS: The play's theatrical device is a museum tour of eleven exhibits that come to life, forcing black stereotypes into the light.

ANALYSIS: The play's inventive milieu presents an excellent opportunity for flashy monologues. The entire cast is African-American. All levels.

SCENES/MONOLOGUES: Male Monologues (1), Female Monologues (2)

COMANCHE CAFÉ
by William Hauptman (revised edition, *Comanche Café and Domino Courts;* Samuel French)

SYNOPSIS: Set in a café in southern Oklahoma during the late 1930s, where Mattie has been a waitress for fourteen years and Ronnie is a newcomer. They sit and peel potatoes, talking about life, love, and leaving Oklahoma.

ANALYSIS: This short play captures the rural southwestern flavor; the language is poetic. All levels.

SCENES/MONOLOGUES: Female/Female Scenes (1), Female Monologues (2)

COME BACK, LITTLE SHEBA
by William Inge (Samuel French)

SYNOPSIS: Lola and Doc have endured a marriage of convenience for twenty years, and both are fixated on their lost youth. Doc's alcoholism has nearly ruined the union and has brought them close to poverty. Sober now and attending Alcoholics Anonymous meetings for almost a year, Doc thinks that things are looking up until he discovers that the couple's boarder, a seemingly innocent young woman, is sleeping with her casual boyfriend. This kind of promiscuity throws Doc into a philosophical tailspin, and he goes on a bender. Lola, for reasons of her own, is also disillusioned to learn that the woman is sleeping around. When Doc dries out, both he and Lola move toward the future with diminished expectations about the prospects for goodness and purity in the world. Little Sheba, by the way, is a puppy Lola used to own that disappeared one day, never to grow old. She wishes it could come back, just as she longs for her youth to be restored.

ANALYSIS: William Inge's first play, *Come Back, Little Sheba* was stylistically influenced by his mentor, Tennessee Williams, and is full of symbols. First performed in 1950, the drama feels dated now but still packs a punch for workshop scenework. Shirley Booth won a Tony for her stage performance as Lola and an Oscar in 1952 for the same film role. All levels.

SCENES/MONOLOGUES: Male/Female Scenes (3), Female Monologues (1)

COME BACK TO THE FIVE AND DIME, JIMMY DEAN, JIMMY DEAN
by Ed Graczyk (Samuel French)

SYNOPSIS: The "Disciples of James Dean" reunite in a tiny, drought-afflicted west Texas town on the twentieth anniversary of the actor's death. They drink, party, and reminisce about how it was to be teenagers in 1955 when *Giant* was filming in nearby Marfa, and many of the locals were extras. Then Joanne arrives, a mysterious woman whom the other women soon discover is former Disciples-member Joe; she underwent a sex-change operation. Joe/Joanne's brutally honest perspective leads to some serious truth-telling among the old gang members. Sissy discloses that she lost her man after she had a mastectomy. Mona admits that James Dean did not father her son after all, and Juanita faces the probability that her late husband was a lecherous alcoholic.

ANALYSIS: A wonderfully theatrical play, jumping back and forth in time between 1955 and 1975 as well as in and out of reality. The work is full of poetry, humor, and magic. For sophisticated actors of all levels.

SCENES/MONOLOGUES: Female/Female Scenes (1), Female Monologues (2)

COUPLA WHITE CHICKS SITTING AROUND TALKING, A
by John Ford Noonan (Samuel French)

SYNOPSIS: The women are unlikely friends: Maude is a reserved lady from Westchester County, New York, and Hannah Mae is a newly arrived, gregarious Texan. Their relationship is oddly strengthened when Maude impulsively makes love with Hanna Mae's husband, Carl Joe. Overcome with guilt, Maude confesses the act to Hannah Mae, who, instead of reacting with anger, contends that they are closer now—and anyway, who could resist a hunk like Carl Joe? Subsequently, Maude confides in her new friend, telling about her troubled marriage to Tyler, who is at that very moment out of town on a romantic fling with his secretary. The women unite to set their respective husbands straight.

ANALYSIS: Very funny two-character comedy, even if a truck could fit through the holes in the plot. Wonderful comedy material. All levels.

SCENES/MONOLOGUES: Female/Female Scenes (1)

COVER
by Jeffrey Sweet with Stephen Johnson and Sandra Hastie (*25 Ten-Minute Plays from the Actors Theatre of Louisville,* Samuel French)

SYNOPSIS: Here's a three-person scene for you. Marty wants Frank to lie and tell his lady friend, Diane, that the two of them were together last night, but the truth is that Marty had a date. Frank doesn't want to lie, but when Diane enters and brings up the issue, he finds the false words coming out of his mouth. Diane sees right through the lie but doesn't challenge the men's story.

ANALYSIS: This entire play is only ten minutes long, but the variety of exchanges to be found within it make it interesting for scenework.

SCENES/MONOLOGUES: Three-Person Scenes (1)

CRIMES OF THE HEART
by Beth Henley (Dramatists Play Service)

SYNOPSIS: A glimpse into the lives of the very eccentric Magrath sisters, Babe, Meg, and Lenny, of Hazlehurst, Mississippi. They rediscover the value of family ties when Babe, the youngest, shoots Zachary, her abusive husband and a prominent local attorney, and faces the prospect of a jail sentence.

ANALYSIS: This pitch-black Southern-Gothic comedy, a 1979 Pulitzer Prize winner, was first produced at the Actors Theatre of Louisville and later on Broadway. It was made into a successful 1986 movie starring Tess Harper, Diane Keaton, Jessica Lange, and Sissy Spacek. All levels.

SCENES/MONOLOGUES: Female/Female Scenes (1), Male/Female Scenes (3)

CROSSING DELANCEY
by Susan Sandler (Samuel French)

SYNOPSIS: Isabelle is an independent, young Jewish woman who, when she isn't working in a bookstore, spends time with her elderly, spunky grandmother on New York's Lower East Side. Bubbie, as the grandmother is known, is a lady with one foot still in the old country. She is concerned about Isabelle still being single and arranges for a matchmaker to cook up a romance. The matchmaker then introduces Isabelle to Sam, a sensitive fellow who works as a pickle-maker. Isabelle, however, has her sights set on a romantic, handsome novelist who frequents the bookstore. As the plot unfolds, she discovers that the novelist is a shallow cad and that Sam has some wonderful virtues, so their match turns out to be a good one after all.

ANALYSIS: Delightful comedy that capitalizes on generational and cultural differences. The play was successfully adapted for the screen in 1988, starring Amy Irving. All levels.

SCENES/MONOLOGUES: Male/Female Scenes (3), Male Monologues (1), Female Monologues (1)

CRUCIBLE, THE
by Arthur Miller (Dramatists Play Service)

SYNOPSIS: Set amid the Salem witch trials in the late seventeenth century, the story involves John Proctor, a man suffering from guilt because he committed adultery with young Abigail Williams. When Abigail and a group of her friends claim to be affected by the devil and accuse various citizens of being witches, Proctor knows she is lying but is afraid to speak up for fear his sin will be disclosed. He tries to ignore the ongoing trials; however, this becomes impossible when his own wife, Elizabeth, is accused of being a witch. Finally, Proctor steps forward and, when he does, is himself accused of being a witch. To save his own life, he shamefully signs a false confession, but when pressed to reveal the names of others who might be witches, he refuses and is led to his death in the gallows.

ANALYSIS: This 1953 drama strongly parallels the struggles against McCarthyism in the United States. It ran for 197 performances on Broadway in 1953 and for more than 500 performances in a later off-Broadway revival. All levels.

SCENES/MONOLOGUES: Male/Female Scenes (3)

DANCE AND THE RAILROAD, THE
by David Henry Hwang (Dramatists Play Service)

SYNOPSIS: In 1867, Chinese laborers working on the American transcontinental railroad launched an unsuccessful strike against their employers. During the strike, two of the men get to know each other in a nearby mountaintop clearing when Ma discovers Lone practicing his dance steps. It turns out that Lone is a trained opera dancer whose parents abruptly took him out of opera school two years ago, sending him to America to get rich. Ma asks to be trained, too, so that he can play the grand role of Gwan Gung, the god of Fighters and the god of Adventurers, in an opera. Lone tests Ma's dedication, leaving him to crouch and imitate a locust overnight. When the strike ends the next morning, Ma has successfully proved that he has the fortitude to learn, but he no longer wants to dance. He wants to get rich in America.

ANALYSIS: David Henry Hwang (the author of *M. Butterfly*) tests elements of Chinese myth against American culture. In this 1981 one-act play, he attacks the image of the passive and subservient "coolie" laborer. All the characters are Asian-American. All levels.

SCENES/MONOLOGUES: Male/Male Scenes (1), Male Monologues (1)

DANNY AND THE DEEP BLUE SEA
by John Patrick Shanley (Dramatists Play Service) (*13 by Shanley*, Applause Books)

SYNOPSIS: Danny and Roberta are violent, battered people. They meet in a Bronx bar and, despite their tough and defensive facades, are drawn to each other. They spend the night together and before dawn, Danny proposes marriage, an act of kindness and hope that neither seems able to accept or tolerate. Finally, their emotional barriers fall, and they face the future together.

ANALYSIS: John Patrick Shanley's insightful, poetic, sensitive characterizations shine a bright light on the heavy toll that childhood abuse and neglect can take. Challenging material for actors of all levels, at times funny, ultimately very moving. Shanley is best known for writing the delightful 1987 film *Moonstruck.*

SCENES/MONOLOGUES: Male/Female Scenes (3), Female Monologues (1)

DARK AT THE TOP OF THE STAIRS, THE
by William Inge (Dramatists Play Service)

SYNOPSIS: The year is 1920, and Cora's friends are getting rich in this oil-soaked Oklahoma town. She longs to climb the social ladder with them, but her husband, Rubin, a simple man and harness salesman by trade, doesn't share the gambling inclinations of the oil drillers. They continually fight about money, and everything comes to a head over the issue of a new party dress for their shy daughter, Reenie, who has been invited to a fancy country-club party. Rubin storms out of the house in frustration, perhaps never to return.

The party turns out to be a disaster, ending in the suicide of Reenie's blind date, a Jewish boy from Hollywood. Cora then asks her sister, Lottie, if she and the children can come live with her and her husband in Oklahoma City. Lottie refuses, saying that her home isn't a happy one either, so the arrangement won't work out. Rubin returns, makes amends with the family and, in a touching speech, explains his frustrations as a man. The family moves forward with greater love and resolve, seemingly more in touch with the values that truly matter.

ANALYSIS: This 1957 drama is dedicated to Tennessee Williams, and his influence is evident throughout the play. Reenie, for example, is very reminiscent of Laura in *The Glass Menagerie*. Beautifully written, if perhaps a little too neat at the end. All levels.

SCENES/MONOLOGUES: Female/Female Scenes (1), Male/Female Scenes (1), Male Monologues (2)

DAY IN THE DEATH OF JOE EGG, A
by Peter Nichols (Samuel French)

SYNOPSIS: Ten-year-old Josephine is spastic, given to frequent seizures, completely dependent on her parents for every imaginable human need, and unable to speak or walk. Her presence in the family has skewed Sheila and Bri's marriage to the point of breaking. Sheila believes that hope springs eternal, and there is always a remote chance that Josephine will still develop normally. Bri, however, has no hope at all. He considers his daughter to be essentially without life and has resorted to black humor to deal with the situation. The playwright employs a theatrical device where Bri and Sheila relive the events of the child's birth and early years, play-acting various characters in their lives, such as a doctor and priest.

ANALYSIS: A very disturbing, sometimes funny two-act drama. Albert Finney starred as Bri during its 1968 Broadway run. Scenework is possible but difficult because of the fast-moving, almost cabaret-style presentation. Written in the British vernacular. All levels.

SCENES/MONOLOGUES: Male Monologues (1), Female Monologues (1)

DAYS OF WINE AND ROSES
by J. P. Miller (Dramatists Play Service)

SYNOPSIS: Joe and Kristen are alcoholics in denial. They marry quickly, have a daughter, and then continue a slow and boozy decline into poverty. Finally, Joe admits his sickness and joins Alcoholics Anonymous. Kristen, however, stays in denial and at the final curtain, the audience realizes that she'll be doomed unless she comes to terms with the truth.

ANALYSIS: Originally a 1958 *Playhouse 90* television production, this drama went on to Broadway and ultimately to film, where Jack Lemmon stopped the clocks with his portrayal of Joe. The dialogue rings true. All levels.

SCENES/MONOLOGUES: Male/Female Scenes (1)

DEATH AND THE MAIDEN
by Ariel Dorfman (*Death and the Maiden;* tie-in edition, Penguin)

SYNOPSIS: Paulina was held in captivity, blindfolded, and brutally tortured by a "doctor" during the reign of a now-collapsed South American military dictatorship. This horror is reborn when her husband, Gerardo, innocently brings home a man who gave him a lift on the road. Recognizing the man's voice as that of her torturer, Paulina takes him prisoner, demanding his confession and repentance. Gerardo, convinced that she is serious about killing the man if he doesn't confess, goes along with her. Although her prisoner passionately denies that he is the torturer, Paulina tricks him into disclosing the truth. The title, by the way, refers to a Schubert quartet that was played during the torture sessions.

ANALYSIS: Intelligent and topical. The Broadway cast included Glenn Close, Richard Dreyfus, and Gene Hackman. Even though the characters have Hispanic names, all roles can be played by non-Hispanics. All levels.

SCENES/MONOLOGUES: Male/Female Scenes (2), Male/Male Scenes (1), Female Monologues (1)

DEATH OF A SALESMAN
by Arthur Miller (Dramatists Play Service)

SYNOPSIS: Willy Loman, an aging traveling salesman, realizes that he is getting too old to be on the road so much. He curtails an unfinished trip through New England and abruptly returns to his Brooklyn home. There he locks horns with his visiting eldest son, Biff, who disagrees with him about which life choices lead to "success." Willy has bought heavily into the American dream, but Biff doesn't believe that working your way up the financial ladder is particularly worthwhile. This conflict, which profoundly changes the relationship between them, is the central issue in the play. Willy is forced to take stock of himself and realizes that he has, indeed, lived his life on false premises. Depressed, he commits suicide in a car crash in order to collect insurance money for the final payment on his home, a home that is a necessary component of the American dream.

ANALYSIS: Arthur Miller's great modern tragedy won the Pulitzer Prize in 1949. As he does in *All My Sons*, he explores a man's basic values. Lee J. Cobb was only thirty-seven years old in 1949 when he created the role of Willy on Broadway, and Dustin Hoffman was in his forties when he later starred in a revival. All levels.

SCENES/MONOLOGUES: Male/Male Scenes (1), Male Monologues (1), Female Monologues (1)

DEATH OF BESSIE SMITH, THE
by Edward Albee (*The Sandbox and The Death of Bessie Smith,* Plume Books)

SYNOPSIS: Two whites-only hospitals near Memphis refuse to treat Bessie Smith, the great blues singer, when she is brought in after a car wreck in 1937. In eight fast-moving scenes, Albee exposes the circumstances and underlying racism of the tragic event.

ANALYSIS: Albee based this 1959 drama on what he thought at the time was the actual story of Bessie Smith's death. It turned out later that she was, in fact, not refused admission to the white hospital. After her car wreck, she was taken directly to a blacks-only hospital and died en route in the ambulance. For sophisticated actors.

SCENES/MONOLOGUES: Male/Female Scenes (3)

DELICATE BALANCE, A
by Edward Albee (Samuel French)

SYNOPSIS: Agnes and Tobias live a highly ordered existence in the spacious suburban home they share with Agnes's sister, Claire. But this isn't a happy domestic scene by any means, for this is a family in strong denial. These are the kind of people who have a civilized drink before breakfast and bury their true emotions in intellectual repartee. One night, longtime friends Harry and Edna arrive, bags in hand. They want to sleep over because they are afraid of some nameless thing, perhaps the darkness of their own home and lives. Harry and Edna retreat into an upstairs bedroom and, days later, announce that they intend to move permanently out of their own place and to live here full time.

Julie (Agnes and Tobias's daughter) arrives home a short time later, licking her wounds from the demise of her fourth marriage. She is pushed to the edge of hysteria and violence by the presence of the strangers who are now residing in her old bedroom. Harry and Edna eventually recognize they aren't welcome and, with deflated spirits, depart.

ANALYSIS: Winner of the Pulitzer Prize, this psychologically dense, mysterious adult drama ran on Broadway in 1967 and again in 1996. Best for experienced actors.

SCENES/MONOLOGUES: Male/Female Scenes (3), Female/Female Scenes (1), Female Monologues (1)

DINNER WITH FRIENDS
by Donald Margulies (Dramatists Play Service)

SYNOPSIS: Karen and Gabe, international food writers, are best friends with Beth and Tom. In fact they introduced them to one another twelve years ago, and they have a summer time-share with them on Martha's Vineyard. Each couple has two kids. The families are, in every sense, intertwined. Therefore, when Beth tells Karen and Gabe that Tom is leaving her for another woman, the news plays havoc with the relationships. It leads to a reevaluation of what marriage and commitment mean, what friendship means, and what it means to lose sexual energy as you get older.

ANALYSIS: *Dinner With Friends* won the Pulitzer Prize for Drama in 2000 and is simply a marvelous play. Donald Margulies has a keen understanding of the nuances in a marriage, and the dialogue rings true virtually one hundred percent of the time. Be warned, however: A play that is this well written is also a trap for actors. It is a great temptation to rely too much on the words and, of course, acting has to do with much more than words. I recall seeing a production of *Dinner With Friends* at Chicago's Goodman Theatre that was flat for precisely this reason. The actors did not do the work.

SCENES/MONOLOGUES: Male Monologues (2), Male/Female Scenes (1), Female/Female Scenes (1)

DIVISION STREET
by Steve Tesich (Samuel French)

SYNOPSIS: Chris Adrian, a Tom Hayden–like former leader of the 1960s radical movement, resurfaces in Chicago in the early 1980s—working as an insurance salesman. After his picture unexpectedly appears in the newspapers, fellow former-radicals converge on his apartment, imploring him to lead a new revolution. But to their surprise, Chris has gone straight and is no longer interested in the great issues of the 1960s. Finally, everyone agrees to get back in touch with the honorable principles that led to the earlier attempt at revolution.

ANALYSIS: Madcap and farcical, this 1980 comedy ran on Broadway for only twenty-one performances. It is full of mistaken identities, pratfalls, disguises, sex changes, and characters with strange international accents. A great deal of fun for actors who can ride this wave. All levels.

SCENES/MONOLOGUES: Male/Female Scenes (2), Male/Male Scenes (1), Male Monologues (3), Female Monologues (1)

DOES A TIGER WEAR A NECKTIE?
by Don Petersen (Dramatists Play Service)

SYNOPSIS: The play is set "in a rehabilitation center for juvenile narcotic addicts located on an island in a river bordering a large industrial city." There is no single plotline, but there are several good scenes and monologues. The work consists of character exploration as incarcerated young people from life's underbelly try to find their way.

ANALYSIS: Al Pacino won a Tony Award in 1969 for creating the role of Bickham. Gritty dialogue and situations, very primal at times. Best for sophisticated actors.

SCENES/MONOLOGUES: Male/Female Scenes (1), Male/Male Scenes (2), Male Monologues (1)

DOLL'S HOUSE, A
by Henrik Ibsen (adapted by Frank McGuinness, Dramatists Play Service)

SYNOPSIS: Nora Helmer forged her father's name to a loan document to get money to pay for her husband, Torvald's, recuperation from a serious illness. She has been secretly repaying the debt out of her meager household allowance for several years. And now that her husband is healthy again and has been promoted to the prestigious position of bank manager, it appears that life is taking a positive turn.

Suddenly, however, on Christmas Eve, Nora finds herself being blackmailed with the old forgery by an unscrupulous and desperate bank employee who is afraid of losing his job when Torvald becomes manager. Torvald discovers Nora's forgery anyway and, rather than protecting his wife, reacts by turning against her, damning her for jeopardizing his job. She concludes that she has been nothing more than a possession—a "doll"—to her husband for all of their eight-year marriage. So at the final curtain, Nora walks out on him and her children, determined to become a self-reliant person.

ANALYSIS: Nora's departure from her family was shocking and outrageous when *A Doll's House* was first staged in 1879. The play was written against a political background of almost zero women's rights. This particular adaptation by Frank McGuinness is excellent.

SCENES/MONOLOGUES: Female/Female Scenes (1), Male/Female Scenes (5)

DOUBT—A PARABLE
by John Patrick Shanley (Theatre Communications Group)

SYNOPSIS: The action takes place in 1964, the year after John F. Kennedy's assassination. The place is St. Nicholas, a Catholic church and school in the Bronx. Sister Aloysius Beauvier is a rigid, rule-driven school principal who convinces herself, on pathetically weak circumstantial evidence, that Father Flynn, the parish priest, has sexually molested one of the young students. Her goal is to ruin him, to bring him down, and, in the end, she succeeds. Along the way to her goal, however, she causes great pain to all parties involved. The boy she suspects of being molested is deprived of the priest's companionship, which he badly needs at this point in his life. Also, the boy's teacher, Sister James, is caught up in a struggle of values because she is convinced Father Flynn is innocent while at the same time aware that Sister Aloysius is her superior.

Analysis: Winner of the 2005 Pulitzer Prize for Drama, this is a superb play that is chock-full of good scenes to work on. Be sure to read the author's preface to the play. He explains in detail what he is trying to accomplish with the work. All levels.
Scenes/Monologues: Male/Female Scenes (2), Female/Female Scenes (2), Three-Person Scenes (1)

DRAMA
by Anton Chekhov (*The Sneeze: Plays and Stories by Anton Chekhov*, translated and adapted by Michael Frayn, Samuel French)

Synopsis: Pavel Vasilevich, a well-known writer, is working at home when an admirer with literary ambitions shows up to get feedback on the drama she has written. Although he agrees to take a look at it if she'll leave it with him, she begins to read it to him right away. Pavel tries diplomatically to stop the reading, but the woman seems oblivious to his growing discomfiture. She goes on and on and, to be truthful, her writing is awful. Finally, when all else fails, he takes out a knife and kills her.
Analysis: Extremely funny eight-page play. Michael Frayn's adaptation is marvelous. All levels.
Scenes/Monologues: Male/Female Scenes (1)

DREAM GIRL
by Elmer Rice (Dramatists Play Service)

Synopsis: Aspiring novelist Georgina Allerton is a daydreamer living a mundane life, finding spice only in her very active fantasies. She confronts this fact about herself when her secret love, her very married brother-in-law, decides to get a divorce and suggests they get together. Finally given the opportunity to act on her fantasy, however, Georgina retreats. Clark Redfield, a hardboiled realist and newspaperman, then enters her life. Although there is chemistry between them, she feels threatened when he accuses her of preferring fantasy to reality. Eventually, however, Georgina falls in love with Clark and, at the play's end, they marry.
Analysis: This 1945 play is the epitome of innocence. Stylistically dated, but still good scene-study material. All levels.
Scenes/Monologues: Male/Female Scenes (1), Female Monologues (1)

DRESSER, THE
by Ronald Harwood (Samuel French)

Synopsis: Sir is an aging actor-manager whose showcase role is King Lear. He travels the English provinces with his entourage, portraying that character and others. *The Dresser* focuses on his final performance, set in war-torn England in 1942, and explores the relationships Sir has formed over the years with his dresser, Norman; the woman he lives with; and others in the ragtag company.
Analysis: A lovely ode to the theater, a valentine to a lifestyle now regretfully long gone, Sir is a role to be cherished. To do it justice, however, an actor needs to have some seasoning, insight, and technical power. Albert Finney played Sir to Tom Courtenay's Norman in the marvelous 1983 movie. Written in the British vernacular.
Scenes/Monologues: Male/Female Scenes (1), Male Monologues (4)

DUET FOR ONE
by Tom Kempinski (Samuel French)

SYNOPSIS: World-famous violinist Stephanie Abrahams finds her career abruptly halted at the premature age of thirty-three when she is afflicted with multiple sclerosis. Losing the skill that literally defines her life, along with her marriage, she becomes suicidal. Seven months after the diagnosis, Stephanie begins psychotherapy. *Duet for One* is a session-by-session diary of her progress. The early denial of her pain turns into hostility, then fury, and finally, acceptance.

ANALYSIS: Very intense material. Stephanie is in a wheelchair for almost the entire play. Anne Bancroft and Max Von Sydow starred in the 1981 production on Broadway.

SCENES/MONOLOGUES: Male/Female Scenes (1), Female Monologues (1)

DYLAN
by Sidney Michaels (Samuel French)

SYNOPSIS: Based on *Dylan Thomas in America* by John Malcolm Brinnin and *Leftover Life to Kill* by Caitlin Thomas, *Dylan* tracks the famous Welsh poet's final American lecture tours, ending with his death at thirty-eight in the White Horse Tavern in New York's Greenwich Village. Journalistic in style, hopping back and forth across the Atlantic and all around the United States on a bare stage, this is very effective theater. Dylan speaks with a Welsh accent, while Caitlin has an Irish accent.

ANALYSIS: This is the kind of material that, if done well, can be theatrical magic. All levels.

SCENES/MONOLOGUES: Male/Female Scenes (2), Male Monologues (1)

ECCENTRICITIES OF A NIGHTINGALE, THE
by Tennessee Williams (Dramatists Play Service)

SYNOPSIS: This later version of *Summer and Smoke* features a much more aggressive and high-strung Alma, and John isn't so obviously a hell-raiser. It also has fewer characters and more focused scenes. Furthermore, Alma actually goes to bed with John on New Year's Eve in a hotel room that is rented by the hour. In the end, however, she still winds up alone, although this version doesn't mention John and Nellie's marriage. The final moments are exactly the same: Alma picks up a traveling salesman at the fountain.

ANALYSIS: Although *Summer and Smoke* is the better-known work, Tennessee Williams preferred this later version. The scenes are more pointed, the conflict more overt, and Alma is a little closer to the edge. All levels.

SCENES/MONOLOGUES: Male/Female Scenes (6), Female Monologues (4)

ECHOES
by N. Richard Nash (Samuel French)

SYNOPSIS: Sam, a high-school history teacher, and Tilda, occupation unknown, share a room in a mental institution. They spend most of their time in a safe, pretend world, excluding the doctors and all the threatening realities they bring with them. Sam, however, is getting better and, as he begins shifting toward lucidity—and away from Tilda—she panics, trying desperately to keep him bound to their pretend world. At the final curtain, he moves into the next room so he can see his wife and three-year-old son, while Tilda is left alone with her fantasies.

ANALYSIS: N. Richard Nash is best known as the author of the play *The Rainmaker*. I like this play, *Echoes,* for scenework because the actors have to construct a credible pretend reality. All levels.

SCENES/MONOLOGUES: Male/Female Scenes (6), Female Monologues (2)

EDUCATING RITA
by Willy Russell (Samuel French)

SYNOPSIS: Like *Pygmalion*, this comedy features an educated but burnt-out literature professor who takes an uneducated but young, spunky, lower-class woman under his wing. Rita excels, perhaps outdistancing Frank in understanding the deeper implications of the assigned material. During the year covered by the play, her shallow husband kicks Rita out because she is trying to better herself, and Frank drifts into and out of a merely comfortable relationship. At the final curtain, it looks like Frank and Rita might get together, now that she is educated.

ANALYSIS: A lovely 1981 two-character, two-act romantic comedy that was the basis for a 1986 movie starring Michael Caine and Julie Walters. Written in the British vernacular, the respective difference between Frank and Rita's upper-and-lower-class accents is important. All levels.

SCENES/MONOLOGUES: Male/Female Scenes (2), Female Monologues (1)

EFFECT OF GAMMA RAYS ON MAN-IN-THE-MOON MARIGOLDS
by Paul Zindel (Dramatists Play Service)

SYNOPSIS: Tillie is an emotionally isolated teenager who is consumed with love for science. She finds a kind of symmetry and beauty in the study of atoms that is missing from her dysfunctional home life. When she becomes a finalist in her school's science fair, the play turns into a family drama in which her alcoholic mother and seizure-prone older sister ruin any possible honors.

ANALYSIS: Winner of the 1971 Pulitzer Prize, this haunting and beautifully written drama is chock-full of metaphors. The colorful role of Tillie's alcoholic mother was created on stage by Sada Thompson and later played by Joanne Woodward in the movie version. All levels.

SCENES/MONOLOGUES: Female/Female Scenes (1), Female Monologues (3)

EMPRESS OF CHINA
by Ruth Wolff (Broadway Play Publishing)

SYNOPSIS: The story of the Dowager Empress Tzu-Hsi (1835–1908) and her rise to power in China. Starting as the Emperor's concubine, she ultimately ruled the country for fifty years, keeping the tentacles of Western civilization at bay.

ANALYSIS: Ruth Wolff specializes in dramas with strong, central female characters. All characters are of course Asian. All levels.

SCENES/MONOLOGUES: Male/Female Scenes (2), Female Monologues (2)

END OF THE WORLD WITH SYMPOSIUM TO FOLLOW, THE
by Arthur Kopit (Samuel French)

SYNOPSIS: A mysterious, wealthy industrialist commissions an out-of-work playwright to write a play based on the premise that the world is going to end because of nuclear proliferation. As the playwright researches the topic, interviewing generals and war experts, he is shocked to learn that nuclear proliferation is, in the final analysis, like a giant M. C. Escher drawing and makes no sense.

ANALYSIS: This 1984 comedy, directed on Broadway by Hal Prince, was written by the prolific and talented Arthur Kopit. All levels.

SCENES/MONOLOGUES: Male/Male Scenes (1), Male Monologues (2)

ENEMY OF THE PEOPLE, AN
by Henrik Ibsen (adapted by Arthur Miller, Dramatists Play Service)

SYNOPSIS: A small Norwegian city seeks financial salvation through the development and promotion of a health spa. Everything moves forward happily until Dr. Thomas Stockmann discovers that the local water is polluted. It is filled with disease-causing bacteria that are washing downstream from a tannery, which, ironically, his father-in-law owns. When it becomes clear that Stockmann intends to publicize the danger, the local power elite, including his brother the mayor, conspire to ostracize and discredit him, officially labeling him an "enemy of the people." Stockmann stands on principle, even though this translates into personal financial ruin and hard times for his family. Despite local hostility, he remains true to his sense of what is right.

ANALYSIS: Henrik Ibsen's most militant play, reportedly based on an actual 1830 incident. Arthur Miller's adaptation is marvelous. All levels.

SCENES/MONOLOGUES: Male/Male Scenes (2)

ENTER LAUGHING
by Joseph Stein (adapted from Carl Reiner's novel, Samuel French)

SYNOPSIS: This play is set in New York City during the 1930s. David Kolowitz is a "nice Jewish boy" with a predictable future as a pharmacist, who has a sweet, simple local girlfriend named Wanda. When David sees an ad for the Marlowe Theatre and School for Dramatic Arts, he thinks that he is better suited for the glamorous life of an actor. The Marlowe school turns out to be a seedy nickel-and-dime operation, the kind of place where an aspiring actor's wallet is more important than his talent. The owner's jaded daughter is the company ingenue. David, who has almost zero talent, is cast opposite the ingenue and has an important (to him) kissing scene. Opening night is almost a disaster but, wonderful or not, David is happy to have made his theatrical debut. Although his parents think he is making a big mistake if he doesn't go to pharmacy school, Wanda believes he is doing the right thing.

ANALYSIS: Joseph Stein is best known as the author of *Fiddler on the Roof.* He has a wonderful feel for physical comedy, and this play is a total delight. All levels.

SCENES/MONOLOGUES: Male/Female Scenes (1)

EQUUS
by Peter Shaffer (Samuel French)

SYNOPSIS: Martin Dysart, a doctor at the Rokesby Psychiatric Hospital in southern England, accepts seventeen-year-old Alan Strang as a patient. Alan has blinded six horses with a metal spike, and the court has ordered him to be treated at the hospital rather than being sent to prison. Dysart and Strang spar like two gladiators in a ring but, in the end, come to respect each other as the young man's complex motives are understood. In the process of working with Alan, Dysart questions his own values.

ANALYSIS: Extraordinarily intelligent script dealing with religion, sexuality, and guilt. Much of the play's power, however, derived from the original, highly theatrical staging by John Dexter.

SCENES/MONOLOGUES: Female Monologues (1)

EVERYTHING IN THE GARDEN
by Edward Albee (adapted from the play by Giles Cooper, Dramatists Play Service)

SYNOPSIS: Richard is outraged to learn that his wife has started earning money by working as a high-priced prostitute, and he threatens to throw her out. On the other hand, they are living beyond their means in an upscale neighborhood, and they could use the money she's making. To complicate matters, several other wives from the country-club set are also working as prostitutes, but their husbands like the money and condone the practice. Then the wealthy man next door is accidentally killed after he discovers the neighborhood secret. The husbands get together and bury him in the backyard. At the final curtain, the women decide to continue hooking, and their very charismatic madam, Mrs. Toothe, sets up shop in the neighborhood.

ANALYSIS: This strange 1968 drama contains some excellent, well-written scenes for actors in workshop. All levels.

SCENES/MONOLOGUES: Male/Female Scenes (2), Female/Female Scenes (1)

EVILS OF TOBACCO, THE
by Anton Chekhov (*The Sneeze: Plays and Stories by Anton Chekhov*, translated and adapted by Michael Frayn, Samuel French)

SYNOPSIS: Nyukhin is the father of seven unmarried daughters and the henpecked husband of a domineering woman who owns and operates a school for girls. In this fifteen-minute monologue, he addresses an assembly of female students on the evils of tobacco. Nyukhin does not, however, really make his points because he gets lost in relating incidental details of his personal life. Toward the end of the speech, he returns to the subject at hand when he hears his wife approaching.

ANALYSIS: A one-act comedy with a poignant edge. The more Nyukhin talks, the more the audience realizes how he has wasted his life. Anton Chekhov initially considered this monologue to be inconsequential, but over the years he revised it many times, which explains its richness. For experienced actors.

SCENES/MONOLOGUES: Male Monologues (1)

EXONERATED, THE
by Jessica Blank and Erik Jensen (Dramatists Play Service)

SYNOPSIS: *The Exonerated* is nonfiction drawn from interviews with former death-row convicts. What they all have in common is that they were first sentenced to death and, before the sentence could be carried out, were discovered to be innocent after all. The point of the whole enterprise of course is that the United States judicial system, particularly as it is applied to the death penalty, is highly imperfect. And just how much margin of error should a country allow when the punishment is the taking of life itself?

ANALYSIS: As compelling as these stories are, I don't think many of them are good for audition purposes. The problem is that they are informative, even dispassionate, a sort of declamatory history remembered. All levels.

SCENES/MONOLOGUES: Male Monologues (1)

EXTREMITIES
by William Mastrosimone (Samuel French)

SYNOPSIS: Marjorie is alone in her house when Raul appears, supposedly looking for "Joe." Quickly, he becomes menacing and tries to rape her. She sprays insecticide in his face, blinding him, and then ties him up with extension cords and shoves him into the fireplace. By the time Marjorie's roommates return, Raul appears to be the victim, not the criminal. Marjorie is wild-eyed and bent on revenge. After an extended psychological game of cat and mouse in which Raul cleverly turns the women against each other, he agrees to confess his crime to the police. Satisfied that he won't walk away free, Marjorie turns him over to the legal system.

ANALYSIS: William Mastrosimone was motivated to write *Extremities* after developing a friendship with a rape victim who lived in constant terror that her rapist would return. He decided to create a scenario that gives the victim the opportunity for revenge. But is Marjorie's desire to hurt the man evil in itself? As the playwright asks in the afterword to the acting-edition of the play, "How does one deal with evil without becoming evil oneself?" Physically violent and erotic material, appropriate for mature actors of all levels.

SCENES/MONOLOGUES: Male/Female Scenes (2)

FALLEN ANGELS
by Noel Coward (Samuel French)

SYNOPSIS: Jane and Julia, friends since childhood, were involved romantically with the same handsome Frenchman before their respective marriages. Now, five years later, their marriages have become merely comfortable; they love their husbands, but there is no spark. Suddenly, the Frenchman arrives in town, throwing both women into a frenzy of romantic anticipation and guilt. In the end, the two couples stay married, but the former lover moves into a flat upstairs, so the audience suspects that the juiciest moments are yet to come.

ANALYSIS: Another vintage piece of fluff from playwright Noel Coward. The plot is ridiculously improbable, but he milks it for all it is worth. Appropriate for all levels.

SCENES/MONOLOGUES: Male/Female Scenes (1), Female/Female Scenes (1)

FAR COUNTRY, A
by Henry Denker (Samuel French)

SYNOPSIS: A dramatization of one of Freud's breakthrough cases, detailing the treatment of an attractive young woman, Elizabeth von Ritter, who is plagued by phantom leg pain. With Freud's encouragement, she puts the pieces together in her memory and…voilà!…she can walk again!

ANALYSIS: This material is a great deal of fun for scenework. Actors who like to pull out all the stops will love it. The great Kim Stanley played von Ritter in the 1961 production. All levels.

SCENES/MONOLOGUES: Male/Female Scenes (2), Male/Male Scenes (1)

FATHER'S DAY
by Oliver Hailey (Dramatists Play Service)

SYNOPSIS: It's Father's Day, so the women in a New York City co-op apartment building are having a get-together while their ex-husbands take the children for the day. Because the play is character-driven rather than plot-driven, the audience learns in Act I about each of the women. They discuss, for example, how they came to marry the way they did, what they think of motherhood and sex, and why they're divorced. In Act II, when the ex-husbands join them on the patio, the audience discovers that, in most cases, the women and men have illusions about one another. Richard, for example, is actually bisexual, but Marian doesn't have a clue. She thinks he is promiscuous with other women. The major event in the play is the custody battle between Louise and Tom. Their seven-year-old son has chosen to live with his father, and Louise is trying to cope.

ANALYSIS: Biting, intelligent, sophisticated comedy/drama. Good scenes. All levels.

SCENES/MONOLOGUES: Male/Female Scenes (1), Female/Female Scenes (1), Female Monologues (2)

FENCES
by August Wilson (Samuel French)

SYNOPSIS: Troy Maxson, the son of a sharecropper, is a powerful, sometimes violent man who understands the virtues of hard work and the value of an education. Here, in Pennsylvania in 1957, he has a home, a good woman, a grown son from a former marriage, and a teenage son from this union. *Fences* covers the years 1957 through 1965, ending with Troy's death. During this time, the audience sees him involved in a standoff with his young son, father a son by another woman, get promoted from garbage collector to garbage-truck driver, and have his simple-minded brother jailed. Troy also finishes putting up a fence around the house, more to keep people in than to keep people out.

ANALYSIS: Winner of the 1987 Pulitzer Prize, *Fences* is a major achievement. The role of Troy Maxson, tailor-made for James Earl Jones, is on a par with that of Willy Loman from *Death of a Salesman*. The entire cast is African-American. All levels.

SCENES/MONOLOGUES: Male/Female Scenes (1), Male/Male Scenes (1), Male Monologues (2), Female Monologues (2)

FIRST BREEZE OF SUMMER, THE
by Leslie Lee (Samuel French)

SYNOPSIS: Gremmar is in her mid-seventies when the audience first meets her, and already her cough and dizzy spells signal that she won't live too much longer. As her children and grandchildren sort out their lives in the present day, Gremmar's story is told in flashback sequences. The audience meets the three men, two black and one white, with whom she had children and finds out why she never married any of them. When Louis, the grandson who dotes on Gremmar the most, learns that the father of his Aunt Edna was a white man, he flies into a rage, embarrassed by what he perceives to be Gremmar's wild sexual past and lack of racial pride. Before she actually gets an opportunity to respond to Louis's rage, however, she is gone.

ANALYSIS: Winner of the Obie for Best Off-Broadway Play in 1975 and later a Tony Award nominee. This is a wise and outstanding drama, well written, and excellent for scenework. All levels.

SCENES/MONOLOGUES: Male/Female Scenes (6), Male Monologues (1)

FOB
by David Henry Hwang (*FOB and The House of Sleeping Beauties: Two Plays,* Dramatists Play Service)

SYNOPSIS: *FOB* (an abbreviation for "Fresh Off the Boat," a derogatory term for a newly arrived Chinese person) is set in the back room of a Chinese restaurant in Torrance, California. Grace, a college journalism student, is a first-generation Chinese American. Her cousin Dale is an American of Chinese descent, second generation. Steve is a Chinese newcomer, a man who mysteriously appears and claims to be Gwan Gung, the Chinese god of warriors, writers, and prostitutes. To Dale, this new fellow is a grinning, pidgin-speaking stereotype of everything Asian-Americans have tried to outgrow; to Grace, who is initially skeptical, Steve becomes part of a Promethean struggle against the loss of divinity.

ANALYSIS: David Henry Hwang, author of *M. Butterfly,* wrote *FOB* while an undergraduate student at Stanford University during the late 1970s. The play is stylistically innovative, blending mythic and contemporary characters, as well as elements of Chinese opera and kitchen-sink drama. *FOB* won the 1981 Obie for Best Play after running at New York's Public Theatre. The entire cast is Asian-American. All levels.

SCENES/MONOLOGUES: Male/Female Scenes (1), Male Monologues (1), Female Monologues (1)

FOOL FOR LOVE
by Sam Shepard (Dramatists Play Service)

SYNOPSIS: May is Eddie's half sister, but they've been romantically involved for fifteen years, living in a trailer in some unnamed place out west. She may have been pregnant at one time, but this isn't clear. Eddie disappears now and then, and the last time he went, May hit the road herself, landing in a motel on the edge of the Mojave Desert. Eddie finds her and wants to take her back but, when he arrives, she is dressing to go out on a date with a local fellow she met. After a while, Martin, her date, arrives and he and Eddie have something of a standoff. Then a mysterious woman in a black Mercedes, perhaps a countess Eddie has been dating, firebombs Eddie's truck and horse trailer in the parking lot outside the motel. When Eddie goes out to confront her, May starts packing her suitcase to move on, telling Martin that Eddie isn't coming back.

ANALYSIS: Actors love to work on Sam Shepard's plays because the characters are so bold. Even though the action is set in modern America, the characters have about them the air of the Old West. Very primal. All levels.

SCENES/MONOLOGUES: Male/Female Scenes (1), Male/Male Scenes (1)

FOX, THE
by Allan Miller (based on D. H. Lawrence's short novel, Samuel French)

SYNOPSIS: The year is 1918. Jill and Nellie purchased the old Bailey Farm and moved there three years ago intending "to live our own lives, without having to strut about to other people's ideas and demands." It has been hard going, how-ever, and the women's experiment is about to end when a young soldier appears unexpectedly at the door. Jill and Nellie invite him to stay for a few days, and he immediately begins to charm and dominate them. Nellie is smitten when he pro-poses marriage to her the next day. Alarmed by this sudden threat to her rela-tionship with Nellie, Jill tries to force him out and to talk Nellie out of marriage. She finally convinces Nellie that he wants only the farm and a couple of women to take care of him. Henry, recognizing that Jill has become his enemy, kills her. At the final curtain, the audience knows that he'll have his way with Nellie, and that Jill was correct about his true purpose.

ANALYSIS: A big question left unanswered in the script is whether or not the women are lovers. It works much better if you come down on the "yes" side. Written in the British vernacular, but can be transposed into American English. All levels.

SCENES/MONOLOGUES: Female/Female Scenes (1), Male Monologues (1), Female Monologues (1)

FRANKIE AND JOHNNY IN THE CLAIR DE LUNE
by Terrence McNally (Dramatists Play Service)

SYNOPSIS: All of the action takes place in Frankie's Tenth Avenue apartment in New York City between 3 A.M. and dawn. She and Johnny, her co-worker at a greasy-spoon restaurant, have made love for the first time, and Frankie is ready for him to put on his clothes and go home. He, on the other hand, has fallen in love. Frankie can handle the sex, but she isn't up for true intimacy because she has been burned before. Their emotionally defensive dating dance nonetheless becomes more intimate. By sunrise, he still has not departed and we know that they will stay together.

ANALYSIS: Terrence McNally is one of our finest playwrights. The dialogue here rings true and is often poetic. Marvelous characters. All levels.

SCENES/MONOLOGUES: Male/Female Scenes (3), Male Monologues (1), Female Monologues (1)

GENIUSES
by Jonathan Reynolds (Samuel French)

SYNOPSIS: A Hollywood movie company is shooting a major motion picture enti-tled *Parabola of Death* (read *Apocalypse Now*) in the Philippines. The hotshot young director is woefully behind schedule because of monsoons, the necessity of coordinating a cast of thousands, an incomplete script, and a Playmate of the Year with the runs.

ANALYSIS: Fun parody of big-time, over-budget moviemaking. All levels.

SCENES/MONOLOGUES: Male/Female Scenes (1), Male/Male Scenes (2)

GETTING OUT
by Marsha Norman (Dramatists Play Service)

SYNOPSIS: After spending most of her young life in jail, Arlene is getting out. But this isn't going to be easy. Her former pimp appears and tells her how much she can make on the streets of New York; a former guard at the prison is hanging around, trying to make time with her; and her mother has no use for her. All

Arlene wants is to stay out of jail and somehow get it together so that she can bring her child to live with her. The child was taken away at birth by prison officials and given up for adoption.

ANALYSIS: The playwright utilizes a theatrical device in which two actresses play Arlene at different ages. The younger, more confrontational one moves into and out of the action. For scene-study purposes, simply eliminate her. Tough, uneducated, streetwise characters populate this challenging play. Best for experienced actors.

SCENES/MONOLOGUES: Female/Female Scenes (1), Female Monologues (1)

GINGERBREAD LADY, THE
by Neil Simon (Samuel French)

SYNOPSIS: Evy arrives home after ten weeks of drying out in a Long Island sanitarium. Her daughter, Polly, moves in with her, and best friends Jimmy and Toby are protective, hovering. Sobriety doesn't last long, however, as Evy quickly falls off the wagon directly into a reprise of an abusive relationship with Lou Tanner. At the final curtain, she resolves to try again—and harder—to get sober.

ANALYSIS: Neil Simon is at his best when he tackles tough subjects like this one. The dialogue and characters are sharply focused, often funny. All levels.

SCENES/MONOLOGUES: Male/Female Scenes (2), Female/Female Scenes (2), Female Monologues (2)

GIRL ON THE VIA FLAMINIA, THE
by Alfred Hayes (Samuel French)

SYNOPSIS: Rome in late 1944 is a war-ravaged city with few economic opportunities for anybody. Many Italian women, therefore, allow themselves to be "kept" by American soldiers that are occupying the country, even though such arrangements are a source of shame. Lisa agrees to be "married" to Robert, and the truth is that they might have been a good match under different circumstances. Before long, however, their sham marriage is exposed. Lisa is officially designated a prostitute and given a yellow government ID card so that she can work the streets.

ANALYSIS: This 1954 drama holds up very well, and the scenes are excellent, full of deep emotion and conflict. All levels.

SCENES/MONOLOGUES: Male/Female Scenes (4), Female/Female Scenes (1)

GLASS MENAGERIE, THE
by Tennessee Williams (Dramatists Play Service)

SYNOPSIS: The play is set in the Depression era during the 1930s in the Wingfields' modest St. Louis apartment. The central event in this classic American drama concerns Amanda's attempts to find a gentleman caller for her crippled and shy daughter, Laura. At Amanda's urging, her son, Tom, brings Jim O'Connor, a co-worker at the shoe factory, home to dinner, not realizing what elaborate and embarrassing attempts his mother would make to impress the visitor. It turns out that Laura once had a crush on Jim in high school and that he is currently engaged. The evening is a major disappointment to Amanda and leaves Laura even more emotionally withdrawn. Tom leaves home shortly after the events of the play in order to pursue a life as a poet.

ANALYSIS: Tennessee Williams's great autobiographical "memory" play, the one that brought him to fame in 1945. Williams modeled Tom on himself. Laura, based on his sister, Rose, and Amanda, based on his mother, Edwina, are major female roles. All levels.

SCENES/MONOLOGUES: Male/Female Scenes (2), Male Monologues (2), Female Monologues (1)

GLENGARRY GLEN ROSS
by David Mamet (Samuel French)

SYNOPSIS: The play is set amid the dog-eat-dog world of unscrupulous Florida real-estate salesmen—the kind of people who sell swampland to unsuspecting buyers. The central event involves Moss and Levene's theft of leads and contracts from the company office.

ANALYSIS: A stunning character study of salespeople and, ultimately, a comment on free enterprise in America. Rough language. Made into a movie in 1992 starring Alan Arkin, Ed Harris, Jack Lemmon, and Al Pacino. All levels.

SCENES/MONOLOGUES: Male/Male Scenes (2), Male Monologues (2)

GOAT, THE (OR, WHO IS SYLVIA?)
by Edward Albee (Dramatists Play Service)

SYNOPSIS: It is revealed during Martin's fiftieth birthday party that he has fallen in love with a goat he has named Sylvia. He tells this surprising news to his long-time friend, Ross, who reacts with repulsion and ultimately sends Martin's wife, Stevie, a letter filling her in on the secret. Stevie is devastated by the news that her husband is in love with a goat, as is the couple's gay son, Billy. At the end of the play, Stevie finds the goat and kills it.

ANALYSIS: This play is insanely funny at times but, like all of Albee's work, it has a dark underbelly. It is not comedy for comedy's sake. Ultimately, he raises the proposition that none among us can even begin to understand love. For sophisticated actors.

SCENES/MONOLOGUES: Male/Female Scenes (1), Male/Male Scenes (2)

GOLDEN BOY
by Clifford Odets (Dramatists Play Service)

SYNOPSIS: Joe Bonaparte plays the violin brilliantly, and his Italian-American, simple-living widower-father is hoping to see him pursue a career as a musician. But Joe lusts after the fast lane, money, and adventure—and also happens to have talent as a boxer. He enters the fight game, getting mixed up with promoters, hustlers, and their women. At first, Joe pulls his punches in the ring to protect his musician hands, but as he emotionally tilts away from his family and toward the lure of the bright lights and big money, he starts giving his all. He works his way up to an important match during which he kills his opponent.

Overcome with grief at the hardened man he has become, a killer of another man, Joe agrees to give it all up and run off with Lorna Moon, the promoter's streetwise girlfriend who has slowly but surely fallen in love with him. Joe and Lorna take a ride in his new car to celebrate their decision, get into an accident, and are both killed.

ANALYSIS: Less political than Clifford Odets's other plays, *Golden Boy* rests on an unlikely premise and sometimes has corny dialogue. Still, this 1937 drama was the biggest commercial success the famed Group Theatre ever had. The cast was stellar, including Lee J. Cobb, Elia Kazan, Frances Farmer as Lorna, Luther Adler as Joe, and Karl Malden in a tiny role. Harold Clurman directed.

SCENES/MONOLOGUES: Male/Female Scenes (2)

GOOSE AND TOMTOM
by David Rabe (Samuel French)

SYNOPSIS: A slice of ugly life with a couple of bleak, miserable, lowlife, women-hating, violent, small-time jewel thieves, presented in the spirit of *A Clockwork Orange* and *Blade Runner*. Buddies Goose and Tomtom are continually trying to prove to one another and the world how tough they are. The action in this two-act play takes place in an underworld apartment the men share with Lorraine, a pretty woman who likes jewels and is impressed with their toughness. After the men's stash of diamonds is stolen, they resort to kidnapping and murder in their attempts to get the gems back.

ANALYSIS: The 1986 Broadway workshop production was directed by playwright David Rabe and featured Sean Penn, Madonna, and Harvey Keitel. Only experienced actors who have a true taste for experimental drama should attempt this material.

SCENES/MONOLOGUES: Male/Male Scenes (2)

HATFUL OF RAIN, A
by Michael V. Gazzo (Samuel French)

SYNOPSIS: Johnny Pope is fighting drug addiction, a habit acquired when he was recuperating in a military hospital after the Korean War. Borrowing money from his brother, Polo, to support a forty-dollar-a-day habit and keeping his addiction secret from his family, Johnny is sinking deeper and deeper into despair. As Johnny becomes more withdrawn and restless, Celia, his pregnant wife, believes that he must be having an affair. After all, he often disappears at night. Longing for affection, she is drawn to Polo, now living with her and Johnny in their small New York City apartment. Polo is also mightily attracted to Celia, so both of them struggle against their inclinations. By the end of the play, Celia learns the truth about Johnny's addiction and calls the police to come get him so he can begin a supervised withdrawal.

ANALYSIS: The quintessential Actors Studio drama, developed by Michael V. Gazzo in the mid-1950s at the studio lab in New York. Many scenes grew directly out of improvisation. This gritty social drama was an important early showcase for Shelley Winters, who played Celia, and Ben Gazzara, who played Johnny. All levels.

SCENES/MONOLOGUES: Male/Female Scenes (3)

HEDDA GABLER
by Henrik Ibsen (adapted by Jon Robin Baitz, Grove Press)

SYNOPSIS: As the first act begins, Hedda and her new husband, George Tesman, are returning to Norway from a loveless six-month European honeymoon. They move immediately into an impressive new house that they cannot afford unless George were to get an expected promotion. In addition, Hedda is already pregnant (though not showing yet).

Things rapidly begin to unravel for Hedda when Thea Elvsted arrives. She has broken with her husband and is in pursuit of her true love, Eilert Lovborg, who is said to be here in town. Unbeknownst to Thea, however, Eilert is Hedda's former main squeeze. The very mention of Eilert's name sends Hedda into a state of anxiety, but she says nothing to Thea about it.

Soon, Eilert arrives at the house, bringing with him the handwritten manuscript of his new book. He immediately begins to declare his feelings for Hedda, but she rebuffs him, telling him she will not cheat on her husband.

Eilert goes with George and Judge Brack to a men's smoker party, leaving Hedda and Thea alone. The night goes by, and still the men do not return. At dawn George comes in carrying Eilert's manuscript, which he says the man dropped while in a drunken stupor en route to a whorehouse.

Eventually, Eilert himself arrives and announces that he has torn his manuscript to shreds. Hedda knows this is not true, but she doesn't tell him that she in fact has the book in her desk drawer. Instead, she gives Eilert a pistol with which to commit suicide.

Eilert leaves, and Hedda burns the manuscript. When George comes in again, he is outraged that she could do such a thing. But it is too late. Soon word comes that Eilert has indeed killed himself.

Judge Brack, a long-time admirer of Hedda, arrives to tell Hedda in private that he knows she gave the pistol to Eilert. His insinuation is that he will tell no one if she will provide him sexual favors. Hedda knows that this man has power over her life and, unable to endure the situation, walks into the next room and shoots herself in the head.

ANALYSIS: Jon Robin Baitz has done a fine job with this translation, which makes a strong statement about feminism.

SCENES/MONOLOGUES: Male/Female Scenes (1), Female/Female Scenes (1), Three-Person Scenes (1)

HEIDI CHRONICLES, THE
by Wendy Wasserstein (Dramatists Play Service)

SYNOPSIS: Beginning in 1965, when Heidi Holland is sixteen, and progressing to 1989, this play follows the evolution of a New Yorker as she chooses a career, searches for the right man, falls in love, falls out of love, sees friends come and go, tries to make sense of the world, and adopts a baby. All of the characters are urbane, witty, and capable.

ANALYSIS: This frequently touching comedy, winner of the 1989 Tony Award for Best Play and the 1989 Pulitzer Prize for Drama, also won the New York Drama Critics Prize, the Drama Desk Award, the Outer Critics Circle Award, and the Susan Smith Blackburn Prize. All levels.

SCENES/MONOLOGUES: Male/Female Scenes (4), Female Monologues (1)

HELLO AND GOODBYE
by Athol Fugard (Samuel French)

SYNOPSIS: After a bitter fifteen-year absence, and having heard that her Afrikaner father is near death, Hester unexpectedly shows up at his lower-class home in Port Elizabeth to claim her share of his meager estate. She discovers that Johnny, her gloomy younger brother, is tending full time to the old man, having given up dreams of a life on his own. The brother won't let her see their father, explaining that he is sleeping in the other room. Hester digs through family belongings, trying to find the insurance money she contends her father collected when he lost his leg years earlier. She finds no money and, when there are no more boxes to be opened, Johnny admits that their father is in fact already dead and that he knew all along there was no money. Johnny has been comforting himself with the delusion that the old man was still alive in the next room. Not wanting further involvement with her emotionally ruined brother, Hester returns to her life in the big city.

ANALYSIS: Powerful two-character drama. Both characters are Afrikaners, so accents would be appropriate. For experienced actors.

SCENES/MONOLOGUES: Male/Female Scenes (4), Female Monologues (1), Male Monologues (1)

HELLO OUT THERE
by William Saroyan (Samuel French)

SYNOPSIS: A drifter/gambler coming off a two-year run of bad luck picks up a woman in a small Texas town. After they have sex, the woman demands money, which he refuses. She cries rape, and the man is arrested. The entire action of this play takes place inside the jailhouse and revolves around the relationship he forms with the young cook/cleaning girl at the jail. Eventually, a lynch mob arrives and kills him, but not before he has given all his money to the girl and urged her to head for San Francisco.

ANALYSIS: Like all of William Saroyan's other plays, this fourteen-page one-act drama, written in 1941, is musical and poetic and evokes a sense of loneliness. All levels.

SCENES/MONOLOGUES: Male/Female Scenes (1)

HERE WE ARE
by Dorothy Parker (*24 Favorite One Act Plays,* edited by Bennett Cerf and Van H. Cartmell, Doubleday/Main Street Books)

SYNOPSIS: A young couple, married precisely two hours and twenty-six minutes, is en route via a Pullman car to New York City for their honeymoon. The groom is eager to consummate the union, but the bride has a bit of anxiety about the prospect. So they talk about everything except the subject at hand.

ANALYSIS: Innocent, well-written 1931 fun from Dorothy Parker. The play is just ten pages long. All levels.

SCENES/MONOLOGUES: Male/Female Scenes (1)

HOOTERS
by Ted Tally (Dramatists Play Service)

SYNOPSIS: Cheryl, a twenty-five-year-old working woman, is entertaining a serious proposal of marriage but isn't sure she is ready for adulthood. She has brought her girlfriend Ronda to Cape Cod for a weekend of sun and serious girl-talk. As it happens, they meet Clint and Ricky, a couple of wild and crazy nineteen-year-olds with sex on their minds and beer in their hands. To Ronda's dismay, Cheryl hops into bed with Clint, evidently trying to hide from responsibility by immersing herself in a party scene. When Clint tells Cheryl that he loves her, however, the party abruptly ends. In the end, Cheryl begins to take a serious look at herself. Clint and Ricky, meanwhile, have come to a Waterloo of their own, facing the same questions about adulthood, responsibility, and friendship.

ANALYSIS: On the surface, *Hooters* is about horny postadolescents on the make. The language is frequently sexist. There is, however, a method to this madness. The immensely talented playwright, Ted Tally, is up to something. He has highlighted and isolated the pursuit of hedonistic pleasures in order to make a deeper point about values. All levels.

SCENES/MONOLOGUES: Male/Female Scenes (1), Female/Female Scenes (2), Male/Male Scenes (2), Female Monologues (1)

HOUSE OF BLUE LEAVES, THE
by John Guare (Samuel French)

SYNOPSIS: Artie's apartment in Sunnyside, Queens, is full of comic madness on account of the imminent visit of the Pope to New York City. Artie, an untalented but hopeful musician, wants the Pope to bless his music; Bunny Flingus, Artie's mistress who lives downstairs, wants the Pope to bless her hoped-for marriage to Artie—even though Artie presently has a mentally deficient wife named Bananas. Artie's maladjusted son, Ronnie, has come home, AWOL from the Army, and intends to blow up the Pope with a homemade bomb. Add to this nutty stew three crazed nuns, a Hollywood producer, and a deaf starlet, and stir well.

ANALYSIS: This comedy is insanely funny and has been often revived since it premiered in 1986. All levels.

SCENES/MONOLOGUES: Male/Female Scenes (1), Male Monologues (1), Female Monologues (2)

HOUSE OF RAMON IGLESIA, THE
by José Rivera (Samuel French)

SYNOPSIS: Dolores and Ramon Iglesia are trying to sell their dilapidated Long Island home so that they can return with their sons to Puerto Rico after years of unsuccessful struggling to make it in the United States. But establishing title to the house is complicated. Untangling the knots involves expensive trips back and forth to Puerto Rico, and Dolores and Ramon are broke. The selling of the house is the central event of the play and, against that, the family tries to determine whether they are essentially Puerto Rican or essentially American. There is a lot of generational conflict.

ANALYSIS: Wonderful material by a very talented playwright. The drama was first broadcast as part of the *American Playhouse* public television series in 1986. The entire cast is Hispanic. All levels.

SCENES/MONOLOGUES: Male/Female Scenes (1), Male Monologues (1), Three-Person Scenes (1)

HOW I LEARNED TO DRIVE
by Paula Vogel (Dramatists Play Service)

SYNOPSIS: The play is told through the onstage narration of a young woman nicknamed "Li'l Bit." It jumps back and forth in time, tracking her life from age eleven until her early thirties, the unifying theme being the sexual relationship she had with her Uncle Peck all during her childhood and adolescence. By any standard, Uncle Peck is a pedophile, but he is surely the most charming one you will ever see on stage. And, though the child is always the victim, the playwright has not let Li'l Bit off scot-free. All in all, the relationship with her uncle is a sorrowful piece of history, one that will stay with her all her life; it is also one that, in all likelihood, leads ultimately to Uncle Peck's early alcoholic death.

ANALYSIS: *How I Learned to Drive* won the Pulitzer Prize in 1998 and is one of the most intriguing plays you are likely to read or work on. An almost-sweet comedy about pedophilia? It doesn't seem possible, but Ms. Vogel pulled it off.

SCENES/MONOLOGUES: Male/Female Scenes (1), Female Monologues (1)

HURLYBURLY
by David Rabe (Samuel French)

SYNOPSIS: Set in the boozy, cocaine-filled world of Hollywood. Two men coming out of failed marriages share a house in the Hollywood Hills. *Hurlyburly* explores their relationships with each other and with various friends and lovers. There is a continual quest for meaning and connection.

ANALYSIS: Bleak, funny, and brilliantly written. The 1984 production had a dream cast, directed by Mike Nichols: William Hurt, Harvey Keitel, Christopher Walken, Jerry Stiller, Cynthia Nixon, Sigourney Weaver, and Judith Ivey. A challenging play for intelligent actors of all levels.

SCENES/MONOLOGUES: Male/Female Scenes (2), Male/Male Scenes (3), Male Monologues (3), Female Monologues (1)

HUSBANDRY
by Patrick Tovatt (Samuel French)

SYNOPSIS: Harry's aging parents are struggling to make ends meet on their Kentucky farm, and they want him to take over the place. But Harry has a life of his own in New York, including a career-oriented wife who has no interest in farming. Harry is ambivalent about moving, and his wife is actively opposed to it.

ANALYSIS: This work explores the plight of the often overlooked American farmer. Well written. All levels.

SCENES/MONOLOGUES: Male/Female Scenes (2), Male Monologues (1), Female Monologues (1)

I AM A CAMERA
by John Van Druten (Dramatists Play Service)

SYNOPSIS: Adapted from *The Berlin Stories* of Christopher Isherwood, this play was ultimately the basis for the hit musical *Cabaret*. It tells the story of Sally Bowles, would-be actress/singer, and her circle of friends and lovers in 1930 Berlin. As John Van Druten explains in his preface to the acting edition, the play lacks a definable plot; the intent was to create the feel of Berlin at the dawn of Nazism and to people it with richly drawn characters. Van Druten succeeded, particularly with the demonstrative and dramatic Sally Bowles, one of the loveliest roles an actress could hope for.

ANALYSIS: All levels.

SCENES/MONOLOGUES: Male/Female Scenes (3)

I HATE HAMLET
by Paul Rudnick (Dramatists Play Service)

SYNOPSIS: Andrew Rally, star of the television hit *L.A. Medical*, returns to New York to "take a few classes, maybe do a play," wanting to edge his way back into the theater. Instead, based on his celebrity, Andrew gets cast in the title role of Hamlet in Shakespeare in the Park. He is terrified, believing the role is beyond his abilities. Both Andrew's girlfriend and his agent are encouraging, but his Los Angeles producer/friend thinks he is a fool not to jump into a new television series. Then things take a wild turn when the ghost of John Barrymore appears in Andrew's apartment and urges him to fulfill his actor's destiny by playing the great role. When finally Andrew does indeed play Hamlet, he does so not very well, but with the knowledge that he has given it his all.

ANALYSIS: Nicol Williamson played John Barrymore on Broadway and evidently didn't get along with the actor playing Andrew. During one highly publicized performance, the latter stormed off the stage and quit on the spot because Williamson had swatted him on the butt with a sword during a mock duel. All levels.

SCENES/MONOLOGUES: Male/Female Scenes (1), Male/Male Scenes (1), Male Monologues (1)

IMMIGRANT, THE
by Mark Harelik (Broadway Play Publishing)

SYNOPSIS: The story begins in Hamilton, Texas, in 1909 and continues to the present day. A young Russian Jewish immigrant, Haskell Harelik, arrives in America through the port of Galveston instead of the usual New York route. Two local residents, Ima and Milton Perry, befriend Haskell and give him a place to live. Subsequently, Milton arranges financing for Haskell's dry-goods business. After Haskell brings his wife over from Russia, the families continue to share a close friendship. The Harelik family ultimately have three sons, the youngest of whom they name after Milton.

Both families prosper and enjoy one another until 1939, when a Shabbos mealtime discussion about Hitler flares up into a full-fledged argument between the men. After that, they stubbornly refuse to talk to one another for years, meeting only once for a brief time shortly before Milton's death. In a curtain speech, Milton Harelik, American through-and-through, speaks warmly of his parents and of Ima Perry, bringing their story up to the present day.

ANALYSIS: Americans may be cut from many different kinds of trees, but they all are planted in the same yard. This is a lovely play. All levels.

SCENES/MONOLOGUES: Male/Female Scenes (1), Male/Male Scenes (1), Female/Female Scenes (1)

IMPASSIONED EMBRACES
by John Pielmeier (Dramatists Play Service)

SYNOPSIS: This play consists of fourteen sketchlike scenes and monologues by the author of *Agnes of God*. There is no particular theme, but Pielmeier is a fine writer and there is worthwhile material here.

ANALYSIS: Some of the pieces came from a program at the Repertory Theatre of St. Louis, and others from the Actors Theatre of Louisville. All levels.

SCENES/MONOLOGUES: Male/Female Scenes (2)

IMPORTANCE OF BEING EARNEST, THE
by Oscar Wilde (Samuel French)

SYNOPSIS: John (Jack), who lives in the country, pretends to have a naughty brother named Earnest who lives in the city. Algernon, who lives in the city, pretends to have an invalid friend named Bunbury who lives in the country. Both men use these fictions as excuses to travel back and forth between city and country, to live two separate existences. This complicated and unnecessary fabrication blows up in the men's faces when they fall in love with Cecily and Gwendolen, who become entangled in the deceit. In the end, the confusion is all straightened out, and everybody gets married, presumably to live happily ever after.

ANALYSIS: This is possibly the most famous comedy ever written. It pokes malicious fun at social manners and pretensions of nineteenth-century England. First performed in 1895. Appropriate for all levels, but novice American actors may have a challenge with the high comedy and sharp, distinctly British repartee.

SCENES/MONOLOGUES: Female/Female Scenes (1)

INDEPENDENCE
by Lee Blessing (Dramatists Play Service)

SYNOPSIS: Kess visits her childhood home in Independence, Iowa, for the first time since moving to Minneapolis four years ago, right after she had her mother committed to a mental hospital. Kess discovers that her sister Jo is pregnant by a man who is about to marry another woman and that their mother, who is out of the hospital and back at home, is planning to raise Jo's baby. Kess's sister Sherry, meanwhile, is engaging in meaningless sex, and no member of the family, it seems, is altogether comfortable with the fact that Kess is a lesbian. This all-female household, in short, is very maladjusted. A competition of sorts commences between Kess and her mother to see who can most strongly influence Jo. Kess wants to get her out of Independence and take her to the big city while there is still time for her to salvage a respectable life.

ANALYSIS: An improbable premise for a play that is very well written. This would be what you might call a "serious comedy." All levels.

SCENES/MONOLOGUES: Female/Female Scenes (2)

I NEVER SANG FOR MY FATHER
by Robert Anderson (Dramatists Play Service)

SYNOPSIS: Gene's elderly father, Tom, is a stern, demanding, financially successful man who has never been very available on an emotional level. After Tom's wife dies unexpectedly, he is forced to confront his own physical frailty, as well as the disjointed relationship he has with Gene. The father and son struggle to find some equilibrium, some common points of communication. Tom believes it proper that Gene be the dutiful son and live close by in case he is needed, but Gene contends that he has a life of his own and wants to return to California and remarry. In the end, Gene leaves, and his father eventually follows him to Los Angeles, where the latter dies while still harboring deep feelings of bitterness.

ANALYSIS: A thoughtful, intelligent exploration of a dynamic father/son relationship. Hal Holbrook played Gene on stage in 1968, and Gene Hackman played the character in the 1970 film. All levels.

SCENES/MONOLOGUES: Male/Female Scenes (1), Male/Male Scenes (1), Male Monologues (1)

IN THE BOOM BOOM ROOM
by David Rabe (Samuel French)

SYNOPSIS: This play, set in the 1970s, tracks the struggle and ultimate descent of Chrissy, an unsophisticated young woman who comes from squalid, abusive origins. She works as a go-go dancer in a small club and is looking for a way out.

Prostitution, childhood incest, and homosexuality are woven into the fabric of this tense story. In the end, Chrissy falls even lower on the social scale, from the relative safety of the go-go cage to becoming a full-tilt stripper.

ANALYSIS: Even though 1970s go-go clubs and go-go cages are a thing of the past, this play still works. It is extremely well written. There is a lot of good workshop material in it. For the latest Samuel French acting edition, David Rabe has revised the play, reverting to its original two-act format.

SCENES/MONOLOGUES: Male/Female Scenes (2), Female/Female Scenes (2), Female Monologues (2)

I OUGHT TO BE IN PICTURES
by Neil Simon (Samuel French)

SYNOPSIS: Blocked Hollywood screenwriter Herb Tucker awakes one morning to discover his nineteen-year-old daughter, Libby, sitting in the living room. He hasn't seen her for sixteen years, since divorcing her mother. Now she announces that she wants to be an actress and asks Herb to introduce her to some important movie people. He tries to tell her that the life of an actress is tough, but she won't hear it. During the next two weeks, Herb and Libby get to know one another, slowly dropping their defenses. They develop the father/daughter relationship that they should have had all along. Finally, Libby gives up the acting idea and returns to her mother in New York, happier now that she has something worked out with Herb.

ANALYSIS: Funny and warm. Good Neil Simon. All levels.

SCENES/MONOLOGUES: Male/Female Scenes (2), Male Monologues (1)

ISN'T IT ROMANTIC?
by Wendy Wasserstein (Dramatists Play Service)

SYNOPSIS: Janie and Harriet are prototypes of the urban, educated, upwardly mobile young women who are trying to solve the career/family puzzle.

ANALYSIS: Wendy Wasserstein addresses this subject better probably than anyone else. The play is set back in the 1980s, but the career/family puzzle is still alive and well. Every scene is brief and breezy. All levels.

SCENES/MONOLOGUES: Female/Female Scenes (3)

I STAND BEFORE YOU NAKED
by Joyce Carol Oates (Samuel French)

SYNOPSIS: This play is composed of a series of monologues by women. There is the cafeteria worker who is married to a serial killer, the prostitute who is upset by the blood blister on her lip, the anorexic young woman with the orange, the mental patient who talks about Jesus, and more.

ANALYSIS: Joyce Carol Oates is a world-renowned novelist whose playwriting ventures are a mixed bag, veering toward the experimental. For sophisticated actors.

SCENES/MONOLOGUES: Female Monologues (2)

IT HAD TO BE YOU
by Renée Taylor and Joseph Bologna (Samuel French)

SYNOPSIS: Vito Pignoli, a New York City advertising agency producer, feels sorry for actress Theda Blau, who rushes into a commercial audition at the last minute and nervously rambles through the rather hysterical story of her life. Afterward, he assures her in private that she did a good job in the audition but says that her type is a little too unconventional for his conservative client. Vito and Theda then share a cab, winding up at her place. One thing leads to another, one night turns into two, and, before you know it, these people with wildly different personalities wind up marrying each other. At the final curtain, Vito plans to quit his coat-and-tie ad-agency job and devote himself to writing plays with Theda.

ANALYSIS: This physical comedy is great material for acting workshops. All levels.

SCENES/MONOLOGUES: Male/Female Scenes (2), Female Monologues (1)

JAR THE FLOOR
by Cheryl West (Dramatists Play Service)

SYNOPSIS: Four generations of women from a single African-American family gather for the great-grandmother's ninetieth birthday in Park Forest, Illinois. This is the main event of the play, but the real story lies in the way each of the women is trying to escape the expectations of her mother and find her own way in the world. Vennie, the youngest woman, arrives with her white girlfriend, Raisa, a single mother who has had a mastectomy. Vennie's mother, Maydee, is a college professor with high hopes for her daughter. Maydee's mother, Lola, is a good-time flashy dresser who, as it turns out, allowed one of her many men friends to molest Maydee when she was thirteen. Lola's mother, Madear, is senile, delightful, frequently wise, and blunt to a fault. By the final curtain, Lola learns that Vennie isn't going to get her college diploma after all, that she intends to pursue a singing career instead. Lola and Maydee overtly acknowledge the sexual abuse. And Madear escapes into her reveries.

ANALYSIS: Cheryl West has a keen ear for the music of language, ranging from the very uneducated vernacular of Madear, to Maydee's sophistication, to Lola's funky talk. In addition, the playwright puts her finger firmly on the pulse of the mother/daughter dance. All levels.

SCENES/MONOLOGUES: Female/Female Scenes (2)

JOE TURNER'S COME AND GONE
by August Wilson (Samuel French)

SYNOPSIS: The place is Seth Holly's rooming house in Pittsburgh, Pennsylvania; the time is 1911. The black men and women who stay here are in transit, physically and spiritually. They're moving between memories of farmhand slavery and the promises inherent in an urban future. Sometimes they still practice voodoo while they pray to a Christian god. Herald Loomis arrives with his eleven-year-old daughter, seeking a room and information on the whereabouts of his wife, Martha. The two were separated when he was incarcerated in Tennessee on Joe Turner's chain gang. It turns out that Martha has come north and is now a devout member of an evangelical church.

When Martha and Herald meet face-to-face, thanks to the assistance of Rutherford Selig, a white "people finder," it is clear they can no longer be husband and wife. In fact, they've grown apart spiritually. She has found God at the same point at which he has come to distrust a white Jesus. Finally, he turns their daughter over to Martha to raise and walks down the road in search of himself.

ANALYSIS: This is a fascinating play on account of the spiritual never-never land it occupies. The 1988 Broadway production garnered several Tony nominations. All levels.

SCENES/MONOLOGUES: Male Monologues (3), Female Monologues (2)

JOINED AT THE HEAD
by Catherine Butterfield (Dramatists Play Service) (*Women Playwrights: The Best Plays of 1992*, Smith & Kraus)

SYNOPSIS: Maggie arrives in Boston on a book-promotion tour and is contacted by her old high-school boyfriend, Jim. She agrees to have dinner with him and his wife, who is coincidentally also named Maggy (but with a different spelling). Maggie arrives for dinner and soon discovers that Maggy has cancer. A relationship develops between the two women, ending with Maggy's death.

ANALYSIS: The theatrical device used by Ms. Butterfield is that Maggie is telling the story of Maggy from Maggie's own perspective, but Maggy often thinks the other Maggie's version is incorrect and interrupts her to set the record straight. There is a shifting in and out of various realities. Very theatrical and beautifully written. All levels.

SCENES/MONOLOGUES: Male/Female Scenes (1), Female/Female Scenes (2), Male Monologues (1), Female Monologues (1)

K2
by Patrick Meyers (Dramatists Play Service)

SYNOPSIS: Mountain climbers Harold and Taylor are stuck on an ice ledge 27,000 feet up the side of K2, the world's second tallest mountain. There are only two hours of daylight remaining, and one more night without the protection of a tent or sleeping bags means certain death for both men. To make matters worse, Harold's leg is badly broken, and they have only one rope to use for their descent. Harold and Taylor struggle to save themselves and, while looking death in the face, address the existential questions of life. After a sudden avalanche destroys their remaining equipment, the men decide that Taylor must descend alone, leaving Harold to die.

ANALYSIS: Life-and-death situations make for excellent human drama. Scenework in this one-act play requires heavy clothing and perhaps a rope to establish authenticity. All levels.

SCENES/MONOLOGUES: Male/Male Scenes (1), Male Monologues (1)

KATHY AND MO SHOW, THE: PARALLEL LIVES
by Mo Gaffney and Kathy Najimy (Dramatists Play Service)

SYNOPSIS: The show consists of fourteen brief sketchlike comedy scenes that were written to be performed by the authors. The two women play all the characters, which range from God's reps overseeing the creation of humans, to a straight couple in a gay bar, to a couple of five-year-olds trying to figure out the Church, to a couple of menstruating men (!). The style is fast-moving and irreverent. There is no central plotline per se, just a theme built on the idea that people of all colors, shapes, sexes, and sizes are equal and should appreciate each other.

ANALYSIS: This material can be a lot of fun in workshops for actors who want to play with sketch comedy à la *Saturday Night Live*. All levels.

SCENES/MONOLOGUES: Female/Female Scenes (5), Female Monologues (1)

KEELY AND DU
by Jane Martin (Samuel French)

SYNOPSIS: Keely was raped and impregnated by her ex-husband, so she decided to have an abortion. On her way to the clinic, she was kidnapped by Operation Retrieval, a Christian anti-abortion organization. Keely soon discovers that she is a prisoner and that the members intend to keep her in chains in a basement room until her pregnancy is too advanced to terminate. Her constant companion is a grandmotherly woman named Du, who takes her orders from a pastor named Walter.

As the months unfold, Keely and Du gradually form a bond, separated only by the fundamental disagreement about the propriety of abortion. On Keely's birthday, Du secretly arranges a little celebration, allowing Keely to drink some beer and change clothes for the first time since she was captured. The next day Keely grabs the wire hanger that her new dress had been hanging on and performs a self-abortion, causing a massive hemorrhage. Du calls an ambulance, an act that results in her eventual arrest as a kidnapper. In the final scene of the play, Keely is visiting Du in prison.

ANALYSIS: The setup for this drama allows Jane Martin to evenhandedly explore both sides of the abortion debate. For sophisticated actors.

SCENES/MONOLOGUES: Female/Female Scenes (1), Female Monologues (2)

KEY EXCHANGE
by Kevin Wade (Dramatists Play Service)

SYNOPSIS: Lisa is looking for a deeper commitment from Philip, so she suggests they exchange apartment keys. Philip interprets this as being fenced in. He likes things the way they are. Meanwhile, Philip's newly married friend Michael is having trouble; his wife has run off to have a fling with a choreographer. The action in *Key Exchange* involves the back-and-forth negotiations in both of these relationships. Ultimately Michael's wife returns home.

ANALYSIS: Well-written comedy that is fun for acting class. All levels.

SCENES/MONOLOGUES: Male/Female Scenes (2), Female Monologues (1)

KILLER JOE
by Tracy Letts (Samuel French)

SYNOPSIS: Set in a trailer park outside of Dallas, this play is populated by a family of persistent losers. Chris, the twenty-two-year-old son, has turned to dealing drugs to make a living after a failed rabbit farming venture. He finds himself in peril because he owes some very bad people $6,000, so he comes to the seedy house trailer that his father, Ansel, shares with his new wife and Dottie, Chris's innocent sister. Ansel, of course, has no money to lend Chris, and so Chris hatches a Plan B. He has recently learned that his mother (Ansel's ex-wife) has a life insurance policy of which Dottie is the beneficiary. His big idea is that he and Ansel should hire an assassin to kill mama, and then divide up the insurance money.

The plan moves forward with surprising twists and violent turns. Mama winds up dead, but it turns out that Dottie is not the beneficiary. In the end, there is a huge bloodbath.

ANALYSIS: The characters in this play are the very definition of lowlife. They are violent, profane, and almost incestuous. Therefore, the material is not for the fainthearted. Still, "Killer Joe" is extremely well written and often darkly funny.

SCENES/MONOLOGUES: Male/Male Scenes (1)

LADY AND THE CLARINET, THE
by Michael Cristofer (Dramatists Play Service)

SYNOPSIS: Luba, a woman in her late thirties, narrates the history of her love life, from the time she was sixteen up through her present entanglements with Jack. A musician is continually on stage with her, providing clarinet accompaniment for whatever mood she requests. Sometimes she addresses the audience, sometimes the musician, and sometimes she is involved in reenactments from her past.

ANALYSIS: Although this play is full of male/female scenes, they are more like musical riffs and, given the narrator's shifting focus, probably aren't the best source material for scenework in acting class. There are, however, a couple of superb monologues. All levels.

SCENES/MONOLOGUES: Male Monologues (2)

LANDSCAPE OF THE BODY
by John Guare (Dramatists Play Service)

SYNOPSIS: Betty is on the Nantucket ferry, trying to understand why so many people in her life—her family, her employers—have died mysterious, untimely deaths. She herself is under suspicion for murdering her own son in New York's Greenwich Village some months earlier. As she talks with the investigating detective who has been trailing her, the play goes into flashback mode, combing through the events that led Betty from Bangor, Maine, to New York City, to South Carolina, back to New York, and then to the ferry. But she didn't kill her son, and she never finds out who did.

ANALYSIS: John Guare, one of our finest playwrights, wrote this comic, cryptic, graphic play in two days back in 1977. All levels.

SCENES/MONOLOGUES: Male/Female Scenes (2), Male Monologues (1)

LARGO DESOLATO
by Václav Havel (Grove)

SYNOPSIS: Professor Nettle's book, *Ontology of the Human Self,* contains a passage that government officials contend "disturbs the intellectual peace," so they pressure him to disown the work. *Largo Desolato,* seven scenes in one act, captures the agony and insanity of this intellectual's dilemma. On one hand, Nettles speaks for many faceless intellectuals when he defies the government; on the other, his life is in shambles. He is a nervous wreck, quickly becoming addicted to drugs and alcohol. In the end, he refuses to cooperate.

ANALYSIS: Václav Havel, a Czech dramatist and essayist, became the president of Czechoslovakia (1989–1992) and later of the Czech Republic (1993–2003). His voice remains an important one in the world. For sophisticated actors.

SCENES/MONOLOGUES: Male/Female Scenes (1), Male/Male Scenes (1)

LARK, THE
by Jean Anouilh (adapted by Lillian Hellman, Dramatists Play Service)

SYNOPSIS: A retelling of the story of Joan of Arc, the fifteenth-century French peasant girl who responded to the voice of God and raised the siege of Orléans. The action moves back and forth in time on a bare stage, beginning with Joan's childhood and ending with her being burned at the stake after standing trial as a heretic.

ANALYSIS: Julie Harris won a Tony as Best Actress in 1956 for her portrayal of Joan. All levels.

SCENES/MONOLOGUES: Male/Female Scenes (1), Female Monologues (2)

LAST OF THE RED HOT LOVERS
by Neil Simon (Samuel French)

SYNOPSIS: After twenty-three years of marriage and having arrived at the ripe age of forty-seven, Barney faces his mortality. He is determined to have one more fling. So, over the course of a year, he brings three women to his mother's New York City apartment. All three attempts flop, but they cause Barney to develop a new appreciation for his wife.

ANALYSIS: This is an early Neil Simon comedy, something of a chestnut now, but it is still entertaining. All levels.

SCENES/MONOLOGUES: Male/Female Scenes (2), Male Monologues (1), Female Monologues (1)

LAST SUMMER AT BLUEFISH COVE
by Jane Chambers (JH Press)

SYNOPSIS: Bluefish Cove, near New York City, has been a lesbian beach colony for thirty years. The rental agent mistakenly presumes that Eva, who is running from a bad marriage, is a lesbian, and rents her a cottage, creating an instant threat to the women at the colony who prefer to remain in the closet. As the action evolves, Eva strikes up a romantic relationship with Lil and is happy to finally discover that she is a lesbian. Then Eva learns the horrible news that everybody else at Bluefish Cove already knows: Lil has cancer and has only a few months to live.

ANALYSIS: Frequently touching, well written. All levels.

SCENES/MONOLOGUES: Female/Female Scenes (3)

LAST YANKEE, THE
by Arthur Miller (one-act play, Dramatists Play Service)

SYNOPSIS: Two men meet for the first time in the waiting room of a state mental hospital where both their wives are being treated for depression. Frick has money, but Leroy, although a direct descendent of Alexander Hamilton and the son of a lawyer, is a carpenter by trade. He has seven children and is living hand-to-mouth. The men's conversation is full of class sensitivities and prejudices. Frick's attitude finally enrages Leroy, and communication breaks down.

ANALYSIS: Note that I am referring here to the one-act play. Arthur Miller also wrote a two-act play with this same title. The one-act is a nine-page, two-character work that Miller wrote for a play festival in New York. As always with his writing, there are complex characters and plenty of subtext. All levels.

SCENES/MONOLOGUES: Male/Male Scenes (1)

LATER
by Corinne Jacker (Dramatists Play Service)

SYNOPSIS: Malachai Dowson died a year ago, and his widow and two daughters have gathered this Labor Day at their beach house on the Rhode Island shore. Each woman relates to the memory of Malachai in different ways, and they each try to come to terms with it during the action of this play.

ANALYSIS: Corinne Jacker is a lovely writer. The script is full of subtle and telling details. All levels.

SCENES/MONOLOGUES: Female/Female Scenes (2), Female Monologues (3)

LAUGHING WILD
by Christopher Durang (Dramatists Play Service)

SYNOPSIS: Two strangers violently confront one another in the tuna-fish aisle of a New York City supermarket. Because the man is blocking the woman's path, she hits him over the head and curses at him. This crazy incident is then revisited repeatedly, as the action moves back and forth in time. Both the man and the woman tell their version of what really happened in the store. In the process, the audience learns that she is a frequent resident of mental institutions.

ANALYSIS: *Laughing Wild* is an outlandishly theatrical experiment more than a play, "breaking the fourth wall" and jumping back and forth in time. But it is very funny. All levels.

SCENES/MONOLOGUES: Male Monologues (1), Female Monologues (1)

LES BELLES SOEURS—REVISED
by Michel Tremblay (translated by John Van Burek and Bill Glassco; Talonbooks, Canada)

SYNOPSIS: Germaine has won a million trading stamps in a contest and is having a stamp-pasting party. Her sisters and friends steal the stamps as they paste them in. There is no plot per se in this all-female comedy-drama set in a small Catholic parish in Canada. The women put most of their energy into such unimportant activities as playing bingo and entering contests.

ANALYSIS: Stylistically, this play is dazzling and often bewildering. It caused a big dustup when first staged in Canada back in 1968 because it gave voice to a class of people usually ignored. It can be grotesquely comic while, at other times, poignant and troubling. The women suggest that the Catholic Church and men are responsible for their sad state of affairs. Scenework is not practical because there is such a large ensemble cast on stage at all times, but there are several excellent monologues.

SCENES/MONOLOGUES: Female Monologues (3)

LES LIAISONS DANGEREUSES
by Christopher Hampton (Samuel French)

SYNOPSIS: The action in this two-act drama takes place in and around Paris during the 1780s and involves wealthy, decadent, sexually cynical members of the aristocracy. The main plotline centers on a deal struck between the dashing and immoral Valmont and his sometimes lover, widow Madame Merteuil. She is seeking revenge against a former lover who jilted her and who now intends to marry Cécile, a virgin. Merteuil enlists Valmont to seduce (i.e., ruin) the younger woman before her wedding night. He at first refuses the assignment because he doesn't see enough sport in the pursuit of a fifteen-year-old. In addition, he is stalking bigger game, namely the virtuous, married, straight-laced Madame de Tourvel. Eventually he agrees and winds up seducing both Cécile and de Tourvel.

The fun, however, goes out of the game for Valmont because he allows himself to fall in love with de Tourvel, a mortal error according to the upside-down code of morals he and his fellow aristocrats share. Entanglements become even more complex as Le Chevalier Danceny beds Merteuil even though he is in love with Cécile. In the end, Valmont is killed in a duel with this man.

ANALYSIS: It is hard to keep all the liaisons on stage in focus, but it is worth the effort. It is wonderful material for sophisticated actors. The play is based on the classic novel by Pierre Choderlos de Laclos.

SCENES/MONOLOGUES: Male/Female Scenes (5)

LIE OF THE MIND, A
by Sam Shepard (Dramatists Play Service)

SYNOPSIS: Jake beat up his wife again, and this time thinks he killed her. He travels south, hiding out with his younger brother, Frankie, in a shabby motel room while he tries to sort out his options. Beth, meanwhile, doesn't die, but suffers brain damage and is being nursed by her parents in Billings, Montana. Jake moves into his childhood room in his mother's house, and Frankie heads to Montana to find out if Beth is dead or alive. He winds up getting shot in the leg by Beth's dad, who mistakes him for a deer. In the end, Jake also shows up in Montana, wrapped in the American flag, only to discover that Beth's mind has snapped, and that she is going to marry the relatively gentler Frankie.

ANALYSIS: Sam Shepard paints with bold colors, mainly red, white, and blue. His plays are full of symbolism as he claws at the underpinnings of the great American myths. Wide-open spaces, good old boys, women who stand by their men—and guns, always and forever, guns. All levels.

SCENES/MONOLOGUES: Male/Female Scenes (1), Female/Female Scenes (1), Male/Male Scenes (1)

LIFE AND LIMB
by Keith Reddin (Dramatists Play Service)

SYNOPSIS: Franklin joined the army to fight in the Korean War, leaving his new wife, Effie, behind. He lost his right arm during the battle at Pork Chop Hill and now, back in the United States, is unable to find work. Franklin descends into a depressed, alcoholic haze. Just when he is at his most desperate, he lands a job at a company that sells prosthetic devices. Gainfully employed at last, Franklin purchases a new television as a surprise gift for Effie, who is by now having an affair with another man. Before she sees the television, however, she and her girlfriend Doina are killed in a freak movie theater accident. Franklin becomes more and more subservient to Tod Cartmell, the owner of the prosthetic device company. At the play's end, Franklin dies and joins Effie in hell. Literally.

ANALYSIS: Keith Reddin has an excellent feel for dialogue and stagecraft, and the milieu of this drama, 1952–1956, is unusual. Most scenes are suitable for actors of any level, but the office confrontation between Franklin and Cartmell involves sexual humiliation and is appropriate for advanced actors only.

SCENES/MONOLOGUES: Male/Female Scenes (3), Female/Female Scenes (1), Male/Male Scenes (1)

LION IN WINTER, THE
by James Goldman (Samuel French)

SYNOPSIS: Henry II still has a deep affection for his wife, Eleanor of Aquitaine, but keeps her in prison because they can't agree on which of their three sons will inherit the English throne. Complicating their long-term dispute is an agreement Henry made with the French king regarding the marriage of Princess Alais to one of his sons in exchange for the grant of an important plot of land located twenty miles outside of Paris. Henry is himself now hopelessly in love with Alais and is unwilling to see her marry anyone but himself. In the end, he disinherits all of his sons and leaves for Rome in order to have his marriage to Eleanor annulled. This will free him to marry Alais. Henry hopes that a new marriage will produce worthier sons.

ANALYSIS: An appealing and fanciful comedy-drama with a peculiar, almost flippant tone in the face of life-and-death stakes. Although the play is set in 1183, the language is contemporary. Immortalized in the 1968 film of the same name, starring Peter O'Toole, Katharine Hepburn, and Anthony Hopkins. All levels.

SCENES/MONOLOGUES: Male/Female Scenes (4)

LIPS TOGETHER, TEETH APART
by Terrence McNally (Dramatists Play Service)

SYNOPSIS: Sally's brother died and left his Fire Island home to her. She, her husband Sam, and another couple, John and Chloe, are spending the Fourth of July weekend there. It turns out that Sally and John have been having an affair for a while, that John has been diagnosed with cancer, and that no one really gets along with each other. Everybody laughs a great deal, but there is always an underlying tension.

ANALYSIS: This comedy-drama displays Terrence McNally's usual excellent ear for dialogue. But note that all four characters are on stage continually, which makes scenework for acting class difficult. All levels.

SCENES/MONOLOGUES: Female Monologues (1)

LISBON TRAVIATA, THE
by Terrence McNally (Dramatists Play Service)

SYNOPSIS: Terrence McNally wrote two different endings for this play, which deals with the shifting relationships among several gay men. In both versions, Stephen is jealous of his lover Mike's involvement with a new man. In one version, he murders Mike; in the other, he doesn't. The first act is the same in both plays, a funny extended scene between Stephen and his friend Mendy.

ANALYSIS: In my view, *The Lisbon Traviata* has something of an identity crisis. The first act is definitely comedy. The second act can't make up its mind. Still, McNally is one of our finest playwrights. He writes dialogue as well as the best of them. All levels.

SCENES/MONOLOGUES: Male/Male Scenes (1)

LITTLE FOXES, THE
by Lillian Hellman (Dramatists Play Service)

SYNOPSIS: Set in the Deep South in 1900, *The Little Foxes* is about a ruthless family that turns on itself and about the innocent people who get hurt in the crossfire. Ben and Oscar Hubbard are brothers who will stop at nothing to make a dollar, including overcharging uneducated blacks and even marrying for money instead of love if necessary. They've arranged the deal of their lives, but they need their sister Regina's assistance to raise the investment. When she can't persuade her ailing husband, Horace, to participate, Oscar's spineless son, Leo, simply steals the money from him. Horace discovers the crime but, before he can take legal steps to do anything about it, he suffers a massive heart attack and dies.

ANALYSIS: This 1939 Broadway drama would have been better titled *The Little Pit Vipers* because of its cast of immoral characters. It is said that Tallulah Bankhead played Regina to the hilt in the original production. All levels.

SCENES/MONOLOGUES: Male/Female Scenes (2), Male/Male Scenes (1), Female Monologues (1)

LOBBY HERO
by Kenneth Lonergan (Dramatists Play Service)

SYNOPSIS: Jeff is a security guard in a midlevel Manhattan high-rise apartment building. He's not the sharpest tack in the box, but he tries hard and wants to do something worthwhile with his life. His role model and inspiration is his up-by-the-bootstraps African-American supervisor, William. The event that kick-starts the action of *Lobby Hero* occurs when William's younger brother is accused by the police of participating in a heinous rape and murder. William confides in Jeff that he doesn't trust the legal system to treat his brother fairly and has provided him with a false alibi. Then come Dawn and Bill, two New York City cops, who make a stop at Jeff's building. It transpires that Bill is visiting an "actress" in apartment 22J on a regular basis while he is sexually involved with his trusting partner, Dawn, on the side. Dawn, meanwhile, is actually in love with Bill and is shocked when Jeff tells her the truth about the woman in 22J. Jeff develops a crush on Dawn, which leads to discussions about their personal lives (while Bill is upstairs in 22J). Ultimately, Jeff has to decide whether or not to "do the right thing" and tell Dawn about William's big lie.

ANALYSIS: This play won the 2000 Outer Critics Circle Best Play. At first glance, it is deceptively simple and straightforward but, if you scratch the surface a bit, you see that all four characters are struggling with questions of ethics and morality. Along the way, the playwright questions the fairness of the legal system, the meaning of love, the obligations of friendship, and one's purpose in life. Lonergan has a wonderful way with dialogue, and his words roll easily off an actor's tongue.

SCENES/MONOLOGUES: Male/Female Scenes (3), Male/Male Scenes (1)

LONELY IMPULSE OF DELIGHT, A
by John Patrick Shanley (*Welcome to the Moon and Other Plays,* Dramatists Play Service). Also in *13 by Shanley* (Applause Books)

SYNOPSIS: Walter is in love with a mermaid that lives in New York's Central Park Reservoir. Late one night, he brings his best friend, Jim, to see her. Jim, understandably, is skeptical of the entire enterprise and isn't crazy about being in dangerous Central Park at midnight. Furthermore, Walter took him away from a fun party where he was just about to score with a pretty woman.

Sally the mermaid doesn't show up no matter how much Walter tries to summon her. Finally Jim gets tired of the whole thing—and worried about his friend's mental health—and he exits. Once he is gone, the mermaid predictably pops up to talk to Walter.

ANALYSIS: This is a delightful piece of fluff and can be great fun for the actors who play it. All levels.

SCENES/MONOLOGUES: Male/Male Scenes (1)

LONG DAY'S JOURNEY INTO NIGHT
by Eugene O'Neill (Yale University Press)

SYNOPSIS: The action takes place during a single day at the Tyrone summer home in 1912. Aging actor James Tyrone is forced to recognize that his wife, Mary, has once again descended into morphine addiction; his youngest son, Edmund, has contracted tuberculosis; and his shiftless eldest son, Jamie, will never reform. Mary is still tortured with guilt over the death of their two-year-old son twenty-five years ago. In addition, she has never been able to adjust to the nomadic lifestyle of an actor. She would rather live with her drug-induced fantasies of a bygone youth than suffer more pain in the real world.

James has saved almost every penny he ever earned and is now quite rich. Still, he lives in fear of poverty and is slow to part with a dollar even when it comes to paying for medical care for his own family. Jamie, at thirty-three, can find no profession he likes or is good at and is still financially dependent on his father. This situation further robs Jamie of his self-esteem. Edmund, though ill with tuberculosis, is actually the healthiest member of the family.

ANALYSIS: Eugene O'Neill wrote this famous autobiographical drama (he based Edmund on himself) in 1940, but it wasn't published until after his death in 1956. This is a major achievement for the American theater and a must-read for all acting students. The difficult material is appropriate for thoughtful and serious actors at all levels.

SCENES/MONOLOGUES: Male/Female Scenes (1), Male/Male Scenes (2), Male Monologues (2), Female Monologues (1)

LOOK HOMEWARD, ANGEL
by Ketti Frings (based on Thomas Wolfe's novel, Samuel French)

SYNOPSIS: World War I is raging in Europe, but time is measured more slowly in Altamont, North Carolina, where young Eugene Gant lives in a ramshackle, family-run boardinghouse. His tight-fisted mother appears to control his destiny just as she has that of Eugene's brother, Ben; sister, Helen; and artistic, alcoholic father, W. O. Gant. Then, one month during the fall of 1916, everything changes. Ben suddenly gets sick and dies, and Eugene falls in love with a pretty boarder named Laura. Their romance, while sweet and pure, is destined to fail because she is older than he—and, unbeknownst to him, is engaged to somebody back home. At the final curtain, Eugene is bound for college, for which his mother only grudgingly agrees to pay. With his imminent departure, she begins to realize how hollow her life has become.

ANALYSIS: Thomas Wolfe's autobiographical novel (he is Eugene) is a treasure of American literature, and Ketti Frings's adaptation, which won a Pulitzer Prize in 1958, does it proud. The role of Eugene, by the way, was an early showcase for Anthony Perkins. All levels.

SCENES/MONOLOGUES: Male/Female Scenes (4), Female Monologues (1)

LOSS OF ROSES, A
by William Inge (Dramatists Play Service)

SYNOPSIS: The life of an actress was rough in 1933, especially if her show folded in a remote city. Lila Green, finding herself stranded in just such a situation and with no employment prospects, temporarily moves in with Helen Baird and her son, a family she worked for years ago as a housekeeper and baby sitter. Although thirty-two years old, Lila is, in many ways, an unsophisticated and immature woman; she needs a man to baby and care for her. Ricky Powers, her current beau, is an insensitive and domineering actor who tries to entice her into performing in blue movies in Kansas City. Lila resists this proposition until an impulsively romantic night with Helen's young son, Kenny, turns into a disappointment the following morning. Forced to confront her advancing age and dismal employment prospects, Lila abandons her dreams of success on the stage, departing with Ricky for Kansas City, where the sordid world of pornography awaits her.

ANALYSIS: William Inge was a protégé of Tennessee Williams, and this drama carries the same air of poetry and symbolism that typifies Williams's work. All levels.

SCENES/MONOLOGUES: Male Female Scenes (2), Female Monologues (1)

LOST IN YONKERS
by Neil Simon (Samuel French)

SYNOPSIS: After Arthur and Jay Kurnitz's mother dies of cancer in 1942, they live for a year with their Grandma Kurnitz in Yonkers while their father works his way out of debt via out-of-town employment. It is through their eyes that the audience meets the family. For the most part, *Lost in Yonkers* is a character-driven work. The primary action centers on the evolution of the relationship between Grandma, an iron-fisted, humorless, old-school German-Jewish immigrant, and Bella, her childlike thirty-five-year-old daughter who lives at home and takes care of her. After the year passes, the boys' father returns to New York City, and they move back in with him.

ANALYSIS: Winner of the 1991 Pulitzer Prize for Drama as well as the Tony for Best Play. Mercedes Ruehl (Bella) and the wonderful Irene Worth (Grandma) also won Tony Awards as Best Actress and Supporting Actress, respectively. The role of Bella is among Neil Simon's finest achievements. She is a vulnerable, hopeful, and eccentric woman-child. All levels.

SCENES/MONOLOGUES: Female/Female Scenes (1), Female Monologues (1)

LOU GEHRIG DID NOT DIE OF CANCER
by Jason Miller (*Three One-Act Plays*, Dramatists Play Service)

SYNOPSIS: Victor Spinilli is the good but demanding coach of the Spinilli Spoilers, a Long Island little-league baseball team sponsored by the Spinilli family business, which Victor's father runs. After Victor gets into an on-field fistfight with an umpire, his father has him fired from the coaching job. This event, coupled with a late-afternoon conversation with the mother of a shy and sensitive boy on the team, leads Victor to serious introspection about his values, his relationship with his overbearing father, and his marriage.

ANALYSIS: This is a haunting, sometimes cryptic one-act drama by the author of *That Championship Season*. The writing here is superb, and the interplay among the characters always rings true. Jason Miller has an excellent ear for dialogue. All levels.

SCENES/MONOLOGUES: Male/Female Scenes (2), Male Monologues (1)

LOVER, THE
by Harold Pinter (Dramatists Play Service)

SYNOPSIS: Sarah and Richard, married ten years, have an unusual arrangement. After he leaves for work, she prepares herself to receive a lover. Richard returns in mid-afternoon, pretending to be the lover. Eventually Richard becomes jealous of the relationship his wife is having with his other, pretend self. He arrives home as Richard and declares that the whole fantasy relationship has to end. By then, however, Sarah is addicted to the arrangement, and so she begins to seduce Richard, who then turns back into the lover. The fantasy relationship will continue, if we can figure out which one is real and which is fantasy.

ANALYSIS: This play can be a lot of fun for sophisticated actors, having been written by one of the world's great playwrights. Just keep in mind that it deals head-on with sexual fantasy. Actors must be secure, trusting, and professional in their approach to it.

SCENES/MONOLOGUES: Male/Female Scenes (1)

LOVERS AND OTHER STRANGERS
by Renée Taylor and Joseph Bologna (Samuel French)

SYNOPSIS: Each of the five sketchy mini-comedies presented under the umbrella title of *Lovers and Other Strangers* deals with romantic relationships. The plots are minimal, but the dialogue is often hilarious.

ANALYSIS: There is an old New York saying: If you're from New York, and you're not Jewish, you're Jewish; if you're from Texas, and you're Jewish, you're not Jewish. Actors who do scenes from this comedy can keep that in mind. Very funny material. All levels.

SCENES/MONOLOGUES: Male/Female Scenes (3), Male Monologues (1), Female Monologues (1)

LOVE SUICIDE AT SCHOFIELD BARRACKS, THE
by Romulus Linney (Dramatists Play Service) (one-act version: *Seventeen Short Plays*, Smith & Kraus)

SYNOPSIS: The commanding general of Schofield Barracks in Hawaii and his wife commit joint suicide in a very public, highly ritualized Japanese ceremony. This play involves the subsequent hearing into the event. Through the words of many who knew and worked with them, it starts to become clear that this was an act of self-sacrifice. Ultimately, it is a call for all of us to get more involved in the political actions of our country.

ANALYSIS: Romulus Linney (side note: His daughter is actress Laura Linney) has a keen ear for dialogue. All levels.

SCENES/MONOLOGUES: Male Monologues (2), Female Monologues (1)

LUDLOW FAIR
by Lanford Wilson (*Balm in Gilead and Other Plays* by Lanford Wilson, Hill & Wang/Noonday)

SYNOPSIS: Rachel is distressed because she turned her boyfriend in to the authorities after she caught him stealing money from her and her roommate, Agnes. Now that he is in jail, Rachel thinks she may have overreacted. Agnes thinks Rachel did the right thing in this case but that she has had entirely too many boyfriends (six) in the last nine months. Still, Agnes admits that Rachel's social life may have been more exciting than her own dull one during the same period. All Agnes has to look forward to is tomorrow's lunch with her boss's skinny son—if she can get over this terrible cold, that is.

ANALYSIS: Excellent interplay between characters, and there is the extra challenge for one of the actors, who must have the mother of all colds. All levels.

SCENES/MONOLOGUES: Female/Female Scenes (2), Female Monologues (1)

LUV
by Murray Schisgal (Dramatists Play Service)

SYNOPSIS: Ellen is married to Milt, who is doing very well in business. Then she divorces him and marries Harry, Milt's old school chum who is climbing up from the depths of depression. Then Ellen divorces Harry and remarries Milt. Everybody tries to figure out the meaning of life, the mysteries of death, and of course, love.

ANALYSIS: Wonderful dark comedy. The characters are rich, full, sad, and funny. All levels.

SCENES/MONOLOGUES: Male/Female Scenes (2), Male/Male Scenes (1), Male Monologues (1), Female Monologues (1)

MAN FOR ALL SEASONS, A
by Robert Bolt (Samuel French)

SYNOPSIS: King Henry VIII wants to have his marriage to Catherine of Aragon annulled by the Catholic Church so that he can marry the young Anne Boleyn, who he hopes will give him a male heir. The Pope, however, turns down his request because he has already been forgiven one previous marriage. Furious, Henry requires his subjects to sign an Act of Supremacy, making him both spiritual and temporal leader of England. Sir Thomas More sympathizes with Henry's plight but will not sign the Act. The monarch puts increasing pressure on him, but More stands on principle. Finally, Henry has him executed.

ANALYSIS: Surely one of the best plays ever written, *A Man for All Seasons* raises questions about the role government versus church should play, and ethics. What price is a person willing to pay for his or her integrity? Thomas More paid with his life. All levels.

SCENES/MONOLOGUES: Male/Male Scenes (2)

MA RAINEY'S BLACK BOTTOM
by August Wilson (Samuel French)

SYNOPSIS: A recording session for Ma Rainey, "the mother of the blues," brings her together with her musicians who discuss, debate, and fight about the plight of the black person in America during the 1930s. After some fits and starts, they finally get the record cut, but that isn't the real point of the play. Among the colorful characters, Levee, the cornet player, has the most interesting development arc. He is a more serious musician than the others and has hopes for a recording contract of his own. When some white record producers thwart that dream, he sinks to the level of a street thug, knifing and killing another musician who accidentally steps on his new shoes.

ANALYSIS: Nominated for several Tony Awards in 1985, *Ma Rainey's Black Bottom* was August Wilson's first play to reach Broadway. The monologues are terrific. All levels.

SCENES/MONOLOGUES: Male Monologues (5)

MARCO POLO SINGS A SOLO
by John Guare (Dramatists Play Service)

SYNOPSIS: This is a comedy in the Absurdist tradition, set in the year 1999 on an iceberg off the coast of Norway. Stony McBride is making a movie about Marco

Polo, starring his own father. Stony's pregnant wife, a celebrated pianist, is involved in an affair with a politician who has gotten his hands on a cure for cancer. During the play, the audience experiences a cataclysmic earthquake that destroys much of Italy (Hawaii is already long gone), the discovery of a new planet, the astral impregnation of a woman by an astronaut, and a sudden change of power in Washington, DC.

ANALYSIS: John Guare intended *Marco Polo Sings a Solo* to be a philosophical counterpoint to his work *The House of Blue Leaves*. While the latter play deals with the limitations the characters face, this comedy presents a world of possibilities. All levels.

SCENES/MONOLOGUES: Male Monologues (2), Female Monologues (1)

MATCHMAKER, THE
by Thornton Wilder (Samuel French)

SYNOPSIS: This play is set in the early 1880s. Horace Vandergelder is a sweet, blustery, unmarried, self-made bag of hot air. Matchmaker Miss Dolly Levi is going to take care of that just as soon as she gets the cupids in place for his niece, Ermengarde, and her beloved, Ambrose the artist. There is a good deal of farcical running here and there, hiding behind screens and under tables, mistaken identities, and all sorts of charming diversions. In the end, everything comes up roses.

ANALYSIS: Was life ever really this simple? *The Matchmaker* is an American classic that was adapted in 1964 as the Barbra Streisand musical *Hello Dolly!* All levels.

SCENES/MONOLOGUES: Male/Female Scenes (1), Male Monologues (2), Female Monologues (1)

M. BUTTERFLY
by David Henry Hwang (Dramatists Play Service)

SYNOPSIS: Inspired by the true 1986 story of a French diplomat who passed state secrets to a Chinese actress who turned out to be not only a spy, but a man. Here Gallimard truly believes the illusion of femininity the opera singer Song Liling creates. The play unites these basic facts with a fable that highlights Western misconceptions and fantasies about Eastern women and their countries. The glue that holds it all together is the parallel story told in the opera *Madame Butterfly*.

ANALYSIS: All levels.

SCENES/MONOLOGUES: Male/Female Scenes (1)

MIDDLE AGES, THE
by A. R. Gurney, Jr. (Dramatists Play Service)

SYNOPSIS: The action takes place in the trophy room of a men's club in a large city from the mid-1940s through the late 1970s. The small cast of characters must age during this lengthy time span, which is a good part of the acting challenge. The club is a symbol of a kind of highly structured, conservative, moneyed lifestyle that the various characters are continually seeking or avoiding, and the play tracks the way their shifting values alternately pull them together and drive them apart.

ANALYSIS: A. R. Gurney is firmly anchored in WASP America, and this comedy holds its underlying values up for examination. All levels.

SCENES/MONOLOGUES: Male/Female Scenes (2), Male Monologues (1)

MIDDLE OF THE NIGHT, THE
by Paddy Chayefsky (Samuel French)

SYNOPSIS: A kindly fifty-three-year-old widower falls in love with a twenty-three-year-old woman who is unhappily married to a musician. No one in their circle of acquaintances approves of this union, but their love is true.

ANALYSIS: Excellent human drama, frequently touching. The actor who plays the widower needs to have a good feel for New York speech patterns. This sensitivity isn't as essential for the part of the young woman. All levels.

SCENES/MONOLOGUES: Male/Female Scenes (2), Female/Female Scenes (1)

MISS JULIE
by August Strindberg (*Six Plays of Strindberg*, translated by Elizabeth Sprigge, Doubleday/Anchor)

SYNOPSIS: During a midsummer night's revelry that takes place while her father, the Count, is away visiting relatives, Miss Julie makes love with Jean, the family valet. Unable to accept the consequences of her actions, she commits suicide, presumably after the final curtain. The sexual interplay between Miss Julie and Jean violates the taboo of class boundaries, provoking a conflict between her "instincts" as a woman and the propriety of her status in society.

ANALYSIS: Eugene O'Neill, accepting the 1936 Nobel Prize for Drama, said of August Strindberg: "(his)…influence runs clearly through more than a few of my plays…For me, he remains, as Nietzsche remains, in his sphere, the master, still to this day more modern than any of us, still our leader." Written in 1888 by a renowned misogynist and controversial in its time, *Miss Julie* is noted for the psychological complexity of its characters, its straightforward approach to sexual realism, and its unusual one-act format. All levels.

SCENES/MONOLOGUES: Male/Female Scenes (2), Male Monologues (1)

MISS LONELYHEARTS
by Howard Teichmann (adapted from Nathanael West's novel, Dramatists Play Service)

SYNOPSIS: A young, cynical, and ambitious newspaper reporter becomes an advice-to-the-lovelorn columnist during the 1930s. Known now as Miss Lonelyhearts, he finds that his life changes dramatically as the terrible problems of his readers force him to examine the concept of a merciful God. In an almost Christlike fashion, he tries to heal everyone who asks for his help. He gives himself sexually to a sad and lonely woman, who then turns on him when he refuses to have relations with her again. Her husband, a handicapped meter reader for the gas company, finds Lonelyhearts and kills him.

ANALYSIS: Nathanael West's 1933 novella is a classic of American literature. This stage adaptation doesn't come close to the disturbing power of the book, but some of the scenes are good. All levels.

SCENES/MONOLOGUES: Male/Female Scenes (3), Male Monologues (1)

MISS MARGARIDA'S WAY
by Roberto Athayde (Samuel French)

SYNOPSIS: A one-woman show in which a domineering teacher harangues the audience, treating them as if they are rather stupid eighth-graders. She sometimes threatens to send them to the principal, from which some people never return.

ANALYSIS: Written by a young Brazilian playwright, this controversial play is likely a metaphor for an imperialistic United States. Estelle Parsons drew raves and received a Tony nomination for her portrayal of the teacher. Rough language, challenging material for experienced actors.

SCENES/MONOLOGUES: Female Monologues (2)

MISTER ROBERTS
by Thomas Heggen and Joshua Logan (Dramatists Play Service)

SYNOPSIS: The action takes place aboard a supply ship operating in the back areas of the Pacific, May 1945. Lieutenant AJG Roberts, otherwise known as Mister Roberts, dropped out of medical school to get into the war and is frustrated by his noncombat assignment on the supply ship. An irreverent free spirit, he has conflicts with the self-made captain, an ambitious high-school dropout who resents college educated know-it-alls. In order to secure a much-needed recreational shore leave for the crew, Roberts strikes a secret deal with the captain, agreeing to be a better team player and to stop requesting transfers. Then, in frustration, he tosses the captain's beloved potted palm overboard.

During the ensuing shouting match between Roberts and the captain, which is inadvertently broadcast over the ship's loudspeakers, the crew learns about the deal and conspires to forge a transfer request to help Roberts get off the ship. Their scheme works: Roberts goes into combat, and is killed. His spirit and courage are inspirational to the crew, who begin to assert themselves in newer, stronger ways.

ANALYSIS: A well-crafted comedy-drama that ran for three years on Broadway, making Henry Fonda a star. All levels.

SCENES/MONOLOGUES: Male/Male Scenes (2), Three-Person Scenes (1), Male Monologues (1)

MODIGLIANI
by Dennis McIntyre (Samuel French)

SYNOPSIS: The police are hunting for the artist Modigliani, who broke the front window of a fancy restaurant in Paris. He desperately tries to borrow money from friends so that he and his lover, Beatrice, can flee to Martinique. In the meantime, Modigliani's agent, Zborowski, has made an appointment to show the artist's work to an important gallery owner. A sale would solve all the couple's financial problems. When the deal doesn't go through, Modigliani's situation gets even worse; his health deteriorates with tuberculosis, and Beatrice leaves him. At the end of the play, he and his friend Utrillo begin again with blank canvases.

ANALYSIS: A lusty, vibrant drama that is filled with historic and colorful characters who care intensely about life. Modigliani died when he was only thirty-five years old. All levels.

SCENES/MONOLOGUES: Male/Female Scenes (1), Male/Male Scenes (2)

MONDAY AFTER THE MIRACLE
by William Gibson (Dramatists Play Service)

SYNOPSIS: This is a sequel to *The Miracle Worker*, which deals with Annie Sullivan and her work with Helen Keller. Here, the action begins when Helen is in her early twenties and Annie is thirty-five, and tracks them for the next fifteen years or so. Annie marries John, a young academic who comes to help Helen with her writing. In time, however, he feels slighted by the growing fame of the two women and turns to drink. His marriage to Annie then founders.

ANALYSIS: Any scenes involving Helen are impracticable for workshop use because of technical requirements. People communicate with her by tapping on her palm, and the words are interpreted over the theater's public address system. There are, however, a couple of excellent scenes between Annie and John. All levels.

SCENES/MONOLOGUES: Male/Female Scenes (2)

MOON FOR THE MISBEGOTTEN, A
by Eugene O'Neill (Samuel French)

SYNOPSIS: After James Tyrone's mother died in California, he escorted her body across the country by rail, spending most of the trip in a drunken stupor and sleeping with the trashiest whore he could find on the train. *A Moon for the Misbegotten* begins a year after that trip. Tyrone feels deeply guilty and seeks forgiveness from Josie Hogan, the daughter of a tenant farmer on Connecticut land owned by Tyrone's family. Josie is nearly six feet tall and weighs 180 pounds. She is a powerful, full-breasted woman, not mannish at all, just big and powerful. She claims to have slept with half the men in the nearby village, but the big secret is that she is actually a virgin. Tyrone sees through her facade, she sees through his, and their confrontation on the porch in Act III is one of the most complex and revealing in dramatic literature. As their defenses fall, Josie realizes that Tyrone is looking for forgiveness, not a lover, and that the romance she hoped for will never be realized. At the final curtain, Tyrone heads down the road, bound for New York City, following the lure of bright lights and Broadway.

ANALYSIS: The last script completed by the Nobel Prize–winning playwright, *A Moon for the Misbegotten* is a sequel to *Long Day's Journey Into Night*. This second play tracks the tragic path of James Tyrone, Jr., a character that O'Neill based on his real-life brother, Jamie. World-class material for serious actors.

SCENES/MONOLOGUES: Male/Female Scenes (1), Male Monologues (1)

MRS. DALLY HAS A LOVER
by William Hanley (Dramatists Play Service)

SYNOPSIS: Mrs. Dally, age thirty-eight, is a closet romantic. She reads John Donne's poetry and longs to experience more of the sensitive possibilities in life. She is trapped, however, in a joyless fifteen-year marriage with a distant, insensitive, blue-collar husband in a small New York City apartment. The play concerns the ongoing sexual relationship she has with Frankie, an eighteen-year-old who lives downstairs in the same tenement building. On the surface, the age difference between Mrs. Dally and the young man makes their union seem almost sordid, but that is not the case.

ANALYSIS: This lovely and unusual one-act play, winner of the Vernon Rice Award for distinguished production off-Broadway, is frequently poetic and always tender. The age difference between the characters causes the audience—and actors—to reevaluate their preconceptions about romantic love. All levels.

SCENES/MONOLOGUES: Male/Female Scenes (3)

MRS. WARREN'S PROFESSION
by George Bernard Shaw (*Plays: Man and Superman; Candida; Arms and the Man; Mrs. Warren's Profession*, Signet Classic)

SYNOPSIS: Vivie Warren, a strong and confident, Cambridge-educated young woman, discovers that her mother has amassed considerable wealth from the operation of brothels. Despite Mrs. Warren's explanations about her impoverished origins and the scarce opportunities afforded women in the business world, Vivie is repulsed by her mother's occupation. At the final curtain, Vivie banishes Mrs. Warren—and her money—from her life.

ANALYSIS: The idea behind this play is to pit the characters of mother and daughter against one another: Mother works in the ditches in order to pay for the best education for her daughter; the educated daughter learns to look down upon the values of her own mother. Shaw wrote this play in 1894. All levels.

SCENES/MONOLOGUES: Female/Female Scenes (1), Female Monologues (1)

MURDER AT THE HOWARD JOHNSON'S
by Ron Clark and Sam Bobrick (Samuel French)

SYNOPSIS: This zany physical comedy tracks the shifting relationships between Arlene Miller; her husband, Paul, a used-car salesman; and their dentist and her lover, Mitchell Lovell. As the play's title suggests, all the action takes place in a Howard Johnson's motel. In Act I, Scene 1, Arlene and Mitchell plot to murder Paul. But in Act I, Scene 2, Arlene and Paul reunite and plot to murder Mitchell, who has begun an affair with his dental assistant. By Act II, Arlene has abandoned both men in favor of a relationship with her guru, so Mitchell and Paul get together and plot her murder. At the final curtain, Arlene and Paul reconcile, and Mitchell resolves to remain just a dentist.

ANALYSIS: A wildly improbable premise can lead to wonderful acting fun if everybody goes along with it. All levels.

SCENES/MONOLOGUES: Male/Female Scenes (2), Male/Male Scenes (1), Three-Person Scenes (1)

NATURE AND PURPOSE OF THE UNIVERSE, THE
by Christopher Durang (*Three Short Plays*, Dramatists Play Service)

SYNOPSIS: Eleanor is having a terrible time. As the curtain goes up, she is sobbing because her oldest son is a dope pusher and pimp; her middle son is a homosexual; and her youngest son, Andy, lost his penis in a freak reaping-machine accident. Then things really start to deteriorate. Sister Annie De Maupassant shows up at the house and announces that she is the new Pope. The census taker (who looks suspiciously like Sister Annie) appears and advises Eleanor to commit suicide because she is such a failure, and the athletic coach at Andy's school insists that since he has no penis, he must compete in girls' gymnastics. And that's not all...the chaos continues.

ANALYSIS: Durang's work just about defies reasonable analysis, but it is a toot to act. His characters are way out there on the comic ledge.

SCENES/MONOLOGUES: Female Monologues (2)

NERD, THE
by Larry Shue (Dramatists Play Service)

SYNOPSIS: Rick Steadman, who saved Willum's life during the Vietnam War, unexpectedly turns up at his home for a visit. Willum, eternally grateful to the man, rolls out the red carpet and tries to be a good host. Rick, however, turns out to be the houseguest from hell: a thoughtless, clumsy, self-involved nerd. After suffering in silence for a week, Willum and his friends plan to get rid of Rick.

ANALYSIS: Dinner-theater comedy, physical, silly, dumb at times, and fun. All levels.

SCENES/MONOLOGUES: Male/Male Scenes (1), Male Monologues (1)

'NIGHT, MOTHER
by Marsha Norman (Dramatists Play Service)

SYNOPSIS: Jessie lives with her mother in a small house on a country road. Having decided that her life isn't worth living, she tells her mother that she has decided to commit suicide and, methodically, begins the final preparation for that event. Jessie contentedly attends to details as her mother's horror and desperation grow. Exactly ninety minutes—in real time—from the opening curtain, Jessie walks into the next room and shoots herself.

ANALYSIS: Winner of the 1983 Pulitzer Prize for Drama, this play is nerve-racking at times, humorous at times, and always insightful. It made Kathy Bates a star. All levels.

SCENES/MONOLOGUES: Female/Female Scenes (1), Female Monologues (1)

NIGHT OF THE IGUANA, THE
by Tennessee Williams (Dramatists Play Service)

SYNOPSIS: The events in this play occur in 1940, during one long day in the off-season of the ramshackle Costa Verde Hotel on the Mexican coast, the kind of resort that attracts drifters and travelers off the beaten path. Reverend T. Lawrence Shannon, a defrocked Episcopal priest, seducer of young girls, and for many years a nickel-and-dime tour conductor, arrives with a busload of unhappy female tourists. He is suffering another of his nervous breakdowns and has come to see his friend, Fred, the owner of Costa Verde. But Fred died a month ago, and now Fred's lusty widow, Maxine, hanging on by a financial thread, is deciding whether to close the place and move to Texas or make a go of it alone. She immediately begins trying to convince Shannon to move in with her.

Then two other unwanted guests arrive: a dying, financially destitute ninety-seven-year-old minor poet from Nantucket and his unmarried sketch-artist granddaughter Hannah. All these lost souls interact, and by the day's end, Shannon agrees to stay with Maxine, the old man composes his final poem and dies, and Hannah decides to continue the world tour alone. Some native boys capture an iguana and tie it under the verandah to fatten it before eating it. The iguana's continual tugging against the rope becomes a metaphor for the predicament of all the guests in the hotel, each struggling against his or her own unseen restraints and trying to escape.

ANALYSIS: Bleak is too happy a word to describe this harrowing Tennessee Williams drama, but its poetry can't be denied. Difficult material for experienced actors.

SCENES/MONOLOGUES: Male/Female Scenes (1), Female/Female Scenes (1), Female Monologues (1)

NORMAN CONQUESTS, THE—TABLE MANNERS
by Alan Ayckbourn (Samuel French)

SYNOPSIS: Sarah and her husband, Reg, arrive in the country to take over the mother-nursing duties from Reg's sister Annie for a weekend while she goes on a romantic holiday, presumably with her longtime friend, Tom. But Sarah soon discovers that Annie is actually planning to spend the time with Norman, her charming and romantic brother-in-law, an arrangement that Sarah contends won't do at all. Annie then reluctantly cancels the trip. Soon, however, everyone in the house knows what she and Norman were up to. This discovery adds to family tensions and produces more embarrassment and confusion during the weekend. When Norman's plans with Annie go awry, he makes a play for Sarah. But in the very final moment of the play, he and Annie get back together.

ANALYSIS: *Table Manners* is part of a trilogy of plays called *The Norman Conquests.* The other two parts, *Living Together* and *Round and Round the Garden,* take place during the same weekend in the same house and involve the same cast of characters. Each comedy stands alone. Written in the British vernacular. All levels.

SCENES/MONOLOGUES: Male/Female Scenes (1), Female/Female Scenes (1), Male Monologues (2)

NOT ENOUGH ROPE
by Elaine May (Samuel French)

SYNOPSIS: Edith wants to borrow some rope from Claude, her new neighbor across the hall, so that she can hang herself. Claude doesn't have any rope, but he has some twine, so she takes that instead. Edith goes back to her apartment and ties herself up. Once she is standing on the chair ready to make the fatal jump, however, she changes her mind and calls for Claude to rescue her, which he is in no hurry to do. He finally cuts her down, however.

ANALYSIS: A silly one-act play that can be loads of fun for acting students because the premise is so outrageous. All levels.

SCENES/MONOLOGUES: Male/Female Scenes (1)

NUMBER, A
by Caryl Churchill (Theatre Communications Group)

SYNOPSIS: Would you have a beloved child cloned if the technology were available? Salter, now in his early sixties, did just that thirty-five years ago and, in this two-actor play, he is brought face-to-face with the consequences of his action. We learn that Salter intended to have only a single clone made, but the scientists secretly made twenty of them. Salter, whose original motivations were colored by depression and alcoholism, personally knows only the original son and the first clone—until the final scene in the play, when he meets one of the other twenty for the first time.

ANALYSIS: Caryl Churchill has written something wonderfully reminiscent of Pinter or Beckett. The subject matter is as fresh and challenging as today's headlines. Stylistically, there are few capital letters and little punctuation in the script, causing the actors to have to figure out thought patterns and emphasis, just as they have to figure out the tough questions that arise from cloning, parenthood,

parental love, sibling rivalry, individuality, genetics, and nature versus nurture. This is excellent material for experienced performers. One actor plays Salter, the father; the other actor plays the original son plus two of his clones.
SCENES/MONOLOGUES: Male/Male Scenes (5)

NUTS
by Tom Topor (Samuel French)

SYNOPSIS: After Claudia's marriage broke up, she became a high-priced call girl for a few months. When she killed an abusive customer, she was arrested and charged with manslaughter. Examined by court psychiatrists, she was found mentally incompetent to stand trial. She believes she acted properly, however, and wants to be found sane so that she can face the charges. The action of this play centers on Claudia's sanity hearing. Her mother and stepfather want her to be found incompetent; then they won't be forced to balance her values against their own.
ANALYSIS: This material is appropriate for sophisticated actors.
SCENES/MONOLOGUES: Male Monologues (2), Female Monologues (4)

ODD COUPLE, THE (FEMALE VERSION)
by Neil Simon (Samuel French)

SYNOPSIS: When Florence's husband leaves her after fourteen years of marriage, she moves in with her good friend, Olive. This new living arrangement quickly degenerates into a situation in which Florence's compulsive cleanliness and worrying drive Olive, a toss-cares-to-the-wind type of person, to distraction.
ANALYSIS: A fun reversal of the male version of the same comedy. All levels.
SCENES/MONOLOGUES: Female/Female Scenes (3)

ODD COUPLE, THE (MALE VERSION)
by Neil Simon (Samuel French)

SYNOPSIS: Oscar and Felix, both recently separated from their wives, are polar opposites. Oscar is a cigar-smoking slob who can't cook a frozen dinner, and Felix is compulsively clean and a gourmet cook. When they decide to share Oscar's eight-room Riverside Drive apartment in New York City, Felix drives Oscar to utter distraction within three weeks.
ANALYSIS: This comedy is almost an industry in itself, having been turned into a successful movie, television series, and having had continual revivals throughout the United States. The roles of Oscar and Felix were originally created by Walter Matthau and Art Carney. All levels.
SCENES/MONOLOGUES: Male/Male Scenes (4), Three-Person Scenes (1)

OF MICE AND MEN
by John Steinbeck (Dramatists Play Service)

SYNOPSIS: George and Lennie are migrant farm workers, always close to broke, and always dreaming of a place of their own. George calls the shots and watches over his physically powerful but childlike friend. Their last job near Weed, California, ended abruptly when Lennie innocently tried to feel the pretty fabric of a woman's dress. She panicked, ran to the law, and cried rape, but their present situation turns into even more of a disaster than the preceding one. Lennie accidentally kills the flirtatious wife of the boss's jealous son. Certain that Lennie will

be lynched by a mob, George decides to kill him first, as an act of pity and love.
ANALYSIS: Gritty 1937 drama about the struggles of migrant Americans. All levels.
SCENES/MONOLOGUES: Male/Female Scenes (1), Male/Male Scenes (1)

OH DAD, POOR DAD, MAMMA'S HUNG YOU IN THE CLOSET AND I'M FEELIN' SO SAD
by Arthur Kopit (Samuel French)

SYNOPSIS: Jonathan's mother shields him from the outside world, so he occupies himself with his large coin and stamp collections and constructs a telescope, hoping that he'll be able to see far-off things. As the curtain rises, he and his mother are arriving in a Caribbean resort city and have brought with them enough luggage to occupy an entire squad of bellboys. In addition, Madame Rosepettle, as usual, carries with her the corpse of her late husband, neatly stuffed and ready to be hung inside the closet. A few days after their arrival, Rosalie, an attractive young woman who housesits for an absentee couple across the way, visits Jonathan. When she turns seductive, Madame Rosepettle kicks her out.

Meanwhile, Madame Rosepettle is courted by Commodore Roseabove, who owns a very long yacht. By the end of this insane comedy, Jonathan kills Rosalie rather than accept her invitation to accompany her into the outside world. Madame Rosepettle continues to shield him, and her husband's corpse keeps falling out of the closet.

ANALYSIS: Written in the Absurdist tradition, this comedy is fun for actors who are willing to jump directly into the deep end of the pool. All levels.
SCENES/MONOLOGUES: Male/Female Scenes (1), Male Monologues (1)

OLD TIMES
by Harold Pinter (Grove Press)

SYNOPSIS: Kate and Deeley spend an evening with Kate's friend Ann, whom she hasn't seen for twenty years. As is typical of many Harold Pinter plays, it is unclear exactly what the relationships are among the three of them. Perhaps Kate and Ann used to be lovers. Perhaps Deeley and Ann were lovers before he married Kate.
ANALYSIS: Pinter can sometimes be a puzzle because he toys with reality. As soon as you think you know where the characters are coming from, they move. When you consider all the famous pauses in Pinter's scripts, you must keep in mind that a pause means something. When you pause, the pause itself becomes a choice; it is not merely silence. All levels.
SCENES/MONOLOGUES: Male/Female Scenes (2)

OLEANNA
by David Mamet (Dramatists Play Service)

SYNOPSIS: John is a successful, published university professor who, on the eve of receiving tenure, is accused of sexual harassment by Carol, a female student. Subsequently, his tenure is denied, he can't afford the house he and his wife were going to purchase with the anticipated salary increase, and his career is put into reverse. The play poses several questions. Was John treated fairly? Did he actually harass Carol, or did she misinterpret the fumbling efforts of a concerned teacher to comfort and encourage her? In the final moments of the play, John discovers that Carol, now being advised by an unnamed group of radical feminists, is planning to press criminal rape charges unless he makes certain concessions to her and the group. He becomes enraged by this and hits her, barely restraining himself from doing her great bodily harm. More difficult questions arise after the final curtain falls.

ANALYSIS: *Oleanna* was a big 1993 Broadway hit for David Mamet. During a December 1992 appearance at the Dramatists Guild in New York City, he explained the play's title: "'Oleanna' was the title of a song about a utopia of that name in western Pennsylvania, a planned community set up in the post–Civil War period by a Norwegian singer who had made a lot of money and wanted to make a beautiful community for Norwegians to come and live in. His name was Ole and his wife's name was Anna, so he called it Oleanna. It failed, and everybody went bust. *Oleanna* is a play about failed utopia, in this case, the failed utopia of academia." All levels.

SCENES/MONOLOGUES: Male/Female Scenes (1), Male Monologues (1), Female Monologues (1)

ON GOLDEN POND
by Ernest Thompson (Dramatists Play Service)

SYNOPSIS: Norman and Ethel have been married for forty-six years and have spent summers at their place on Golden Pond for forty-four of them. This year, however, it is clear that time is catching up with them. Norman, a retired college professor, is almost eighty, is having heart palpitations, and his memory isn't what it used to be.

Their divorced daughter, Chelsea, arrives with her fiancé and his teenage son, who stays the summer with Norman and Ethel while they go to Europe. Suddenly, the elderly couple have the grandchild they always wanted, and they dote on him. The summer ends all too soon and is accompanied by another scare—Norman has a mild heart attack. These yearly trips to Golden Pond are surely coming to an end.

ANALYSIS: *On Golden Pond* ran on Broadway in 1979 and was made into a wonderful movie starring Henry Fonda, Jane Fonda, and Katharine Hepburn that won several Academy Awards. All levels.

SCENES/MONOLOGUES: Female/Female Scenes (1), Male/Male Scenes (1)

ONLY GAME IN TOWN, THE
by Frank D. Gilroy (Samuel French)

SYNOPSIS: Fran and Joe live and work in Las Vegas. She is a dancer at the Tropicana and he is a lounge singer. Both are trying to overcome addictions: Joe to gambling and Fran to Tom Lockwood, a wealthy married man with whom she has carried on a ten-year affair. Joe moves in with Fran, and they form a convenient sexual relationship in which they're mutually supportive but emotionally undemanding. When Tom shows up unexpectedly and says that he is finally ready to get a divorce and marry Fran, she refuses him because she has fallen in love with Joe—although she won't say that out loud.

Joe and Fran continue to live together for two more years, each of them keeping their emotional distance, each afraid of deeper commitment. Then, in a touching scene that comes at the end of a traumatic day and night during which Joe starts gambling again, he tells her for the first time that he loves her and asks her to marry him. Fran resists at first but eventually says yes.

ANALYSIS: Although this play feels a lot like a soap opera, it is good for scenework. It was the basis of a 1970 movie starring Elizabeth Taylor and Warren Beatty. All levels.

SCENES/MONOLOGUES: Male/Female Scenes (2), Male Monologues (1)

ON THE OPEN ROAD
by Steve Tesich (Samuel French)

SYNOPSIS: Set in the burned-out, post–civil war landscape of some future time, Al and Angel forge a friendship and make their way toward the Land of the Free. Along the way, they salvage precious paintings and art treasures from gutted churches and museums, goods they hope to use to barter their way into the Land of the Free. When they get there, though, they are informed that, as a price of their admission, they have to assassinate Jesus Christ, who is in the midst of His Second Coming. They can't bring themselves to do it, so the monk in charge takes care of that and then has the two men executed.

ANALYSIS: This is a dark satire, frequently horrific and always philosophical. It presents some excellent challenging scenes for intelligent, physical actors.

SCENES/MONOLOGUES: Male/Male Scenes (2)

OPEN ADMISSIONS
by Shirley Lauro (Samuel French)

SYNOPSIS: Calvin, an eighteen-year-old African-American sophomore in New York State's university system, reads at a fifth-grade level but consistently gets Bs. When he figures out that he has been promoted from year to year without learning anything, he seeks out Ginny, one of his teachers. She is a well-intentioned, overworked woman with her own personal problems. Both she and Calvin are, in a way, victims of an inflexible educational system, and by the final curtain, they manage to come to a deeper understanding of each other's situations. In the last scene, Ginny sits down with Calvin and quietly begins to teach him on a level he can grasp, intent on giving him an education at last.

ANALYSIS: A "message" drama with some explosive scenes. All levels.

SCENES/MONOLOGUES: Male/Female Scenes (3)

ORPHANS
by Lyle Kessler (Samuel French)

SYNOPSIS: Treat, who is streetwise, violent, and continually in trouble with the law, has raised Phillip, his childlike, reclusive younger brother, since their mother's death. Their father deserted the family long ago. Treat gets by primarily through robbing people and committing petty crimes in North Philadelphia. One night, he brings home Harold, a well-dressed drunk he met in a bar, intent on robbing him. Harold, who turns out also to be an orphan, can't be restrained, and the next morning takes over the household, becoming something of a father figure.

Harold evidently has a great deal of money, but it comes from murky, unexplained sources, probably from the Chicago underworld. He buys the brothers clothes, encourages the younger one to expand his horizons, teaches him how to read maps so he'll never be lost again, and hires Treat as his personal bodyguard. Then, during a walk with Treat, some mysterious men from Chicago show up, forcefully take Harold aside, and mortally wound him. He finds his way back to the house and dies, leaving the brothers alone again.

ANALYSIS: This drama has a David Mamet feel to it and plenty of subtext. All levels.

SCENES/MONOLOGUES: Male/Male Scenes (2), Male Monologues (1)

OTHER PEOPLE'S MONEY
by Jerry Sterner (Samuel French)

SYNOPSIS: Garfinkle is an investor who wants to take over conservatively run New England Wire and Cable, dismantle it, and sell it off piece by piece. The parts of the company are currently worth more than the stock quote. If he succeeds, of course, a lot of people at the old company are out of a job. This play pits the values of a "green-mailer" against those of an old-fashioned businessman.

ANALYSIS: Well written. Made into a 1991 movie starring Danny DeVito. All levels.

SCENES/MONOLOGUES: Male/Female Scenes (2), Female/Female Scenes (1), Male Monologues (2)

OTHERWISE ENGAGED
by Simon Gray (Samuel French)

SYNOPSIS: Simon Hench settles in to listen to his new recording of Wagner's *Parsifal*. But before he can begin enjoying it, the upstairs boarder drops by; followed by Simon's brother, Stephen, who is anxious about a job promotion; and then Simon's friend, Jeff, who wants to discuss the complications in his love life. In short order, Jeff is followed by Davina, who displays no apparent modesty as she lounges topless while her blouse is drying. Next, Bernard Wood appears to find out whether Simon has in fact seduced his fiancée (he has). Then Simon's wife, Beth, comes home from a tryst and asks for a divorce. All this happens in about an hour and a half. Simon never does get to listen to *Parsifal*.

ANALYSIS: Biting, frequently mean comedy. Written in the British vernacular. All levels.

SCENES/MONOLOGUES: Male/Female Scenes (1), Male/Male Scenes (1), Female Monologues (1)

OUR LADY OF THE TORTILLA
by Luis Santeiro (Dramatists Play Service)

SYNOPSIS: Dolores finds an image of the Virgin Mary in a slab of tortilla dough, bringing excitement and notoriety to the New Jersey home she shares with sister, Dahlia, and her sons, Eddy and Nelson. Nelson is embarrassed by the implications of the discovery because his very non-Hispanic college girlfriend is visiting for the weekend. Eddy, on the other hand, wants to exploit the event to make a quick buck. Reporters and miracle-seekers camp out in the front yard.

ANALYSIS: This good-natured comedy, with its cast of appealing Hispanic characters, has been widely produced since it first appeared in 1987. All levels.

SCENES/MONOLOGUES: Three-Person Scenes (2)

PAINTING CHURCHES
by Tina Howe (Samuel French)

SYNOPSIS: Artist Margaret (Mags) Church comes home to Boston to paint a portrait of her elderly parents, Fanny and Gardner. Her father is becoming senile, so he and Fanny are packing to move from their large old house into a small, more manageable cottage. Against this background of packing and painting, the three family members come to see each other in new, more respectful terms.

ANALYSIS: This gem is beautifully written. Unfortunately, it doesn't contain any two-character scenes involving the daughter. Fanny does, however, have one lovely monologue. All levels.

SCENES/MONOLOGUES: Female Monologues (1)

PHILADELPHIA STORY, THE
by Philip Barry (Samuel French)

SYNOPSIS: Tracy Lord, of the Philadelphia Lords, married and quickly divorced C. K. Dexter Haven last year, and is going to marry successful, self-made businessman George Kittredge this weekend. A gossip magazine sends a reporter and a female photographer to cover the society wedding, and Tracy winds up in a moonlit romantic encounter with the reporter. The next morning, which is the day of the wedding, everything gets worked out: Tracy and her fiancé decide to call off their marriage, the reporter proposes, Tracy demurs at first, and—surprise of surprises—Tracy remarries Dexter!

ANALYSIS: The moral of this play is that the rich are as decent (or as morally neutral) as the rest of us. This was, of course, a major vehicle for Katharine Hepburn. *The Philadelphia Story* ran for more than 400 performances on Broadway and, in 1940, was adapted as one of Hollywood's most famous comedies. All levels.

SCENES/MONOLOGUES: Male/Female Scenes (1)

PIANO LESSON, THE
by August Wilson (Plume Drama)

SYNOPSIS: The action is set in Pittsburgh, 1936. Boy Willie wants to buy the land down south that his ancestors used to work as slaves, but he needs first to sell the old, ornately carved family piano to raise the initial investment. But Boy Willie's sister, Berniece, has possession of the instrument and won't hear of selling it. She points out that there is too much family history in those carvings, and that if you don't have history, you don't have anything.

ANALYSIS: Winner of the 1990 Pulitzer Prize. Beautifully written. Entire cast is African-American. All levels.

SCENES/MONOLOGUES: Male/Female Scenes (1), Male Monologues (4)

PICNIC
by William Inge (Dramatists Play Service)

SYNOPSIS: It is Labor Day weekend in a small Kansas town. The action takes place in the joint backyards of two widows whose families and boarders are all female. Hal Carter, a handsome, earthy drifter, wanders into this environment and sweeps Madge Owens off her feet. Suddenly, Madge's picture-perfect life, complete with plans to marry the town's most eligible bachelor, is turned upside down; at the final curtain, she leaves home to follow Hal into an uncertain future. Against the same background, spinster schoolteacher Rosemary Sydney finally succeeds in getting Howard Bevens to agree to marry her.

ANALYSIS: Winner of the 1953 Pulitzer Prize and later adapted for a movie starring William Holden and Kim Novak, this play is romantic and poetic. All levels.

SCENES/MONOLOGUES: Male/Female Scenes (2)

PILLOWMAN, THE
by Martin McDonagh (Faber and Faber)

SYNOPSIS: Set in an unnamed Eastern European totalitarian state, this play evokes the terrifying feeling of walking into a dark and unknown room. The given circumstances are that a man named Katurian has been arrested because the stories he writes may be the basis for copycat crimes, particularly the murder of young children. The sadistic authorities have also arrested Michal, Katurian's dim-witted brother, and have him in a room down the hall. In the end, we learn that Michal is the one that committed the child-murders; or maybe not.

ANALYSIS: This is violent, difficult, profane material that is only appropriate for advanced actors. The playwright is Irish, and the script has been written in an Irish—or British—vernacular. You should, however, easily be able to convert it to standard American speech. I have attempted to break down a few of the very long scenes into segments that would be manageable for a scene-study workshop.

SCENES/MONOLOGUES: Male/Male Scenes (4)

PIZZA MAN
by Darlene Craviotto (Samuel French)

SYNOPSIS: Julie and Alice are frustrated by their careers and romantic lives. In a moment of misguided impulse, they decide to pick a man, any man, and rape him. They select the pizza-delivery guy as a good victim and begin an awkward seduction. When that doesn't work, Julie and Alice turn more violent, tying up the man. Finally, after much back-and-forth discussion about power and the respective options for men and women in this world, the women release the man unharmed.

ANALYSIS: Rape is a rough subject matter on which to build a comedy, and Darlene Craviotto's effort might not be fully justified. Still, she has created some interesting possibilities for scenework, and the larger issues about violence and power are worth examining on their own merits. For sophisticated actors.

SCENES/MONOLOGUES: Female/Female Scenes (1), Three-Person Scenes (1), Female Monologues (1)

PLAY MEMORY
by Joanna M. Glass (Samuel French)

SYNOPSIS: The sad plot of *Play Memory* is offset by a deft, frequently humorous, and skillful theatrical presentation. A family in Saskatoon, Saskatchewan, Canada in 1944 is torn apart by the husband's stubborn refusal to rebuild his life after he is betrayed by three friends. He goes into an alcoholic decline for ten years, moving steadily from prosperity to poverty, and dragging his wife, Ruth, and their young daughter, Jean, with him. The relentless descent finally ends when Ruth and Jean leave the husband in 1955, moving to a safe, nonviolent home. After they go, he trades in the kitchen stove for more liquor, locks the front door, and proceeds to drink himself to death. The women become adult survivors. This play, which is about memory, is told in flashback sequences. So when the audience first meets Ruth and Jean, they've developed a sense of humor about their lives.

ANALYSIS: Hal Prince's 1984 production was nominated for a Tony. For sophisticated actors.

SCENES/MONOLOGUES: Male/Female Scenes (2), Male Monologues (2), Female Monologues (1)

PORCH
by Jeffrey Sweet (Samuel French)

SYNOPSIS: Amy has traveled from New York City to her small Midwestern hometown to be with her widower father while he undergoes exploratory surgery. Their conversation on the front porch of the old house quickly exposes the reasons she has stayed away all these years. Amy is a disappointment to her father. He reflects on the untimely death of his only son ten years earlier and voices regret that Amy won't carry on the small family business or have children.

Then Sam, Amy's high-school flame, drops by unexpectedly. As she quickly surmises, her father arranged this get-together in the hope that those long-cold sparks might fly again, resulting in perhaps a grandchild for him. Even though Sam still has feelings for Amy, she has no interest in taking up with him again. Furthermore, Amy still believes that her decision to have an abortion after Sam made her pregnant while they were in school was the right one.

ANALYSIS: Jeffrey Sweet writes engaging dialogue, with plenty of emotional subtext. All levels.

SCENES/MONOLOGUES: Male/Female Scenes (3), Female Monologues (1)

PRELUDE TO A KISS
by Craig Lucas (Broadway Play Publishing)

SYNOPSIS: A very old man, living out the final chapter of his life and distressed by the recent death of his wife, happens upon Rita and Peter's wedding. The man joins the festivities, kisses Rita, and magically, his spirit moves into her body, and her spirit into his. Peter then goes on his honeymoon with the woman who looks like Rita but who is suddenly behaving like the old man. By the time they return home, Peter has figured out that a switch has taken place. So he orchestrates another meeting between Rita and the old man, hoping that the transformation can be reversed. Success! Their spirits are switched back, and the young couple begins their marriage all over again. The old man, meanwhile, faces his mortality with dignity.

ANALYSIS: The reversal-of-bodies theatrical device is one of the most unusual you'll ever encounter. Having a young woman's personality in an old man's body, and vice versa, leads to some charming and funny encounters. Most scenes are quite short. Nominated for a Tony in 1990 and turned into a 1992 movie starring Alec Baldwin and Meg Ryan. All levels.

SCENES/MONOLOGUES: Male/Female Scenes (1), Three-Person Scenes (2), Male Monologues (1)

PRIMARY ENGLISH CLASS, THE
by Israel Horovitz (Dramatists Play Service)

SYNOPSIS: Debbie Wastba attempts to teach English as a second language to a roomful of adult students who not only don't understand a word she is saying, but also don't understand each other. Members of the class include a Polish man, an Italian man, a Frenchman, a German man, a Chinese woman, and a Japanese woman. Only Wastba speaks English, and her modus operandi is to teach English by "total immersion." This means that she refuses to speak any language except English to her students. The result: a comedy based on confusion.

ANALYSIS: This play is actually a comment on the insensitivity of Americans to other cultures. Hysterically funny, but unfortunately without scene possibilities. All levels.

SCENES/MONOLOGUES: Female Monologues (1)

PRISONER OF SECOND AVENUE, THE
by Neil Simon (Samuel French)

SYNOPSIS: Mel is having a midlife crisis. He has high blood pressure; takes Valium to relax; hates living in New York City with its endless labor strikes, irate neighbors, and general hassles; and hates the small, overpriced apartment on Second Avenue that he shares with his wife, Edna. When Mel gets laid off from his job at a big ad agency, he can't find another job, and suffers a nervous breakdown. Expensive therapy doesn't help him recover, nor do well-intentioned visits from his brother and sisters. Edna takes a job, but then she too is fired. Finally, Mel decides to fight back against the system, to no longer be a victim. At the final curtain, the audience knows that he and Edna will survive, but they still seem beleaguered.

ANALYSIS: An in-your-face, one-liner, zinger comedy that hangs on a simplistic plot. In other words, vintage Neil Simon. It is good material for actors who want to work on comedy. All levels.

SCENES/MONOLOGUES: Male/Female Scenes (1)

PRIVATE LIVES
by Noel Coward (Samuel French)

SYNOPSIS: Elyot and Sybil are on their honeymoon in the south of France. The terrace of their hotel room overlooks the water, and moonlight pours in—the perfect picture of bliss. Then Elyot discovers that his ex-wife, Amanda, and her new husband are honeymooning in the adjacent hotel room. Naturally, all hell breaks loose. Amanda and Elyot fall into one another's arms, admitting that they never should have broken up in the first place. They unceremoniously abandon their respective new spouses and head for Paris and an even-more-romantic reunion. For a while it is touch-and-go, with Elyot and Amanda reverting to their former love/hate relationship. Then their respective ex-newlywed spouses show up in Paris, and all hell breaks loose all over again. In the end, however, Elyot and Amanda decide to stay together forever.

ANALYSIS: Noel Coward is at his best in this honey of a comedy, which is routinely revived for Broadway productions. He and Gertrude Lawrence became the toast of two continents for their portrayals of Elyot and Amanda. Written in the British vernacular. All levels.

SCENES/MONOLOGUES: Male/Female Scenes (4)

PROMISE, THE
by José Rivera (Broadway Play Publishing)

SYNOPSIS: Set in the backyard of Guzman's working-class home in Patchogue, New York, the central events in this delightfully theatrical play involve Lilia's wedding to a man she doesn't love and her father's commitment to winning independence for Puerto Rico. Mainly, however, *The Promise* is a mélange, mixing pageantry, magic, superstition, possession by spirits, and religion; the playwright refers to this style as "magical realism."

ANALYSIS: A striking work by an increasingly important playwright, *The Promise* unfortunately contains no scenework. Two monologues, however, are excellent for workshops. All characters are Hispanic. All levels.

SCENES/MONOLOGUES: Male Monologues (1), Female Monologues (1)

PROOF
by David Auburn (Dramatists Play Service)

SYNOPSIS: Catherine, twenty-five-years old today, has spent the last several years caring full time for her brilliant but unstable mathematician father, Robert. Now she must bury him and come to terms with her own demons. Has she inherited his genius for mathematics? Has she inherited his emotional fragility? Basically, this is the setup of *Proof,* with Catherine being courted by Hal, one of her father's former students, while simultaneously being pressed by her estranged sister to abandon the old family house and move to New York. Hal discovers a complicated proof in an upstairs desk, and Catherine claims authorship. At first he disbelieves that she would be capable of such an accomplishment, figuring the proof was really written by her father. But in the end, we learn that it is true. She is the author.

ANALYSIS: This extraordinarily well-written play makes the world of higher mathematics almost user-friendly. The structure of the play is as complicated as a mathematical equation itself, bouncing back and forth in time and into and out of dreams. Winner of the 2001 Pulitzer Prize and Tony Award for Best Play.

SCENES/MONOLOGUES: Male/Female Scenes (2), Female/Female Scenes (1)

PROPOSAL, THE
by Anton Chekhov (*The Sneeze: Plays and Stories by Anton Chekhov,* translated and adapted by Michael Frayn, Samuel French)

SYNOPSIS: Lomov has finally gotten up enough nerve to ask Natalya Stepanovna to marry him. He puts on his finest suit and makes the trip to the neighboring farm that she lives on. Alone with his beloved, Lomov begins his proposal with an itemized list of his financial assets, primary among which is Ox Lea Meadows, the property where he lives. Natalya points out that the property isn't really his; in fact, it belongs to her family. He begs to differ and, before you know it, they're involved in an argument and the proposal is no longer on the table.

Natalya's father enters and joins the fray, at which time Lomov storms out. Everybody calms down, and Lomov comes back to try again. This time, however, he and Natalya start arguing about who has the better hunting dog. Finally, Lomov faints dead away from the sheer anxiety of it all. This alarms the father, who presumes that Lomov is actually dead. Suddenly, Lomov revives and, before anything else can go wrong, Natalya's father urges the disoriented lovers to make the leap into marriage. They kiss. Curtain.

ANALYSIS: If anybody thinks that Anton Chekhov can't be funny, he needs to read this hysterical one-act play. All levels.

SCENES/MONOLOGUES: Male/Female Scenes (1), Three-Person Scenes (1)

P.S. YOUR CAT IS DEAD
by James Kirkwood (Samuel French)

SYNOPSIS: Vito, a bisexual burglar with a good sense of humor, breaks into Jimmy's Greenwich Village apartment on New Year's Eve—the very night that

Jimmy's girlfriend, Kate, has chosen to leave him. Surprised by Kate and Jimmy's return to the apartment, Vito hides under the bed and eavesdrops on their problems. All of this is the setup for the two men to get to know one another. Jimmy winds up capturing Vito and tying him up. By the final curtain, they have become friends and potential lovers.

ANALYSIS: This very offbeat comedy is quite black at times. Playwright James Kirkwood says that it is "a play about two losers who meet at a certain crucial time in their lives. Will they help each other?" Sal Mineo's final performance was his portrayal of Vito. For sophisticated actors.

SCENES/MONOLOGUES: Male/Female Scenes (1), Male/Male Scenes (1), Male Monologues (1)

RAINMAKER, THE
by N. Richard Nash (Samuel French)

SYNOPSIS: A con man named Starbuck arrives in a drought-stricken western town one August and promises to make it rain. The Curry family pays him one hundred dollars to do just that and, within the next twenty-four hours, he makes believers of everyone. In the process, Starbuck teaches the Currys' plain daughter, Lizzie, to believe in herself. This new relationship also deeply affects Starbuck, and after a single night of lovemaking, he admits to Lizzie that he is a con artist.

ANALYSIS: A wonderful 1954 romantic comedy. The roles are bold and colorful; the play, an actor's delight, was turned into a star movie vehicle for Burt Lancaster. All levels.

SCENES/MONOLOGUES: Male/Female Scenes (3), Male Monologues (1)

RAISIN IN THE SUN, A
by Lorraine Hansberry (Samuel French)

SYNOPSIS: Big Walter Younger worked hard all his life to keep his insurance premiums paid, and now that he is dead, the members of his family are torn about how to spend the $10,000 payout. This was a significant amount of money in 1958. Walter Lee, Big Walter's son, sees himself becoming a big businessman by investing the money in a liquor store. Mama, Big Walter's widow, would rather escape the Chicago ghetto by making a down payment on a nice home somewhere. With the money left over, she wants to pay for daughter Beneatha's college education. Walter Lee's wife, Ruth, favors getting the house, primarily so that their son, Travis, can have a better life. Beneatha wants the money to go toward her education so that she can serve humanity by becoming a doctor.

After acrimonious debate, Mama secretly makes a down payment on a house in a white neighborhood. When Walter Lee finds out what she has done, he drinks himself into a stupor. Seeing his reaction, Mama has misgivings about her actions and entrusts the rest of the money to him. She tells him to go ahead and buy the liquor store, but to be sure to save part of the money for Beneatha. Walter gives the money to his would-be partner, who promptly skips town with it. Just as suddenly as the money appeared, it is gone. The only part the family still has is the amount used for the down payment on the house.

Enter Karl Lindner, a representative from the white community in which the house is located. He offers the Youngers a bribe not to move into his neighborhood. At first Walter Lee is tempted to accept the bribe, but when the family unites against the offer, he stands up to Karl, telling him that the Youngers will move in anyway.

ANALYSIS: *A Raisin in the Sun,* the first Broadway play written by an African-American woman, was also the first to be directed by an African-American man, Lloyd Richards. It won the 1959 New York Drama Critics' Circle Award for Best Play and was made into a movie with Sidney Poitier, who also portrayed Walter Lee on stage. All levels.

SCENES/MONOLOGUES: Male/Female Scenes (1), Three-Person Scenes (1), Male Monologues (3)

RED COAT, THE
by John Patrick Shanley (*Welcome to the Moon and Other Plays,* Dramatists Play Service)

SYNOPSIS: Although seventeen-year-old John is at a festive party, he still feels lonely. He goes outside to sit in the light of the full moon. Mary, who is sixteen, arrives, and they talk. Their conversation quickly becomes an exultant declaration of mutual love.

ANALYSIS: John Patrick Shanley is arguably best known as the author of the 1987 film comedy *Moonstruck,* and the same kind of lunar magic is at work here. Very innocent. All levels.

SCENES/MONOLOGUES: Male/Female Scenes (1)

REUNION
by David Mamet (*Reunion and Dark Pony,* Grove Press)

SYNOPSIS: A father and daughter reunite after a twenty-year separation. During this mostly quiet and tentatively probing conversation, which takes place in Bernie's apartment, they try to fill in the blanks. He is no longer drinking, but alcoholism has taken a terrible toll on his life; Carol is married to a man who has two children from an earlier marriage. Bernie regrets missing his brother's funeral, and Carol is close to her half-sister. Bernie has settled into a blue-collar restaurant job and is about to remarry; Carol smokes too much, and her sex life isn't great.

ANALYSIS: This is an early David Mamet work that demonstrates his keen ear for the flow of dialogue and negotiation within a scene. All levels.

SCENES/MONOLOGUES: Male/Female Scenes (2)

ROAD TO NIRVANA
by Arthur Kopit (Samuel French)

SYNOPSIS: Arthur Kopit extends satire to its grotesque extreme as he takes audiences into a world where a common locker-room vulgarity ("I'd give my left ball for a piece of that deal.") becomes the literal price of doing business in Hollywood. Al and Lou, former producer/partners, reunite to produce the filmed autobiography of rock's biggest female star, Nirvana (who is a ringer for Madonna). What Jerry doesn't know is that Nirvana's loyalty test—and her price for anchoring the deal—is whether or not he'll give up a testicle, or preferably both of them. Al, as it turns out, gave her one of his just to get the option, which is actually a recopied, erotic version of Melville's *Moby Dick.*

ANALYSIS: With this plot, Arthur Kopit was courting censorship trouble from the start, and he got it. *Road to Nirvana* has been greeted with diverse reactions from protest to praise wherever it has played. Kopit is a serious and consistent contributor to American theater and is arguably one of America's finest playwrights. Be warned that every scene in this play contains graphic images and plenty of vulgarity. All levels.

SCENES/MONOLOGUES: Male/Female Scenes (1), Male/Male Scenes (3)

ROSENCRANTZ AND GUILDENSTERN ARE DEAD
by Tom Stoppard (Samuel French)

SYNOPSIS: Turning *Hamlet* upside down, Tom Stoppard has made stars of two minor characters and made supporting players of the lead roles Hamlet, Gertrude, Claudius, Polonius, Ophelia, Laertes, and the rest. Most of the time, Rosencrantz and Guildenstern don't know where they are or why they are there. All they understand is that they were "sent for" because they are Hamlet's old school chums. After the players act out *The Murder of Gonzago* and Hamlet kills Polonius, the hapless pair escort him to England, where presumably he will be executed. Then they discover that the letter they're carrying to the King of England demands their own immediate execution. Rosencrantz and Guildenstern don't realize that Hamlet has switched it in order to escape his own death. The events are all predetermined, and Rosencrantz and Guildenstern have no say in the matter.

ANALYSIS: Clever is too modest a word for this 1967 delight, which immediately placed Tom Stoppard on the map as a major talent. The philosophical premise of the play is best summed up by one of the players: "Uncertainty is the normal state." All levels.

SCENES/MONOLOGUES: Male/Male Scenes (2), Male Monologues (2)

SCENES AND REVELATIONS
by Elan Garonzik (Samuel French)

SYNOPSIS: The drama opens in 1894 on a Pennsylvania farm as four sisters are about to depart for England and Uncle Jacob's inheritance rather than follow the popular western migration. In nineteen short scenes, the action covers the preceding years and finally returns to the farm in 1894. Along the way, the women fall in love, decide whether or not to pursue careers, and have children. When Uncle Jacob dies, leaving them a fortune in British textile mills, they head for the boat.

ANALYSIS: Innocent, earnest dialogue and scenes.

SCENES/MONOLOGUES: Male/Female Scenes (3), Female Monologues (1)

SCENES FROM AMERICAN LIFE
by A. R. Gurney, Jr. (Samuel French)

SYNOPSIS: Spanning the years from 1930 to 1970, the play tracks generational changes in an upper-class WASP family in Buffalo, New York. Most of the scenes are very short and flow into one another, with actors playing multiple roles.

ANALYSIS: A. R. Gurney takes potshots at hypocritical attitudes and behavior in America in this breezy offering, which is really a series of unrelated scenes from American life brought together under a single title. As always, he is a master when it comes to writing dialogue. All levels.

SCENES/MONOLOGUES: Female/Female Scenes (1), Female Monologues (2)

SEAGULL, THE
by Anton Chekhov (a new version by Jean-Claude Van Itallie, Dramatists Play Service)

SYNOPSIS: Playwright Anton Chekhov described *The Seagull* as "a comedy with three female parts, six male, a landscape, much talk about literature, little action, and tons of love." A modern reader will have difficulty understanding how this play (in which Konstantine, one of the central characters, commits suicide) could be called a comedy at all. Indeed, nothing seems to encourage laughter. It is important to understand that this comedy revolves around posturing—it is really a study of tedious people who don't know they are being tedious.

ANALYSIS: First produced in 1889, *The Seagull* made both Anton Chekhov and the Moscow Art Theatre famous. It was his first attempt at a play of "indirect action," in which the psychology of the characters takes precedence over the action. The complex characters were the perfect vehicle for Stanislavsky's new acting techniques, which were designed to find "inner truth, the truth of feeling and experience." All levels.

SCENES/MONOLOGUES: Male/Female Scenes (1), Male Monologues (2), Female Monologues (1)

SEA HORSE, THE
by Edward J. Moore (Samuel French)

SYNOPSIS: Gertrude Blum is the owner/proprietor of The Sea Horse, a small-town saloon on the California coast. It is a rough place, catering to seamen only—not to their women. Gertrude herself is a physically big woman, weighing some 200 pounds, fat but firm. She runs the bar with an iron hand, laughing and cussing with the best of them and taking the occasional favorite upstairs for the night. For the past year, she has been sharing her bed with one Harry Bales whenever he is in port. Harry has come to adore her and wants to marry her, but Gertrude is not big on true intimacy. The play explores their evolving relationship and their attempts to grow closer.

ANALYSIS: Originally written as an exercise in Uta Hagen's New York City acting class, *The Sea Horse* went on to be published, and Edward Moore won the 1974 Vernon Rice Drama Desk Award for Outstanding New Playwright. All levels.

SCENES/MONOLOGUES: Male/Female Scenes (2), Male Monologues (1), Female Monologues (1)

SEXUAL PERVERSITY IN CHICAGO
by David Mamet (*Sexual Perversity in Chicago and the Duck Variations*, Samuel French)

SYNOPSIS: A fast-moving one-act play that explores the deceits of the dating game. Danny and Bernard are very much "into" women, but their approaches toward them are radically different. Danny, an assistant office manager, is a nice guy who treats women with respect, while his buddy and co-worker Bernard thinks the way to women's hearts is to "treat 'em like shit."

The action of the play takes place over a couple of months, during which the men are dating two roommates, Joan and Deborah. Bernard may think he is hip and that he knows all the moves, but it is nice-guy Danny who winds up connecting, if only for a brief moment of intimacy, with Deborah. In the end, the men return to girl-watching, while the women continue as roommates.

ANALYSIS: This early comic work by Mamet has plenty of rough language, mainly because he is holding up sexual stereotypes for ridicule. All levels.

SCENES/MONOLOGUES: Male/Female Scenes (1), Male/Male Scenes (2)

SHADOW BOX, THE
by Michael Cristofer (Samuel French)

SYNOPSIS: The action occurs in three cottages on the grounds of a large hospital in California. Terminally ill patients are allowed to use the cottages for visits with their families. Joe is using Cottage Number One to spend some time with his wife and fourteen-year-old son. Brian is living with his lover, Mark, in Cottage Number Two and receives an unexpected visit from his ex-wife. Felicity and her daughter are in Cottage Number Three. The play explores the complex relationships that become more complex—or simpler—as death approaches.

ANALYSIS: This beautiful drama won both the 1977 Tony Award and Pulitzer Prize for Best Play. All levels.

SCENES/MONOLOGUES: Male/Female Scenes (4), Male Monologues (1), Female Monologues (3)

SHAPE OF THINGS, THE
by Neil Labute (Faber and Faber)

SYNOPSIS: Evelyn concocts the ultimate college thesis project. She will turn an unsuspecting person into a work of art. "Can I install x-amount of change in this creature," she asks, "using only manipulation as my palette knife?" Her project of course plays havoc with the minds and emotions of the people around her, who have no idea what she is up to.

ANALYSIS: Neil Labute wants to explore the parameters of art and love in this provocative play. The plot is appropriately outrageous and can be fun for sophisticated actors.

SCENES/MONOLOGUES: Male/Male Scenes (1), Male/Female Scenes (2)

SHIRLEY VALENTINE
by Willy Russell (Samuel French)

SYNOPSIS: Shirley Valentine, a forty-two-year-old Liverpool housewife with two grown children and a complacent husband, goes on an impulsive fortnight vacation in sun-drenched Greece, has a romance with a Zorba-like tavern owner, and decides not to return home. In the process, she takes stock of her life, marriage, and unrealized dreams.

ANALYSIS: Shirley is the only character in this insightful and touching comedy. *Shirley Valentine* won England's Olivier Award for Best Comedy, and Pauline Collins won a Tony for Best Actress during the Broadway run. Written in the British vernacular. All levels.

SCENES/MONOLOGUES: Female Monologues (2)

SHIVAREE
by William Mastrosimone (Samuel French)

SYNOPSIS: Chandler is a hemophiliac living in seclusion, protected from the world by his domineering mother. Shivaree, a southern belly dancer, sublets an apartment in the building across the way and strikes up a relationship with Chandler, much to his mother's chagrin.

ANALYSIS: The very talented Mastrosimone must have been in a strange state of mind when he wrote this odd comedy. All levels.

SCENES/MONOLOGUES: Female Monologues (1)

SIGHT UNSEEN
by Donald Margulies (Dramatists Play Service)

SYNOPSIS: On the occasion of his first major exhibit outside of North America, artist Jonathan Waxman looks up his former lover, Patricia, who is now married and living with her archaeologist husband, Nick, in Norfolk, England. Although fifteen years have passed, Jonathan finds that Patricia is still smarting from the way he dropped her, and that Nick has no use for him at all, professionally or personally. Jonathan's visit with Patricia provides a platform for revisiting their early days together, going over the reasons they broke up, including the incompatibility between his Jewish heritage and her Gentile background. Jonathan is also forced to defend his artistic integrity and financial success when attacked by Nick and, later at the exhibit, by a German art critic/interviewer.

ANALYSIS: Winner of the 1992 Obie Award for Best New American Play, *Sight Unseen* works on several levels and is structurally very clever. It is a broad, intellectual debate about the merits of art, set against a background of a failed love affair and mixed with questions about Jewish assimilation. All levels.

SCENES/MONOLOGUES: Male/Female Scenes (2), Male/Male Scenes (1), Three-Person Scenes (1), Male Monologues (1)

SILENT NIGHT, LONELY NIGHT
by Robert Anderson (Samuel French)

SYNOPSIS: Katherine and John first meet in a New England inn on Christmas Eve when they discover that they occupy adjoining rooms. She is distressed because her husband, who is in England on a business trip, has been having affairs. John is sad because his wife has been institutionalized for insanity for the past five years. Both of them are lonely, needing to be held and loved, and near dawn they finally give in to this yearning. The next day, Katherine leaves for England with her son, and John returns to the vigil he keeps with his wife. Surprisingly, she is under a temporary spell of lucidity. It is Christmas Day.

ANALYSIS: In the end, this lovely play, which starred Henry Fonda, evokes a poetic, adult mood. The main characters are the kind of vaguely well-off, educated people that seem to populate a number of plays from the 1950s. Audiences get a sense that the characters spend a great deal of time gazing reflectively out a picture window at the freshly fallen snow as they sip a Scotch and water. Robert Anderson is a wonderful writer. All levels.

SCENES/MONOLOGUES: Male/Female Scenes (2)

SISTER MARY IGNATIUS EXPLAINS IT ALL FOR YOU
by Christopher Durang (Dramatists Play Service)

SYNOPSIS: The title of this play says it all. Sister Mary Ignatius, a Catholic nun, lectures the audience on the pros, cons, and history of the world from a Catholic perspective. Some of her former students appear to talk about how the nun's

teachings have affected them, but the focus of the play is the Sister's lectures.
ANALYSIS: Wonderful one-act satire of Catholicism. All levels.
SCENES/MONOLOGUES: Female Monologues (1)

SIX DEGREES OF SEPARATION
by John Guare (Dramatists Play Service)

SYNOPSIS: Paul, a young, charming African-American man, maneuvers his way into the lives of Louisa and Flanders Kittredge and two other high-living, white New York families, each time masquerading as the son of famous actor Sidney Poitier. In each case, once Paul's deception is discovered and he has disappeared, no one can figure out what possible motive he could have had for carrying out such a charade because he didn't steal any valuable property. The mystery deepens when Paul befriends Rick and Elizabeth, a couple of aspiring actors, this time pretending to be Flanders Kittredge's illegitimate son.

In short order, Paul seduces Rick, who has never before had a homosexual experience, and cons him out of all the money he and Elizabeth have saved: $250. When Rick realizes he has been duped, he commits suicide. After Paul's escapades show up in a newspaper article, he telephones the Kittredge residence, claiming remorse and saying that he wants to go straight. Even more, he wants Flanders to be his mentor, training him to buy and sell fine art. Louisa and Flanders agree to help Paul, but when they go to meet him at a prearranged location he isn't there. They never see him again.

ANALYSIS: This clever, fast-moving comedy-drama is crammed with metaphor, ultimately becoming a comment on identity, pretension, and America's supposed classless society. The plot is presented in flashback, narrated by Louisa and Flanders, one quick scene melding into another on an open stage. Playwright John Guare based the work on an actual New York incident in which a young man pretended to be Sidney Poitier's son.

SCENES/MONOLOGUES: Male Monologues (1), Female Monologues (1)

SNOWANGEL
by Lewis John Carlino (*Cages,* Dramatists Play Service)

SYNOPSIS: Connie is a prostitute, so she presumes that John wants to have sex when he shows up at her shabby hotel room on the Lower East Side at 4 A.M. Soon, however, she discovers that he longs for more than that. John wants true romance and affection, and he expects her to reenact the first meeting he had years ago with the only woman he ever loved. Connie resists this charade, drinking heavily as he continues to elaborately set the stage. Finally, the fantasy falls apart as she turns on John, demanding that he honor her memory of the first time she was in love. He then begins to reenact her fantasy.

ANALYSIS: A poetic, frequently moving one-act drama. Good material for sophisticated actors.

SCENES/MONOLOGUES: Male/Female Scenes (2), Female Monologue (1)

SOCIAL EVENT, A
William Inge (*Eleven Short Plays by William Inge,* Dramatists Play Service)

SYNOPSIS: Randy and Carole, two up-and-coming Hollywood actors, consider it imperative that they be "seen" at the funeral of a recently deceased famous movie star even though they didn't care overmuch about him. As the play begins, they are extremely frustrated, having been up all night trying to figure out how to get an invite. When it appears that the situation is just impossible, they discover that their hotel maid has been invited. They use double-talk to get the sweet woman to let them go to the funeral with her.

ANALYSIS: A delightful trifle, all of ten pages long, from William Inge. Actors will recognize that the pretensions of would-be stars are timeless. All levels.

SCENES/MONOLOGUES: Male/Female Scenes (1)

SORROWS OF STEPHEN
by Peter Parnell (Samuel French)

SYNOPSIS: Stephen loves Christine, and Christine loves Stephen. Christine also loves William, Stephen's best friend. In the end, Christine marries William, leaving Stephen to read Balzac instead of Goethe. All characters are contemporary, upwardly mobile, educated, witty New Yorkers.

ANALYSIS: Sweet comedy. All levels.

SCENES/MONOLOGUES: Male/Female Scenes (4), Male/Male Scenes (1)

SPEED-THE-PLOW
by David Mamet (Samuel French)

SYNOPSIS: Bobby Gould, the head of production for a big Hollywood movie studio, listens favorably to a pitch his longtime friend Charlie Fox is making. The proposed movie, designed for hot star Doug Brown, is sure to make money. Also on Bobby's desk is a book by a serious East Coast writer that deals with radiation, the end of civilization, and eroding values. He gives the radiation book to Karen, his sexy temp, to read, asking for her private and personal recommendation. (Actually, Bobby just wants to sleep with her. Surprise, surprise.) She reads it and convinces Bobby to give the green light to the radiation book rather than to the Doug Brown project. Karen then sleeps with Bobby. Charlie flips out when he discovers his pet project has been killed. After a violent confrontation with Bobby and a scene with Karen, the projects revert again. At the end, Karen is out, and Charlie is back in with the Doug Brown vehicle.

ANALYSIS: It seems like every playwright has to do his own send-up of crazy Hollywood values. This is David Mamet's attempt. Well written, of course. All levels.

Mamet, in a 1993 talk at the Dramatists Guild, said, "*Speed-the-Plow* was the title of a four-hundred-year-old play by Thomas Middleton, and it was also a motto written on English barns and displayed on English cups. It's also in a poem that ends, 'God speed the plow/Good health and success to the farmer.' In other words, may God speed—help—the farmer. It's about *work*. That's why I chose the title."

SCENES/MONOLOGUES: Male/Female Scenes (2), Male/Male Scenes (2)

SPINNING INTO BUTTER
by Rebecca Gilman (Dramatic Publishing)

SYNOPSIS: An African-American freshman student at Belmont College in Vermont begins to receive hate mail, driving the school administration and student body into shock and self-assessment. At the center of the maelstrom is the dean of students, Sarah Daniels, who comes to acknowledge her own racism.

ANALYSIS: This is an issue play that explores how latent racism can exist even among people who consider themselves to be liberal and open-minded. It also explores the traps inherent in political correctness. Very well written.

SCENES/MONOLOGUES: Male/Female Scenes (4)

SPLENDOR IN THE GRASS
by William Inge (Dramatists Play Service)

SYNOPSIS: Deanie Loomis and Bud Stamper are young lovers whose passions and ambitions are thwarted continually by the prejudices and ignorance of their elders. The action takes place in a small oil-boom town in Kansas during the 1920s.

ANALYSIS: William Inge's popular screenplay makes it to the stage. There is a bang-up scene between Bud and his father, Ace. All levels.

SCENES/MONOLOGUES: Male/Male Scenes (1)

SPLIT SECOND
by Dennis McIntyre (Samuel French)

SYNOPSIS: Val Johnson is an African-American cop in New York City. When a white car thief he has captured begins to spew racial epithets, Val snaps and kills the man, shooting him cleanly through the heart. Then, realizing what he has done, he restages the event to make it look like a case of self-defense. Subsequently, Val has confrontations with his wife, who urges him to continue with the deception rather than risk jail; his father, a retired cop, who wants him to tell the truth; his buddy, who confesses that he also once killed a man in cold blood; and the investigating officer, who knows Val is lying but can't prove it. At the official hearing (and on the very last page of the script), Val hesitates only briefly, considers changing his story, and then stands by his lie.

ANALYSIS: Though the basic dramatic situation is contrived, this drama has some powerful scenes. All levels.

SCENES/MONOLOGUES: Male/Female Scenes (2), Male/Male Scenes (2)

SPOILS OF WAR
by Michael Weller (Samuel French)

SYNOPSIS: Set in the mid-1950s in New York City, the action in this play centers on sixteen-year-old Martin's efforts to orchestrate a reconciliation between his parents, who have been separated for ten years. Before World War II, Elise and Andrew were part of the very active political left, so when he joined the Army and went off to fight, Elise felt betrayed and abandoned. When Andrew returned, he was a changed man in her eyes and part of "the system." She then left with their young son to follow a bohemian way of life. Since then, Andrew has bounced from one vocational pursuit to another, making a pretty good living and getting by with low-commitment romantic relationships. Martin manages to get his parents together at a party, but the meeting turns disastrous. These two ships will continue to pass in the night.

ANALYSIS: This 1989 drama might surprise you. We don't have a lot of material that is set in the politically confused 1950s, and Michael Weller has a keen ear for realistic dialogue. Excellent material for scenework. All levels.

SCENES/MONOLOGUES: Male/Female Scenes (3), Female/Female Scenes (1), Three-Person Scenes (1)

STEEL MAGNOLIAS
by Robert Harling (Dramatists Play Service)

SYNOPSIS: Shelby Eatenton-Latcherie is the prettiest young woman in Chinquapin, Louisiana. She marries the most eligible young man around, and her life would be perfect if she didn't have diabetes. Against her doctor's advice, Shelby has a baby; a short while later, her body begins to fail. Ultimately, she has to have a kidney transplant, and her own mother is the donor. The operation is unsuccessful, and Shelby dies. This is the core plotline.

ANALYSIS: This comedy is set in the town beauty parlor and is chock-full of southern humor and wisdom, as well as several stereotypical southern women. This work by actor/writer Robert Harling was later made into a successful big-budget movie starring Olympia Dukakis, Sally Field, Darryl Hannah, Shirley MacLaine, Dolly Parton, Julia Roberts, and Tom Skerritt. All levels.

SCENES/MONOLOGUES: Female/Female Scenes (1), Female Monologues (1)

STILL LIFE
by Emily Mann (Dramatists Play Service)

SYNOPSIS: This play was based on actual conversations the playwright had with survivors of the Vietnam War. The actors individually address the audience directly, telling overlapping stories about the war and its effect on them. The playwright attempts to connect the violence of the war with violence in our society. Cheryl and Mark are married, and Nadine is his mistress.

ANALYSIS: Many of the Vietnam-era plays feel dated now in the twenty-first century, but there is something lasting about this one. Somehow, I can foresee the same kinds of reactions coming out of the United States's Middle Eastern military ventures. Extremely well written. All levels.

SCENES/MONOLOGUES: Female Monologues (1), Male Monologues (2)

STRANGE SNOW
by Steve Metcalfe (Samuel French)

SYNOPSIS: Megs and Dave were in Vietnam together and share a deep secret. One day when they were to be dropped by helicopter into a battle, Dave froze in terror, jumped badly, and broke both ankles. Megs was hit by enemy fire when he jumped. Their buddy Bobby came to their aid and was killed. Both men still feel guilty. While Dave has become an alcoholic, Megs has dealt better with his guilt, coming to terms with himself, Bobby, and the war.

One day, years after the war has ended, Megs unexpectedly shows up at the house Dave shares with his sister Martha, explaining that he and Dave have a long-standing date to go fishing. Martha and Megs are immediately attracted to each other, and Dave just wishes Megs would go away. They work everything out, however, and at the final curtain, the audience knows that Dave will finally emerge from the shadow of his nightmares and that Megs and Martha will be together romantically.

ANALYSIS: One of the better post-Vietnam dramas. It was made into a movie called *Jackknife* starring Robert DeNiro, Kathy Baker, and Ed Harris.

SCENES/MONOLOGUES: Male/Female Scenes (2) Male/Male Scenes (1)

STRANGEST KIND OF ROMANCE, THE
by Tennessee Williams (*The Theatre of Tennessee Williams, Volume 6*; New Directions)

SYNOPSIS: A man, referred to throughout the play as "The Little Man," takes a room in a seedy rooming house in the Midwest, where the lonely landlady wants him to satisfy her sexually because her husband is an invalid. The man forms a closer bond, however, with a cat left behind by the last boarder. A few months after moving in, the man has a nervous breakdown and is hospitalized. When he gets out, he discovers that the woman has rented his room to a new man and, much worse, gotten rid of the cat.

ANALYSIS: An early, thoroughly odd one-act play from Tennessee Williams. Very interesting seduction scene, though. For sophisticated actors.

SCENES/MONOLOGUES: Male/Female Scenes (1), Male Monologues (1)

STREETCAR NAMED DESIRE, A
by Tennessee Williams (Dramatists Play Service)

SYNOPSIS: An aging Blanche DuBois, having lost the family plantation and all her money, arrives in the French Quarter of New Orleans to visit her younger sister, Stella, who is pregnant and happily married to a crude and forceful working-class lug named Stanley Kowalski. Hiding her destitution and the details of her sexually sordid past behind a false-happy facade and illusions of southern gentility, Blanche immediately has conflicts with Stanley, who sees through her pretensions. She is simultaneously horrified by and attracted to his base manners and animal magnetism, while her false airs and deceits repulse Stanley.

Blanche then sees a last hope for emotional refuge in Stanley's good-hearted co-worker Harold Mitchell, and sets about seducing the bachelor. Mitch falls hard for Blanche and speaks of marriage but, before that can happen, Stanley unravels the truth about her sexual past. This disclosure destroys her relationship with Mitch and catapults her into an emotional breakdown. After a final confrontation with Stanley that turns violently sexual, Blanche retreats totally into her fantasy life and must be institutionalized.

ANALYSIS: Tennessee Williams's crown jewel, the best of the best, the play that made Marlon Brando a star. Winner of the 1948 Pulitzer Prize. All levels.

SCENES/MONOLOGUES: Male/Female Scenes (3), Female/Female Scenes (2), Female Monologues (1)

SUBJECT WAS ROSES, THE
by Frank D. Gilroy (Samuel French)

SYNOPSIS: After being discharged from the Army in 1946, Timmy returns to the Bronx apartment where he grew up and where his parents still live. The folks are glad to see him and are grateful that he wasn't killed or injured as so many other soldiers were, so they launch into a round of family parties, dinners out, and visits with relatives. On the surface, the play is the perfect picture of a happy family reunion, but old currents run strong and deadly underneath. Timmy's father, John, is an emotionally distant, penny-pinching, self-made man who exists in a sexless marriage. Nettie, Timmy's mother, is a long-suffering woman whose affection is reserved for her own mother and her cousin. Both parents continually struggle for their son's loyalty. Over the course of the first weekend at home, all of this erupts, culminating in an honest acknowledgment of love and Timmy's decision to move out on his own.

ANALYSIS: This 1964 drama is a dandy. Martin Sheen rose to stardom after playing the son in the 1965 Broadway production, which won a Tony Award for Best Play. All levels.

SCENES/MONOLOGUES: Male/Female Scenes (2), Male/Male Scenes (2), Female Monologues (1)

SUBSTANCE OF FIRE, THE
by Jon Robin Baitz (Samuel French)

SYNOPSIS: Isaac Geldhart, a refugee of Nazi-occupied Europe, owns a publishing house in New York City, printing "serious" literary works. Increasingly out of step with the public's fast-food tastes, Kreeger/Geldhart Publishers is on the verge of bankruptcy when Isaac's children pool their stock in order to take control and publish more popular books. Their takeover is successful and Isaac is forced into retirement.

In the second act, which takes place several years after Isaac has retired, he has to face the prospect of being committed to an institution by his children. A social worker arrives, and he must convince her that he is sane.

ANALYSIS: Urban, caustic drama from a very bright young playwright. The characters tear at each other with literary references. All levels.

SCENES/MONOLOGUES: Male/Female Scenes (1), Male Monologues (2)

SUMMER AND SMOKE
by Tennessee Williams (Dramatists Play Service)

SYNOPSIS: The play is set in Mississippi during the early 1900s. Alma, the town minister's prim and proper daughter, has always loved John, the womanizing, hell-raising son of the local doctor, but she has never declared or acted on her feelings. John goes away to college, returning with a medical degree and still intent on sowing wild oats and having fun. Ultimately, he is transformed into a caring and talented physician, partly because of Alma's example and partly because his irresponsibility contributes to his father's death. Alma finally decides that her lifestyle of fanatical purity isn't healthy, declares her love to John, and agrees to go to bed with him, but it is too late. He already has plans to marry Nellie, a sweet, practical, carefree local woman, formerly one of Alma's piano students. This turn of events changes Alma's life forever.

ANALYSIS: A Tennessee Williams classic that pits soul against body. Alma is smoke, while John is the heat of summer. See also *The Eccentricities of a Nightingale*, which is Williams's later revision of *Summer and Smoke*. All levels.

SCENES/MONOLOGUES: Male/Female Scenes (3), Female/Female Scenes (1), Female Monologues (2)

SUMMER BRAVE
by William Inge (Dramatists Play Service)

SYNOPSIS: This 1962 work is the final revised edition of William Inge's successful play *Picnic*. Set in Kansas, this is the exact same story about Madge and her romance with Hal, a handsome rogue. The only difference between *Summer Brave* and *Picnic* is that this later play is a bit more cinematic in style.

ANALYSIS: William Inge, like Tennessee Williams, enjoyed tinkering with his plays long after they were produced. In the case of *Summer Brave,* Inge was clearly influenced by the film adaptation of his original play and tried to incorporate some of the elements that he thought worked in the movie. However, he was only moderately successful. All levels.

SCENES/MONOLOGUES: Male/Male Scenes (1)

SURE THING
by David Ives (*All in the Timing: Six One-Act Comedies* by David Ives, Dramatists Play Service)

SYNOPSIS: Bill and Betty meet in a café and fall in love. What makes this scene so delicious to play is the inclusion of an offstage bell-ringer. Every time Bill or Betty makes a false start, a gaffe, or a faux pas, the offstage bell rings. They do not acknowledge the sound of the bell, but every time it rings, it causes them to back up and start again.

ANALYSIS: Make sure you get somebody sharp to ring the bell offstage. And make sure the bell is loud enough to be heard by the audience. Keep the pace brisk.

SCENES/MONOLOGUES: Male/Female Scenes (1)

SWAN SONG
by Anton Chekhov (*The Sneeze: Plays and Stories by Anton Chekhov,* translated by Michael Frayn, Samuel French)

SYNOPSIS: The acting company has left the theater for the evening when Svetlovidov, an elderly comic actor, wakes from a nap and walks out onto the stage. The only other person remaining in the building is the prompter. The two men discuss the life of an actor.

ANALYSIS: One of Anton Chekhov's first popular successes in the theater, adapted from one of his own short stories, "Calchas." Charming and ultimately moving. Like all of Michael Frayn's adaptations of Chekhov, this is glorious. All levels.

SCENES/MONOLOGUES: Male Monologues (2)

SWEET BIRD OF YOUTH
by Tennessee Williams (Dramatists Play Service)

SYNOPSIS: Chance Wayne still has his chorus-line good looks even though he is in his late twenties. The aspiring actor and sometime gigolo arrives in his home-town of St. Cloud as the "escort" of Princess Kosmonopolis, better known to the world as the aging actress Alexandra Del Lago. Chance plans to parlay Alexandra's Hollywood influence into important introductions out west and a ticket out of Louisiana for his true and only love, Heavenly Finley. But her father, a corrupt segregationist politician, has put word out to kill or castrate Chance if he is caught because he infected Heavenly with a venereal disease during an earlier visit.

Although time has passed by most of the characters in this play, they continue to grasp for success. It is too late for Chance to be a star, too late for Alexandra to make a true comeback, and too late for Heavenly to have children or happiness. For all of them, the sweet bird of youth has flown away. At the end of the play, Chance refuses to run any more. He stands awaiting castration at the hands of Boss Finley's henchmen as Alexandra departs for Hollywood.

ANALYSIS: Despite some structural weaknesses, primarily the fact that Alexandra barely appears in the second act at all, the play drew kudos from the critics and has become a staple of American theater. The original 1960 Broadway production starred Paul Newman as Chance Wayne and Geraldine Page as Alexandra. Bruce Dern made his Broadway debut in a small role. All levels.

SCENES/MONOLOGUES: Male/Female Scenes (1), Male/Male Scenes (1), Male Monologues (1), Female Monologues (1)

SYLVIA
by A. R. Gurney, Jr. (Dramatists Play Service)

SYNOPSIS: Greg is facing a midlife crisis, questioning the value of his job and his marriage, when he brings home a stray dog he found in New York City's Central Park. His relationship with the dog (Sylvia) develops to the point where it becomes a threat to his marriage with Kate. In the end, however, the three of them live happily ever after.

ANALYSIS: *Sylvia* is what you would call a gimmick play, the trick being that an actress plays the role of a talking dog. It is the kind of idea that would normally make one roll one's eyes, but as written by master playwright A. R. Gurney, the story has plenty of charm.

SCENES/MONOLOGUES: Male/Female Scenes (2)

TAKE ME OUT
by Richard Greenberg (Dramatists Play Service)

SYNOPSIS: Darren Lemming is an immensely popular, highly paid star center-fielder for the New York Empires baseball team. When he publicly announces that he is gay, he assumes the news will be taken in stride by the public and his team-mates. It looks like it will indeed turn out that way until the Empires sign on a new pitcher. Shane Mungitt turns out to be a racist and bigot of the worst stripe. He makes racial and homophobic comments on a TV interview, leading to a public backlash for Darren and general discontent on the team. Darren emotionally retreats and then strikes up a friendship with Mason Marzac, his new financial adviser.

ANALYSIS: Winner of the 2003 Tony Award, this play is both an ode to baseball and an examination of American values.

SCENES/MONOLOGUES: Male/Male Scenes (3), Male Monologues (1)

TAKEN IN MARRIAGE
by Thomas Babe (Dramatists Play Service)

SYNOPSIS: Annie is getting married tomorrow in this small New Hampshire church, so her various female relatives have come into town for what is supposed to be a rehearsal. The rehearsal never happens because the groom's family is out at a bar somewhere. Instead, the women spend time together, sharing intimacies. We get to know all of them pretty well.

ANALYSIS: Upper-class people are interesting to watch when they begin to get insightful. Thomas Babe has an excellent ear for dialogue. All levels.

SCENES/MONOLOGUES: Female Monologues (1)

TALKING WITH...
by Jane Martin (Samuel French)

Synopsis: A compilation of eleven monologues for women, all credited to Jane Martin. There is no plot or obvious theme, just some riveting monologues.

Analysis: These well-written monologues are probably too long for audition purposes, but they're very good for class. All levels.

Scenes/Monologues: Female Monologues (11)

TAPE
by José Rivera (*Ten-Minute Plays: Volume 3 from Actors Theatre of Louisville*, Samuel French)

Synopsis: A person is led into a dark room by an attendant. The only thing inside is a table, an old tape recorder, a glass, and a pitcher of water. In truth, the dark room is really purgatory, and this person is there to listen to tape recordings of every lie he ever told in his life. He learns that there are ten thousand boxes of tapes.

Analysis: For scenework, I love this little play. Neither of the characters knows one another at the start but, within ten minutes, they begin to have mutual understanding. The script calls for an old reel-to-reel tape recorder, but you can work around that.

Scenes/Monologues: Male/Female Scenes (1)

TASTE OF HONEY, A
by Shelagh Delaney (Grove Press)

Synopsis: Jo moves into a slumlike flat in Salford, Lancashire, with her barhopping, whorish mother. Almost immediately, the mother moves out to marry a younger boyfriend, and Jo takes up with a black sailor. Their romance is intense and brief, leaving her pregnant and alone once he ships out. A gay student then moves in, caring for Jo as her pregnancy progresses. Late in her ninth month, Jo's mother comes back after her marriage falls apart, so the good-hearted student is forced out. At the final curtain, Jo is going into labor for a home delivery.

Analysis: Unsentimental and powerful, this perceptive drama was written by Shelagh Delaney when she was only eighteen years old.

Scenes/Monologues: Male/Female Scenes (3), Female/Female Scenes (1)

TENTH MAN, THE
by Paddy Chayefsky (Samuel French)

Synopsis: Everything is in an uproar at the tiny Orthodox synagogue of the Congregation Atereth-Fiferth Yisroel in Mineola, a Long Island town. Not only is the sexton facing the usual trouble of finding a tenth Jew for morning prayer, Foreman has just shown up with his schizophrenic granddaughter and announced that she is, in fact, possessed by a dybbuk. This is a migratory soul that lands in the body of another human being in order to return to heaven. Foreman suggests an exorcism. After some debate, the sexton agrees to conduct the service, and preparations get under way. By the end of the play, when the exorcism takes place with some very surprising results, the granddaughter has fallen in love, a Jew who is grabbed from the street to make the quorum finds salvation, and the elders' faith is strengthened.

ANALYSIS: Funny, poignant, and instructive, this 1959 comedy still delivers. Paddy Chayefsky was one of America's greatest playwrights. All levels.

SCENES/MONOLOGUES: Male/Female Scenes (1), Male Monologues (2), Female Monologues (1)

THAT CHAMPIONSHIP SEASON
by Jason Miller (Dramatists Play Service)

SYNOPSIS: The 1952 Pennsylvania High School Basketball champions are having their annual reunion at the coach's house. Plenty of liquor and horseplay only temporarily cover the explosive tensions and violence simmering within the men. No longer a close team under the strict but loving guidance of their leader, it is now every man for himself in the game of life.

ANALYSIS: This stunning drama, the winner of the 1973 Tony Award for Best Play, holds up well. There are two glorious monologues for the coach. All levels.

SCENES/MONOLOGUES: Male Monologues (2)

TIME OF YOUR LIFE, THE
by William Saroyan (Samuel French)

SYNOPSIS: In 1939 Nick's Saloon, a waterfront honky-tonk bar in "the lousiest part" of San Francisco, is a gathering place for eccentric characters. Joe is a fellow bent on finding the good and gentle in people; he is trying to live a life in which he doesn't hurt anyone. There are also two young lovers, an aspiring comic, a piano player, a cop who doesn't like his work, a prostitute with a heart of gold, and a few men who aren't nice at all. In the end, good conquers evil, at least for now and at least in spirit, and love promises to prevail.

ANALYSIS: *The Time of Your Life* was awarded both the 1940 New York Drama Critics' Circle Award and the 1940 Pulitzer Prize. The scenes in this play are gentle and evocative, and the play reflects William Saroyan's personal slant on life more than it centers on a plotline. The characters are, for the most part, endearing eccentrics. All levels.

SCENES/MONOLOGUES: Male/Female Scenes (1), Male Monologues (3)

TOPDOG/UNDERDOG
by Suzan-Lori Parks (Theatre Communications Group)

SYNOPSIS: Two African-American brothers, cruelly named Lincoln and Booth by their father, live together in a run-down rooming house. Booth is a street hustler, his game Three-Card Monty; Lincoln used to be an even better street hustler but gave up cards to work in an arcade as a Lincoln impersonator—in whiteface. Lincoln is actually the smarter of the two men, which makes Booth even more competitive toward him. The action in the play revolves around Lincoln's loss of his arcade job and Booth's attempts to become a master at Three-Card Monty, like his brother. The climax is unexpected and violent.

ANALYSIS: This is a remarkable and insightful play. Ms. Parks has created a microcosm of American values in a single family, in much the same way that Sam Shepard does with *True West*. The brothers here are capable of real violence, and that is what gives their relationship its punch. The play won the 2002 Pulitzer Prize for Drama.

SCENES/MONOLOGUES: Male/Male Scenes (1), Male Monologues (2)

TOP GIRLS
by Caryl Churchill (Samuel French)

SYNOPSIS: After Marlene is promoted to manager at the Top Girls Employment Agency, she hosts a celebration lunch that is attended by six women from the pages of history: Isabella Bird (1831–1904), Lady Nijo (born 1258), Dull Gret (subject of a Brueghel painting), Pope Joan (thought to have been Pope between 854 and 856 while disguised as a man), and Patient Griselda (a character from *The Canterbury Tales* by Chaucer). There are roasts and lunch and much talk about how each of these women fared in her lifetime.

In subsequent scenes, the actresses who play the six historical figures now play office co-workers and Marlene's relatives. What the audience learns, finally, is that Marlene has refashioned herself despite her upbringing in order to achieve success in a man's world and, in the process, has acquired the worst traits of successful men. The Top Girls Employment Agency coaches its job-seekers using these same tactics. In the last scene of the play, it becomes clear that the ultra-ambitious Marlene went so far as to abandon her own offspring, giving the child, who is now sixteen years old, to her sister Joyce to raise.

ANALYSIS: This is, frankly, a brilliantly conceived play that holds up quite well. All levels.

SCENES/MONOLOGUES: Female/Female Scenes (1), Female Monologues (1)

TOUCH OF THE POET, A
by Eugene O'Neill (Dramatists Play Service)

SYNOPSIS: Cornelius Melody, to the Irish manor born, has wound up struggling late in life to make ends meet in a small Massachusetts tavern. Although he was once a military hero in the Napoleonic Wars, he can now only relive those distant glories at an annual party during which he puts on his old officer's uniform and holds court for the local lowlife and his own embarrassed family.

The events of this story take place on such a day, and there is no major plot. As Eugene O'Neill does in other dramas such as *Long Day's Journey Into Night,* the central character is presented on the cusp of a revelation and, in a few short hours, his life has changed forever. In this case, Melody schemes to see his daughter marry the wealthy son of a neighboring landowner. When the young man's parents respond by threatening to cut off his inheritance and by offering Melody a bribe to move away, he turns violent. Forced to confront the fact that he has become a shell of a man, Melody goes into a dark, drunken rage and shoots his prized mare, a symbol of his aristocratic origins and his self-deception.

ANALYSIS: This play was published after Eugene O'Neill's death and didn't reach Broadway until 1958. The language is rich, the literary references myriad, and the dialogue challenging. Best suited for serious, literate actors.

SCENES/MONOLOGUES: Male/Female Scenes (3), Female Monologues (1)

TOYER
by Gardner McKay (Samuel French)

SYNOPSIS: This two-character psychological thriller centers on the question of whether or not a male intruder into a woman's home in the Hollywood Hills is a rapist, a voyeur, an actor, or a serial mutilator—or all of the above. The woman, a psychiatrist at a local hospital, is at first convinced that she is facing a voyeur, so she uses her knowledge of scopophilia to neutralize the potentially dangerous situation.

But then the situation turns deadly as the intruder admits to being the notorious Toyer, a serial mutilator whose modus operandi is to give his victim an animal tranquilizer and then sever her spinal cord, rendering her his "toy." After terrorizing the psychiatrist with this possibility for a while, he suddenly turns jovial and says he is actually an actor practicing his character work. She is relieved, disoriented, and emotionally drained. They then drink some liquor and head for the bedroom. The next morning, however, she learns that he is the Toyer after all. When he tries to drug her, she turns the tables on him and, at the final curtain, has him tied up and is about to cut his spinal cord.

ANALYSIS: This play was originally published as a novella and inspired a movie of a different name. Tony Richardson directed Kathleen Turner and Brad Davis in a production at the Kennedy Center in Washington, DC, and there was a production of it at the Actors Studio. For intense, advanced actors who want to delve into the darkest psychological wilderness within, this tightly written play is ideal. Some scenes include justified nudity.

SCENES/MONOLOGUES: Male/Female Scenes (5)

TOYS IN THE ATTIC
by Lillian Hellman (Dramatists Play Service)

SYNOPSIS: Julian Berniers, brash and full of bravado, arrives in New Orleans one day in the 1940s for a visit with his budget-minded, simple-living sisters, bringing with him the wonderful news that he has struck it rich. It turns out, however, that he is involved in a romantic affair with Charlotte Warkins, a woman who helped him arrange a crooked real-estate deal in order to get money from Cyrus, her rich, ruthless husband. Julian intends to leave his clinging young wife, Lily, to marry Charlotte, but before that can happen, Lily tells Cyrus about his wife's extramarital romance. Outraged, Cyrus arranges for a vicious retaliation against Julian and Charlotte.

ANALYSIS: A sprawling three-act drama—the kind no one writes anymore—*Toys in the Attic* opened on Broadway in 1960 and ran for more than a year, garnering Tony nominations for Anne Revere, Jason Robards, Maureen Stapleton, and Irene Worth. All levels.

SCENES/MONOLOGUES: Female/Female Scenes (1)

TRIBUTE
by Bernard Slade (Samuel French)

SYNOPSIS: Wisecracking, fun-loving Scottie Templeton is diagnosed with a form of leukemia at the age of fifty-one and told to get his affairs in order. He decides to keep the diagnosis a secret and, without any appeal for pity, tries to salvage the strained relationship he has with Jud, his twenty-year-old son. As this relationship evolves, Scottie also comes to a deeper appreciation of his former wife and the true meaning of friendship. The dramatic device in the play is a tribute to Scottie, which is being given at a downtown theater by friends from all over the country. The action moves back and forth between the stage of that theater and Scottie's apartment.

ANALYSIS: A lovely comedy, guaranteed to make audience members cry. Jack Lemmon portrayed Scottie on Broadway and in the subsequent movie. All levels.

SCENES/MONOLOGUES: Male/Female Scenes (1), Male/Male Scenes (1), Female Monologues (1)

TRIP BACK DOWN, THE
by John Bishop (Samuel French)

SYNOPSIS: The play is set in Mansfield, Ohio, where most folks work at the Westinghouse plant. Bobby Horvath escaped all of that to become a big-time stock-car driver on the southern circuit. Now, eight years later, it is clear that he'll never be "number one" as a driver, so he has returned to his hometown in order to reestablish ties with the wife and child he left behind.

ANALYSIS: Ran briefly on Broadway, starring John Cullum. The best part of the play is the stock-car racing/factory-town/blue-collar milieu. John Bishop's dialogue rings true.

SCENES/MONOLOGUES: Male/Female Scenes (1), Male Monologues (1)

TRUE WEST
by Sam Shepard (Samuel French)

SYNOPSIS: Austin is housesitting near Los Angeles for his mother who is on vacation in Alaska. Because he is a successful screenwriter, he is using the time to cement a new deal with movie producer Saul Kimmer. Then Austin's older brother Lee, a vagabond and petty thief, shows up. The usual air of tension between these dissimilar men becomes even more highly charged when Lee decides to pitch a movie idea of his own to Saul and, wonder of wonders, Saul buys it.

ANALYSIS: Probably Sam Shepard's most accessible play and a favorite in scene-study workshops. All levels.

SCENES/MONOLOGUES: Male/Male Scenes (3), Three-Person Scenes (1)

TWENTY-SEVEN WAGONS FULL OF COTTON
by Tennessee Williams (*The Theatre of Tennessee Williams, Volume 6;* New Directions)

SYNOPSIS: Jake is a sharecropper whose income has been hurt by the encroaching syndicate. In retaliation, he secretly burns down the syndicate's big cotton gin and then innocently makes himself available to gin all the cotton that is sitting around after the fire. Silva Vicarro, the superintendent of the Syndicate Plantation where the fire occurred, comes to Jake's place to give him the gin business. Left alone with Jake's childlike wife, Silva quickly discovers who set the fire and then responds by cruelly seducing the woman. Later, Jake gloats about all this new-found business, oblivious to his wife's disheveled, sexually ravaged appearance. She tells him that Silva is planning to come back with loads of cotton (and presumably plans for more seduction) all summer.

ANALYSIS: An early one-act play from Tennessee Williams that is realistic and gritty. You can almost feel the perspiration and smell the dust on these rural, uneducated southern people as they do one another in. For sophisticated actors.

SCENES/MONOLOGUES: Male/Female Scenes (1)

TWICE AROUND THE PARK
by Murray Schisgal (Samuel French)

SYNOPSIS: These two one-act plays were a showcase for Anne Jackson and Eli Wallach. In the first, *A Need for Brussels Sprouts,* Leon is an actor practicing loudly for an audition as an opera singer. His upstairs neighbor complains to no avail.

Then a police officer shows up to give him a summons for disturbing the peace. It turns out that the officer is Margaret, the upstairs neighbor Leon has never seen; she is actually a very nice widow with two teenagers. Leon is currently single, having been married three times before. In short order, a love affair is born.

The second one-act play, *A Need for Less Expertise,* involves a married couple, Gus and Edie, who are having sexual problems. Edie is neck-deep in therapy, self-help groups, and counselors, but Gus only grudgingly cooperates. The first time we see Gus and Edie, they are comically trying to follow the recorded instructions of sex counselor Dr. Oliovsky; each of his exercises is designed to lead couples one step closer to the bedroom. After several embarrassing stops and starts, Gus admits that he has had a number of affairs, all one-night stands, but that this errant behavior is all over. Edie gets mad, leaves, and then comes back. As the curtain falls, they begin to practice Dr. Oliovsky's foot-massage exercise.

ANALYSIS: New York humor, very funny. All levels.

SCENES/MONOLOGUES: Male/Female Scenes (3), Female Monologues (1)

TWO ROOMS
by Lee Blessing (Dramatists Play Service)

SYNOPSIS: Michael Wells was kidnapped from Beirut Lebanon University, where he was teaching. As the play opens, he has been in captivity for a year, and his wife, Lainie, has constructed a shrine to him in her home in the United States. The room is as identical as she can make it to the prison in which she imagines he is being held, with only a mattress on the floor. Ellen Van Oss, a State Department representative, often visits Lainie, imploring her to remain silent, not to speak to the press about her husband's situation. She tells her threateningly that to do so would increase the danger for him; that the best option is to allow the government to work silently to free him. Walker Harris is another visitor. He is a reporter who encourages Lainie to go public because the government is in fact not doing enough to free her husband. In the end, the reporter wins, and Lainie does indeed go public. It is too late, however, because her husband's captors execute him.

ANALYSIS: When this play was published in 1988, who would have thought that the United States would still be involved in a conflict in the Middle East two decades later? Provocative and challenging. All levels.

SCENES/MONOLOGUES: Male/Female Scenes (1), Female/Female Scenes (1)

TWO SMALL BODIES
by Neal Bell (Dramatists Play Service)

SYNOPSIS: Two young children disappear from their bedroom during the night, and Lieutenant Brann is assigned to the case. He immediately suspects their mother, Eileen, who is estranged from her husband and working as a cocktail waitress in a strip joint. He interrogates her aggressively and, in the end, she confesses to the killings. Only she didn't do it, a fact that becomes clear when the children's bodies are found and the vagrant who killed them is taken into custody.

The real underbelly of this play is the complex love/hate relationship that develops between Brann and Eileen during the course of the interrogations. He is a straight-arrow conservative-leaning cop; she is doing what she has to do in the world to survive. He is simultaneously sexually attracted to her and repulsed by her. Their conversations take on aspects of masochism and religious guilt.

ANALYSIS: Adult material, plenty of subtext, sexually loaded, frequent rough language. For experienced actors.

SCENES/MONOLOGUES: Male/Female Scenes (4)

VALUE OF NAMES, THE
by Jeffrey Sweet (Dramatists Play Service)

SYNOPSIS: New York City–based actress Norma Silverman arrives in Hollywood to appear in a play and to visit with her elderly father, Benny. When the play's director suffers a stroke, Norma is put in an awkward position by his replacement, Leo Greshen, the man who named her father as a communist sympathizer in testimony before the House Un-American Activities Committee during the 1950s. Out of respect for her father, Norma feels that she can't continue in the show without his blessing. Leo visits Benny's home to meet with Norma and try to reconcile with Benny. They heatedly kick the subject of "naming names" back and forth, arriving at no satisfactory conclusions. In the end, Norma proceeds with the play, but Benny doesn't forgive Leo for what he did. Some wrongs, he contends, can never be undone.

ANALYSIS: Originally commissioned by the Actors Theatre of Louisville in 1982, the first production of this drama was directed by Emily Mann, herself a prolific and talented playwright. All levels.

SCENES/MONOLOGUES: Male/Female Scenes (2), Male Monologues (1)

VIEUX CARRÉ
by Tennessee Williams (New Directions)

SYNOPSIS: For part of 1938, Tennessee Williams lived in a French Quarter rooming house in New Orleans. *Vieux Carré* is more of a tableaux of the sad but colorful occupants of that house than it is a play. Nightingale is an aging, gay, tubercular painter; Mrs. Wire, a demented opportunistic landlady; Tye McCool, a drug-addicted barker at a strip-show joint; his lover, Jane Sparks, a fashion illustrator from up north whose leukemia is at first in remission but then returns. These and other characters move in and out of the house, their stories being narrated by a young writer, a role clearly based on Williams himself.

ANALYSIS: This play is useful for actors in search of powerful scenes and monologues but doesn't hold together as a complete work. In fact, it closed after only five performances on Broadway and is rarely revived. Best suited for advanced actors.

SCENES/MONOLOGUES: Male/Female Scenes (1), Male/Male Scenes (1), Male Monologues (1), Female Monologues (1)

VIEW FROM THE BRIDGE, A
by Arthur Miller (Dramatists Play Service)

SYNOPSIS: Eddie Carbone is a longshoreman of Italian descent, working the docks from the Brooklyn Bridge to the breakwater. He helps two of his wife's cousins emigrate illegally from Sicily to the United States, putting them up in the small apartment he and Beatrice share with her beautiful orphaned niece, Catherine. The older of the immigrant brothers turns out to be hardworking and dependable, but the younger one is evidently cut from a different cloth. Rodolpho sings and cooks, and can even repair a dress—skills that make him suspect in Eddie's eyes.

Then when Rodolpho and Catherine fall in love, Eddie is driven almost crazy with repressed jealousy. In his efforts to break up the couple, he accuses Rodolpho of being homosexual, of courting Catherine only to gain American citizenship. When it becomes clear that Catherine will marry Rodolpho, Eddie turns the brothers in to the Immigration Bureau. Before being deported, Marco, the older brother, seeks out Eddie and kills him. Rodolpho ultimately marries Catherine.

ANALYSIS: In his autobiography, *Time Bends,* Arthur Miller explains that he wrote this famous drama originally as a one-act companion piece to *A Memory of Two Mondays.* The playwright found the 1955 production unsatisfactory because Van Heflin didn't have a seat-of-the-pants feel for the character of Eddie Carbone, but the 1965 off-Broadway revival was excellent because of the presence of Robert Duvall and Jon Voight as the immigrant brothers. All levels.

SCENES/MONOLOGUES: Male/Female Scenes (4), Female/Female Scenes (1), Male/Male Scenes (1)

VISIT, THE: A TRAGI-COMEDY (Evergreen Original, #344)
by Friedrich Durrenmatt (translated by Patrick Bowles, Grove Press)

SYNOPSIS: Claire Zachanassian, the richest woman in the world, returns to her Central European hometown, which is suffering from economic depression and disrepair. She offers £1 million to the town and its residents on a single condition—that they murder a beloved local citizen: Alfred Ill, the man who done her wrong many years ago. The offer alone makes the town prosperous, as the citizens begin to purchase goods on credit. In the end, murder is rationalized in the name of justice, and poor Alfred dies from fright.

ANALYSIS: Written by a major German dramatist, this parable is a vicious indictment of the power of greed. All levels.

SCENES/MONOLOGUES: Male/Female Scenes (1), Male/Male Scenes (1)

VITAL SIGNS
by Jane Martin (Samuel French)

SYNOPSIS: The play is a series of short monologues performed by six young women, sometimes relating to one another or to one of the two men who assist them, and sometimes to the audience. There is no discernible plot or theme except an effort to figure out, or comment on, colorful or poignant life situations. One woman talks about working as a waitress in an all-nude diner; another supervises unruly children at a playground; and still another describes a fun but rare excursion to Coney Island with her father.

ANALYSIS: For actresses who like to use cute stories for monologue material, *Vital Signs,* which was born at the Actors Theatre of Louisville, is a gold mine because it has thirty-nine of them. Only a few contain obvious conflict or tension. All levels.

SCENES/MONOLOGUES: Female Monologues (2)

WAITING FOR LEFTY
by Clifford Odets (Dramatists Play Service)

SYNOPSIS: The year is 1935, and a group of taxi drivers are gathered in a smoke-filled room to vote whether or not to go on strike. As they wait for their leader, Lefty, to show up, the men take turns going to center stage to tell their stories. These episodes dramatize families being torn apart, economic hardship, and corruption in the business place, and constitute the body of the drama. In the end, word comes that Lefty has been murdered, and the workers finally unite, demanding with one voice, "Strike! Strike! Strike!"

ANALYSIS: This kind of political theater (sometimes known as *agitprop*: a combination of "agitation" and "propaganda") was common during and after the Great Depression. Clifford Odets wrote *Waiting for Lefty*, a five-scene, one-act play, intending it to be performed in labor halls as well as theaters. It was an immediate success, putting him and the Group Theatre firmly on the map. Odets and Sanford Meisner jointly directed that first production.

SCENES/MONOLOGUES: Male/Female Scenes (2), Male Monologues (1)

WAITING FOR THE PARADE
by John Murrell (Talonbooks, Canada)

SYNOPSIS: A group of women in Calgary, Canada, do their part to support the men, young and old, who are overseas fighting in World War II. In twenty-four scenes presented in a single act, spanning three years, they cope with the pressures of war at home, sometimes with humor, sometimes with tears.

ANALYSIS: Even though the play is set in Canada and makes many references to that country's government and local life, much of the material can be adapted for workshops anywhere. All levels.

SCENES/MONOLOGUES: Female/Female Scenes (1), Female Monologues (2)

WASH, THE
by Philip Kan Gotanda (Dramatists Play Service)

SYNOPSIS: After forty-two years of marriage, at the age of sixty-seven, Masi Matsumoto has left her husband, Nobu, thirteen months ago. The play tracks them as they attempt to live alone or with new lovers, and try to redefine their relationships with their adult children. Masi and Nobu are both Nisei, second-generation Japanese Americans, and divorce is rare among these people.

ANALYSIS: Well-written drama that shines a light on generational differences in Japanese-American culture. All levels.

SCENES/MONOLOGUES: Male/Female Scenes (1), Male Monologues (2), Female Monologues (1)

WHAT I DID LAST SUMMER
by A. R. Gurney, Jr. (Dramatists Play Service)

SYNOPSIS: During the summer of 1945, fourteen-year-old Charlie is happily under the influence of Anna the Pig Woman, a local free spirit and self-styled mentor who is determined to develop his very hidden talents. Maybe he is a sculptor! A painter! None of the above?

Charlie's mother, Grace, meanwhile, who was herself once under Anna's influence, is threatened by this laissez-faire philosophy. She would rather he join the country-club set and mark out a more conventional life path. The matter finally comes to a head when Grace and Anna decide to let Charlie choose for himself. He opts for Anna, moving into her barn. The arrangement is short-lived, however, because he soon wrecks her car, which he is too young to be driving. This event leads to legal and financial problems for Anna, and she is forced to sell her home and move into a trailer. This ends her time with Charlie. He then leaves for boarding school, his apprenticeship to Anna a fond memory.

ANALYSIS: If you liked the movie *Harold and Maude,* you're going to love this play. Anna the Pig Woman is a lovable eccentric, the kind of person who disregards just about every rule and guideline society has to offer so that she can march along in her unorthodox but highly moral fashion. Clearly, A. R. Gurney is suggesting that everyone would be better off with a little bit of what Anna has. All levels.

SCENES/MONOLOGUES: Female/Female Scenes (1)

WHO'S AFRAID OF VIRGINIA WOOLF?
by Edward Albee (Dramatists Play Service)

SYNOPSIS: George came to teach history at a small New England college twenty-three years ago and shortly after arriving married Martha, the college president's daughter. As George's prospects for academic prominence dimmed, however, their relationship, while remaining vivid and loving in its own way, has become cloaked in illusion and perverse game-playing. The action takes place between 2 A.M. and 5 A.M. one Sunday morning after a faculty reception at Martha's father's house. George and Martha "entertain" Nick, the new, young, handsome biology professor, and Honey, his simpering wife.

Everyone is slightly drunk as the curtain goes up, and a continual flow of alcohol fuels round after round of vicious game-playing, truth-telling, deception, seduction, and verbal brutality. Martha tries to seduce Nick, but he is too drunk to perform; Honey spends most of her time throwing up and sleeping in the bathroom; and George retaliates against Martha in an unexpected game where he "kills" their imaginary twenty-one-year–old son.

ANALYSIS: George and Martha, probably the most famous couple in modern drama, continually lash out at one another, cutting away layer after layer of facade, exposing raw nerve. All scenes require extreme honesty and vulnerability. The play walked off with almost all the Tony Awards when it premiered on Broadway in 1963, including Best Actress for Uta Hagen as Martha. Sophisticated, demanding material that is appropriate for advanced actors.

SCENES/MONOLOGUES: Male/Female Scenes (4), Male/Male Scenes (2), Female Monologues (1)

WHOSE LIFE IS IT ANYWAY?
by Brian Clark (Dramatic Publishing Company)

SYNOPSIS: Ken Harrison, sculptor and art teacher, suffered a spinal-cord injury in a car accident and is paralyzed from the neck down. After learning that the damage is permanent, he announces to the hospital staff that he would rather die than live this way. The physician in charge of the intensive-care ward contends that it is his duty to keep injured people alive and refuses to facilitate a suicide. A court hearing to determine Ken's sanity is conducted, after which the judge orders the hospital to let him die if he wants to. Dignity begins not with life, but with choice.

ANALYSIS: Tom Conti first played the role of Ken Harrison in London and then won a Tony Award for Best Actor in the 1979 Broadway production. Richard Dreyfus starred in an excellent 1981 movie version. The script is written in the British vernacular but can easily be adapted to standard American usage. All levels.

SCENES/MONOLOGUES: Male/Female Scenes (2), Male/Male Scenes (1)

WILD HONEY
by Michael Frayn (adapted from an early, untitled play by Anton Chekhov; Samuel French)

SYNOPSIS: Anton Chekhov's original play, discovered in a Moscow safe-deposit box after his death, would, in Michael Frayn's estimate, run "over six hours" and has too many sprawling plotlines and characters. Taking a great deal of liberty with the original manuscript, he has centralized the story along a premise that would later show up in *The Cherry Orchard*, namely, the pending loss of a family estate. The primary subject of the moment, however, is love. Set during the first balmy days of summer, romance is in the air, and all manner of intrigue is woven throughout. Everyone here is madly in love with someone who loves or is married to someone else, creating delicious comedic scenes.

ANALYSIS: Unlike Chekhov's major plays, no one will argue that this modern adaptation is anything but a comedy. Michael Frayn has cleverly managed to maintain the spirit of Chekhov's style with a subtle adaptation. All levels.

SCENES/MONOLOGUES: Male/Female Scenes (4), Male Monologues (1)

WIT
by Margaret Edson (Dramatists Play Service)

SYNOPSIS: Vivian Bearing is a fifty-year-old professor of seventeenth-century poetry, specializing in the Holy Sonnets of John Donne, and she is dying of advanced metastatic ovarian cancer. In this extraordinary one-act multiple-vignette play, Vivian narrates her own demise. She is alternately witty, dominant, submissive (to her disease), vulnerable, and strong. She has no family and no husband to comfort her at this time, but she relies instead on the poetry of John Donne and reflections on her life's journey.

ANALYSIS: Does anybody really like to face human mortality head on? When confronted with the inevitability of death, most people will turn away. But I contend that actors are shamans and have a special obligation to consider such things. *Wit*, which won the 1999 Pulitzer Prize for Drama, certainly presents an excellent opportunity. The character of Vivian Bearing is dynamic, funny, painful, and multilayered. Portraying her will be emotionally exhausting and spiritually uplifting for any actor who takes on the job. Technical note: When we first meet Vivian, chemotherapy has already caused her to lose her hair. Actresses in workshop will have to figure out a way to deal with this, perhaps with a head-covering of some kind.

SCENES/MONOLOGUES: Male/Female Scenes (1), Female/Female Scenes (1), Female Monologues (1)

WOMEN, THE
by Clare Boothe Luce (Dramatists Play Service)

SYNOPSIS: Sweet and trusting Mary is shocked to discover that her wealthy husband, Stephen, is having an affair with Crystal Allen, a sales clerk at Saks. Mary's gossipy friends spread the word all over town and, finally, a Reno divorce results. Two years later, Crystal, now married to Stephen, is bored and begins an affair with yet another man. Mary finds out about it and, having learned how to survive in the female jungle, helps sabotage their marriage. At the final curtain, Crystal and Stephen have divorced, while Mary and Stephen are reuniting.

ANALYSIS: No one writes plays like this anymore. *The Women,* with its massive forty-four-character, all-female cast, would cost a fortune to stage professionally today. Still, it is a polished gem with its claws out, and a delight for scene-study purposes. All levels.

SCENES/MONOLOGUES: Female/Female Scenes (3)

WOOLGATHERER, THE
by William Mastrosimone (Samuel French)

SYNOPSIS: Cliff is stuck in Philadelphia overnight while he waits for repairs on his big-rig truck. He starts talking with Rosie, a candy-counter clerk at a local five-and-dime store. When they wind up at her apartment, Cliff expects that they're going to sleep together. But he soon realizes that Rosie is a bit odd, that she has no intentions of sleeping with him, and that she collects men's sweaters. He leaves at the end of Act I but returns later in the night, drawn by some kind of unnamed attraction. At this point, Cliff discovers that Rosie has an entire closetful of men's sweaters and, in fact, has never recovered from an earlier nervous breakdown. She prefers a fantasy love life to the risks of involvement with real flesh-and-blood men. The play ends with Rosie beginning to have another breakdown and Cliff comforting her.

ANALYSIS: William Mastrosimone, who also wrote *Extremities,* has a wonderful way with working-class language and manners. This strange play is very funny at times. All levels.

SCENES/MONOLOGUES: Male/Female Scenes (2), Male Monologues (1), Female Monologues (1)

ZOOMAN AND THE SIGN
by Charles Fuller (Samuel French)

SYNOPSIS: Reuben and Rachel's twelve-year-old daughter Jinny was killed in urban-gang crossfire as she sat on the front porch of her home. Although it is likely that several neighbors witnessed the tragedy, no one comes forward to identify the killer. So Reuben hangs a large sign over the front of his house that reads, "The Killers of our daughter Jinny are free on the streets because our neighbors will not identify them." The sign becomes a subject of disagreement in the family and the object of anger in the neighborhood. Finally, the same hoodlum who shot Jinny comes to the house to rip down the sign and is killed by Uncle Emmett. Another death, however, doesn't bring Jinny back or solve anything.

ANALYSIS: As tragic as today's headlines, this well-written drama was first presented in 1980 at New York City's famous Negro Ensemble Company. All the characters are African-American. All levels.

SCENES/MONOLOGUES: Male Monologues (2), Female Monologues (1)

ZOO STORY, THE
by Edward Albee (*Zoo Story and The Sandbox: Two Short Plays,* Dramatists Play Service)

SYNOPSIS: Peter is enjoying a warm afternoon in New York City's Central Park when a stranger walks up and announces that he has been to the zoo. Peter and Jerry get into a conversation that begins on friendly terms but soon takes on overtones of dominance and control. Jerry becomes increasingly volatile, finally drawing a knife. Then he inexplicably tosses the knife to Peter and, when Peter tries to defend himself with it, Jerry lunges, impaling himself on the knife and committing suicide.

ANALYSIS: Albee's first play, *The Zoo Story* premiered in Berlin in 1950 and is routinely revived.

SCENES/MONOLOGUES: Male/Male Scenes (1)

PART TWO

MALE MONOLOGUES

ABSENT FRIENDS
by Alan Ayckbourn (Samuel French)
Comedy: Act I, p. 29, Colin (30s)

Colin's former friends have invited him to a tea party to cheer him up after the untimely death of his fiancée. At the very end of Act I, he delivers this exquisitely sensitive and touching speech about how much he loved the woman, how much he cherishes her memory, and how much he appreciates this group of good friends. As they listen to him, they descend into abject depression and tears. Fun for workshops, but less suitable for auditions. Depending on the delivery, this monologue is either very funny or very sad. Start: "It's a funny thing about somebody dying—you never know, till it actually happens, how it's going to affect you." End: "I just want you to know that, despite everything that happened, in a funny sort of way, I too am very happy."

ABSURD PERSON SINGULAR
by Alan Ayckbourn (Samuel French)
Comedy-Drama: Act II, pp. 41–44, Geoffrey (30s)

Oblivious to the fact that his wife, Eva, is trying to commit suicide at the precise moment he is talking to her, Geoffrey, an unrepentant womanizer, suggests that they legally separate. She sits at the kitchen table, clinging to her partially written suicide note and staring blankly at him the whole time. For audition use, excerpt the section that deals specifically with the separation. For workshops, it is probably more interesting to work on Geoffrey's transitions, starting with his entrance and initial complaints about his job, then moving to the couple's marriage trouble, and finally getting into the imminent arrival of their Christmas-party guests. Written in the British vernacular. Start: "God, I think I need a drink. You want a drink?" End: "What I lack in morals, I make up in ethics."

Comedy-Drama: Act III, pp. 79–80, Ronald (40s)

On the surface, this monologue doesn't look like much, just a man explaining to his friends that he doesn't understand women. To do it justice, an actor needs to address issues of mortality, life changes, and shifting expectations. As Ronald speaks on this apparently cheerful Christmas Eve, his second wife is sitting upstairs in alcoholic isolation, and his business has fallen apart. Written in the British vernacular. Eliminate Geoffrey's lines here. Start: "You seem to have got things pretty well organized on the home front." End: "Couldn't do without them, could we, I suppose...."

AFTER THE FALL
by Arthur Miller (Dramatists Play Service)
Drama: Act I, pp. 38–39, Quentin (40s)
Quentin tells Louise about meeting a young woman in the park. He was fascinated by her because she "wasn't defending anything, upholding everything, or accusing—she was just there." Start: "I sat by the park for a while." End: "This city is full of lovers."

AH, WILDERNESS!
by Eugene O'Neill (Samuel French)
Comedy: Act III, Scene 2, pp. 106–108, Richard (16)
As Richard waits on a moonlit beach for his true love to sneak out of her home and join him, he carries on a dialogue with himself. He kicks himself for stupidities, recites some poetry, and declares his most ecstatic love. Probably not the best choice for auditions, but this is a charming theatrical moment—excellent workshop material for a young actor working on self-stimulation and the uses of imagination. Start: "Must be nearly nine...I can hear the Town Hall clock strike, it's so still tonight." End: "Let her suffer for a change!"
Comedy: Act IV, Scene 3, pp. 124–126, Miller (50)
A father/son lecture about the birds and the bees, circa 1906. Dad bumbles and mumbles his way through it, illuminating nothing. Start: "But listen here, Richard, it's about time you and I had a serious talk." End: "I never had anything to do with such women, and it'll be a hell of a lot better for you if you never do!"

ALL MY SONS
by Arthur Miller (Dramatists Play Service)
Drama: Act I, pp. 30–31, Chris (32)
Trying to explain why he is having trouble committing himself fully to Annie, Chris recalls his experiences in the war and his dedication to his brother. Omit Annie's lines at the beginning of Chris's speech. Start: "You remember, overseas, I was in command of a company?...Well, I lost them....Just about all of (them)....It takes a little time to toss that off." End: "I didn't want to take any of it. And I guess that included you."

AMADEUS
by Peter Shaffer (Samuel French)
Drama: Act II, pp. 72–73, Mozart (25–30)
Baron Van Swieten is horrified to learn that Mozart wants to write an opera based on the play *The Marriage of Figaro*. Mozart blasts the Baron and his contemporaries for their loftiness and artistic pretensions, arguing in favor of "flesh and blood" opera—stories of real people, not gods and goddesses. Start: "I don't

understand you! You're all up on perches." End with either: "and turn the audience into God" or "my tongue is stupid. My heart isn't."

AMEN CORNER, THE
by James Baldwin (Samuel French)
Drama: Act II, p. 52, David (18)
David talks to Luke, his musician father who is on his deathbed. David explains
how the prospect of being a professional musician has drawn him away from his
mother's church. The space that used to be filled by God is now filled by music.
Eliminate Luke's line. Start: "A few months ago some guys come in the church and
they heard me playing piano and they kept coming back all the time. Mama said
it was the Holy Ghost drawing them in. But it wasn't." End: "And I was trying to
find some way of preparing Mama's mind."

Drama: Act II, pp. 52–53, Luke (40–50)
Luke, on his deathbed, tells his son that it is okay to be a professional musician.
He tells David that it wasn't music that messed up his life. Start: "you got to won-
dering all over again if you wanted to be like your daddy and end up like your
daddy. Ain't that right?…Well, son, tell you one thing.…" End: "So don't you
think you got to end up like your daddy just because you want to join a band."

Drama: Act III, p. 88, David (18)
After a traumatic confrontation with his mother, David tells her why he has to
leave home and be his own man. Great monologue. Start: "And if I listened—
what would happen? What do you think would happen if I listened?" End with
either: "Mama—you knew this day was coming" or "I ain't going to be hanging
around the house. I'll see you before I go."

AMERI/CAIN GOTHIC
by Paul Carter Harrison (*Totem Voices: Plays from the Black World Repertory*, edited by Paul Carter Harrison, Grove Press)
Drama: Act II, I. W. Harper (mid-30s)
Cass and Harper met in a seedy Memphis motel room yesterday and surprised
themselves by making explosive love. In the afterglow, Harper tells Cass that she
shouldn't get the wrong idea about what happened and that he doesn't intend to
stick around. Cass guesses that he is married, and he admits that he used to be but
no longer is. She then presses him to talk about his ex-wife. Start: "I did everything
in my power to win that woman's respect, and she showed me no more appreciation than a common whore!" End: "I grabbed her in the throat!…And kissed her!"

AMERICAN PLAN, THE
by Richard Greenberg (Dramatists Play Service)
Drama: Act I, Scene 6, pp. 34–35, Nick (20s)
Eva, the mother of Nick's fiancée, confronts him with the litany of untruths he
has told her daughter during their courtship. In this very stark and well-written
speech, Nick explains how his father lost his fortune, suffered a nervous breakdown, and committed suicide. At this point in the play, Nick's homosexuality is
still a secret. Start: "After my mother died, my father more or less lost control of
things." End: "Well, this has been a marvelous party, you've been a perfect host-
ess, and I've had a splendid time."

ANDERSONVILLE TRIAL, THE
by Saul Levitt (Dramatists Play Service)
Drama: Act II, Scene 1, p. 69, Chipman (31)
Chipman implores the military court to address questions of moral responsibility, not merely the technical matter of conspiracy. Start: "General, I do not enter that area of my own free will." End: "Let us have a human victory in this room."

ANOTHER ANTIGONE
by A. R. Gurney, Jr. (Dramatists Play Service)
Drama: One-act play, pp. 17–18, Henry (40–50)
Outraged that one of his students is persisting in writing an antiwar adaptation of the Greek classic *Antigone,* Henry defends his opposition and explains his concept of tragedy in this wonderful speech delivered to the dean of Humane Studies. Eliminate Diana's single line. Start: "Do you know what tragedy is, Diana?…I don't think you do." End: "That is just troublemaking. And I cannot give her credit for it."

AUTUMN GARDEN, THE
by Lillian Hellman (Dramatists Play Service)
Drama: Act III, pp. 93–94, Ned Crossman (46)
Years ago, Ned Crossman would have jumped at the chance to marry Constance Tuckerman, but she was holding a secret flame for her first love, Nick Denery, who married another woman a long time ago. A moment earlier, in sadness and despair, Constance asked if Ned would have her at this late date. Struck speechless at first, this monologue is his answer. The speech comes at the very end of the play and carries a heavy subtext. It could be a rich selection for an actor willing to fully explore it. Cut Constance's few lines that interrupt the speech. Start: "I live in a room and I go to work and I play a game called getting through the day." End: "And I've never liked liars—least of all those who lie to themselves."

BEAR, THE
by Anton Chekhov (*The Sneeze, Plays and Stories by Anton Chekhov,* translated and adapted by Michael Frayn, Samuel French)
Comedy: One-act play, pp. 52–53, Smirnov (45–55)
Smirnov arrives at the widow Popova's home in order to collect a debt owed to him by her late husband. When she is unable to pay him, Smirnov goes into a rage but at the same time finds himself attracted to the widow Popova. In this speech, he tells her how awful all women are. Start: "Oh, but this is amazing! How do you want me to talk to you?" End: "Tell me, in all honesty—have you ever in your life seen a woman who could be sincere and constant and true? You haven't!"

BEDROOMS: FIVE COMEDIES
by Renée Taylor and Joseph Bologna (Samuel French)
Comedy: "David and Nancy," pp. 7–8, David (35–45)
David is the nervous father of the bride. In the middle of the night, he wakes Nancy up to tell her that he has changed his mind about allowing her to marry. Although father and daughter embrace at the end, this speech is basically a crazed monologue. For a cute audition-length excerpt, start midspeech. Start: "Look,

Nancy, I can't see how you can really be in love with this guy." End: "Nancy, I beg you. Don't marry Melvin."

BIRDY
Adapted from the William Wharton novel by Naomi Wallace (Broadway Play Publishing)
Drama: Act I, Scene 7, p. 29, Sergeant Al (22)
Sergeant Al tells his uncommunicative friend, Birdy, about the time his mother poisoned all of his pet birds. His purpose in the telling is to snap Birdy out of his mental withdrawal. It doesn't work. Start, "It doesn't matter, does it, Birdy?" End, "Are you crazy, Birdy?"
Drama: Act I, Scene 11, pp. 41–42, Young Birdy (16) (Note: This monologue will work for actors in their early to mid-20s)
Birdy talks to his birds about how he came to identify so closely with them. The actor will have a lot of latitude in regard to handling this material for audition purposes. You can crouch like a bird, or maybe not. You can talk to the birds, or maybe not. Whatever you do, the speech is beautifully written and should roll easily off your tongue. Start, "It's hard to know you're dreaming." End: "There's a feeling of being lifted from the top, of moving up into an emptiness."
Drama: Act II, Scene 9, p. 62, Dr. White (50)
Dr. White tells Sergeant Al his idea of a real man and a real soldier. The vision is frightening, but White is deadly sincere, and that's how to play it. Start: "It's not your friend I hate, Sergeant." End: "Nor that spiritless, vacated friend of yours you don't even have the courage to abandon."

BOYS' LIFE
by Howard Korder (Dramatists Play Service)
Comedy: Scene 6, pp. 31–32, Phil (late 20s)
Phil confides in his best friend, Jack, how much he needs this woman he has been seeing for the past few weeks and why he is afraid of being alone. They have a lot in common, hit it off on the first date, and once talked about God for three hours straight. This is the perfect relationship—except she isn't reciprocating. Even worse, when Phil declared his need for her after a couple of intense weeks, she was repulsed. She claimed that no one should ever need anyone else that much. Start: "I would have destroyed myself for this woman." End: "Plus, my hair is falling out, that really sucks."
Comedy: Scene 8, pp. 40–41, Don (late 20s)
Lisa is furious and ready to leave after discovering that Don recently slept with another woman. In an attempt to charm her and calm her down, he tells about this very strange dream. Start: "Okay...okay...now...I was...flying. In a plane. I mean a rocket." End: "And we died. And the ocean ate our bones."

BREAKING THE CODE
by Hugh Whitemore (Samuel French)
Drama: Act II, Scene 2, pp. 71–72, Knox (60)
Concerned about Turing's homosexuality and unorthodox work practices, Knox, his boss at the Government Code and Cipher School, admonishes him in this speech. Knox quotes the philosopher Wittgenstein, drawing a comparison between the limits of science and those of humanity. Eliminate Turing's single

line. Start: "All right! Let me give you an example." End: "the problems of life remain completely unanswered."

BURN THIS
by Lanford Wilson (Dramatists Play Service)
Comedy-Drama: Act I, Pale (36)

Pale's entrance. He is angry about a guy that wanted the same parking space outside. This monologue is full of profanity and is appropriate only for an actor willing to go full-tilt. Definitely not for the timid. Start: "Goddamn this fuckin' place." At the end of this passage, pick up again with, "I mean no personal disparagement of the neighborhood in which you have your domicile, honey, but this street's dying of crotch rot." End: "Trans Am and go beep-beep, you know?"

CHERRY ORCHARD, THE
by Anton Chekhov (*Chekhov, The Major Plays;* translated by Ann Dunnigan, Signet Books)
Drama: Act III, Lopakhin (40–50)

Born to serfs, Lopakhin is a self-made man. He surprises everyone by purchasing at auction the very estate that his father and grandfather were slaves on. Start: "I bought it. Kindly wait a moment, ladies and gentlemen, my head is swimming." End: "Music! Strike up!"

CHILDREN OF A LESSER GOD
by Mark Medoff (Dramatists Play Service)
Drama: Act II, pp. 67–68, James (30)

In the final moments of the play, James and his deaf wife, Sarah, have a huge argument over whether or not she is playing a control game by refusing to try to speak; she is willing to communicate only by signing. In this speech, James sums up his position, demanding that she speak. Very powerful material that absolutely must be delivered with love. Start: "You think I'm going to let you change my children into people like you who so cleverly see vanity and cowardice as pride? You're going nowhere, you're achieving nothing." End: "Now come on! I want you to speak to me. Let me hear it. Speak! Speak! Speak!"

COASTAL DISTURBANCES
by Tina Howe (Samuel French)
Comedy: Act II, Scene 2, pp. 63–65, Leo (28)

Leo the lifeguard tells Holly a humorous, fantastic story about Juanita Wijojac, a girl with six fingers that he knew in school. Start: "I was thirteen and she was eleven." End: "I'll tell you one thing—she could have given one hell of a back rub." For monologue purposes, cut Holly's lines and Leo's direct responses to them.

COLORED MUSEUM, THE
by George C. Wolfe (Grove Press)
Drama: "A Soldier with a Secret," Junie Robinson (20s)

Junie, a young soldier, tells a horrific story about dying on the battlefield and coming back to life. Since then, he has been able to see the future hurt in people's faces and so has been giving them the hypodermic needle to prevent their pain. Do the whole speech for classwork; shorten it for audition purposes. Start: "Pst.

Pst. Guess what? I know the secret. The secret to your pain." End: "The secret to yours, and yours. Pst. Pst. Pst. Pst."

CROSSING DELANCEY
by Susan Sandler (Samuel French)
Comedy-Drama: Act II, pp. 66–67, Sam (early 30s)
Sam is wooing Isabelle and, in this lovely monologue, speaks of the value that exists in simple virtues. He tells her how fortunate she is to have an elderly, wise grandmother like Bubbie. Then Sam tells her that he would like to be with her in an open, honest fashion. His intentions are clear. Not much conflict here and probably not the most dynamic choice for audition purposes, but plenty of mood and texture. Excellent for workshops. Cut and paste at the beginning, eliminating Isabelle's line. Start: "This is the most wonderful thing you can do for yourself, Isabelle, to be with her like this." End: "…I want very much to show you the best I got, Isabelle. Please let me do this. Maybe I talked too much—but I been saving up."

DANCE AND THE RAILROAD, THE
by David Henry Hwang (Dramatists Play Service)
Comedy-Drama: Scene 4, pp. 29–30, Ma (18)
Looking for proof of his dedication to be a dancer, Lone has left Ma alone in the woods to crouch and imitate a locust all night. At some point during the night, he delivers this monologue directly to the audience. Ma talks about Second Uncle, whose life was ruined by locusts, and the revenge he took against grasshoppers. Start: "Locusts travel in huge swarms, so large that when they cross the sky, they block out the sun." End: "But then again, Second Uncle never tortured actual locusts, just weak grasshoppers." Remember, you're supposed to deliver this speech while crouching like a locust.

DARK AT THE TOP OF THE STAIRS, THE
by William Inge (Dramatists Play Service)
Drama: Act II, pp. 48–49, Sammy (16)
Reenie's blind date, a Jewish boy from Hollywood, tells her family how he has spent his whole life living in military academies. Although Sammy tries to be cheerful, the audience sees how sad and lonely he really is. Later this evening, Sammy will commit suicide. Cut Reenie's line at the top of Sammy's speech. Start: "I've never been to many parties, have you?" End: "I guess I've bored you enough, telling you about myself."
Drama: Act III, pp. 72–73, Rubin (36)
Rubin, an uneducated but sincere man, tells his wife, Cora, why he feels like a stranger in his own town, a man out of place and time. Cut Cora's lines and Rubin's direct responses to them. Start: "Goddamn it! What have I got to give 'em?" End: "How can I feel I've got anything to give my children when the world's as strange to me as it is to them?"

DAY IN THE DEATH OF JOE EGG, A
by Peter Nichols (Samuel French)
Drama: Act II, pp. 62–63, Bri (33)
Bri and Sheila's spastic daughter had a major seizure, and though Bri delayed seeking medical help in the hope that the child would die peacefully, she survived.

In this monologue, delivered directly to the audience, Bri describes the hectic trip to the hospital and Joe's later return home. He says that, at last, his marriage to Sheila is over, that he is leaving. Written in the British vernacular. Start: "Sheila and I went with Joe in the ambulance." End: "Want a nice slow job—game warden—keeper at Regents Park—better still, Kew Garden. Well, cheers."

DEATH OF A SALESMAN
by Arthur Miller (Dramatists Play Service)
Drama: Act II, pp. 58–59, Willy (over 60)
Willy begs for his job by telling his young boss, Howard, why he has spent his life being a salesman. Cut Howard's single line. Start: "Business is definitely business, but just listen to me for a minute." End: "They don't know me any more."

DINNER WITH FRIENDS
by Donald Margulies (Dramatists Play Service)
Comedy-Drama: Act I, Scene 3, pp. 37, Tom (40s)
Tom is explaining to his best friend, Gabe, why he is leaving his wife of twelve years for another woman. Stunning monologue, a man trying to justify actions that he well knows are, on some level, a cop-out. Start: "No, Gabe, there were no other women." End: "…Who would you choose?"
Comedy-Drama: Act II, Scene 3, pp. 64–65, Gabe (40s)
Gabe tells Tom why, even if his relationship with Karen is not as hot as it was when they first dated, he would not break up their marriage. This is another revealing monologue, one of those moments of sudden insight that we all experience from time to time. This is a man getting in touch with his own mortality and the value of relationships. Start: "You don't get it. I *cling* to Karen.…" End: "I'm taking piano."

DIVISION STREET
by Steve Tesich (Samuel French)
Comedy: Act I, pp. 26–27, Sal (30s)
Dianah's Legal Aid lawyer, Sal, tells her how rotten his life has been and how she should show pity by paying romantic attention to him. But she isn't even listening. Start: "You are looking at a desperate, homeless, friendless creature, Dianah." End: "This is the single longest uninterrupted speech I have ever made, Dianah, and I hope it moved you."
Comedy: Act I, pp. 28–29, Chris (37)
Chris tells his ex-wife, Dianah, that he no longer cares about 1960s causes and that he isn't interested in being a radical leader any longer. Cut Dianah's lines and Chris's direct responses to them. Start: "We're not we, Dianah." End: "I want it now!"
Comedy: Act I, pp. 37–38, Roger (mid-30s)
Roger tells Chris, a former leader of the 1960s radical movement, how he has sold out and that he is full of shame for deserting the revolution. Omit Chris's lines and Roger's direct response to them. Start: "You should spit on me!" End: "If I had an orgasm, I'd give it to them just so they'd leave me alone!"

DOES A TIGER WEAR A NECKTIE?
by Don Petersen (Dramatists Play Service)
Drama: Act II, Scene 2, pp. 64–65, Bickham (20)
A bitter, violent speech in which Bickham tells the staff psychiatrist at the detention

center how, after a long search, he found his father—and brutally beat him. Rough material. Start: "I was sick to my stomach. He made me puke…Just like you do. That lousy sonofabitch!" End: "You cured me, doctor, and now I belong to you."

DRESSER, THE
by Ronald Harwood (Samuel French)
Drama: Act I, pp. 13–14, Norman (35–45)
Sir is an elderly actor in the Old School tradition, and his big role is King Lear, which he has played hundreds of times in the provinces. Tonight, however, as curtain time approaches, Sir is confined to a nearby hospital in a state of emotional collapse. It appears that, for the first time, a performance will have to be canceled. In this poignant monologue, Norman, Sir's longtime dresser, lovingly tells Her Ladyship how he came to be in the actor's employ. Written in the British vernacular. Start: "Sixteen years. I wish I could remember." End: "Next day he asked if I'd be his dresser."
Drama: Act II, pp. 61–62, Sir (about 60)
Tired and increasingly philosophical, Sir explains to Her Ladyship why he identifies with King Lear. Start: "I thought tonight I caught sight of him." End: "I'll see a locked door, a sign turned in the window, closed, gone away, and a drawn blind."
Drama: Act II, p. 68, Norman (35–45)
Norman is concerned that Sir is becoming overly excited by Irene's flirtations and that this may be bad for his health. Alone with Irene, Norman insists that she tell him precisely what she has been doing with the old actor. She tries to pull away from Norman, threatening to tell Sir if he doesn't let go of her arm. He scoffs, telling her how very well he knows his boss and how futile it is for her to make such a threat. Start: "Tell Sir? On me? I quake in my boots." End: "I have to know all he does."
Drama: Act II, pp. 79–80, Norman (35–45)
The final speech in the play. Norman is drunk and Sir has been dead only a few moments. Norman reflects on his relationship with the actor, bemoaning the fact that it was "always a backseat." Start: "He never once took me out for a meal." Continue to the end of the play.

DYLAN
by Sidney Michaels (Samuel French)
Drama: Act I, pp. 42–43, Dylan (38)
Midway during his final American lecture tour, Dylan Thomas is tiring of the constant adoration. At a party given in his honor, he retreats to a bedroom where he hears a child crying. Dylan gets the boy to go back to sleep as another poet comes in to discover him sitting quietly by the crib. He explains that he lulled the child to sleep by reciting his favorite poem, "Baa, Baa, Black Sheep." Then he explains what the poem means to him personally. Dylan speaks with a Welsh accent. Start: "…one of my favorite poems and the story of my life." End as he recites the poem a second time: "*And one for the little boy who lives down the lane.*"

END OF THE WORLD WITH SYMPOSIUM TO FOLLOW, THE
by Arthur Kopit (Samuel French)
Drama: Act III, pp. 87–89, Stone (60s)
Stone recalls what it was like to witness nuclear testing on Christmas Island

before World War II. After the explosion, flying birds that were nearby caught on fire. Start: "In any event, there we were on this ship, this battleship, not far from where the detonation was to take place." End: "And I thought: This is what it will be like at the end of time. And we all felt…the thrill of that idea."

Drama: Act III, pp. 89–91, Trent (35–45)

Trent remembers picking up his newborn son in his arms and being tempted to throw him from the apartment window. It was a seductive moment, and he was drawn to that window—but he resisted. In telling the story, he makes the point that countries with nuclear power deal with the threat of war the same way. Start: "Now I know where we met!…It was at our place." End: "if doom comes…it will come in that way."

EVILS OF TOBACCO, THE
by Anton Chekhov (*The Sneeze: Plays and Stories by Anton Chekhov*, translated and adapted by Michael Frayn, Samuel French)

Comedy: One-act play, pp. 61–66, Nyukhin (50–55)

Nyukhin sets out to lecture young female students on the evils of using tobacco, but he gets off the track easily. The more he talks, the more the girls learn about his private life. Nyukhin has been married for thirty-three years to a domineering woman who has borne him seven daughters who don't appreciate him. Toward the end of this speech, he hears his wife approach and abruptly brings himself back to the assigned topic. This monologue isn't good for auditions, but it is wonderful for classwork. For advanced actors. Start: "Ladies and, if I may say so, gentlemen." End: "That is all I have to say, and I am very pleased to have had the opportunity to get it off my chest."

EXONERATED, THE
by Jessica Blank and Erik Jensen (Dramatists Play Service)

Drama: pp. 51–52, Delbert (50–60, African-American)

As written, Delbert is sixty years old, but there really is some leeway with his age. I can see an actor even in his late thirties delivering this monologue, which is Delbert's final speech in the play. In it, he expresses his mixed feelings for the United States of America. Start: "Mahatma Gandhi said that once he discovered who God was, all fears left him…" End: "What's *wrong* with it is what we better deal with."

FENCES
by August Wilson (Samuel French)

Drama: Act I, Scene 1, pp. 16–17, Troy (53)

Troy tells Rose and Bono about the time in 1941 he wrestled with "Mr. Death" and won. Omit Rose and Bono's lines and Troy's direct responses to them. Start: "I looked up one day and Death was marching straight at me." End: "He's gonna have to fight to get me. I ain't easy."

Drama: Act I, Scene 3, pp. 39–40, Troy (53)

In this short monologue, Troy tells his young son, Cory, that it is his responsibility to take care of the boy and that he doesn't do it because he likes Cory. Start: "Like you? I go outta there every morning…bust my butt." End: "You understand what I'm saying, boy?"

FIRST BREEZE OF SUMMER, THE
by Leslie Lee (Samuel French)

Drama: Act I, pp. 20–21, Sam (20s)

The setting: the Deep South in the late 1920s. Sam, an African-American, got into a confrontation with a white man at the train station when he came to the defense of an elderly porter who had dropped the man's bags. Rather than being grateful to Sam, the porter began to apologize to the traveler, thereby humiliating Sam. That was two days ago, and he walked off the job on the spot. Now he is telling his girlfriend, Lucretia, about the event as he prepares to move on to the next town. Begin midway through Sam's speech. Start: "Colored people weren't ready for colored doctors, or maybe colored doctors weren't ready for colored people." End: "Baby, I'm so miserable, it's funny…miserable."

FOB
by David Henry Hwang (*FOB and The House of Sleeping Beauties: Two Plays*, Dramatists Play Service)

Comedy: Act II, p. 35, Dale (20s)

In this short speech at the top of the act, delivered directly to the audience, Dale describes the differences between himself and his very Chinese parents. Start: "I am much better now." End: "I'm making it in America."

FOX, THE
by Allan Miller (based on D. H. Lawrence's short novel, Samuel French)

Drama: Act III, Scene 1, p. 61, Henry Grenfel (20s)

Henry Grenfel, a mysterious young soldier, has been a guest at Nellie and Jill's farm for only one day and has already asked Nellie to marry him. Jill feels threatened by this turn of events and has been warning Nellie to be wary of Henry. He realizes that Jill is his enemy and, in this speech, presses Nellie hard for a commitment. Henry ultimately ends up killing Jill. She was right to be suspicious. You'll have to cut and paste, eliminating Nellie's lines. Written in the British vernacular. Start: "What's holding you in, Nellie, say what's on your mind!" End: "You want the feel of me. You need it! Say you'll have me, Nellie. Say it!"

FRANKIE AND JOHNNY IN THE CLAIR DE LUNE
by Terrence McNally (Dramatists Play Service)

Drama: Act II, p. 60, Johnny (46)

Johnny tells Frankie that he is her Prince Charming. Very nice monologue in which a man who isn't great with words finds eloquence. Start: "You don't want to hear anything you don't already know." End: "I know this thing, Frankie."

GLASS MENAGERIE, THE
by Tennessee Williams (Dramatists Play Service)

Drama: Act I, Scene 3, p. 24, Tom (21)

Tom is furious with his mother, Amanda, for prying into and controlling his life. Start: "I'm going to opium dens." End: "You ugly—babbling old—witch."

Drama: Act II, Scene 8, p. 68, Tom (21)

At the end of the play, Tom talks to the audience, revealing that he hasn't been able to separate himself from his sister, Laura. Start: "I didn't go to the moon." End: "Blow out your candles, Laura—and so good-bye."

GLENGARRY GLEN ROSS
by David Mamet (Samuel French)

Drama: Act I, Scene 3, pp. 27–29, Roma (40s)
Super salesman Roma sets up a sucker. He is going to sell him some Florida swampland. Cut Lingk's few lines and Roma's direct responses to them. Start: "All train compartments smell vaguely of shit." End: "It's been a long day."

Drama: Act II, pp. 43–44, Levene (50s)
Levene made a big sale last night, or so he believes: eight units of property for $82,000 to an unsuspecting couple. Here, he gloats about how he put one over on them. What he doesn't realize is that this same couple regularly signs contracts to buy property but doesn't have any money. Cut Roma's few other lines and Levene's direct responses to them. Start: "What we have to do is admit to ourselves that we see that opportunity...." End: "...and we toast. In silence." Roma's line, "Always be closing..." can be spoken by Levene. Both of these monologues from *Glengarry Glen Ross* are too long for audition purposes but are very good for workshop.

HELLO AND GOODBYE
by Athol Fugard (Samuel French)

Drama: Act II, p. 50, Johnny (late 20s)
Johnny tells his sister about the day years ago when he left home to go to railroad school, got as far as the bridge, and turned back to be with his father. Having a career wasn't important, but being devoted to his father was. Johnny is a white Afrikaner, so an accent is appropriate. Start: "Yes, I wanted to go. They are the most beautiful things in the world!" End: "I sweep, I wash, I wait...it was me. What I wanted."

HOUSE OF BLUE LEAVES, THE
by John Guare (Samuel French)

Comedy: Act II, Scene 1, pp. 35–37, Ronnie (18)
Ronnie is building a bomb in order to blow up the Pope while telling the audience about the terrible humiliation he felt when Artie's Hollywood producer buddy visited six years ago. Start: "My father tell you all about me?" End: "I'll show you all. I'll be too big for any of you."

HOUSE OF RAMON IGLESIA, THE
by José Rivera (Samuel French)

Drama: Act I, Scene 1, pp. 14–15, Ramon (49)
Ramon has just returned from Puerto Rico, where he tried to locate Doa Prez, the legal owner of his Long Island home. The family is hanging on Ramon's every word as he first leads them on, suggesting that Doa Prez is dead, and then delightedly admits that he found her and had the papers signed. You have to piece this monologue together, cutting out the other characters' responses to Ramon's story, but it works. Start: "When I landed in San Juan, I took a bus to Adjuntas." End: "They think she can fly and bring the dead to life! They are always making stories about her!"

HURLYBURLY
by David Rabe (Samuel French)

Comedy-Drama: Act I, Scene 2, pp. 49–50, Mickey (mid-30s)
Feeling caught in a romantic triangle, Mickey tells Eddie and Darlene that they should continue their relationship without him. Start: "You know what I'm going to do?" End: "Am I totally off base here, Eddie, or what?"

Drama: Act I, Scene 3, pp. 67–69, Phil (30s)
Edging close to a nervous breakdown, Phil describes for Eddie how he sees Los Angeles and the world from his moving car. An intense monologue, full of haunting, stark imagery. Start: "Eddie, for God's sake don't terrify me." End: "I got to stay married. I'm lost without her."

Drama: Act II, Scene 1, pp. 116–117, Eddie (mid-30s)
Eddie, who is very drunk, has been engaging in some truth-telling repartee with his good friend, Phil. Eddie then abruptly announces that he is depressed by the news about the neutron bomb in today's paper. His speech is a drunken harangue, but there is a sad logic to it. Start: "The aborigine had a lot of problems." End: "…we have emptied out the heavens and put oblivion in the hands of a bunch of aging insurance salesmen whose jobs are insecure."

HUSBANDRY
by Patrick Tovatt (Samuel French)

Drama: One-act play, Scene 2, pp. 19–20, Harry (37)
Harry tries to get his wife, Bev, to understand the plight of the American farmer in general and of his parents in particular. Start: "I am absolutely pissed off about…and feeling shit worthless about a whole lot of stuff." End: "…and there are mysteries, by God, not yet penetrated by Purdue University."

I HATE HAMLET
by Paul Rudnick (Dramatists Play Service)

Comedy: Act II, Scene 2, p. 67, Andrew (27–34)
Andrew tells John Barrymore (actually, the ghost of Barrymore) about a brief moment of inspiration during the performance last night, a moment in which he transcended himself and "became" Hamlet. In order to really pull this monologue off, an actor needs to be able to play Shakespeare. He has to perform five lines of the "To be or not to be" soliloquy, and he must do it well so as to make a point. You might want to add even a few more lines of that famous speech, to flesh out the monologue for audition purposes. Start: "Last night, right from the start, I knew I was bombing." End: "And only eight thousand lines left to go."

I NEVER SANG FOR MY FATHER
by Robert Anderson (Dramatists Play Service)

Drama: Act II, p. 62, Gene (40)
This is the final speech in the play, very moving and introspective. Gene summarizes the final years of his father's life and the complex relationship they had. He discovers that death ends a life but not a relationship. Start: "That night I left my father's house forever." End: "But, still, when I hear the word Father…It matters."

I OUGHT TO BE IN PICTURES
by Neil Simon (Samuel French)

Comedy: Act II, Scene 3, pp. 61–62, Herb (45)

After learning that his daughter, Libby, has a job working as a parking valet and that she is promoting herself as an actress by writing her name and number on the back of the valet-parking tickets, Herb tells her why this is a dumb idea. Cut Libby's lines and Herb's direct responses to them. Start: "Libby, can I ask you a serious personal question?" End: "I'll contact her first thing in the morning and hope and pray that someone else with spareribs in their teeth didn't get to her before me."

JOE TURNER'S COME AND GONE
by August Wilson (Samuel French)

Drama: Act I, Scene 4, pp. 72–73, Bynum (60s)

Bynum is a "conjure man" who is pretty wise in the ways of women. Here, he advises young Jeremy Bynum, who is intent on chasing women, to look a little deeper than surface beauty. Good speech. You can probably make two monologues out of this text with some editing. Start: "You just can't look at it like that. You got to look at the whole thing." End: "You got to learn how to come to your own time and place with a woman."

Drama: Act II, Scene 2, pp. 106–107, Bynum (60s)

Another wise speech from the conjure man, having to do with how a man needs to find his own "song" in life. Cut and paste the monologue, eliminating Loomis. Start: "Mr. Loomis done picked some cotton. Ain't you, Herald Loomis? You done picked a bunch of cotton." End: "That's why I can tell you one of Joe Turner's niggers. 'Cause you forgot how to sing your song."

Drama: Act II, Scene 2, pp. 108–109, Loomis (32)

Loomis tells Bynum and Seth how he came to be incarcerated on Joe Turner's chain gang, lost his wife, and came to be traveling these past four years in search of her. Start: "Joe Turner caught me when my little girl was just born. Wasn't nothing but a little baby sucking on her mama's titty when he caught me." End: "When I find my wife that be the making of my own."

JOINED AT THE HEAD
by Catherine Butterfield (Dramatists Play Service) (*Women Playwrights: The Best Plays of 1992,* Smith and Kraus)

Drama: Act II, pp. 59–60, Jim (late 30s)

Jim addresses the audience for the first time in the play, explaining in calm detail his emotional reactions to his wife's progressive cancer and her imminent death. This is a crusher of a speech, breathtakingly poignant, and the playwright explicitly advises that actors not give in to maudlin impulses when playing it. Start: "Here's what you won't hear from them about me. You won't hear about the nights I lie awake looking at Maggy." End: "I just thought you should know."

K2
by Patrick Meyers (Dramatists Play Service)

Drama: One-act play, pp. 21–22, Harold (mid-30s)

After listening to Taylor expound on his rather racist view of the world, Harold levels him with this monologue. Harold describes an American society obsessed with the production and sale of gizmos. Cut Taylor's lines and Harold's direct responses to them. Start: "Let me tell you who you really do it for...You do it for the gadgets." End: "That's all part of the gizmo plan, baby. It's all a part of the gizmo plan."

LADY AND THE CLARINET, THE
by Michael Cristofer (Dramatists Play Service)
Comedy: Act I, pp. 32–33, Jack (40s)

Jack's mistress is pressing him to separate from his wife, Marge. In a spasm of self-disclosure, he suddenly acknowledges that he is a stranger in his own life, that he doesn't recognize himself. You'll have to cut and paste this speech. Just eliminate Luba's lines. Start: "I don't feel anything about them any more. The kids, I look at them—they're bright." End: "I'm telling you they're wrong, because that isn't me! It isn't! It isn't me!"

Comedy: Act I, pp. 35–36, Jack (40s)

Jack finally got up enough nerve to leave his wife. Now he stands in the living room of his astonished girlfriend and gives her a blow-by-blow description of the Grand Farewell. He tells her how Marge helped him pack and how, before that, they got the giggles and made the best love ever. He is still trembling from the excitement of it all, in fact. Start: "Well, I did it. It's done. Finished. I finished it. I did it. Jesus." End: "And then, after, we went upstairs, she helped me pack. I packed the suitcase, kissed her good-bye, and here I am."

LANDSCAPE OF THE BODY
by John Guare (Dramatists Play Service)
Comedy: Act I, pp. 25–26, Raulito (33–45)

Raulito, an opportunistic and flamboyant Cuban refugee, is the owner/operator of a small New York City travel agency. He tells Betty, the sister of his former employer/lover, how he came to be what he is today—and why he happens to be wearing a gold lamé dress over his business suit. Start: "That is exactly what your sister Rosalie said to me the first time we met." End: "Then she would let me sleep with her after, and dreams would come out of our heads like little Turkish moons."

LAST OF THE RED HOT LOVERS
by Neil Simon (Samuel French)
Comedy: Act I, pp. 29–30, Barney (47)

Barney brings Elaine to his mother's apartment and tells her why he wants to have a one-day fling. The complete monologue is too long for audition purposes and probably too long for class, so I suggest you shorten it. Start: "I started getting the urge about five years ago." End: "For once, I didn't just exist—I lived!"

LAUGHING WILD
by Christopher Durang (Dramatists Play Service)
Comedy: One-act play, Scene 2, pp. 21–22, A Man (any age)

The man talks directly to the members of the audience, telling them about a violent encounter he had recently with a strange woman at the supermarket. A short (about one-and-a-half-minute long), intense monologue excerpt from a very long speech. It's funny because it is outrageous. Start: "I was in the supermarket the other day about to buy some tuna fish when I sensed this very disturbed presence right behind me." End: "It makes me want to never leave my apartment ever ever again."

LONG DAY'S JOURNEY INTO NIGHT
by Eugene O'Neill (Yale University Press)

Drama: Act IV, James Tyrone (65)
James tells his drunk son, Edmund, about his glory days as a young actor and how he sold out his artistic integrity by purchasing a vehicle-play for himself. This role became his trademark, a fate he accepted because of the money. Now he is full of regret. Start: "Yes, maybe life overdid the lesson for me, and made a dollar worth too much." End: "What the hell was it I wanted to buy, I wonder, that was worth— well, no matter. It's a late day for regrets."

Drama: Act IV, Edmund (23)
Edmund tells his very drunk father about some "high spots" in his memory, specifically the times he spent at sea; these were the moments when he came closest to finding God. Start: "You've just told me some high spots in your memories." End: "I will always be a stranger who never feels at home."

LOU GEHRIG DID NOT DIE OF CANCER
by Jason Miller (*Three One-Act Plays* by Jason Miller, Dramatists Play Service)

Drama: One-act play, pp. 55–56, Victor (32)
Victor gives a personal treasure, a baseball autographed by Lou Gehrig, to Barbara with instructions that she is to pass it on to her young son. While Victor gives it to her, he recounts how the ball came to be autographed by the great player, how he and his father experienced that particular day at the ballpark so many years ago. Start: "You're a strong woman…a little strange but strong." End: "…give this ball to Jeffrey…I've had it too long."

LOVERS AND OTHER STRANGERS
by Renée Taylor and Joseph Bologna (Samuel French)

Comedy: "Mike and Susan," pp. 245–26, He (Mike, 30s)
Four days before his wedding, Mike gets cold feet. He comes to Susan's apartment at about 4 A.M. to call it off. After Mike delivers an impassioned monologue that she casually ignores, they continue with their wedding plans as before. Start: "What do you expect me to do, carry on a long conversation at four in the morning?" End: "That's it. It's all over. Goodbye. I'm sorry. That's it." For a shorter version, start: "India's overpopulated! We'll all be sterilized soon." Continue to the same end.

LOVE SUICIDE AT SCHOFIELD BARRACKS, THE
by Romulus Linney (Dramatists Play Service) (one-act version: *Seventeen Short Plays*, Smith & Kraus)

Drama: Dramatists Play Service, pp. 13–14, Ruggles (45–50)
Ruggles, an old-school, blood-and-guts Army sergeant major, testifies about his in-your-face relationship with the general and the last meeting they had before the general and his wife committed suicide. He is on the stand for a couple of pages, so you can construct monologues from his dialogue in various ways. One choice is to begin toward the end, when Ruggles starts talking about nostalgia. He hits emotional peaks, describing how his son died. The language is graphic, too

rough perhaps for audition purposes, but it rings true. Start: "Nostalgia. Maybe he thought that would be safe." End: "And that was the end of the interview."

Drama: Dramatists Play Service, pp. 31–34, Roundhouse (50s)

A former university president and now restaurant owner, Roundhouse testifies about his close friendship with the general. He tells how his own homosexuality led to his downfall in the American educational system, and how the general helped him pick up the pieces of his life. This beautifully written speech is too long for most audition purposes but perfect for class. Start: "I was President of two American universities." End: "In an age where everyone else is innocent, Michael chose the terrible right to be guilty." For a shorter, audition-length excerpt, start: "So here I am, better off than ever, a closet queen Midwestern college president." Continue to the same end.

LUV
by Murray Schisgal (Dramatists Play Service)
Comedy: Act I, pp. 11–12, Harry (late 30s)

Just moments ago, Milt discovered his old classmate, Harry, preparing to jump from a bridge and talked him down. Harry explains that the really big issues in life are troubling him. He believes that everything is summed up in one episode: A dog walked up to him one day in the park and lifted its leg on his pants leg. As he tells it, you can see that Harry is a haunted man and has reached the point where he is seeing significance in absolutely everything around him. You'll have to cut and paste a lot, completely eliminating Milt's lines, but it works. Start: "…I'm at the end of the line. Everything's falling apart….The world, Milt. People. Life…." End: I became aware…aware of the whole rotten senseless stinking deal. Nothing mattered to me after that. Nothing."

MA RAINEY'S BLACK BOTTOM
by August Wilson (Samuel French)
Drama: Act I, Toledo (45–55)

Toledo is the only person in the recording studio who can spell *music,* so when he wins a dollar from Levee on a wager, no one is impressed. Trying to get the others to see how ludicrous their ignorance is, Toledo tells this story about the Lord's Prayer. Start: "Alright. Now I'm gonna tell you a story to show just how ridiculous he sound." End: "Only 'cause I knowed how to spell *music,* I still got my dollar."

Drama: Act I, Cutler (35–45)

Cutler tells the other musicians how Slow Drag got his nickname during a dance contest when his dance partner's boyfriend walked in with a knife. Omit Slow Drag and Levee's interruptions. Start: "Slow Drag break a woman's back when he dance." End: "The women got to hanging around him so bad after that, them fellows in that town ran us out of there."

Drama: Act I, Toledo (45–55)

Toledo gives the other musicians a brief lesson in black history, humorously comparing black people to leftovers from a stew on a white person's table. Start: "Now I'm gonna show you how this goes…Where you just a leftover from history." End: "So go on and get off the plate and let me eat something else." If you use this selection for an audition, it might be more effective to end the monologue a line earlier in midsentence. End: "He'll tell you he done ate your black ass."

Drama: Act I, Levee (32)

Stung because the other musicians believe he is sucking up to the white record producers, Levee launches into this impassioned defense of his independence and integrity. He describes how, as a child, he tried to save his mother from being raped by a gang of white men. Start: "Levee got to be Levee!" End: "You all just leave Levee alone about the white man." To shorten this monologue for audition purposes, begin halfway through the speech. Start: "My mama was frying up some chicken."

Drama: Act II, Toledo (45–55)

Toledo starts talking about how many ways he has been a fool during his life, particularly with women. Start: "Now, I married a woman. A good woman." End: "So yeah, Toledo been a fool about a woman. That's part of making life."

MARCO POLO SINGS A SOLO
by John Guare (Dramatists Play Service)

Comedy: Act I, p. 16, Stony (36)

Stony explains that he is sensitive to the needs of plants and can hear their anguished cries. He concludes that people are really plants, not animals. A thoroughly odd and wonderful monologue, good for class. Stony's twisted logic is an entertaining workout for actors. Start: "Theory? You call scientific fact theory?" End: "My plant nature. I celebrate that."

Comedy: Act I, p. 27, Stony (36)

Stony shares his very revisionist take on the plot of Henrik Ibsen's A Doll's House. His view is that Nora doesn't really leave at the end of the play, that her husband keeps building new rooms to contain her. As always, Stony marches to a different drummer; he has a frenetic inner rhythm and sees things that others don't. A challenging and fun monologue. Start: "Nora never left." End: "…her closet crammed with clothes, her possessions, her life sat waiting for her in a rocking chair."

MATCHMAKER, THE
by Thornton Wilder (Samuel French)

Comedy: Act I, pp. 18–19, Horace Vandergelder (60)

Horace Vandergelder is a self-made, blustery old fool who intends to remarry. In this speech to the audience, he outlines his amusingly parental views about the other sex. Remember, this play is set in the 1880s. Start: "Ninety-nine per cent of the people in the world are fools and the rest of us are in great danger of contagion." End: "Yes, like all you other fools, I'm willing to risk a little security for a certain amount of adventure. Think it over."

Comedy: Act II, pp. 47–48, Cornelius (33)

Cornelius is the head clerk in Vandergelder's Yonkers store. He has snuck out to have some fun and has fallen hard for Miss Molloy, the owner of the hat shop. Cornelius is a very innocent man; at thirty-three, he has never even been kissed. In this speech, delivered to the audience, he is ecstatic about the wonders of women, particularly Miss Molloy. Start: "Isn't the world full of wonderful things? There we sit cooped up in Yonkers." End: "Even if I have to dig ditches for the rest of my life. I'll be a ditch digger who once had a wonderful day."

MIDDLE AGES, THE
by A. R. Gurney, Jr. (Dramatists Play Service)
Comedy: Act II, pp. 44–45, Charles (60s)

Charles, a distinguished, upper-class WASP, defends the virtues of a private men's club, comparing its very civilized service to the treatment men receive in public places. Start: "Barney, I want you to go down to the pool, and ask your friends to put on their clothes." End: "That's what Barney wants apparently. And I'm sorry."

MISS JULIE
by August Strindberg (*Six Plays of Strindberg*, translated by Elizabeth Sprigge, Doubleday/Anchor)
Drama: One-act play, Jean (30)

Jean tells Miss Julie about the time he hid in the Count's privy on the castle grounds where she lived. Not knowing the purpose of the building, he had snuck in to look at the opulent interior. When people approached, he had only one escape: through the opening used for excrement. Finally safe again, Jean hid in a nearby hedge of raspberry canes and, for the first time, caught sight of Miss Julie, practically the vision of a young angel. He subsequently watched her from afar and, because a romance between them was impossible, he attempted suicide. Keep in mind that Jean might be lying about everything. At this point in the play, he is intent on seducing Julie, and the anecdote may be seen as a device to endear himself to her. Start: "One time I went into the Garden of Eden with my mother to weed the onion beds." End: "There was no hope of winning you…you were simply a symbol of the hopelessness of ever getting out of the class I was born in."

MISS LONELYHEARTS
by Howard Teichmann (adapted from Nathanael West's novel, Dramatists Play Service)
Drama: Act II, Scene 4, p. 71, Miss Lonelyhearts (26)

In this strong, brief speech, Lonelyhearts speaks of his father, a preacher who brought no love to his own home. Then he tells his employer, the very cynical Mr. Shrike, that he despises him. Start: "My father stood in the pulpit every Sunday." End: "Two things I don't want: to be like him, to be like you."

MISTER ROBERTS
by Thomas Heggen and Joshua Logan (Dramatists Play Service)
Drama: Act I, Scene 6, p. 41, The Captain (40–50)

The up-by-his-own-bootstraps Captain tells Mister Roberts why he hates know-it-all college guys and how much he wants to be a full commander in the Navy. Start: "I think you're a pretty smart boy." End: "Now get out of here!"

MOON FOR THE MISBEGOTTEN, A
by Eugene O'Neill (Samuel French)
Drama: Act III, pp. 88–90, Tyrone (early 40s)

Tyrone has a secret. While escorting his mother's body cross-country a year ago, he spent his time drinking heavily and sleeping with the trashiest whore he could find on the train. In this painful monologue, Tyrone confesses his sins to Josie, seeking her forgiveness. Only experienced actors should attempt this challenging speech. You'll have to edit this monologue a bit, but it works. Start: "When mama died, I'd been on the wagon for nearly two years. Not even a glass of beer." End: "I suppose I had some mad idea she could make me forget—what was in the baggage car ahead."

NERD, THE
by Larry Shue (Dramatists Play Service)
Comedy: Act II, pp. 49–50, Willum (34)
Burnt out from hassling with Rick, his unwanted houseguest, for a week, Willum tells a horror story about an airplane trip the two of them took together. Start: "Six days. Has it been just six days?" End: "I think he only escaped because the ones who really had the grounds didn't want to stand up."

NORMAN CONQUESTS, THE—TABLE MANNERS
by Alan Ayckbourn (Samuel French)
Comedy: Act I, Scene 2, pp. 21–22, Norman (30s)
Everyone in the family knows that Norman intended to take his wife's sister, Annie, away for a romantic weekend, so he is being ostracized at breakfast. After making repeated efforts to get someone to talk to him, he resorts to reading their minds. This excerpt, which is written in the British vernacular, begins after Norman reads aloud from the Puffa Puffa Rice cereal box. Start: "Hang on, I've got another game. Mind reading. I'll read your minds." End: "I knew you wouldn't come. You didn't have the guts."
Comedy: Act I, Scene 2, pp. 22–23, Norman (30s)
This excerpt comes later in the breakfast speech discussed above. Everyone except Reg has left the table at this point, so Norman talks to him as Reg glumly eats his cereal in silence. The speech is touching and funny. Norman describes his marriage, one that is efficient but unromantic. Start: "I suppose you think I'm cruel, too, don't you? Well, I've damn good cause to be, haven't I?" End: "…The real me. Look at me…."

NUTS
by Tom Topor (Samuel French)
Drama: Act II, p. 46, Arthur Kirk (60s)
Arthur Kirk is a self-made, no-nonsense millionaire whose stepdaughter, Claudia, has been arrested for prostitution and murder. Testifying on the stand during her sanity hearing, Arthur succinctly puts forth his philosophy on love, marriage, and the propriety of getting "a little something on the side." Start: "Let me finish would ya." End: "As far as I'm concerned, a man can chase sheep, just so long as he comes home and takes care of his family. Bill didn't. Bill took a walk."
Drama: Act II, p. 53, Arthur Kirk (60s)
Testifying on the stand, Arthur Kirk has just been asked why it is so important to him that his stepdaughter be found incompetent to stand trial. In response, he lashes out at the entire legal system and denies that Claudia is a prostitute. To his way of thinking, that is impossible; she must be mentally ill. Start: "We're thinking about a trial." End: "You get that straight."

OH DAD, POOR DAD, MAMMA'S HUNG YOU IN THE CLOSET AND I'M FEELIN' SO SAD
by Arthur Kopit (Samuel French)
Comedy: Act I, Scene 2, pp. 19–20, Jonathan (17–25)

Jonathan, a fellow with zero social skills, is smitten with Rosalie, the pretty young woman who babysits for the absentee couple in the penthouse across the way. He has been watching her through his homemade telescope. In this speech, Jonathan haltingly but excitedly tells us how to construct such a telescope. Eliminate Rosalie's single line. Start: "Well, I made it out of lenses and tubing. The lenses I had because Ma-Ma—Mother gave me a set of lenses so I could see my stamps better." End: "Even if I didn't see anything else, I did see you. And—and I'm—very glad."

OLEANNA
by David Mamet (Dramatists Play Service)
Drama: Act II, pp. 33–34, John (35–45)

John is a college professor facing sexual-harassment charges. As his exasperation grows, he tries to explain to Carol, the student accusing him, what communication really is. You'll have to cut and paste the dialogue a bit. Start: "Wait a second, will you, just one moment. Nice day today." End: "I don't think we can proceed until we accept that each of us is human. And we still can have difficulties."

ONLY GAME IN TOWN, THE
by Frank D. Gilroy (Samuel French)
Drama: Act II, Scene 2, pp. 69–70, Joe (30–35)

Joe asks Fran to marry him. When she hesitates, he levels her with this monologue, accusing her of being afraid to make a deeper commitment. Start: "For two years, I've slinked through these corridors as the villain in Apartment 2C." End: "Do I perceive the hint of a smile—the trace of a tear?…Say it."

ORPHANS
by Lyle Kessler (Samuel French)
Drama: Act II, Scene 1, pp. 50–51, Harold (40–50)

Harold gives the boys a lecture on the value of moderation. He tells a story from his boyhood. Cut Treat and Phillip's lines and Harold's direct responses to them. Start: "You know who you remind me of, Treat?" End: "…How far a man will go for financial gain."

OTHER PEOPLE'S MONEY
by Jerry Sterner (Samuel French)
Comedy-Drama: Act II, pp. 63–64, Garfinkle (40–45)

Kate has just offered Garfinkle twenty dollars per share "greenmail" if he'll cease his efforts to take over New England Wire and Cable. Garfinkle scoffs at the offer, setting his price at twenty-five dollars per share and claiming that he would rather talk about Kate's good looks. As it becomes evident that Kate isn't authorized to pay twenty-five dollars, her mood sinks. He considers her for a moment and then delivers this short, cynical monologue. Cut Kate's single interruption of the speech. Stage directions indicate that Kate exits in the middle of Garfinkle's monologue and that he keeps talking, presumably to the audience. For audition/workshop purposes, he should continue speaking directly to Kate; eliminate her exit.

Comedy-Drama: Act II, pp. 86–88, Garfinkle (40–45)

Garfinkle addresses stockholders in the company he is taking over. Start: "You just heard the prayer for the dead, and fellow stuckholders (sic), you didn't say 'Amen' and you didn't even get to sip the wine." End: "Now that is a funeral worth having."

PIANO LESSON, THE
by August Wilson (Plume Drama)

Comedy-Drama: Act I, Scene 1, Doaker Charles (47)

During the twenty-seven years Doaker Charles has worked for the railroad, he has made some keen observations about all the travelers he has seen coming and going. After Boy Willie butters him up by suggesting that women are always waiting for him at every depot down south, Doaker starts talking about what he has seen and learned over the years. You'll have to cut and paste. Start: "I'm cooking now, but I used to line track." End: "It'll come back every time."

Comedy-Drama: Act I, Scene 1, Avery Brown (38)

Avery Brown migrated north and got a job running the elevator in a skyscraper downtown. He also became a preacher and has been trying to raise the money to start his first church. In this speech, Avery tells a very skeptical Boy Willie, who used to work alongside him picking cotton, how he came to be a preacher in the first place. Start: "It came to me in a dream." End: "So I became a preacher."

Comedy-Drama: Act I, Scene 2, Boy Willie (30)

Boy Willie explains that he intends to sell the family's heirloom piano because he wants to purchase the land his ancestors worked on as slaves. His sister Berniece is adamantly opposed to this plan. Start: "Now, I'm gonna tell you the way I see it." End: "But that's why I'm gonna take this piano out of here and sell it."

Comedy-Drama: Act II, Scene 1, Wining Boy (56)

Wining Boy just sold Lymon his "all-silk" suit for three dollars, as well as a sharp pair of Florsheim shoes for the same price. As Lymon happily goes upstairs to get dressed so that he and Boy Willie can go downtown and find some women, Wining Boy muses about how he almost was Lymon's daddy; he had that close a relationship with the young man's mother. Start: "That's all Lymon thinks about is women." End: "Fellow walked in and shot him thinking he was someone else."

PLAY MEMORY
by Joanna M. Glass (Samuel French)

Drama: Act II, pp. 61–62, Cam (late 50s)

Cam is evidently determined to drink himself to death and to drag his wife and young daughter, Jean, down with him. A few moments ago, Jean came home from school and told him that she longs for a normal life. In this speech, which is tinged with self-pity, Cam defends his life choices. Rather than seeing his stubborn nature as a liability, he considers it an asset. You'll have to cut and paste a little. Start: "You know what normal is? Normal is where nothing happens." End: "And when they go to bed at night they say, 'God, when will you stop me? When will you send someone in to stop me?'"

Drama: Act II, p. 66, Cam (late 50s)

Cam is in the process of rejecting his sponsors from Alcoholics Anonymous. They accuse him of having a superiority complex, and he responds by justifying his behavior, claiming to have higher standards than everyone else. You'll have to cut and paste, eliminating Ross's lines. Start: "…I'm trying like hell to hold onto something. And I've realized that all I've got to hold onto is what I carry around in my head." End: "The sound of their coats, turning. And I will never recover from that!"

PRELUDE TO A KISS
by Craig Lucas (Broadway Play Publishing)
Comedy: Act II, The Old Man (60s)

Rita's soul is in the Old Man's body, and she has learned a great deal from the experience. Here, the Old Man (really Rita) tells Peter what life means to him/her in very existential terms. In portraying the Old Man, actors should not make any effort to speak in a woman's tone or style. Start: "You know…if you think how we're born and we go through all the struggle." End: "So we might as well have a good time while we're here, don't you think?"

PROMISE, THE
by José Rivera (Broadway Play Publishing)
Comedy-Drama: Act II, Scene 2, Guzman (about 40)

Guzman encourages Hiberto, a sickly, fearful, awkward—but quite possibly wealthy—man to marry his daughter, Lilia. Guzman promises to make a gift of his book, *Tales of Marcario,* which contains stories of magical happenings in the small Puerto Rican town. It might be effective to precisely mime the book when using this speech for audition purposes. Start: "You marry her, my friend, and tonight you touch her." End: "This book will come in handy when you liberate Puerto Rico for me."

P.S. YOUR CAT IS DEAD
by James Kirkwood (Samuel French)
Comedy: Act II, pp. 60–61, Jimmy (38)

Jimmy has let Vito talk him into sharing some marijuana and is completely stoned. Jimmy tells his prisoner about a recent commercial audition that was awful. Start: "Now get this scene: Nine men and three women glued together behind this long conference table.…" End: "No, you see, there was a little speck of shit in the pool—you!"

RAINMAKER, THE
by N. Richard Nash (Samuel French)
Drama: Act I, pp. 41–42, Starbuck (30s)

Starbuck tells the skeptical Curry family precisely how he intends to make it rain. He is a spellbinding orator, and utterly charismatic. Omit Lizzie and Noah's interruptions. Start: "What do you care how I do it, sister, as long as it's done!" End: "And me? I'm ridin' right through the rainbow!—Well, how about it? Is it a deal?"

RAISIN IN THE SUN, A
by Lorraine Hansberry (Samuel French)
Drama: Act II, Scene 2, pp. 87–88, Walter (35)

When Ruth and Mama discover that Walter hasn't been at his work for the past three days, they ask him what he has been doing instead. He tells them that, basically, he has been driving around Chicago and getting drunk at the Green Hat. Start: "Mama—you don't know all the things a man got leisure can find to do in this city." End: "You can just sit there and drink and listen to them three men play and you realize that don't nothing matter worth a damn, but just being there."

Drama: Act II, Scene 2, pp. 90–91, Walter (35)

Walter tells his ten-year-old son, Travis, what life is going to be like in about seven years, at which point he plans to be a big business executive. Start: "You know what, Travis? In seven years you are going to be seventeen years old." End: "You just name it, son…And I hand you the world."

Drama: Act III, pp. 123–124, Walter (35)

Walter's "friend" and would-be business associate has disappeared with all of Walter's money. As he reflects on the tragic turn of events, he discovers a hard lesson in life. In this short and extremely bitter monologue, Walter tells Mama about the difference between "the takers and the 'tooken.'" Start: "You all always telling me to see life like it is." End: "He's taught me to keep my eye on what counts in this world. Yeah—thanks, Willy!"

ROSENCRANTZ AND GUILDENSTERN ARE DEAD
by Tom Stoppard (Samuel French)

Comedy: Act II, pp. 54–55, Rosencrantz (20–30)

Up to this point, Rosencrantz has been bewildered about where he is and why he is there. He just wants to go home, but he can't because he and Guildenstern were "sent for." Here, Rosencrantz grapples with whether it is possible to conceive of one's own death. You'll have to cut and paste this amusing speech a bit. Start: "Do you ever think of yourself as actually dead, lying in a box with a lid on it?" End: "Eternity is a terrible thought. I mean, where's it going to end?"

Comedy: Act II, pp. 55–56, Rosencrantz (20–30)

This monologue is actually a continuation of the "dead in a box" speech discussed above, but you can treat it as a separate monologue. Rosencrantz tells a couple of bad jokes as he tries to understand the meaning of time, consciousness, and death. He orders someone in the wings to come out, but no one does. Then he orders the person to keep out, and no one enters. In this way, Rosencrantz gains control of the situation. Start: "Two early Christians chanced to meet in Heaven." End: "Keep out, then! I forbid anyone to enter!…That's better."

SEAGULL, THE
by Anton Chekhov (version by Jean-Claude Van Itallie, Dramatists Play Service)

Drama: Act I, p. 8, Treplev (25)

Treplev, an aspiring playwright and the son of a famous actress, talks about the difference between his view of theater and his mother's. In this speech, he tells his uncle how frustrating it has been to live in her shadow and how much he disagrees with her conventional attitudes toward the theater and acting. Start: "You see, my mother doesn't love me. Why should she?" End: "I imagined I could read their thoughts, and I was going through agonies."

Drama: Act II, pp. 25–27, Trigorin (late 30s)

Trigorin tells Nina, who adores him, how difficult it is to be a famous writer. This long speech is good for classwork. Eliminate Nina's interruption and Trigorin's response. Start: "I hear you talk about fame and happiness and a bright interest-

ing life, but to me those are words which if you'll forgive me are about as meaningful as sugar plums." End: "Oh how horrible that all was. It was really torture."

SEA HORSE, THE
by Edward J. Moore (Samuel French)

Drama: Act I, pp. 15–16, Harry (late 30s)

Harry has spent his life as a sailor. In this lovely monologue—which is really a
marriage proposal—he tells Gertrude about his dream of a son, a home, and his
own boat. Start: "A while back…I get relieved of the midwatch." End: "And he'll
have a great mom!…Well…what do ya think?"

SHADOW BOX, THE
by Michael Cristofer (Samuel French)

Drama: Act II, pp. 68–69, Mark (25–30)

Mark tells Beverly about how he was selling his ass on Market Street when he first
met her ex-husband, Brian. Mark's love for Brian is apparent. Cut Beverly's lines.
Start: "…when I met Brian, I was hustling outside a bar in San Francisco." End:
"And he never stopped talking. Never."

SIGHT UNSEEN
by Donald Margulies (Dramatists Play Service)

Drama: Act I, Scene 1, pp. 16–17, Jonathan (35–45)

Jonathan tells Patricia about how his father, who died last week, covered an entire
wall of the family home with photographs, stapling them right to the wall.
Eliminate Patricia's lines and Jonathan's direct responses to them. Start: "I went
to pack up his house the other day." End: "That's all gone now. It's all gone."

Drama: Act II, Scene 6, p. 48, Jonathan (35–45)

Trying to answer the question, "What is good art?" Jonathan tells an interviewer
why he was disgusted by the huge turnout for the Van Gogh exhibit in New York.
Start: "Okay, let me ask you something: When we talk about good art, what are we
talking about?" End: "The art was just a backdrop for the real show that was happening. In the gift shop!" You can extend the monologue a bit more. Cut Grete's
lines. End: "…'cause the media told them so!"

Drama: Act II, Scene 6, pp. 49–50, Jonathan (35–45)

Now a famous and wealthy painter, Jonathan tells an interviewer how basically
stupid his fame really is. He points out that eight years ago, he was painting
houses, not canvas. Start: "What I am today? What am I today?" End: "The work
loses its importance, the importance becomes 'Waxman.'"

SIX DEGREES OF SEPARATION
by John Guare (Dramatists Play Service)

Drama: One-act play, p. 50, Rick (early 20s)

Rick is an aspiring actor in New York City, having recently arrived from Utah with
his girlfriend. He falls under Paul's spell and winds up depleting his bank account
for the con man and having sex with him. This monologue, delivered directly to
the audience, reveals Rick's embarrassment, disillusionment, and shame. A short
time after this speech, he commits suicide by jumping from a building. Start: "He
told me he had some of his own money and he wanted to treat me." End: "My
father said I was a fool and I can't have him be right. What have I done?"

STILL LIFE
by Emily Mann (Dramatists Play Service)

Drama: Act III, Scene 6, p. 45, Mark (28)

Mark, a burned-out Vietnam vet, observes that criminals on the evening news go to jail for doing what he did legally during the war. A short, powerful speech. Start: "I don't know. I just don't know." End: "I need to tell them what I did."

Drama: Act III, Scene 7, pp. 46–47, Mark (28)

In an anguished, deeply introspective confession, Mark reveals how he executed an entire Vietnamese family. He is haunted and tortured by his act. Very difficult material that is compellingly written. Unfortunately, this speech is too long for most audition purposes. Start: "I killed three children, a mother and a father, in cold blood." End: "I'm shell shocked."

STRANGEST KIND OF ROMANCE, THE
by Tennessee Williams (*The Theater of Tennessee Williams, Volume 6*; New Directions)

Drama: Scene 3, Old Man (65–75)

Tennessee Williams describes this character named The Old Man as looking like Walt Whitman. The character is the lonely boardinghouse landlady's father-in-law, and he visits one of the boarders. In a striking speech, he talks about visiting the plant where he used to work and demanding a job. This short piece is good audition material. Start: "The day before yesterday, I went down to the plant." End: "The Superintendent…said, 'Hush up, be still! I'll send for the wagon!'"

SUBSTANCE OF FIRE, THE
by Jon Robin Baitz (Samuel French)

Drama: Act I, pp. 32–33, Martin (late 20s)

Martin tells his family how books have ruined his life. The challenge for the actor is to avoid a one-note harangue. Martin is angry—he is summing up the frustration of a lifetime spent with his too literary family. Start: "Poison! You want to talk about poison?" End: "I hear the book chains are now selling preemptive strike video games, so why bother anyway? I'm out."

Drama: Act II, pp. 64–65, Isaac (60s)

Isaac tells Marge, a psychiatric social worker sent by his sons to determine his mental competence, about the memories he has of his family apartment. Start: "Listen to me. You come here with an agenda." End: "The silence, Miss Hackett. The silence. Pointless."

SWAN SONG
by Anton Chekhov (*The Sneeze: Plays and Stories by Anton Chekhov*, translated and adapted by Michael Frayn, Samuel French)

Comedy: One-act play, pp. 73–75, Svetlovidov (68)

An elderly comic actor wearing a clown costume wakes from a liquor-induced nap to discover that everyone has left the theater except Nikita the prompter and himself. Before Svetlovidov realizes that anyone else is there, he talks to himself. Start: "Well, here's a fine how-do-you-do! Here's a fine state of affairs!" End: "I'm not fit to be seen! Better go and get dressed."

Comedy: One-act play, pp. 77–78, Svetlovidov (68)

Svetlovidov tells Nikita how actors are consistently ostracized by the public, remembering a romance that ended years ago when he refused to give up his profession. This is a very touching speech. Start: "When I was a young actor, when I was just starting to get my teeth into it, I remember there was a woman who loved me for my art." End: "Don't trust them an inch!"

SWEET BIRD OF YOUTH
by Tennessee Williams (Dramatists Play Service)
Drama: Act I, Scene 2, pp. 28–30, Chance (29)
Chance is an aging Adonis with a good body. He is still clinging to the hope of Hollywood success, but he makes his money by sleeping with wealthy women. In this frank speech, Chance tells one of them about his life and aspirations. Cut Princess's lines and Chance's direct responses to them. Start: "Here is the town I was born in." End: "And that was when Heavenly became more important to me than anything else." For a shorter audition version, start with: "I'm talking about the parade."

TAKE ME OUT
by Richard Greenberg (Dramatists Play Service)
Comedy-Drama: Act I, pp. 25–27, Mason (30–50)
Mason is a rather uptight gay man, a financial advisor by trade. He gains a new client, one of the young superstars of baseball. As a result, he begins to follow the game and falls in love with it. This is a terrific monologue, a true ode to baseball. It is a little long for an audition, but there are several places to shorten it. Start: "So I've done what was suggested. I continued to watch and I have come (with no little excitement) to understand that baseball is a perfect metaphor for hope in a democratic society." End: "…well, does any other game do that?"

TENTH MAN, THE
by Paddy Chayefsky (Samuel French)
Comedy-Drama: Act I, pp. 13–14, Foreman (60s)
Foreman has surprised the other elderly Jews who are gathered in the tiny synagogue for morning prayers by showing up with Evelyn, his schizophrenic granddaughter, who is currently waiting in the rabbi's office. Clearly in a state of high anxiety, he composes himself and then tells the amazed men that his granddaughter is possessed by a dybbuk, a spirit, and that the voice of a woman he dishonored years ago has come out of her throat. Start: "She is possessed, Alper. She has a dybbuk in her." End: "May God strike me down on this spot, Alper, if every word I tell you is not true."

Drama: Act II, Scene 1, pp. 45–46, Arthur (30s)
During a moment of lucidity between schizophrenic departures, Evelyn has been talking to Arthur about her illness. Then, in a remarkably introspective speech, he tells her about himself, explaining why life is unsatisfactory for him, why he'll probably commit suicide one day even though he has enjoyed all the accoutrements of success. Toward the end of the speech, Arthur is on the verge of tears. Start: "Life is merely dreary if you're sane, and unbearable if you are sensitive." End: "As you see, I have quite a theatrical way when I want to."

THAT CHAMPIONSHIP SEASON
by Jason Miller (Dramatists Play Service)

Drama: Act II, p. 26, Coach (60s)

The coach implores his boys to stop squabbling, not to fall apart on him now. He says he never got married because coaching basketball was more than a profession—it was a vocation. A strong monologue. Start: "Booze and women. I tried to protect you from it." End: "You, boys, are my real trophies, never forget that. Never."

Drama: Act III, pp. 46–47, Coach (60s)

In one devastating speech in the final moments of the play, the coach sums up his life, remembering the innocent optimism of childhood and the agony of the stock-market crash, and blaming the Jews. His team, his pathetically glorious championship high-school basketball team, is his life, but a memory of greatness is all that is left. This monologue is long but stunning. Start: "We don't need them, boys…It's history now." End: "I made you winners. I made you winners." For audition purposes, start: "Jesus, I can still see buckets of ice cream. Great red slabs of beef."

TIME OF YOUR LIFE, THE
by William Saroyan (Samuel French)

Comedy: Act II, p. 68, Harry (20s)

Harry is an energetic comic and dancer whom most people don't find funny. Here, he tries one of his routines on a patron of Nick's Saloon. Start: "This is it. I'm up at Sharkey's on Turn Street. It's a quarter to nine." End: "I turn around. Everybody's behind the eight ball."

Comedy: Act II, pp. 74–76, Kit Carson (58)

Probably the most colorful character in the play, Kit Carson is a throwback to the American West, and tells fantastic tales, most of which aren't true. In the end, he does something very heroic. This particular anecdote, which you'll have to cut and paste, deals with his outrageous adventures in Gallup. Start: "I don't suppose you ever fell in love with a midget weighing thirty-nine pounds?" End: "I don't suppose you ever had to put a dress on to save your skin, did you?"

Drama: Act V, pp. 99–100 (Joe 25–35)

Joe tells his friend Tom about money, where it comes from and what it does to people. Start: "Now don't be a fool, Tom. Listen carefully." End: "Now, don't ever bother me about it again."

TOPDOG/UNDERDOG
by Suzan-Lori Parks (Theatre Communications Group)

Comedy-Drama: Scene 3, p. 47, Lincoln (mid-20s, African-American)

Lincoln describes his daily work at the arcade where, in whiteface, he pretends to be Abe Lincoln. People come in and pay to go through a mock assassination, shooting Lincoln at the theater. Start: "It's pretty dark. To keep thuh illusion of thuh whole thing." End, "It'll cut costs."

Comedy-Drama: Scene 4, p. 54–55, Lincoln (mid-20s, African-American)

Lincoln recalls what a good street hustler he used to be, a master at Three-Card Monty. Start, "Hustling. Shit, I was good. I was great.…" End: "…But I was good."

TRIP BACK DOWN, THE
by John Bishop (Samuel French)
Comedy: Act II, pp. 75–76, Chuck (24)

Chuck has a big case of hero worship and is beside himself when he gets a chance to talk to stock-car driver Bobby Horvath. Excited, Chuck describes in detail the very first time he saw Bobby race. You'll have to eliminate the other characters' lines and piece this speech together, but it works well. Start: "You know you was in the first stock car race I ever saw." End: "Man, what a race."

VALUE OF NAMES, THE
by Jeffrey Sweet (Dramatists Play Service)
Drama: One-act play, p. 41, Leo (late 60s)

Late in this one-act play, Leo complains about how everyone wants him to prove he is repentant for having named names before the House Un-American Activities Committee. Although he considers what he did to be wrong, he doesn't think public apologies will help anything. Start: "Look, I've been through this before." End: "And believe me, you're about the only reason I'd think of doing it."

VIEUX CARRÉ
by Tennessee Williams (New Directions)
Drama: Part 1, Scene 2, Writer (28)

In the preceding scene, Nightingale goes to the writer's rooming-house cubicle to comfort him after hearing sobs. They talk of loneliness, death, and love and then they have sex. As the lights fade on that scene, the writer steps out and speaks to the audience as the play's narrator. In an extraordinarily poetic speech, he says that, as he lay in his bed with Nightingale, a vision of his grandmother as a saint appeared to him. He muses about her reaction to the two entwined men. Start: "When I was alone in the room, the visitor having retreated beyond the plywood partition between his cubicle and mine..." End: "An almost invisible gesture of...forgiveness?...through understanding?...before she dissolved into sleep...."

WAITING FOR LEFTY
by Clifford Odets (Dramatists Play Service)
Drama: Scene 3, "The Young Hack and His Girl," Sid (25–35)

Sid tells his girlfriend, Florrie, why he is disgusted with the 1935 American system of government and economics. He claims that the cards are stacked against the little guy and that, in the end, the big guys with the money just want those on the bottom to go fight wars. A speech full of moral outrage and passion. Start: "We worked like hell to send him to college—my kid brother, Sam, I mean—and look what he done—joined the navy!" End: "They'll teach Sam to point the guns the wrong way, the dumb basketball player!"

WASH, THE
by Philip Kan Gotanda (Dramatists Play Service)
Drama: Act I, Scene 3, p. 12, Sadao (65)

Sadao, a widower, is seeing Masi, who is recently separated after forty-two years of marriage. She is making coffee for them when he suddenly tells this very personal story. During a visit with a group of widows, one of them asked Sadao why he was still wearing a wedding ring, seeing his wife was dead and he was actively trying to meet a new woman. He broke down and cried, and then took off the ring. Start: "We were all sitting around in somebody's living room, when someone said, 'How come you're still wearing your wedding ring?'" End: "Because you're not married any more."

Drama: Act II, Scene 2, pp. 35–36, Sadao (65)
Sadao and Masi lie in bed together. He speaks of his deceased wife, the challenges of aging, and how fortunate he is to have a second chance at romance. Start: "She just slept all the time." End: "Can you imagine what the kids are thinking?"

WILD HONEY
by Michael Frayn (adapted from an early, untitled play by Anton Chekhov; Samuel French)
Comedy: Act I, Scene 2, pp. 44–45, Platonov (28–32)
Back in their university days, Sofya and Platonov were idealistic lovers. Today, married to different partners, they meet unexpectedly, and the old flame still burns. But Sofya wounds Platonov when she asks why he hasn't done more with his life. In this speech, he responds and then attacks her choice of a husband. Eliminate Sofya's lines. Start: "Is every man you meet really such a threat to your Sergey?" End: "What in all the wide world made you marry that man?" For an audition-length excerpt, start: "Why haven't I done better? The first thing you asked me!"

WOOLGATHERER, THE
by William Mastrosimone (Samuel French)
Comedy-Drama: Act I, pp. 36–37, Cliff (25–35)
Cliff tells Rosie about the awful life of a trucker. This long monologue runs four-and-a-half pages. For audition purposes, begin about three pages into the speech with Cliff. Start: "You swear this is your last run." End: "Lose touch. Lose yourself in the road."

ZOOMAN AND THE SIGN
by Charles Fuller (Samuel French)
Drama: Act II, pp. 46–48, Zooman (18)
Zooman, the inner-city gang member who accidentally killed Jinny, has been hiding from the police ever since. Throughout the play, he represents a street-level counterpart to the civility and basic decency of the victim's family. He delivers all five of his monologues directly to the audience; these are rough stuff, full of violent, graphic images. The following excerpt is fine for special audition purposes. In it, Zooman talks about what it is like to be on the run. Start: "It kin be fun being on the run." End: "Niggahs can't be heroes, don't he know nothin'?"

Drama: Act II, p. 58, Victor (15)
Victor's twelve-year-old sister, Jinny, was accidentally killed three days ago when caught in inner-city-gang crossfire. In this short speech, he tells the audience about the special relationship they shared. Start: "They always tell me that I've got a better education than they had." End: "I know it, but I'll never tell them!"

PART THREE

FEMALE MONOLOGUES

ABSENT FRIENDS
by Alan Ayckbourn (Samuel French)
Comedy: Act II, p. 41, Diana (30s)

Actually, this is a sad and touching monologue in the middle of a very funny play. Diana begins this speech by recalling a pretty red coat she owned as a child. She liked red because she wanted to join the Canadian Royal Mounted Police, but then she found out that "girls don't do that kind of thing." They type and knit and marry and have babies. So Diana married and had babies, but now she sees how empty all of this is and wishes that she could have joined the Royal Mounted Police anyway. At the end of the speech, she breaks into sobs. This unusual monologue could be a showstopper at an audition. Written in the British vernacular. Start: "I'd seen it in the window of this shop when I walked to school. It was red." End: "I know I should have joined the Mounted Police. (Starting to sob) I want to join the Mounted Police. Please."

AGNES OF GOD
by John Pielmeier (Samuel French)
Drama: Act I, Scene 4, pp. 19–20, Agnes (21)

Agnes tells her court-appointed psychiatrist where she believes "good" and "bad" babies come from. This is an interesting speech, full of inner conviction and logic that is apparent only to Agnes. Start: "Well, I think they come from when an angel lights on their mother's chest and whispers into her ear." End: "God loves you!…God loves you."

Drama: Act I, Scene 10, pp. 48–49, Mother Superior (50s)

It is becoming clear that the psychiatrist intends to probe Agnes's mind more deeply, and that the Mother Superior feels threatened. In this reflective speech, she describes her adult life as a time of pointless drifting. After joining the convent, she didn't find meaning…until the night she heard Agnes singing in an upstairs room. Suddenly, Mother Superior felt connected to God. She asks the doctor not to jeopardize her faith. Start: "When I was a child I used to speak with my guardian angel." End: "Those years after six were very bleak."

AMEN CORNER, THE
by James Baldwin (Samuel French)
Drama: Act III, pp. 87–88, Margaret (35–45)

Margaret begs her son not to pursue the life of a professional musician, not to turn out like his daddy. A short, strong speech. Eliminate Odessa's line. Start: "David, I'm older than you. I done been down the line." End: "You think I want you one day lying where your daddy lies today?"

AMERI/CAIN GOTHIC
by Paul Carter Harrison (*Totem Voices, Plays from the Black World Repertory,* edited by Paul Carter Harrison, Grove Press)
Drama: Act I, Cass (30s)

Cass is a reclusive woman who lives in a Memphis rooming house across the street from the motel where Martin Luther King will soon stay. As history will show, he will also die there. In this haunting speech, Cass tells I. W. Harper, a security agent who has been sent to check out the motel for King, why she is afraid that someone is pursuing her. Start: "I was leaving that department store on Main Street where the old Gayoso Hotel used to be." End: "When I awoke, a man's hand was around my throat."

ANNA CHRISTIE
by Eugene O'Neill (*Anna Christie, The Emperor Jones, The Hairy Ape;* Vintage Books)
Drama: Act III, Anna (20)

In an impassioned speech, Anna confesses to Mat and her father, who believe she had been reared as an innocent farm girl, that she has in fact been a prostitute. You'll have to piece together the monologue a bit, but it works. Cut the men's few lines and Anna's direct responses to them. Start: "It was one of them cousins that you think is such nice people—the youngest son—Paul—that started me wrong." End: "Like hell you will. You're like all the rest."

ANOTHER ANTIGONE
by A. R. Gurney, Jr. (Dramatists Play Service)
Drama: One-act play, pp. 37–39, Judy (early 20s)

Judy Miller is a college senior who has written a modern antiwar adaptation of the Greek drama *Antigone,* but the Professor of Classics has refused to accept it for grading. In defiance, she has mounted a campaign for a university production of her play, causing factions for and against her to form on campus. In the scene leading up to this monologue, Judy learned from Diana Eberhart, the dean of Humane Studies, that the professor has agreed to give her a C, which will enable her to graduate on time. Judy won't accept this, however, opting for a stand on the principle of the issue. When Diana tells Judy that if she doesn't graduate, she'll lose the Wall Street job that is awaiting her, Judy lashes out at the older woman with this speech. In it, Judy attacks feminist values in general and the dean personally, positioning herself against what she perceives to be a feminist stereotype. Start: "What's a job anyway? Is it the most important thing in the world?" End: "And now here I am, about to graduate, or rather not graduate, because I've come up with the first vaguely unselfish idea I've ever had in my life, and this place, this institution—in which my family has invested at least seventy thousand dollars—won't give me credit for it."

APPROACHING ZANZIBAR
by Tina Howe (Samuel French)
Comedy: Act II, pp. 108–110, Olivia (81)
Olivia is a famous avant-garde artist living in Taos, New Mexico. She delivers this speech on her deathbed to her nine-year-old great-niece. Olivia is a crusty old woman, full of life, energy, and fun, and this definitely isn't a last-gasp kind of monologue. At the end of the speech, Olivia and the girl start jumping up and down on the bed. Start: "I was on a train somewhere between Paris and Tangier." End: "I thought my heart would burst. Zanzibar!"

BAD HABITS
by Terrence McNally (1990 revised edition, Dramatists Play Service)
Comedy: "Dunelawn," pp. 24–25, Dolly (late 20s)
Dolly tells Dr. Pepper why she and her husband, Harry, have been trying to kill each other. According to Dolly, Harry is compulsive, worries too much, reads road signs out loud, and follows her around with coasters. Start: "His hobby is tropical fish. I hate tropical fish." End: "That incident with the lawn mower was just the straw that broke the camel's back."

BETWEEN DAYLIGHT AND BOONVILLE
by Matt Williams (Samuel French)
Comedy: Act I, pp. 35–36, Marlene (30s)
Trying to prove that she and Big Jim have bigger fights than Carla and Larry, Marlene describes one humdinger they had when they wound up throwing every stick of furniture out in the yard. Start: "This one time, before the kids were born, Big Jim was workin' construction before goin' to work for the company." End either: "Left everything in the yard and went up and went to bed." Or: "Don't never go to bed angry."

BLUE WINDOW
by Craig Lucas (Samuel French)
Drama: Scene 3, pp. 62–65, Libby (33)
Libby tells Norbert about the accident in which she and her new husband fell from a seventh-floor New York apartment balcony. She was seriously injured, and he was killed. You'll have to piece together the monologue to make it work. Start: "When I first came to New York?" End: "I'm thirty-three years old. I can't have anybody hold me. I can never be held."

BOSOMS AND NEGLECT
by John Guare (revised edition, Dramatists Play Service)
Comedy-Drama: Act One, pp. 35–36, Deirdre (30s)
Deirdre describes the violent event that landed her in long-term psychotherapy. It involved the breakup of a romance. She hit the guy on the head with an ashtray, which sent his lighted match sailing into some Orlon pajamas that in turn caused

the suitcase on the bed to catch fire. She called 911. Start: "…This married person sat in a hotel room and told me this person is going back to their mate." End: "…and in a secret way found Dr. James and have been going to him every day since that day." (Cut Scooper's single line on p. 36.)

Comedy-Drama: Act One, pp. 66–68, Henny (83)
Henny is dying and blind but still has a mouth on her. She's a caustic, lovable old New York broad in every sense of the word. This monologue is the final speech in the play. In workshop, you can go ahead and do the whole thing; for audition purposes, I suggest you cut it down by half. For auditioning, you might want to eliminate the blindness in the character. A trait like that can upstage an audition if you are not careful. For an audition cut, I suggest starting about a third of the way into the speech and going to the end. Start: "We loved each other. I felt my father in heaven was paying attention to me…" End: "…I want that for you…"

BURN THIS
by Lanford Wilson (Hill & Wang/Noonday; HarperCollins Canada, Ltd.)
Comedy-Drama: Act I, Anna (32)
Anna tells Larry what a disaster Robbie's wake was, especially since no one in Robbie's family seemed to know that he was gay and presumed she was his girlfriend. And then, to top it off, she had to sleep in a bedroom that contained a collection of butterflies pinned to the wall. Cut Larry's lines and Anna's direct responses to them. Start: "In about eight seconds I know they have no idea that Robbie's gay." End: "There's these two bag ladies yelling at each other, apparently they're rivals. I fit right in."

CANDIDA
by George Bernard Shaw (Signet)
Comedy-Drama: Act III, Candida (33)
This speech, in which Candida chooses between her husband and the lovesick young poet, Marchbanks, comes at the end of the play. In it, she firmly establishes herself as a strong, fiercely independent woman. She decides that she'll stay with her husband, "the weaker of the two," not out of duty and obligation, but out of free choice. You'll have to cut and paste the speech a bit, but it will make an excellent monologue, particularly if you want to demonstrate your command of language and breath. Shaw requires a lot of breath, as does Shakespeare. Start: "I give myself to the weaker of the two." End: "I am mixing up your beautiful cadences and spoiling them, am I not, darling?"

CHAPTER TWO
by Neil Simon (Samuel French)
Comedy-Drama: Act II, Scene 7, pp. 119–121, Jennie (32)
Jennie tells off her new husband, George, for putting her in the untenable position of having to compete with the memory of his recently deceased first wife. This is a very strong, stop-you-in-your-tracks kind of speech. Start: "You know what you want better than me, George." End: "Sometimes I don't know when to stop talking. For that I'm sorry, George, and I apologize. I am now through!"

CHEATERS
by Michael Jacobs (Samuel French)
Comedy: Act I, Scene 2, pp. 15–16, Grace (50)

Grace and Sam met in a movie theater earlier tonight, felt electricity, and have guiltily made their way to a motel room, complete with X-rated movies on the television. They begin an affair, the first for each of them. Here, Grace recalls the first time she ever went to bed with a man. Actually, she is stalling because she is quite nervous about cheating on her husband. Begin with Grace singing "Amazing Grace" or start: "I was remembering the first time I ever went to bed with a man—I was almost twenty years old." End: "What could I tell them? I didn't feel a thing."

COASTAL DISTURBANCES
by Tina Howe (Samuel French)
Comedy: Act I, Scene 5, pp. 54–55, Holly (24)

Holly exuberantly fantasizes about what the world would have been like if dolphins had legs and behaved like people. The more she talks, the more amused she becomes with herself. Cut Leo's lines and Holly's direct responses to them. Start: "You know what I read in a book? That the island of Atlantis was really inhabited by dolphins." End: "Boy, do I feel weird…I'm so light-handed all of a sudden…I mean, headed."

COLORED MUSEUM, THE
by George C. Wolfe (Grove Press)
Comedy-Drama: "The Party," Topsy Washington (20–30)

Topsy comes on funky, dancing. She describes a wild party she went to uptown the other night and how that party is always going on in her brain. Whenever she walks down the street, she sashays all over the place "'cause I'm dancing to the music of the madness in me." This is a truly stunning, show-stopping speech for the right actress. It requires a lot of boldness. Start, "Yoho! Party! Party!" End: "So, hunny, don't waste your time trying to label or define me 'cause I'm not what I was ten years ago or ten minutes ago. I'm all of that and then some. And whereas I can't live inside yesterday's pain, I can't live without it."

Comedy-Drama: "Lala's Opening," Lala (30–45)

Lala is a famous opera singer and something of a flamboyant character. This is a good monologue for an actress who can do a French accent and sing a bit—just a bit. You don't have to be an opera singer. Fine audition material in the right hands, not for beginners. Start: "Yes, it's me! Lala Lamazing Grace!" End: "I am going away."

COMANCHE CAFÉ
by William Hauptman (revised edition, *Comanche Café and Domino Courts;* Samuel French)
Comedy: One-act play, pp. 10–11, Mattie (40–50)

Mattie gently tells Ronnie, who is younger and very unsophisticated, what it is like to make love with a man who is special to you. Drawing on a finely etched memory, she describes her most loving adventure in precise detail. Cut Ronnie's lines and Mattie's direct responses to them. Start: "When we started driving that morning…" End: "You're still young. But one day everything's happened. Then the night's no different from the day."

Comedy: One-act play, pp. 12–13, Ronnie (teens to early 20s)

Ronnie has a humorously distorted idea of what the world is like because she has never left her small Oklahoma town. In fact, she has gotten all her information from movie magazines and cheap tabloids. In this very funny speech, Ronnie tells Mattie about the strange and wonderful places she intends to visit. Start: "I'll never be like you…There's a whole mysterious country out there." End: "Just let me go anyplace but here—in Oklahoma."

COME BACK, LITTLE SHEBA
by William Inge (Samuel French)

Drama: Act II, Scene 4, pp. 75–76, Lola (39)

In this moving speech, which comes at the very end of the play, Lola tells her husband about a dream she had last night in which he was a hero and their dog, Little Sheba, died. Eliminate Doc's lines and Lola's direct responses to them. Start: "You know what, Doc? I had another dream last night." End: "We got to go on. Now isn't that strange?"

COME BACK TO THE FIVE AND DIME, JIMMY DEAN, JIMMY DEAN
by Ed Graczyk (Samuel French)

Drama: Act II, pp. 67–71, Mona (30s)

As she has done many times before, Mona tells the story of how she came to make love with James Dean on the set of the movie *Giant* many years earlier. This is a fantasy of course, but she has embroidered it and believes in it deeply. You'll have to cut, paste, and alter some lines to make the speech work, but the result is worth the effort. Wonderfully poetic. Start: "It was like a regular parade. People from all over these parts headed for Marfa, bumper to bumper, to be in that movie." End: "We spent that whole entire night together…until the sun started to peek out from over the edge of the earth, turnin' the sky into the brightest red I ever saw." For a shorter audition-length excerpt, start: "That night, I laid there in the back seat of the Buick and kept thinkin' about how I was chosen above all them thousands of others." End in the same place.

Drama: Act II, pp. 82–83, Joanne (30s)

At this point, everyone knows that Joanne is really Joe, who has undergone a sex-change operation. In this speech, which you'll have to cut and paste, Joanne talks about an interlude she had with Lester T. a couple of years earlier. It transpires that he'd abandoned his lover, and Joanne's friend, Sissy because she had a mastectomy. Start: "I went there with the intention of seeing you…I had heard you were living there and thought I would show up on your doorstep." End: "…one day the watermelons just disappeared…went away, and…so did (he)."

CROSSING DELANCEY
by Susan Sandler (Samuel French)

Comedy-Drama: Act II, p. 69, Bubbie (80s)

Bubbie is a Jewish grandmother who lives on the Lower East Side of New York but still has one foot in the old country. She has employed a matchmaker to cook up a romance between her granddaughter, Isabelle, and Sam the pickle-maker. After some false starts, the romance has taken off and this very sweet speech is directed toward Sam. Bubbie tells him how she came to marry Shiah, a tailor's son, and that she intends to dance at Sam's wedding. Start: "You're some big-time operator, Sammy." End: "You'll buy the schnapps. We'll have a good time."

DANNY AND THE DEEP BLUE SEA
by John Patrick Shanley (Dramatists Play Service) (*13 by Shanley*, Applause Books)

Drama: One-act play, Scene 2, Dramatists Play Service pp. 26–27, Roberta (31)
Roberta, an emotionally complex but undereducated woman, tells Danny about a dream she once had while under the influence of opium. She dreamed of the deep blue sea and of whales jumping out of the water all around her. Then they stopped, and the sea was calm. Start: "There's boats right up by Westchester Square." End: "…'cause I knew it had all them whales in it."

DAY IN THE DEATH OF JOE EGG, A
by Peter Nichols (Samuel French)

Drama: Act I, pp. 28–29, Sheila (35)
While speaking about Josephine, her spastic daughter, Sheila tells the audience about something that took place nine years ago. This event caused Sheila and her husband, Bri, to believe that their daughter had a will of her own. The celebration was brief, however, because Josephine had another grand-mal seizure and regressed. This is a lovely speech that illustrates a mother's unconditional love. Start: "I join in these jokes to please him." End: "Perhaps it's being a woman."

DEATH AND THE MAIDEN
by Ariel Dorfman (Penguin)

Drama: Act II, Scene 1, Paulina (40)
Paulina tells her husband, Gerardo, what kind of revenge she seeks against Roberto for raping and torturing her. Cut Gerardo's lines and Paulina's direct responses to them. Start: "When I heard his voice last night, the first thought that rushed through my head, what I've been thinking all these years…" End: "That's what I want."

DEATH OF A SALESMAN
by Arthur Miller (Dramatists Play Service)

Drama: Act I, pp. 40–42, Linda (late 50s)
Linda tells her sons why their father is a good man, why she loves him. To construct this monologue, omit Biff and Happy's lines and Linda's direct responses to them, and then rewrite around them. This can be a powerful monologue if you patch it together the right way. Start: "I don't say he's a great man. Willy Loman never made a lot of money." End: "When does he get a medal for that?"

DELICATE BALANCE, A
by Edward Albee (Samuel French)

Drama: Act III, pp. 81–82, Agnes (late 50s)
Family friends Harry and Edna have moved into an upstairs bedroom, apparently intending to live there permanently, an intrusion that has brought Agnes's family to the edge of hysteria and violence. She contends that Harry and Edna have brought "the plague" with them, a "disease" to which only a few are immune.

Powerful speech. You'll have to piece it together, cutting out the other characters' lines, but it works. Start: "Thank you, Claire. I was merely waiting—until I'd heard, and thought a little, listened to the rest of you." End: "Or shall we burn them out, rid ourselves of it all…and wait for the next invasion. You decide, my darling."

DIVISION STREET
by Steve Tesich (Samuel French)
Comedy: Act I, p. 25, Dianah (30s)
Dianah, still marching after all these years, tells her adoring Legal Aid lawyer, Sal, how exciting her ex-husband, Chris Adrian, used to be when he led the protest movement. In her eyes, he was a cross between Che Guevara and Chuck Mangione, smelling of mimeo ink and Cuban cigars, standing like a titan with a bullhorn in his hands. According to Dianah, Chris was beautiful. This is a difficult comic monologue but can be a showstopper if played full tilt. Cut Sal's lines and Dianah's direct responses to them. Start: "We met in Chicago." End: "I let his spark die…The flame of the rebel became a charcoal lighter on the Bar-B-Que Pit of History."

DREAM GIRL
by Elmer Rice (Dramatists Play Service)
Comedy: Act I, pp. 12–14, Georgina (23)
As Georgina dresses for work and puts on her makeup, she talks to herself in the mirror, assessing her life, her physical assets, the status of her unpublished novel, and the possibility that she is too much of a daydreamer. Start: "All right, Mother. I'm practically dressed." End: "Well, if I'm going to play with fire, I may as well look my best. So here goes."

DUET FOR ONE
by Tom Kempinski (Samuel French)
Drama: Act I, Session 2, p. 13, Stephanie (33)
Stephanie is a world-famous violinist whose career was cut short by multiple sclerosis. She tells her psychiatrist, Dr. Feldmann, how she met her husband, who is a prominent composer. She happily describes the evening he approached her after one of her concerts and they played an impromptu Beethoven duet backstage. Stephanie relates the story through rose-colored glasses, however, and the last line is a leveler. Omit Feldmann's one-line interruption. Written in the British vernacular. Start: "It was lovely, actually. I was at the BBC." End: "The papers called it a fairy story, but it wasn't…Fairy stories don't happen, do they?"

ECCENTRICITIES OF A NIGHTINGALE, THE
by Tennessee Williams (Dramatists Play Service)
Drama: Act I, Scene 2, p. 17, Alma (25–29)
Alma itemizes for her father the many community services she performs. Start: "Father, I do all I can. More than I have the strength for. I have my vocal pupils." End: "Oh, I've had to bite my tongue so much it's a wonder I have one left."
Drama: Act II, Scene 3, p. 41, Alma (25–29)
It is 2 A.M., and Alma is having a panic attack. Her feelings were hurt by John's earlier departure from her "group" where he was an invited guest. She knows now that he left on a false pretense. A moment ago, John told her that she is lonely, a diagnosis that made her angry. In this speech, Alma accuses him of avoiding her and her

"eccentric" friends and of planning to marry a "Northern beauty" someday. This is a difficult speech because Alma is distraught, and you don't want it to degenerate into a rant. Keep in mind that she feels like a woman scorned, even though she and John have never been intimate. Eliminate John's lines. Start: "Oh, how wise and superior you are! John Buchanan, Junior, graduate of Johns Hopkins, magna cum laude!" End: "But everything perfect and regular as the tick of that—clock!"

Drama: Act III, Scene 1, Alma (25–29)

In what is probably the most significant monologue in the play, Alma confesses to John that she has always loved him and that she has fantasized about being intimate with him. You'll have to cut and paste, eliminating John's lines. Start with: "Oh, I always say too much or say too little. The few young men I've gone out with have found me…" or "Look. My ring has cut my finger. No! I shall have to be honest! I can't play any kind of a game!" End: "Would I have sprung from my seat, or would I have stayed?" (This monologue doesn't appear in the Dramatists Play Service acting edition. You can, however, find it in earlier library compilations.)

Drama: Epilogue, pp. 54–55, Alma (25–29, playing mid-to-late 30s)

John is long gone from Alma's life, and she has turned into a lonely woman, seeking comfort from occasional involvement with traveling salesmen. In this speech, she describes the landmarks in Glorious Hill. Each one Alma mentions has particular meaning to her at this point in her life, which is the key to playing the piece. When she tells one salesman about that part of the city known as "Tiger Town," she is making a thinly veiled proposition. You'll have to cut and paste a bit, eliminating the man's lines. Start: "Sit down and I'll point out a few of our historical landmarks to you." End: "Tiger Town, it's the part of town that a traveling salesman might be interested in. Are you interested in it?" or "Oh!—There goes the first skyrocket! Look at it burst into a million stars!"

ECHOES
by N. Richard Nash (Samuel French)
Drama: Act I, pp. 23–24, Tilda (20–25)

Tilda and Sam share a room in a mental institution. In this speech, she tells him how she first started inventing imaginary friends and how the doctor ("The Person") caused her to drive them away. Omit Sam's single line. Start: "When I first came here, there was nobody here." End: "…and one day I opened my eyes a little…and you were there…and you've never hurt me…and never gone away."

Drama: Act II, pp. 51–52, Tilda (20–25)

Tilda, afraid that Sam is edging too close to sanity (in which case he will leave the hospital), passionately warns him about the doctor's therapeutic tricks and the false values that await him outside. Start: "Now listen to me, Sammy. Don't you see what the technique is?" End: "And you'll be right back there, where you started from…playing a part that somebody assigned you…making other people's motions because you're too frightened to be still."

EDUCATING RITA
by Willy Russell (Samuel French)
Comedy-Drama: Act I, Scene 7, pp. 31–32, Rita (26)

Frank invited his student Rita to a dinner party at his place last night, but she was embarrassed by her lower-class origins and didn't show up. In the morning, during their regular session, she explains what happened and makes a new commitment to improving herself. Written in the lower-class British vernacular, which is important to Rita's portrayal. Cut Frank's single line. Start: "I'm all right with you, here in this room; but when I saw those people you were with, I couldn't come in." End: "…and that's why I came back. And that's why I'm staying."

EFFECT OF GAMMA RAYS ON MAN-IN-THE-MOON MARIGOLDS
by Paul Zindel (Bantam)
Drama: Act I, Beatrice (30s)
Although this telephone conversation is not, strictly speaking, a monologue, it presents unique challenges and is particularly well written. Beatrice is talking to and flirting with Mr. Goodman, her daughter's high-school science teacher. Start: "Hello. Yes it is. Who is this?…I hope there hasn't been any trouble at school." End: "It's been a true pleasure speaking with you. Goodbye."

Drama: Act I, Beatrice (30s)
This is another telephone conversation between Beatrice and Mr. Goodman. She is concerned about the radiation-exposed marigold seeds her daughter brought home. Start: "Hello—Mr. Goodman, please…How would I know if he's got a class?" End: "You know, really, our schools need more exciting young men like you. I really mean that. Really. Oh, I do. Goodbye, Mr. Goodman."

Drama: Act I, Beatrice (30s)
Beatrice has just calmed down her daughter after the latter has had a violent nightmare, and they're talking about Beatrice's childhood. You'll have to do some cutting and pasting, but the result is a very textured monologue. Eliminate Ruth's lines. Start: "My father made up for all the other men in this whole world, Ruth. If only you two could have met." End: "I see the face of my father and my heart stands still."

EMPRESS OF CHINA
by Ruth Wolff (Broadway Play Publishing)
Drama: Act I, Tzu-Hsi (60s)
In this short speech, Tzu-Hsi tells the Pearl Concubine Ying how she came to seize the reins of power; she started out as a dutiful wife but found it necessary to take charge because of her ineffectual husband. Start: "When I first came to this palace, I was ready to be the perfect feminine complement to my masculine lord." End: "Where are the women today who would dare what I dared? They do not exist!"

Drama: Act II, Tzu-Hsi (60s)
Having elevated herself to the throne, Tzu-Hsi refuses to receive the British ambassador because she hates all that Britain stands for. In an unusual charade carried out with a costumed actor, she demonstrates for Li Lien-Ying, the Chief Eunuch, and General Jung Lu, how she would speak to the ambassador if she were to see him. Playing out the scene with actor Shen Tai, who is dressed as Sir Claude MacDonald, she blasts the British for their imperialistic ways in China. Start: "White Christians! What you are saying is we should become prejudiced, intolerant and despotic—like you." End: "We were here long before you existed, and long after you are gone we shall remain."

EQUUS
by Peter Shaffer (Samuel French)
Drama: Act II, Scene 23, p. 69, Dora (37–43)

Dora implores her son's psychiatrist to understand that parents aren't merely instigators of psychological problems in their children. She is confused by and ashamed of her young son's awful actions, but she loves him deeply. This is a very powerful and moving selection. Start: "Look, Doctor: you don't have to live with this." End: "I only know he was my little Alan, and then the Devil came."

FATHER'S DAY
by Oliver Hailey (Dramatists Play Service)
Comedy-Drama: Act I, p. 17, Louise (30–35)

In her black-humor style, Louise tells Marian and Estelle how awful her marriage was, how she and Tom tried to kill each other all the time, and why they got a divorce. Eliminate the brief interruptions by Marian and Estelle. Start: "Marian, I'm going to explain divorce to you one more time." End: "When I say that is why we get divorced."

Comedy-Drama: Act II, pp. 60–61, Estelle (25–30)

At the end of the play, Estelle sums up her philosophy on family life and vows not to hate Harold, even though he is remarrying. Start: "I admire Marian very much." End: "Marian doesn't hate. I'm not going to either. I wish you wouldn't."

FENCES
by August Wilson (Samuel French)
Drama: Act II, Scene 1, pp. 67–68, Rose (43)

After Troy tells Rose that he made another woman pregnant, she tells him why she has stayed with him for eighteen years. Start: "I been standing with you! I been right here with you, Troy." End: "You take…and don't even know nobody's giving!"

Drama: Act II, Scene 5, pp. 90–91, Rose (43)

When Cory informs his mother that he doesn't intend to go to Troy's funeral, Rose tells him why he should respect his father and why she loved him. Start: "You can't be nobody but who you are, Cory." End: "And if the Lord see fit to keep up my strength…I'm gonna do her just like your daddy did you…I'm gonna give her the best of what's in me."

FOB
by David Henry Hwang (Dramatists Play Service)
Comedy: Act I, Scene 2, pp. 33–34, Grace (20)

Grace, a first-generation Chinese American, describes her unsuccessful childhood efforts to blend in with the white children. Start: "Yeah. It's tough trying to live in Chinatown." End: "So I drove home."

FOX, THE
by Allan Miller (based on D. H. Lawrence's novel, Samuel French)
Drama: Act III, Scene 2, p. 71, Jill (29)

Jill tries to convince Nellie not to marry the strange young soldier who has come to live with them. Written in the British vernacular, but you may want to convert it to American English. Start: "Listen to me, Nellie, please." End: "Call it off. Call it off before it's too late!"

FRANKIE AND JOHNNY IN THE CLAIR DE LUNE
by Terrence McNally (Dramatists Play Service)
Drama: Act II, pp. 43–44, Frankie (40)

Frankie tells Johnny about how when she was a young girl her grandmother would come into her room and close the blinds at night. A truly lovely speech. Frankie can speak Johnny's line: "It's supposed to make them romantic." Cut Johnny's second line that interrupts the speech. Start: "I've always been very suspicious of what moonlight does to people." End: "I just want my Nana back."

GETTING OUT
by Marsha Norman (Dramatists Play Service)
Drama: Act I, pp. 9–10, Arlie (20s)

Arlie is southern, tough, streetwise, and just out of prison. Here, she talks about the time she and her young friends threw another child's pet frogs at cars. Start: "So, there was this little kid, see, this creepy little fucker next door." End: "I never had so much fun in one day in my whole life."

GINGERBREAD LADY, THE
by Neil Simon (Samuel French)
Comedy-Drama: Act II, pp. 52–54, Toby (40)

Toby tells Jimmy and Evy that her husband wants a divorce, that he isn't interested in her sexually anymore. Then she recites her impressive sexual resumé. Cut Jimmy and Evy's lines and Toby's direct responses to them. Start: "Martin has grown accustomed to my face…accustomed to my voice." End: "Then let him get out, I don't need him!"

Comedy-Drama: Act III, p. 68, Toby (40)

Evy arrived back in her apartment a few moments ago, hungover and sporting a black-and-blue eye. Her daughter, Polly, and her good friend, Toby, were anxiously waiting for her. Relieved by the knowledge that Evy is at least safe after being gone all night, Toby lashes out at her for being so self-destructive, and for not owning up to who and what she really is. Cut Evy's line. Start: "Damn you, Evy. Damn you for being so goddamned honest all the time. Who needs the truth if this is what it gets you?" End: "That's the first time in my entire life I ever told anyone off. I think I'm going to be sick."

GLASS MENAGERIE, THE
by Tennessee Williams (Dramatists Play Service)
Drama: Scene 6, pp. 43–44, Amanda (40s)

Amanda enters, wearing "a girlish frock of yellowed voile with a blue silk sash…carrying a bunch of jonquils," all in preparation for the arrival of Laura's gentleman caller. In this monologue, Amanda tells Laura the history of the dress. Start: "Now, Laura. Just look at your mother." End: "I hope they get here before it rains."

HEIDI CHRONICLES, THE
by Wendy Wasserstein (Dramatists Play Service)
Comedy: Act II, Scene 4, pp. 59–62, Heidi (playing 37)

The occasion is a 1986 luncheon for Miss Crain's School East Coast Alumnae Association at the Plaza Hotel in New York City, and Dr. Heidi Holland, a prominent art historian, is the featured speaker. She talks extemporaneously about how the women's movement has fragmented. This monologue is far too long for audition use, but it is so succinct, intelligent, and well constructed that it is wonderful for the workshop. Start: "Hello. Hello." End: "Thank you."

HELLO AND GOODBYE
by Athol Fugard (Samuel French)
Drama: Act II, pp. 46–47, Hester (late 30s)

Hester tells her brother how frightened their mother was and then recalls what it was like to see their mother's body in a casket. You'll have to piece together this monologue a bit, eliminating Johnny's lines. Hester is a white Afrikaner, so an accent is appropriate. Start: "What did you know about her? You wasn't even five years when she died." End: "There was something I wanted to do, but it was too late."

HOOTERS
by Ted Tally (Dramatists Play Service)
Drama: Act II, Scene 6, pp. 64–65, Cheryl (25)

This monologue is probably the redeeming moment in *Hooters*. Cheryl has been running away from adulthood and all its implications. She allowed herself to be picked up and taken to bed by a hot and horny nineteen-year-old guy at the beach, who, after the lovemaking, told her he loved her. Now he is asleep on Cheryl's arm, and she talks to him even though he can't hear her. With true insight, she speaks of her history as a sex object and says she intends to stop being one. For audition purposes, simply wake the boy up and talk to him. You always want to talk to someone who can hear you. Start: "Hey, Clint. You file your shirts in the closet?" End: "So hey!…Welcome to the top."

HOUSE OF BLUE LEAVES, THE
by John Guare (Samuel French)
Comedy: Act I, pp. 9–10, Bunny (late 30s)

Bunny, who tends to talk nonstop, tells Artie about the wonderful excitement along the parade route where the Pope will soon travel. Start: "Oooo, it's freezing out there. Breath's coming out of everybody's mouth like a balloon in a cartoon." End: "…like a burglar's torch looking all through the sky—Everybody's waiting, Artie—everybody!"

Comedy: Act I, pp. 12–13, Bunny (late 30s)

Bunny gleefully tells Artie how she plans to get the Pope's attention as he passes by in the parade so that he will perform a marriage ceremony for the two of them. Start: "Miss Henshaw's saving us this divine place by the cemetery so the Pope will have to slow down." End: "And nobody'll believe it. Oh, Artie, tables turn."

HOW I LEARNED TO DRIVE
by Paula Vogel (Dramatists Play Service)

Drama: pp. 44–45, Aunt Mary (30s)

You'll notice that, in the script, Aunt Mary is portrayed by a member of the play's "Greek Chorus." Never mind about that, just play it as Aunt Mary, a woman who is convinced her husband is behaving inappropriately with his high-school-aged niece. Start: "My husband was such a good man—is." End: "I am counting the days."

HURLYBURLY
by David Rabe (Samuel French)

Comedy-Drama: Act II, Scene 1, pp. 93–95, Bonnie (late 30s)

Bonnie talks about a phone conversation she had earlier in the day with a strange guy. Building on the theme that cocaine is superior to est as a mood enhancer, she says that she finally hung up on the man. This impassioned, mentally frenetic monologue would be wonderful for auditions if est and cocaine weren't so passé. Still, it is a toot to work on. Start: "I'm telling this guy on the phone that drugs are and just have been as far as I can remember, an ever-present component of my personality." End: "…and slam down the phone and hang it up."

HUSBANDRY
by Patrick Tovatt (Samuel French)

Drama: One-act play, Scene 2, pp. 27–28, Dee (55)

Dee gets a little tight and tells her son Harry that his aging father is having a tough time running the family farm. Her objective is to convince Harry to take it over. You'll have to change or cut a line here and there, but the monologue works. Eliminate Harry's lines, and connect Dee's speeches. Start: "…Les and I had a humdinger of a fight." End: "I think this one more year business is the silliest thing I ever heard of."

IN THE BOOM BOOM ROOM
by David Rabe (Samuel French)

Drama: Act I, pp. 39–40, Susan (25–35)

Susan, who is a lesbian, tells Chrissy about the time she shot her high-school foot-ball-hero boyfriend. Start: "All through my sophomore year in high school, I was in love with a boy and we were sleeping together." End: "It's somethin', though, how once you shoot a man, they're none of them the same any more, and you know how easy, if you got a gun, they fall down."

Drama: Act II, p. 104, Chrissy (early 20s)

Chrissy, a very unsophisticated young woman, summons up her courage and tells her abusive husband, Al, that she thinks she is going crazy. The tension escalates as she accuses him of being a lousy sex partner. Short, venomous, graphic sexual language. Start: "Listen to me what I'm saying!" End: "Am I making myself clear, Big Al?"

I STAND BEFORE YOU NAKED
by Joyce Carol Oates (Samuel French)

Drama: "Little Blood Button," Girl (20s)

A prostitute addresses the audience, complaining about the blood blister on her lip, a result of the too-intense lovemaking she engaged in the previous night. About midway into this sexually graphic speech, she shifts into a provocative one-on-one mode, presumably talking to the man who did this to her. Appropriate for sophisticated actresses. Start: "One of you's to blame—I could name which!" End: "That's the God's honest truth, guaranteed. Says so on the label."

Drama: "The Boy," Woman (30s)

A substitute public-school teacher addresses the audience, telling them about the romance she struck up with a teenage boy. She took him to a motel, they drank, and she got turned on, but he was impotent. This sexually graphic speech is appropriate for sophisticated actresses. Start: "This boy named Kit—soon as I started subbing for his class he pestered me with love, called out 'Hey, good-lookin' on the street, eyeing me every chance he could." End: "...he was laughing too, maybe he was crying, nose running like a baby's, and I just lay there thinking, All right, kid, all right, you bastards, this is it."

IT HAD TO BE YOU
by Renée Taylor and Joseph Bologna (Samuel French)
Comedy: Act I, pp. 9–11, Theda (28–35)

Rushing into an audition for a commercial, Theda nervously rambles through her life story, crying, laughing, dancing and singing. (By the way, this could never ever happen at a real-world commercial audition. But never mind. The routine Theda goes through is hysterically funny.) This monologue can be a showstopper if you play it for all it's worth. It is very New York. Start: "I had to get up early to go to a funeral this morning." End: "I have the power to make my dreams come true. It's not too late for me."

JOE TURNER'S COME AND GONE
by August Wilson (Samuel French)
Drama: Act II, Scene 1, pp. 95–97, Molly (22)

Molly tells Mattie why she doesn't trust men. You'll have to cut and paste, but this monologue is very effective. Eliminate Mattie's lines, and adapt a few others. Start: "I don't trust none of these men, Jack or nobody else." End: "That's why I don't trust nobody but the good Lord above, and I don't love nobody but my mama."

Drama: Act II, Scene 3, pp. 111–112, Bertha (40s)

Bertha gives Mattie a pep talk about men and spiritual advisers. Start: "If I was you, Mattie, I wouldn't go getting all tied up with Bynum in that stuff. That kind of stuff, even if it do work for a while, it don't last." End: "You got your time coming. You watch what Bertha's saying."

JOINED AT THE HEAD
by Catherine Butterfield (Dramatists Play Service) (*Women Playwrights: The Best Plays of 1992*, Smith & Kraus)
Drama: Act I, Dramatists Play Service pp. 9–11, Maggie (late 30s)

This play takes the form of a narration by Maggie, as she steps into and out of the action. You'll have to paste together this speech, which is in two pieces. In a very reflective mood, Maggie recalls a walk down a crowded Boston street and how overhearing snippets of the conversations of passersby prompted a philosophical revelation. This isn't a passionate, showstopper kind of speech, simply an introspective, straightforward, and beautifully written monologue. Start: "I was walking down Newbury Street in Boston on a very brisk, very clear day, late afternoon." Cut from the end of this speech directly to the beginning of Maggie's next speech, eliminating the comments of the passersby. Continue with: "Fragments of conversations. Who knows where they were meant to lead?" End: "And convinced that, really, deep down in the truest part of life, we are nobody's backdrop."

KATHY AND MO SHOW, THE: PARALLEL LIVES
by Mo Gaffney and Kathy Najimy (Dramatists Play Service)
Comedy: "Hank and Karen Sue," pp. 100–101, Karen Sue (28–35)
Set in a country-and-western bar, Hank has been coming on to Karen Sue as he always does, telling her how pretty she is and asking her when she is going to give up that other guy and marry him. Then Hank passes out face down on the bar. At this point, Karen Sue tells the waitress how she would have married him if she thought he was serious. Hell, she would do anything to get her life off the dime. Start: "Yeah, I'd marry him—if I thought he meant a goddam word of what he was sayin.'" End: "I think a nut job is what you call it, Adele. Oh, turn this song up. I love it."

KEELY AND DU
by Jane Martin (Samuel French)
Drama: One-act play, Scene 8, pp. 26–27, Keely (early 30s)
Keely has responded to her antiabortion captor by remaining silent—until now. In this emotional speech, she tears into Du, the grandmotherly woman assigned to care for and guard her; Du has just finished quoting some scripture as justification for Keely's imprisonment. Cut Du's lines and Keely's responses to them. Start: "Hey, I didn't choose to have this baby." End: "You're criminal filth, and I will see to it that you get yours. Now, leave me alone."
Drama: One-act play, Scene 13, p. 40, Keely (early 30s)
Keely is no longer yelling at her captor, Du, though she is still hoping to escape from her basement prison. After Du graphically describes the horrors of abortion, Keely responds with this quiet, intense speech, trying to explain why she shouldn't be made to carry this baby to term. Start: "I can't raise this baby." End: "So I guess it's me or the baby, so I guess that's crazy, but you don't…I don't show you…just how…how angry I really am. I don't. I don't."

KEY EXCHANGE
by Kevin Wade (Dramatists Play Service)
Comedy-Drama: Scene 3, p. 18, Lisa (late 20s)
Lisa tells her friend Michael about her mother's death from cancer. This isn't as macabre a story as it sounds. After relating it, Lisa cracks a joke. Start: "When I was very young, my mother got cancer." End: "It was a long time before I could even give a decent kiss without somewhere asking myself whether or not this guy would stand outside my window for six months while I died."

LARK, THE
by Jean Anouilh (adapted by Lillian Hellman, Dramatists Play Service)
Drama: Act I, pp. 6–7, Joan (18)
Joan is being tried as a heretic. In this speech to the court, she recalls her simple origins, tending sheep in the field. She also explains how she began to hear

"voices," instructions from God to raise an army and fight the British. The speech runs about one-and-a-half pages, but you can easily shorten it. Eliminate Warwick and Cauchon's lines. Start: "Then I'll start at the beginning. It's always nicer at the beginning." End: "And that was the day I was saddled with France. And my work on the farm."

Drama: Act II, p. 54, Joan (18)
Now in her prison cell, Joan recants her confession, knowing as she does that she'll face death by burning at the stake. Start: "And I will wear cast-off brocade and put jewels in my hair and grow old. I will be happy that few people remember my warrior days." End: "Call your soldiers, Warwick. I deny my confession."

LAST OF THE RED HOT LOVERS
by Neil Simon (Samuel French)
Comedy: Act I, pp. 26–27, Elaine (late 30s)
Barney brought Elaine to his mother's apartment to have sex. Instead, she tells him off. In this speech, Elaine angrily defends her basic philosophy of life. Start: "You hypocrite!" End: "If you can't taste it, touch it or smell it, forget it!"

LATER
by Corinne Jacker (Dramatists Play Service)
Drama: Act I, Scene 1, pp. 24–25, Molly (55–65)
Molly's husband, Malachai, died a year ago, and she and her daughters are gathered at their Rhode Island summer place. Here in the moonlight on the beach, Molly sits alone, in profound pain, remembering the day he died as well as happy times and the distinctive birthmark on his shoulder. She misses Malachai terribly and can't get him out of her mind. Start: "There's no privacy in this house." End: "Well, he's in the ground. I won't see it again."

Drama: Act I, Scene 2, pp. 35–36, Laurie (35)
Laurie has just finished washing her hair and is laughing with her mother. Alone now in the bathroom, she reflects on how hard it is to sleep now that her father, Malachai, is dead. She tells of lying awake in the night, next to her husband, Norm, listening to him snore and trying to sleep. Then, just as Laurie dozes off, Malachai's face looms before her, his lips stitched shut, just as she remembers seeing him in the mortuary—and she is awake again. Start: "Hell no…It wouldn't hurt." End: "His equipment is definitely no more than half the size of mine."

Drama: Act II, pp. 37–38, Kate (37–40)
Kate is an expert sailor, thanks to her father, Malachai. She came close to being the boy that her father secretly wanted, and they shared a different kind of bond than he did with her sister. Here, she sits quietly in her anchored sailboat and reflects on the relationship she had with her dad and how she felt after he died. Start: "I can sail." End: "Well…Katey's a girl after all."

LAUGHING WILD
by Christopher Durang (Dramatists Play Service)
Comedy: One-act play, Scene 1, pp. 5–6, A Woman (any age)
The woman talks directly to the audience, telling them about a violent encounter she recently had with a man in the supermarket aisle. A short—perhaps one-and-a-half-minute—intense excerpt from a very long speech. This monologue is funny because it is outrageous and because the woman is such a New York character.

Start: "I want to talk to you about life." End: "I'll take a taxi to the Metropolitan Museum of Art. I need to be surrounded with culture right now, not tuna fish."

LES BELLES SOEURS—REVISED
by Michel Tremblay (translated by John Van Burek and Bill Glassco; Talonbooks, Canada)
Comedy-Drama: Act I, Des-Neiges Verrette (40–50)
Des-Neiges Verrette has fallen in love with a door-to-door brush salesman and defensively explains to her friends how that came to happen, confessing how much she needs someone to love. Start: "The first time I saw him I thought he was ugly." End: "If he goes away, I'll be all alone again, and I need…someone to love.…I need a man."
Comedy-Drama: Act II, Angeline Sauv (59)
Angeline reveals, to the horror of the other women, that she has been frequenting a nightclub (read: den of iniquity) for four years. She turns to the audience, justifies these simple pleasures, and then promises not to behave this way anymore. Start: "It's easy to judge people." End: "I guess the party's over."
Drama: Act II, Rose (44)
A bitter, venomous speech in which Rose condemns men for the way they exercise power over women. According to her, life isn't like a pretty French movie. In reality, women get pregnant and are lost for life. Rose hates her sex-craving husband, her marriage, all of it. Start: "Life is life and no Goddamn Frenchman ever made a movie about that." End: "They get grabbed by the throat, and they stay that way, right to the end!"

LIPS TOGETHER, TEETH APART
by Terrence McNally (Dramatists Play Service)
Comedy-Drama: Act II, pp. 44–45, Chloe (40)
Chloe is the kind of person who is always being helpful, refilling your cup, and checking to see if you are okay. Her husband just told her to "shut up" and not to talk for six hours. Embarrassed in front of their friends, she defends herself in this speech and then exits toward the house. Start: "Before I go into my six-hour exile…" End: "We'll have bugs galore. Pussy Galore! Remember her?"

LITTLE FOXES, THE
by Lillian Hellman (Dramatists Play Service)
Drama: Act III, pp. 58–59, Birdie (40)
High-strung Birdie has had just enough of Addie's elderberry wine to loosen her tongue. She recalls her first big party twenty-two years ago, the one where she met her future husband, Oscar. From the start, Mama didn't like Oscar , she remembers, and perhaps she should have listened to her mother. Cut Addie's interruption of the speech. Start: "Mama used to give me elderberry wine when I was a little girl. For hiccups." End: "And so she had. They were all gone."

LONG DAY'S JOURNEY INTO NIGHT
by Eugene O'Neill (Yale University Press)
Drama: Act III, Mary (54)
In a morphine-induced reverie, Mary tells her maid, Cathleen, what it was like to be young and in love with a famous actor like James Tyrone. As she tells the story,

the audience gets a glimpse of the innocent young girl Mary once was. Start: "If you think Mr. Tyrone is handsome now, Cathleen…" End: "It has made me forgive so many other things."

LOOK HOMEWARD, ANGEL
by Ketti Frings (based on Thomas Wolfe's novel, Samuel French)
Drama: Act III, pp. 80–81, Laura (23)

For reasons of her own, Laura didn't tell Eugene that she is engaged to a man in another town, perhaps because she hoped against hope that her relationship with Eugene would work out even though he was too young for her. Their romance blossomed and, less than an hour ago, he asked her to marry him. Believing that she has accepted, Eugene runs off to pack, but Laura knows that she can't do it. In this speech, she tells Eugene's irate mother that she won't marry him and is, in fact, leaving on the afternoon train. Eliminate Eliza's few lines at the beginning of this scene. Start: "Mrs. Gant, I am not marrying Eugene. I'm not." End: "Some day you're going to have to let him go, too. Good-bye, Mrs. Gant."

LOSS OF ROSES, A
by William Inge (Dramatists Play Service)
Drama: Act II, Scene 2, p. 74, Lila (32)

Lila's prospects as an actress are dim, and she has agreed to go to Kansas City and perform in blue movies with her boyfriend. As she prepares to depart, she shares with Helen, who knows nothing of Lila's future plans, a memory of her first day in the first grade. Lila recalls how she approached the event with childlike innocence and joy, only to be jerked into reality when the teacher slapped her. It was her first major lesson in life. Start: "I remember my first day of school." End: "There's so many things I still want back."

LOST IN YONKERS
by Neil Simon (Samuel French)
Drama: Act II, Scene 2, pp. 83–84, Bella (35)

Bella grew up with an unnamed learning disability and, in some ways, is childlike. Still, love has found her, and she wants to marry an usher at a local movie theater. She finally gets the courage to ask her stern mother and other family members for their approval. When they respond negatively, Bella yells at them, telling them how much she longs to be in love with someone who will love her back. A very touching speech, not funny at all, which is something unusual for Neil Simon. Start: "You think I can't have healthy babies, momma?" End: "Hold me.…Somebody please hold me."

LOVERS AND OTHER STRANGERS
by Renée Taylor and Joseph Bologna (Samuel French)
Comedy: "Bea, Frank, Richie and Joan," p. 40, Bea (45–55)

Bea's son and his wife have surprised everyone by announcing their separation. To head off this catastrophe, Bea takes Joan to the bedroom for a mother-in-law/daughter-in-law chat. This is the funniest of a couple of monologue possibilities. Start: "And Joan, of all the pictures in your wedding album, my favorite is this one." End: "…and they're still together."

LOVE SUICIDE AT SCHOFIELD BARRACKS, THE
by Romulus Linney (Dramatists Play Service)

Drama: One-act play, pp. 28–30, Mrs. Bates (34)

In a remarkable monologue that is too long (one-and-a-half pages) for most auditions, Mrs. Bates tells the court how she first met the late general and his wife, how they saved her life, rescued her from a life of prostitution, and introduced her to her current husband. She is grief-stricken by their joint suicide. Start: "I met them first outside Miami, in a place called Slim's, on Route One." End: "That's what they mean to me, the General and his wife."

LUDLOW FAIR
by Lanford Wilson (*Balm in Gilead and Other Plays* by Lanford Wilson, Hill & Wang/Noonday)

Comedy: Agnes (20s)

At the very end of this sixteen-page one-act play, Agnes talks to her roommate, who falls asleep in the middle of the speech. After that, she sort of talks to herself and to an imaginary dinner date. Agnes is concerned about the sad state of her love life, and she is trying to get over a bad cold. Fun for classwork. A great deal of detail and subtext. If you are ambitious, you can do the entire two-page monologue. Start: "I don't know why you should worry any more about Joe than you did about whoever it was before." For a shorter monologue, start: "You know what Charles looks like? He looks like one of those little model men you make out of pipe cleaners." End: "I've got to quit saying that."

LUV
by Murray Schisgal (Dramatists Play Service)

Comedy: Act I, pp. 29–30, Ellen (early 30s)

In this gloriously dark speech, Ellen explains her dilemma to her new husband, Harry. On one hand, she has a cold, calculating mind that frightens men away and, on the other, she is a woman, warm and passionate. You'll have to cut and paste quite a bit, eliminating all of Harry's lines and adjusting Ellen's responses. Start: "I was lonely, Harry; I was always lonely." End: "…She loses her dream and…It makes an animal of her, a vicious little creature who thinks only of scratching and biting and getting revenge."

MARCO POLO SINGS A SOLO
by John Guare (Dramatists Play Service)

Comedy: Act I, p. 29, Diane (30s)

In this wild and woolly monologue, Diane tells Tom about her childhood music training, by now hopelessly interlaced with surreal erotic fantasy. Start: "I really started cookin' when I was eight." End: "Diane de la Nova and her Massage Parlor of Melody."

MATCHMAKER, THE
by Thornton Wilder (Samuel French)

Comedy: Act IV, pp. 109–110, Dolly Levi (40–50)

Dolly Levi has the unsuspecting Horace Vandergelder just about ready to pop the question. Before the big moment, however, she stops—and is alone on stage to talk privately to the spirit of her late husband, explaining to him that she is going to marry for money and that she doesn't want to remain a recluse. They don't write them like this anymore. Start: "Ephraim Levi, I'm going to get married again. Ephraim, I'm marrying Horace Vandergelder for his money." End: "Anyway, that's the opinion of the second Mrs. Vandergelder."

MISS MARGARIDA'S WAY
by Roberto Athayde (Samuel French)
Comedy-Drama: pp. 9–13, Miss Margarida (30–50)
This is a one-woman, two-act play in which the theater audience is treated like an undisciplined, rather stupid eighth-grade class. Miss Margarida instructs, harangues, seduces, and berates the audience members. You can draw excerpts from almost any section. One option is to start at the top of the play where she introduces herself and continue for about two-and-a-half pages. Start: "Good evening to all of you." End: "There is a very nice nursery rhyme that goes: '*The deserving ones, who are they? They are those who obey.*'"

   Another option is to begin where the first selection ends (pp. 13–15), just after Miss Margarida writes the following on the blackboard: "*The deserving ones, who are they? They are those who obey.*" Her very next line is: "I want to take advantage of this first class." Continue for about one-and-a-half pages. End: "…any Holy Ghosts in class? None, right? Fuck you then! You can go to hell."

MRS. WARREN'S PROFESSION
by George Bernard Shaw (Signet Classic)
Drama: Act IV, Mrs. Warren (40–50)
Once Vivie learned that her mother is still operating a chain of brothels, she refused to accept any more money from her. Mrs. Warren visits Vivie, telling her that her Cambridge-education values are false. Omit Vivie's single line and Mrs. Warren's direct response to it. Start: "Vivie, listen to me. You don't understand. You've been taught wrong on purpose." End: "Can't you see that you're cutting your own throat as well as breaking my heart in turning your back on me?"

NATURE AND PURPOSE OF THE UNIVERSE, THE
by Christopher Durang (*Three Short Plays*, Dramatists Play Service)
Comedy: One-act play, pp. 24–25, Elaine (25–45)
God has sent Elaine to impersonate the census taker who lambastes Eleanor for leading a "lousy life," suggesting that she consider suicide. A very funny speech because it is so off-the-wall and demented. Point by point, Elaine tells Eleanor why her life is such a failure. Start: "You phony liar. Your oldest son pushes dope and is a pimp." End: "Why do you continue living, Mrs. Mann!? Why don't you do yourself a favor!?"
Comedy: One-act play, pp. 28–29, Elaine (25–45)
Elaine, formerly the census taker and Sister Annie De Maupassant, the radical nun of Bernardsville, is the Pope now. In this speech, she stands on a tabletop and speaks in a grand and holy fashion, sharing her thoughts and insights on the subject of death. Start: "Death comes to us all, my brothers and sisters in Christ." End: "For we are the little people of the earth, and His is the power and the glory, and never the twain shall meet. Hubb-ba, hubb-ba, hubb-ba."

'NIGHT, MOTHER
by Marsha Norman (Dramatists Play Service)
Drama: One-act play, p. 50, Jessie (37–43)
Jessie tells her mother why suicide is the best option, explaining how she has lost her identity somewhere along the way. Start: "I am what became of your child." End: "…so there's no reason to stay, except to keep you company, and that's…not reason enough because I'm not…very good company. Am I?"

NIGHT OF THE IGUANA, THE
by Tennessee Williams (Dramatists Play Service)
Drama: Act III, Hannah (39)
Hannah is an unusually perceptive sketch artist who supports herself and her poet grandfather in a hand-to-mouth existence as they travel from tourist resort to tourist resort. In this haunting and poignant speech, she tells Shannon of the beauty—and evidence of God—she has seen in the eyes of the dying in Shanghai. She also mentions that she has recently begun to see that same expression in the eyes of her grandfather. Start: "You see, in my profession I have to look hard and close at human faces in order to catch something in them before they get restless and call out, 'Waiter, the check, we're leaving!'" End: "Lately my grandfather's eyes have looked up at me like that." (Note: This monologue does not appear in the Dramatists Play Service acting edition. You can, however, find it in earlier library compilations.)

NUTS
by Tom Topor (Samuel French)
Drama: Act II, pp. 43–44, Rose (60s)
Although her daughter is the accused, Rose behaves as if she were herself on trial. She is defensive about her record as a mother. In this monologue, she begins by telling the court how lovely Claudia's wedding was. Then she goes into a venomous attack on her former husband, who cheated on her. Cut Claudia's few lines and Rose's direct responses to them. Motivate the transitions internally. Start: "Your honor, I know it's a terrible thing to hear a mother say her daughter is…" End: "That's how much he loved me: six dollars and thirty-one cents worth."
Drama: Act III, pp. 75–76, Claudia (early 30s)
Claudia faces the court and graphically outlines her fee structure for various prostitution services. Explicit sexual language. Appropriate for sophisticated actresses. Start: "I get a hundred for a straight lay, a hundred for a hand job." End: "Do you all get what I'm telling you?"
Drama: Act III, pp. 82–83, Claudia (early 30s)
In answer to the question, "Do you love your mother?," Claudia tells the court what she thinks about love. An insightful monologue, very well written. Start: "When I was a little girl, I used to say to her, I love you to the moon and down again and around the world and back again." End: "It's too much and not enough."
Drama: Act III, pp. 83–84, Claudia (early 30s)
The final speech in the play is a blast furnace of a monologue. Cut the judge's lines and Claudia's direct responses to them. Start: "Wait a second, wait one goddamn second. What is this?" End: "Get it straight: I won't be nuts for you. Do you get what I'm telling you?"

OLEANNA
by David Mamet (Dramatists Play Service)
Drama: Act III, pp. 39–40, Carol (20)
Carol accused her professor of sexual harassment, and his flourishing career subsequently has been put on hold. Now the student becomes a demanding teacher as she lectures him on his transgressions. Start: "The issue here is not what I 'feel.' It is not my 'feelings,' but the feelings of women." End: "You worked twenty years for the right to insult me. And you feel entitled to be paid for it."

OTHERWISE ENGAGED
by Simon Gray (Samuel French)
Comedy-Drama: Act II, p. 36, Beth (30s)
Beth has just discovered that her husband, Simon, has known for months that she has been having an affair and that, rather than enjoy her guilt, he opted for silence. In this highly charged monologue, she tells him what she thinks of his deceit. What Simon doesn't know is that Beth is pregnant, but she doesn't know who the father is. Written in the British vernacular. Start: "You know the most insulting thing, that you let me go on and on being unfaithful without altering your manner or your behaviour." End: "Damn. Damn you…Oh, damn…So you might as well listen to your Wagner."

PAINTING CHURCHES
by Tina Howe (Samuel French)
Drama: Act II, Scene 1, pp. 72–73, Fanny (60s)
Fanny tells her daughter, an artist, that if she is going to paint the family, to do it truthfully. Start: "…and to you who see him once a year, if that…what is he to you?" End: "If you want to paint us so badly, you ought to paint us as we really are. There's your picture."

PIZZA MAN
by Darlene Craviotto (Samuel French)
Comedy-Drama: Act II, Scene 2, pp. 75–76, Julie (late 20s)
Julie has become frustrated in her efforts to rape a man. This started as a kind of misdirected lark, but it has turned ugly, almost violent. She complains to her roommate and their potential victim that fairy tales don't, in fact, exist and that life is a kick in the teeth. Then Julie continues in a bittersweet fashion, describing how she learned that a pretty smile isn't enough to get you through. Start: "I'm unemployed. I've had ten jobs in the last eight years. I live in a crappy one-bedroom apartment." End: "But can you see what a nice smile it used to be? Can you see how nice things used to be?"

PLAY MEMORY
by Joanna M. Glass (Samuel French)
Drama: Act II, pp. 76–77, Jean (20)
Jean's father is an unrepentant alcoholic, evidently intent on destroying his life along with his family's. Here, Jean tells him how much she loved him when she was a young girl, how much she adored going on a business trip with him. They drove places, saw wild horses, met people, and ate candy. Within the context of

the play, the actress is actually in her early teens when she makes this speech. The material can, however, work very well for actresses in their mid-20s. A very touching, beautiful monologue. You'll have to cut and paste a bit, omitting Cam's lines and references to the horses being sold for dog food. Start: "I remember the first time I knew I loved you." End: "I haven't been able to love you since then, because you're making me sick."

PORCH
by Jeffrey Sweet (Samuel French)
Drama: One-act play, p. 34, Amy (early 30s)

Amy resents her widower father for pressuring her to marry and have a family and for continually comparing her unfavorably to the memory of her late brother. In this poignant speech, she talks about the decision she made to have an abortion, how that affected her relationship with her father, and why she resents her brother for dying. Start: "My father's daughter. That sounds so possessive." End: "Christ, talk about selfish!"

PRIMARY ENGLISH CLASS, THE
by Israel Horovitz (Dramatists Play Service)
Comedy: Act I, pp. 28–29, Debbie Wastba (25–40)

Facing a classroom filled with students who know no English, Debbie tries to introduce herself and explain what is going to happen in class. She has zero sensitivity to other cultures, and that is what makes this speech funny. A blackboard would make a good prop, but you can easily mime that. Start: "Listen, now. I'll just go really slow. My name is Debbie Wastba." End: "Now then: Questions?"

PROMISE, THE
by José Rivera (Broadway Play Publishing)
Drama: Act II, Scene 8, Lilia (18)

Lilia's father, now old and feeble and on his way to a nursing home, listens as she declares her independence from him. She tells him that because he robbed her of the only man she ever loved, she'll make sure he never knows his future grandchildren. Start: "I talked to the home. You're getting the one-bedroom on the first floor." End: "…a broken promise makes us free of each other. You set me free."

SCENES AND REVELATIONS
by Elan Garonzik (Samuel French)
Drama: Scene 10, pp. 35–36, Helena (25)

It is 1893, and Helena is feeling romantic toward her new farm manager, Samuel. After a scene during which they dance around the questions of commitment and marriage, he asks why she so often sits on the back-porch steps with that air of longing about her. In response, she delivers this speech, telling him about a former love and how he vanished from her life during the period when her father was dying. Helena admits that this took the air right out of her. Start: "There are some things in life, Samuel, that are so private. Things that should…shouldn't be said to just anyone." End: "And am as you find me today: Sitting on the back porch. Pulling stems off blades of grass."

SCENES FROM AMERICAN LIFE
by A. R. Gurney, Jr. (Samuel French)
Comedy: Act I, pp. 32–33, Woman (50 plus)

A nervous resident of an upscale town addresses a neighborhood-council meeting, protesting the potential construction of a fence around the area. The character, an older woman, isn't used to public speaking and refers frequently to 3 s 5 index cards throughout her speech. Good contemporary, comic material for a Waspy actress. Start: "Um. I want to make three quick points about this whole business of the fence." End: "I mean, I'm just not sure a fence is the best solution."

Comedy: Act II, p. 51, Mrs. Hayes (50 plus)

A woman explains to her pianist why she has taken up singing at this late age. Interesting monologue material for the actress who can effectively create the illusion of the pianist. Start: "Before we begin, you probably want to know, don't you, why I'm taking up singing lessons at my age?" End: "I'm singing my heart out!" You can also try to sing a bar or two and end: "I'm terribly sorry. I'm terribly, terribly sorry."

SEAGULL, THE
by Anton Chekhov (a new version by Jean-Claude Van Itallie, Dramatists Play Service)
Drama: Act IV, pp. 51–52, Nina (21)

Nina, nervous and hungry, has appeared unexpectedly in Treplev's study. Ecstatic to see her, he declares his love once again. Nina, however, tells Treplev that she is here for only a moment and that she has accepted a winter acting engagement in a distant province. Suddenly, hearing Trigorin's voice in the next room, she pulls back and, in this monologue, tells Treplev that she is still in love with Trigorin even though he abandoned her. Nina then explains how she'd lost faith in herself after Trigorin treated her so badly, but now she has found her true self on the stage—and in acting. Somehow, though, her words sound hollow and desperate. Start: "Why did you say you kiss the ground I walk on?" End: "When I think about my work I'm not so afraid of life any more."

SEA HORSE, THE
by Edward J. Moore (Samuel French)
Drama: Act II, pp. 51–52, Gertrude (late 30s)

Gertrude describes the events surrounding her father's death when she was a little girl, her subsequent upbringing, and how she came to own and run The Sea Horse saloon. Although in the context of the play a "big woman" must portray this role, the actress's size doesn't matter for this isolated monologue. Start: "I was sitting on the pier one day, doing my homework." End: "...and I didn't need...anyone...anymore."

SHADOW BOX, THE
by Michael Cristofer (Samuel French)
Drama: Act II, pp. 71–72, Beverly (mid-30s)

Beverly is disgusted by Mark's self-serving tone as he tells her how he and her ex-husband, Brian, became lovers. When Mark continues to enumerate in graphic and putrid detail the way he has had to care for the dying man these last few months, Beverly levels him with this impassioned speech. Start: "Let me tell you something, as one whore to another." Cut Mark's line and Beverly's direct response to it. End: "My God, why isn't that ever enough?"

Drama: Act II, pp. 77–78, Maggie (38–45)

Maggie pleads with Joe, her husband, to come home from the hospital, knowing full well he can't because he is dying. Cut Joe's line and Maggie's direct response to it. Start: "For Christ's sake, don't make me say things I don't understand." End: "I want you to be there because I want you to come home." Or end: "Come home. That's all. Come home."

Drama: Act II, pp. 58–60, Agnes (44–50)

Agnes's mother, Felicity, seemed to cross over suddenly into old age the day word came that her daughter Claire had been killed in an accident. Felicity's health deteriorated as she became increasingly despondent. After many months of emotional and financial decline, she began to fantasize that Claire was still alive. That was when Agnes began to write fictitious letters to Felicity, signing Claire's name to them, hoping they would lift the woman's spirits. In a poignant speech, Agnes tells the offstage Interviewer why she has deceived her mother. Once you cut and paste, eliminating the Interviewer's lines, you'll have a wonderful monologue. Start: "We were very close. Our whole family." End with Agnes's admission that she has been writing the letters. Rework her lines and the Interviewer's so that the material reads: "So...So I've been writing these letters for almost two years...You're not angry with me, are you?"

SHIRLEY VALENTINE
by Willy Russell (Samuel French)
Comedy: Act I, Scene 1, Shirley (42)

Since *Shirley Valentine* has only one character, the entire play is a monologue, much of which is literally addressed to the walls of Shirley's kitchen. For the most part, Shirley talks about past events and although they still affect her, the speeches don't have enough tension for audition purposes. Still, this is wonderfully rich material, frequently touching. Written in the British vernacular.

You have many excerpts to choose from. You can do the last part of Shirley's story about having tea with Marjorie Majors. This section begins on a light note and takes an introspective, perhaps tearful turn at the end. Start: "The waitress was just puttin' the tea an' cakes on the table." End: "...who turned me into this? I don't want this." For a touching excerpt, try beginning immediately after this point. Start: "Do you remember her, wall? Remember Shirley Valentine? She got married to a boy called Joe." End: "I've always wondered why it is that if somebody says 'I love you' it seems to automatically give them the right to treat you worse."

Drama: Act I, Scene 2, Shirley (42)

This is the only section of the play that finds Shirley in the throes of a dilemma in the present moment. As such, it makes arguably the best material for audition purposes. She is waiting in her kitchen for her friend Jane to pick her up in order to go to the airport and fly to Greece. Start: "Guess where I'm going?" End: "...and keep Joe safe. Please." For a longer excerpt, continue to this point: "...got hold of a pen an' wrote, across the wall, in big letters—GREECE."

SHIVAREE
by William Mastrosimone (Samuel French)
Comedy: Act I, pp. 33–34, Shivaree (20s)

Shivaree tells Chandler how she makes a living as a belly dancer. This character is southern to her toes, apparently rural, displays a sophisticated vocabulary, and is bright, sassy, sexy, and very much in her own energetic orbit—in other words, a free spirit. Start: "Well, sport, you can dance for dance and get a flat rate, or you can dance for tips." End: "And that's m'story bub, now where's this wine?"

SISTER MARY IGNATIUS EXPLAINS IT ALL FOR YOU
by Christopher Durang (Dramatists Play Service)
Comedy: One-act play, pp. 30–31, Sister Mary Ignatius (40–60)

This funny play contains a couple of possible monologues, but this is the best because it includes some outrageous Catholic doctrine. The actress should wear a traditional nun's habit if possible—or at least put a black/gray scarf on her head. Start: "I have your questions here on little file cards." End: "If you die instantaneously and are unable to say a good act of contrition, you will go straight to hell."

SIX DEGREES OF SEPARATION
by John Guare (Dramatists Play Service)
Drama: One-act play, p. 45, Ouisa (43)

Ouisa has just discovered how the young intruder managed to learn so many personal details of her private family life. This causes her to reflect on how "everybody on this planet is separated by only six other people. Six degrees of separation." Start: "Can you believe it? Paul learned all that in three months. Three months!" End: "Six degrees of separation between me and everyone else on this planet. But to find the right six people."

SNOWANGEL
by Lewis John Carlino (*Cages*, Dramatists Play Service)
Drama: One-act play, pp. 24–25, Connie (mid-to-late 30s)

As dawn approaches and the liquor heightens her reverie, Connie, a prostitute, tells her john about her first love, a Mexican laborer named Paco. He was a gentle man with a special smile. This is really a lovely and well-written monologue. Start: "He came to me while I was workin' in a house in Stockton." End: "That's what I remember, mister. That's what I imagine."

STEEL MAGNOLIAS
by Robert Harling (Dramatists Play Service)
Drama: Act II, Scene 2, pp. 66–67, M'Lynn (50ish)

M'Lynn tells her friends about the final hours of her daughter's life. The monologue is peaceful, accepting, and loving—not a crying scene. Start: "No, I couldn't leave my Shelby." End: "It was the most precious moment of my life thus far."

STILL LIFE
by Emily Mann (Dramatists Play Service)
Drama: Act III, Scene 4, p. 42, "The Spaghetti Story," Cheryl (28)

On the surface, this is simply a funny story of a wife trying to cope with her husband's wild and wacky yearly spaghetti feast for forty of his closest friends. But underneath the surface lies the disturbing edge and manic quality of a woman who is just barely hanging on. The following excerpt is appropriate for audition purposes. Start: "I hate to cook. Probably because he likes to cook." End: "I can't take it."

STREETCAR NAMED DESIRE, A
by Tennessee Williams (Dramatists Play Service)
Drama: Act II, Scene 2, pp. 67–68, Blanche (early 30s)
A romance between Blanche and Mitch is blossoming, but he doubts his feelings for Blanche because his mother views the union with skepticism. Returning from a date, the lovers flirt in the dim lantern light. Suddenly, Mitch asks Blanche exactly how old she is; this is a dangerous question because Blanche is several years older than she has led him to believe. Afraid that he might be slipping from her grasp, Blanche goes into this story about her long-ago marriage to a boy who turned out to be gay. His ultimate suicide made her very needy for someone exactly like Mitch. Blinded by love, Mitch buys Blanche's story completely. Start: "He was a boy, just a boy, when I was a very young girl." End: "And then the searchlight which had been turned on the world was turned off again and never for one moment since has there been any light stronger than this kitchen candle...."

SUBJECT WAS ROSES, THE
by Frank D. Gilroy (Samuel French)
Drama: Act II, Scene 3, p. 64, Nettie (45)
Nettie tells her son how she came to marry his father. Tinged now with bitterness and regret, she still can remember the appeal her husband had as a young man. A good monologue, with plenty of subtext. Start: "I think it was his energy...a certain wildness. He was not like my father at all." End: "The baker from Paterson was all tongue-tied outside, but in the home he would have been beautiful...Go to bed now."

SUMMER AND SMOKE
by Tennessee Williams (Dramatists Play Service)
Drama: Part I, Scene 1, pp. 17–18, Alma (25–29)
Alma has been in love with John since childhood, but they've evolved into radically different kinds of adults. She is shy, proper, and nervous, while he is something of a hell-raiser and a rogue. In this speech, motivated by her feelings of unrequited love, Alma blasts John for wasting his considerable talents and his life. Start: "I'm afraid you and I move in different circles." End: "You know what I call it? I call it a desecration!"
Drama: Part II, Scene 5, p. 73, Alma (25–29)
Alma has come to John's office to tell him that she'll sleep with him and that she loves him. When she kisses him, however, he pulls back, explaining that what he now feels for her is spiritual, not physical. In this emotional speech, Alma tells John that she has loved him since childhood. Start: "But I don't want to be talked to like some incurably sick patient you have to comfort." End: "Why did you come almost close enough—and no closer?"

SWEET BIRD OF YOUTH
by Tennessee Williams (Dramatists Play Service)
Drama: Act I, Scene 1, pp. 19–20, Princess Kosmonopolis (50–60)
The Princess tells her lover, Chance, about the disastrous Hollywood screening of her "comeback" film. People laughed in the wrong places, and she fled from the theater. Cut Chance's lines and the Princess's direct responses to them. Rewrite around Chance this way: "If I could paint deserts and nomads, if I could paint...smoke...but you come after the comeback." Start: "Stars in retirement sometimes give acting lessons." End: "Flight, just flight, not interrupted until I woke up this morning."

Drama: Act I, Scene 1, pp. 25–26, Princess Kosmonopolis (50–60)
Princess Kosmonopolis tells Chance that she can't be blackmailed, but that she'll give him money in exchange for sex. You'll have to cut and paste, eliminating Chance's lines and rewriting around him. Start: "You are trembling and sweating...you see this part doesn't suit you...." End: "I'm sending a young man down with some travelers' checks to cash for me...."

TAKEN IN MARRIAGE
by Thomas Babe (Dramatists Play Service)
Comedy: Act I, pp. 19–20, Ruth (late 50s)
At the rehearsal for Annie's upcoming wedding, her various female relatives chat about what marriage and love actually mean. In this crusty speech, Annie's Aunt Ruth explains to Annie and the others why she stayed with her late husband for twenty-five years, despite his infidelities. Loyalty, you see, is the key. Start: "I may seem the smallest part of a fool, and Anne and Andrea may think worse, but I'm not." End: "I want you to remember that, Anne."

TALKING WITH...
by Jane Martin (Samuel French)
Comedy-Drama: "Fifteen Minutes," pp. 7–10, Actress (any age)
An actress spends the final moments before going on stage putting on her makeup and talking to the audience about how strange it is to be part of a theatrical transaction.

Comedy-Drama: "Scraps," pp. 13–16, Actress (35)
A housewife lives a fantasy life as the Patchwork Girl of Oz, from the seventh Oz book. Each day, after her husband leaves for work and her daughter goes off to high school, she dresses up in her colorful patchwork-quilt outfit and cleans the house. In this monologue, she tells the audience why this escape is necessary for her sanity.

Drama: "Clear Glass Marbles," pp. 19–22, Actress (20–30)
A woman talks about the final days of her mother's life. During this monologue, she drops marbles, one at a time, on the floor, symbolizing the passing of each day.

Comedy: "Audition," pp. 25–27, Actress (late 20s)
An actress goes on stage to audition. She brings a cat on a leash with her. The more she talks, the stranger she seems. She threatens to kill the cat right there if she doesn't get the job.

Comedy-Drama: "Rodeo," pp. 31–34, Actress (late 20s)
A woman named Lurlene, former rodeo rider, complains about modern-day merchandising of the rodeo. During this speech, the actress works on a piece of tack.

Comedy-Drama: "Twirler," pp. 37–40, Actress (20–30)
A young woman wearing a spangled one-piece swimsuit and carrying a baton talks about the glories of being a twirler. She elevates the twirler to the rank of a deity.

Drama: "Lamps," pp. 43–45, Actress (65)
Surrounded by lamps, perhaps a dozen or so, a woman talks about old age. She turns off the lamps one at a time until, finally, there is darkness.

Comedy: "Handler," pp. 49–52, Actress (20–30)
Here, a rural woman discusses the pros and cons of religious snake handling.

Drama: "Dragons," pp. 55–57, Actress (20–30)
This woman is nine months pregnant and in labor as she speaks. Prenatal tests indicated that her baby is abnormal, but she is having it anyway.

Comedy: "French Fries," pp. 61–63, Actress (60s)
A bag lady rambles on in a funny but touching manner about how wonderful it would be to actually live in a McDonald's fast-food restaurant. In the middle of her long speech, there is a nice one-and-a-half-minute excerpt that is appropriate for auditions. Start: "I saw a man healed by a Big Mac." End: "Healed by a Big Mac. I saw it."

Comedy: "Marks," pp. 67–69, Actress (early 40s)
A woman talks about all the tattoos on her body. They represent various people and events in her life.

TENTH MAN, THE
by Paddy Chayefsky (Samuel French)
Comedy-Drama: Act II, Scene 1, pp. 43–44, The Girl (Evelyn, 18)
This speech begins in a lucid fashion, but midway through the girl stops making sense. She starts by talking about life in the mental institution and shifts into descriptions of her secret life as a movie actress. Probably not a wise choice for auditions, but very good for workshop. Start: "I'm being institutionalized again. Dr. Molineaux's Sanitarium in Long Island. I'm a little paranoid." End: "He's really Mr. Hirschman the Cabalist. He's making a golem. You ought to come here, Rabbi."

TOP GIRLS
by Caryl Churchill (Samuel French)
Comedy-Drama: Act I, Scene 1, p. 27, Lady Nijo (30s)
Lady Nijo is one of the historical guests at Marlene's celebration lunch. Born in 1258, Nijo was the Emperor's concubine and later a Buddhist nun. In this short speech, she tells how her young lover impregnated her before she became a concubine. The Emperor thought she was four months pregnant when she was actually in her sixth month. When the baby was born, Nijo's lover, Akebono, cut the cord and took the baby away. Nijo told the Emperor that she had miscarried. Start: "I too was often in embarrassing situations, there's no need for a scandal." End: "Then I told the Emperor that the baby had miscarried because of my illness, and there you are. The danger was past."

TOUCH OF THE POET, A
by Eugene O'Neill (Dramatists Play Service)
Drama: Act IV, Nora (40)

Nora's husband stormed off hours ago, bent on defending his honor in a duel. Now, at midnight, she is worried that a terrible fate might have befallen him. She confides to her daughter that perhaps this is God's way of punishing the family. The speech requires a slight Irish brogue. This is a good dramatic monologue for a versatile actress of power and intelligence. Start: "Don't tell me not to worry. You're as bad as Mickey." End: "Oh, if I only had the courage!"

TRIBUTE
by Bernard Slade (Samuel French)
Comedy: Act I, pp. 28–29, Hilary (30s)

Hilary, a former call girl who is now a successful travel agent, speaks to the audience about her affection for and relationship with Scottie Templeton, who has been diagnosed with a terminal illness. She explains how he arranged for her former clients to raise the money so that she could start her own travel agency. Start: "Okay, maybe it's about time I introduced myself." End: "I'm here for the same reason you are. I love him."

TWICE AROUND THE PARK
by Murray Schisgal (Samuel French)
Comedy: "A Need for Brussels Sprouts," pp. 26–28, Margaret (40s)

Margaret is a New York City cop who is mad because her downstairs neighbor plays his opera music too loud. After complaining to him on the telephone to no avail, she puts on her uniform and knocks on his door to issue a summons for disturbing the peace. It turns out that he is a widower, and since she is a single mother, they hit it off in an insulting kind of way. In a very funny speech, she tells him about her awful marriages. This is a good monologue for an actress who has a feel for New York humor. You'll have to cut and paste, eliminating Leon's lines. In its entirety, the speech is probably too long for most audition purposes, but it is easy to cut it down. Start: "Three short marriages, huh? You think that's funny?" End: "…and that, Mr. Rose, is the story of two short marriages that were not so funny."

VIEUX CARRÉ
by Tennessee Williams (New Directions)
Drama: Part II, Scene 9, Jane (20s)

The story Jane relates in this speech may or not be true. What Tye doesn't know is that Jane's blood count has "taken a turn for the worse," signaling a return of leukemia, and she is deeply depressed. In the preceding scene, Jane has ordered the lowlife Tye out because he has begun shooting heroin again. Then she begins this speech, telling him how she came to meet a wealthy Brazilian in a bar—a man she is expecting momentarily, and a man who will pay for her services. You'll have to cut and paste a bit, omitting Tye's lines. Start: "I know what I said, I said a buyer to look at my illustrations, but what I said was a lie." End: "The bed bit is finished between us. You're moving out today."

VITAL SIGNS
by Jane Martin (Samuel French)
Drama: pp. 57–58, "Abortion Lawyer," Woman (25–40)
Vital Signs is composed of more than thirty monologues for women on a variety of contemporary topics. One particularly intense speech focuses on the abortion issue. A female prosecutor is being replaced by a male attorney in an abortion-clinic protest case. In this speech, she demands that she be the one to try it. Start: "Suitable? No, actually that doesn't seem 'suitable' to me." End: "You can't do anything about number one and you are cordially invited to number two, my treat. How about it?"

Drama: p. 79, "Endings," Woman (25–40)
This monologue is also quite compelling. Here, a woman takes her bag out to the car, intending to leave her companion while he is sleeping. But she can't do it. Instead, she returns to the house and climbs into the bed with him. Maybe she'll leave next time. The speech should be directed to the audience. Start: "I sat in the chair by the bed watching him sleep until I ached from sitting and then went out to the toolshed where I had hidden the suitcase." End: "And as I fell asleep I thought, well, that's all right, it's going on then. It's going on."

WAITING FOR THE PARADE
by John Murrell (Talonbooks, Canada)
Drama: Scene 14, Catherine (early 30s)
Earlier today, Catherine received word that Billy, her husband, is missing in action in World War II, and she has been hitting the bottle a little heavy ever since as the other women try to comfort her. In this touching speech, she recalls the fights she and Billy had in the early days of their marriage and how those are her most vivid memories. Eliminate Margaret's line. Start: "When Billy and I were first married—we fought all the time." End: "Losing him—a little at a time."

Comedy-Drama: Scene 20, Margaret (mid-to-late 50s)
As she draws a stocking seam up her leg with an eyebrow pencil, Margaret talks about the sadness of getting old, as well as the fact that her imprisoned youngest son didn't want to see her the last time she visited him in jail. Finally, she cries out in pain against it all, resolving to overcome the bad thoughts. Because of the eyebrow pencil, this might not be the best piece for audition purposes, but it is excellent for workshop use.

WASH, THE
by Philip Kan Gotanda (Dramatists Play Service)
Drama: Act II, Scene 7, p. 44, Masi (67)
Masi tells her adult daughters why she left their father after forty-two years of marriage. She confesses that he didn't find her sexually desirable. Furthermore, he considered her to be stupid. She is now very happy with a new man, Sadao. An excellent monologue. Start: "Here are things you kinds don't know." End: "I like Sadao. I like Sadao very much."

WHO'S AFRAID OF VIRGINIA WOOLF?
by Edward Albee (Dramatists Play Service)
Drama: Act III, p. 88, Martha (52)

Martha took the new biology teacher to her bedroom, but he was unable to perform because he was too drunk. Now, back in the living room, she tells him that all men except her husband are flops, describing the futile seductive dance she has endured so many times. Rough material, appropriate for advanced actresses. By this point in the play, Martha has been drinking steadily for many hours and is seeing through an alcoholic veil. Start: "You're all flops." End: "There is only one man in my life who has ever…made me happy. Do you know that? One!"

WIT
by Margaret Edson (Dramatists Play Service)
Drama: One-act, pp. 43–44, Vivian (50)

This monologue begins with Vivian reciting six lines from a John Donne poem. Then, speaking directly to the audience, she relates the poem to her present situation in which her life expectancy is so tenuous. Start: (quoting Donne) "This is my played last scene…" End: "…It would be a relief to be a cheerleader on her way to Daytona Beach for Spring Break."

WOOLGATHERER, THE
by William Mastrosimone (Samuel French)
Drama: Act I, p. 28, Rosie (mid-20s)

Rosie is tortured by the memory of hoodlums viciously breaking the legs of the pretty cranes in the zoo. Here, she tells Cliff about the circumstances, describing it in vivid detail. The terror is still real for her. Start: "You may think it's funny but I was the last one to see them last summer." End: "They can't make the birds come alive again."

ZOOMAN AND THE SIGN
by Charles Fuller (Samuel French)
Drama: Act II, pp. 33–34, Rachel (mid-30s)

Still in mourning over the violent death of her twelve-year-old daughter, Rachel describes the step-by-step deterioration of this formerly safe African-American neighborhood. This is an extremely well-written and powerful monologue. Start: "What is it about men, they won't let well enough alone?" End: "I just want to move."

PART FOUR

MALE/MALE SCENES

AMEN CORNER, THE
by James Baldwin (Samuel French)
Drama: Act II, pp. 49–54, Luke (40–50) and David (18)

David hasn't seen his father, Luke, for ten years, ever since the day his mother took him and walked out on the man. But like his father, David is born to be a musician. It is in his blood, and he has identified with his father from afar. Until last week, however, David always thought his father had left his mother, not the other way around. It makes a difference. Luke is dying, and the father/son relationship is more important than ever. In this wonderful scene, Luke tells David that it is possible to be a good musician without screwing up your life the way he has. Both characters have good monologues. Start, Luke: "Hello there." End, Luke: "Oh yes."

AMERICAN BUFFALO
by David Mamet (Samuel French)
Drama: Act I, pp. 5–10, Don (late 40s) and Bob (30–40)

Bob's job was to tail the man with the coin collection and not to let him out of sight. When the man went into a building, however, Bob lost him and came slinking back to the junk shop to report his failure to Don, the mastermind behind the coin heist. Don is worried that Bob's failure to follow instructions to the letter might jeopardize the entire caper, so he tries to teach Bob the principles of successful street survival. Start, Don: "So?…So what, Bob?" End, Don: "Well, we'll see."

Drama: Act I, pp. 22–32, Don (late 40s) and Teach (35–45)

Teach presses Don for details of his plan to steal the coin collection. When Teach finds out that the heist might result in a great deal of money, he maneuvers to cut Bob out of the picture. Start, Teach: "So what is this thing with the kid?" End, Teach: "…you can take your 90 dollars for a nickel, shove it up your ass—the good it did you—and you want to know why? (And I'm not saying anything…) Because you didn't take the time to go first class."

Drama: Act II, pp. 54–60, Don (late 40s) and Teach (35–45)

Teach and Don make last-minute plans for pulling off the coin-collection robbery. Ultimately, however, they don't go through with it. The entire scene between
the men runs eighteen pages and is too long for most workshops. Try this excerpt,
which begins after Bob's exit. Start, Don: "Fuckin' kid." End, Teach: "Because I got
the balls to face some facts? You scare me sometimes, Don."

AMERICAN PLAN, THE
by Richard Greenberg (Dramatists Play Service)

Drama: Act II, Scene 2, pp. 44–49, Nick (20s) and Gil (28–35)

When Gil kisses Nick briefly on the mouth in this scene, the moment shocks
audience members because, up until this point, they thought both men were heterosexual. The truth is that Gil and Nick are lovers, and Gil has followed Nick to
a Catskills resort in an effort to rekindle their romance. Complex characters, well-
written scene. Start, Gil: "I sat at the bar through last call. This woman in a grey
beehive kept ordering Brandy Alexanders." End, Nick: "I'm a man who chooses
moats."

ANDERSONVILL TRIAL, THE
by Saul Levitt (Dramatists Play Service)

Drama: Act I, Scene 2, pp. 47–49, Chipman (31) and Hosmer (30–45)

Two weeks into the trial of Confederate Army officer Henry Wirz, Colonel
Chipman still isn't sure whether he made a good case for the charge of conspiracy. More to the point, he wants to find a way to get the court to address the
broader question of moral responsibility. In this scene, Chipman and Hosmer, the
assistant judge advocate, consider whether or not to call a witness both men suspect is lying. His testimony will help convict Wirz, but the men wonder if they'll
be compromising their principles by calling him. Start, Hosmer: "Don't you see
what he's trying to do? Provoke you into playing the idealist here?" End, Hosmer:
"Sometimes, you make me feel so old."

ANGELS IN AMERICA: A GAY FANTASIA ON NATIONAL THEMES, PART I: MILLENNIUM APPROACHES
by Tony Kushner (Theatre Communications Group)

Drama: Act I, Scene 4, Louis (about 30) and Prior (30)

Louis and Prior are longtime lovers. After the funeral service for Louis's grandmother, they sit on a bench and talk about being Jewish and being gay. Then Prior
shows Louis a Kaposi's sarcoma lesion on his arm, an irrefutable sign of the pro-
gression of AIDS. Start, Louis: "My grandmother actually saw Emma Goldman
speak. In Yiddish. But all Grandma could remember was that she spoke well and
wore a hat." End, Louis: "Then I'll come home."

Drama: Act II, Scene 7, Joe (early 30s) and Louis (about 30)

Joe and Louis met by accident on the steps of the Hall of Justice. Louis is
depressed because his longtime lover is dying of AIDS, and Joe is tormented by
his shifting sexual preferences and crumbling marriage. As the men talk about
values during the Reagan era, their conversation takes on increasingly erotic
undertones. Start, Joe: "Can I...?" End, Louis: "You're scared. So am I. Everybody
is in the land of the free. God help us all."

ART
by Yasmina Reza (Faber and Faber)
Comedy: One-act play, pp. 1–5, Serge (30–40) and Marc (30–40)

Serge proudly shows Marc the new Antrios painting he has purchased. Instead of seeing a modern masterpiece, Marc sees only an outrageously expensive white-on-white waste of time. His reaction offends Serge. Start, Marc: "Expensive?" End, Marc: "…Obviously."

Comedy: One-act play, pp. 5–11, Marc (30–40) and Yvan (30–40)

Marc goes to Yvan's apartment to tell him about Serge's new purchase. Yvan's reaction frustrates Marc even more. Rather than express astonishment and disapproval with the purchase, Yvan says, "Well, if it makes him happy"—refusing to take an aesthetic position. Start with Marc's entrance, when Yvan is on his hands and knees searching for the cap to the felt pen. Marc: "What are you doing?" End, Yvan: "He'll laugh, you just wait."

BABY DANCE, THE
by Jane Anderson (Samuel French)
Comedy-Drama: Act II, Scene 1, pp. 50–56, Richard (30s) and Ron (30–50)

Richard and his wife, Rachel, have purchased the as-yet-unborn child of Wanda and Al, a dirt-poor Louisiana couple. Wanda has gone into labor, so Richard and Rachel have come to the hospital to witness the birth of "their" baby. Al shows up, however, and tries to ask for more money. Here, Richard and Ron, his lawyer, discuss tactics. Start, Richard: "Hello? Oh…yes, I'm trying to dial out." End, Richard: "I agree, my friend, I agree."

BENT
by Martin Sherman (Samuel French)
Drama: Act I, Scene 4, pp. 36–43, Max (34) and Rudy (30)

Hiding from the Gestapo, Max and Rudy pitch a tent in a camp near Cologne. Although they're broke and desperate, they still have their love. (At the very end of this scene, the offstage voice of a police officer orders Max and Rudy to surrender. It interrupts their song, riveting them. It would be effective to include that moment if possible.) Start, Rudy: "Cheese! Max!" End, Max and Rudy: "Will you forget me? Was I ever really there?"

Drama: Act I, Scene 6, pp. 51–57, Max (34) and Horst (30–40)

Max becomes friends with Horst in the camp. The audience learns that Max, a non-Jew, has managed to get a yellow star, which permits the wearer more camp privileges, instead of a pink star, which indicates he is a homosexual, by providing entertainment for the Nazi guards. Begin with Max's entrance as he crawls up next to Horst. Start, Max: "Hi…Here." Continue until the end of the scene. End, Max: "One. Two. Three. Four. Five. Six. Seven. Eight. Nine. Ten."

Drama: Act II, Scene 2, pp. 68–77, Max (34) and Horst (30–40)

Max and Horst are assigned to rock detail, which consists of moving a pile of heavy rocks from one place to another. After they move the pile, they must move it back to its original position. Then they do it again—all day, every day, with a three-minute break every two hours, during which they must stand at attention. This scene begins with Max and Horst moving the rocks and continues into the break. While at attention, they verbally go through an entire act of lovemaking.

Very graphic and sexual material. Start, Horst: "It's so hot." End, Max: "Do it in three minutes."

Drama: Act II, Scene 3, pp. 78–84, Max (34) and Horst (30–40)
As the men move rocks from one place to another and back, Horst tells Max that he has fallen in love with him. Start, Horst: "I'm going crazy. I'm going crazy." End, Horst: "Poor you, you don't love anybody. It's getting cold. Winter's coming."

BETRAYAL
by Harold Pinter (Dramatists Play Service)

Drama: One-act play, Scene 2, pp. 12–16, Jerry (30s) and Robert (30s)
Jerry is guilt ridden because Emma, his longtime lover, informed her husband, Robert, who is also Jerry's best friend, about their now-defunct affair. He asked Robert to drop by his home this evening for a private chat. During the scene, Robert discloses that he knew about the affair for years but opted to maintain a discreet silence. He tells Jerry that, at any rate, his marriage to Emma is on the rocks. Start, Jerry: "It's good of you to come." End, Jerry: "The Lake District."

BIRDY
Adapted from the William Wharton novel by Naomi Wallace (Broadway Play Publishing)

Drama: Act I, Scene 8, pp. 32–35, Doctor White (50) and Sergeant Al (22)
Dr. White is an Army doctor/psychiatrist, a by-the-book sort of man that is short on patience and long on arrogance. Sergeant Al is a mentally troubled young man, first as a result of an abusive childhood and most recently from the battles of World War II. Sergeant Al has been sent to Dr. White's Kentucky hospital for personal treatment and, not coincidentally, because Al's lifelong friend, Birdy, is being treated there. Birdy's case is a major frustration to Dr. White because Birdy will not communicate and has withdrawn into a mental space that White cannot fathom. The doctor hopes that Al might be able to help. In this scene, White presses Al to talk about the time he became violent with a fellow soldier; then he presses Al to talk about Birdy. During the scene, a character known as "Young Al" is also on stage. Cut him and eliminate his lines. Start, Dr. White: "Do you have any idea about the bizarre cringing positions he gets into?" End, Dr. White: "Just sit on the pot and shit. It's as simple and straightforward as that."

BITTER SAUCE
by Eric Bogosian (*Love's Fire—Seven New Plays Inspired by Seven Shakespearean Sonnets,* William Morrow)

Comedy: One-act play, Herman (20s) and Red (20s)
Red has been carrying on a sex-only relationship with Herman's fiancée, Rengin. He has arrived at her apartment intent on a pre-marriage roll in the hay with her since she is getting married tomorrow. Instead of Rengin, he encounters Herman, and so the two men have it out. Physically, Red is 100 percent Hell's Angels biker, and Herman is more of the accountant type, so when Herman dispatches Red, it is through his wits, not his brawn. This is only a three-page scene, but it is a toot. Start with Red's entrance. Red: "The fuck?" End, Herman: "You're dead."

BORN YESTERDAY
by Garson Kanin (Dramatists Play Service)
Comedy: Act I, pp. 34–37, Harry Brock (40s) and Ed Devery (50s)

Self-made millionaire and con man Harry Brock is worried that his dumb-but-beautiful girlfriend will embarrass him as he tries to wine and dine the Washington, DC, elite in an attempt to get them to pass legislation that is in his own best interest. Against the advice of his alcoholic lawyer, Ed Devery, Harry decides to hire the serious-minded journalist who lives down the hall to tutor the woman, to show her the ropes in Washington. Start, Brock: "She's gonna be in the way, that dame." End, Brock: "I don't believe in nothin' on no friendly basis."

BREAKING THE CODE
by Hugh Whitemore (Samuel French)
Drama: Act I, Scene 6, pp. 39–46, Turing (39) and Ron (20)

Turing picked up a young man, brought him home for a tryst and, this morning, discovers that he wants to be paid for his services. Start, Ron: "What's the time?" End, Turing: "Down the road, turn left."

Drama: Act I, Scene 8, pp. 55–60, Turing (39) and Ross (30–50)

Detective Sergeant Ross is investigating a minor burglary at Turing's home. He has learned that the pieces of Turing's story about the event don't hold together and figures that Turing must be lying to protect someone. In this scene, Turing reluctantly admits he was trying to conceal a homosexual relationship. Ross immediately responds to this new information by telling Turing that he has committed a crime by having sex with another man. Start, Turing: "Sergeant Ross." End, Turing: "Anyway…all right…Yes. I'll make a statement. You'll want me to go to the police station. I'd better get dressed."

BUTLEY
by Simon Gray (Samuel French)
Comedy-Drama: Act I, pp. 15–22, Ben (35–40) and Joey (mid-20s)

Ben's jealousy plays close to the surface in this confrontation with his lover/student, Joey. The scene is quite long, but this excerpt captures the flavor and underlying tensions of their relationship. Start, Ben: "You're in trouble, Joey." End, Joey: "That's right, he's a butcher."

Comedy-Drama: Act II, pp. 48–52, Ben (35–40) and Joey (mid-20s)

After a big argument with Anne, his estranged wife, Ben turns his hostility on his student/lover, Joey. Start, Ben: "If it's Anne you were hiding from, she's gone. If it's Edna, she hasn't arrived." End, Joey: "It doesn't matter. Let it go."

Comedy-Drama: Act II, pp. 57–66, Ben (35–40) and Reg (mid-30s)

Reg, Joey's new lover, has come to Ben's office to explain that Joey will be moving out of Ben's flat and in with him. What Reg doesn't know is that Ben has just learned that his wife, Anne, has announced that she's moving in with a new man, too. In fact, as Reg enters the scene, Ben is completing a mischief-making telephone call to Kent Vale Comprehensive, the school where his wife's new lover works. The scene bristles with jealousy. Start, Ben: "Come." End, Reg: "It's worked out quite well though, hasn't it?" For a shorter version of the dialogue, end the first time they toast each other. End, Reg: "Cheers."

CANDIDA
by George Bernard Shaw (Signet)

Comedy-Drama: Act III, Marchbanks (18) and Morell (40)

Morell's wife, Candida, has just left the room. Marchbanks and Morell get into a full-tilt argument about which of them is the better man for her. Finally, Marchbanks proposes that Candida choose. This is a dynamic five-page scene. Start, Morell: "Well?" End, Marchbanks: "Send for her, Morell. Send for her and let her choose between us."

CAT ON A HOT TIN ROOF
by Tennessee Williams (Dramatists Play Service)

Drama: Act II, pp. 47–59, Brick (27) and Big Daddy (65)

Brick tells Big Daddy why he drinks so much. For workshop purposes, try this excerpt from the act-long confrontation between the men. Eliminate the lines of the various family members who come and go. Start, Big Daddy: "What makes you so restless?" End, Brick: "I'm sorry, Big Daddy."

CHAPTER TWO
by Neil Simon (Samuel French)

Comedy-Drama: Act I, Scene 9, pp. 59–68, George (42) and Leo (40)

George surprises Leo, his brother, with the news that he is marrying Jennie after a two-week courtship. Leo is very worried and tries to talk George into waiting. Update Leo's reference to Jimmy Carter. Start, Leo: "George, will you let somebody else in New York use the phone?" End, Leo: "I don't know what the hell I'm doing in publicity. I was born to be a Jewish mother."

CHASE, THE
by Horton Foote (Dramatists Play Service)

Drama: Act II, Scene 1, pp. 33–37, Sheriff Hawes (40–45) and Damon (40–45)

The outlaw everyone is hunting for broke into Damon's store last night, ripping up clothes and trashing the place. Damon is scared and angry, and he accuses Sheriff Hawes of not properly protecting him. Hawes pleads for patience and says he'll get the criminal. Using a Texas accent is helpful but not essential. Start, Damon: "Did you see my store?" End, Damon: "All right."

Drama: Act II, Scene 1, pp. 38–40, Sheriff Hawes (40–45) and Edwin (early 30s)

Edwin Stewart, the nervous, high-strung son of the town banker, wants the sheriff to guard his house, but Hawes can't spare anybody. Edwin threatens to reject Hawe's loan application. Omit the reference to Ruby. Start, Edwin: "Hello…Hawes." End, Edwin: "And my wife has a lot of friends, and every one of them is gonna hear of your treatment of us."

CLOSER
by Patrick Marber (Dramatists Play Service)

Drama: Act II, Scene 10, pp. 93–101, Dan (35) and Larry (mid-30s)

Note: Brief telephone/intercom sequences interrupts this scene twice. Simply eliminate them both. Dan shows up at Larry's office, saying that he wants Anna back. By the end of the scene, Larry has convinced Dan that he actually loves Alice. Dan breaks down and cries, then he exits to go find Alice. This is a very strong and difficult scene with a good deal of subtext. It is absolutely essential that actors in workshop carefully study the *entire* play before attempting it. Start, Larry: "So?" End after Dan's exit. Dan: "I'm just…not…big enough to forgive you."

DANCE AND THE RAILROAD, THE
by David Henry Hwang (Dramatists Play Service)
Comedy-Drama: Scene 3, pp. 23–29, Lone (20) and Ma (18)
To pass the time during a labor strike against the railroad, Lone, one of the Asian-American workers, has gone off by himself to practice opera dances. Ma, another worker, watches from the bushes for a while and then asks for instruction. In this scene, Lone tells Ma how much dedication being in the opera requires. Start, Ma: "How long will it be before I can play Gwan Gung?" End, Ma: "If you do, you're crazy. Lone? Come back here."

DEATH AND THE MAIDEN
by Ariel Dorfman (Penguin)
Drama: Act II, Scene 2, Gerardo (45) and Roberto (50)
Gerardo feeds the captive Roberto, who is tied to a chair, and tells him that he is going to have to confess to the crimes Paulina is accusing him of if he wants his freedom. Roberto professes his innocence. Eliminate Paulina's brief appearance in the scene. Start, Gerardo: "You're not hungry, Doctor Miranda?" End, Gerardo: "I'm going to tell her that you need to piss."

DEATH OF A SALESMAN
by Arthur Miller (Dramatists Play Service)
Drama: Act I, pp. 12–18, Biff (34) and Happy (32)
Brothers Biff and Happy are in their bedroom, talking about their aspirations, their relationship with their father, and the past. Start, Happy: "He's going to get his license taken away." End, Biff: "I was the only one he'd let lock up the place."

DINNER WITH FRIENDS
by Donald Margulies (Theatre Communications Group)
Comedy-Drama: Act I, Scene 3, pp. 37–42, Tom (40s) and Gabe (40s)
Gabe is dismayed to learn that his best friend, Tom, is leaving his wife after twelve years (and two kids) of marriage. He is encouraging Tom to see a therapist or family counselor and work things out. Tom is trying to get Gabe's tacit approval for the divorce. Start after Karen exits. Gabe: Boy, if this is any indication of what it would be like if *I* ever…" End, Tom: "See ya."
Comedy-Drama: Act II, Scene 3, pp. 70–79, Tom (40s) and Gabe (40s)
Gabe and Tom meet in a Manhattan bar five months after Tom has separated from his wife, Karen. During the conversation, it becomes clear that the men's longtime friendship—going all the way back to college—is over. They have come to that fork in the road. Excellent scene, mainly for all that is left unsaid. Start, Tom: "Gabe!" End, Gabe: "Bye."

DIVISION STREET
by Steve Tesich (Samuel French)
Comedy: Act I, pp. 33–39, Chris (37) and Roger (mid-30s)
Roger, dressed as an old bum, complete with gray wig, shows up in Chris's apartment. Full of guilt for selling out, Roger wants Chris to take up the 1960s left-

wing banner again and lead a new revolution. Chris wants no part of it; he has gone straight and is no longer a radical. Start, Chris: "Who's there? Who are you?" End, Roger: "You go right ahead, man…Dream on, man!"

DOES A TIGER WEAR A NECKTIE?
by Don Petersen (Dramatists Play Service)

Drama: Act II, Scene 1, pp. 43–51, Winters (35) and Bickham (20)
Of all the inmates, Bickham has the biggest chip on his shoulder and is the one most likely to start a fight. In this scene between Bickham and Pete Winters, the English teacher, the audience discovers that he is also remarkably sensitive and has the makings of a writer. Start, Bickham: "Gimme your wallet, lame, or I'll break your back." End, Bickham: "You know what I really want, Pete? I'll tell ya what I want…I want…I can't remember."

Drama: Act II, Scene 2, pp. 55–67, Werner (40s) and Bickham (20)
This scene is almost a one-act play in itself. Bickham tells Werner, the staff psychiatrist, how, after a long search, he found his father working in a barbershop and how he came to brutally beat up the man. This emotionally violent, sometimes physical scene definitely isn't suited for novice actors. Start, Werner: "Well? Come in Bickham." Continue through the end of Act II. End, Bickham: "Ayieeeee!! God! God!" For a shorter version, try this excerpt. Start, Bickham: "You ain't the Great White Doctor you think you are!" Continue to the same end.

END OF THE WORLD WITH SYMPOSIUM TO FOLLOW, THE
by Arthur Kopit (Samuel French)

Comedy-Drama: Act I, pp. 26–32, Trent (35–45) and Stone (60s)
Stone is trying to commission Trent to write a play about the imminent end of the world. Trent is convinced that Stone is crazy and, despite the offer of money, he wants no part of this. You'll need a pistol for this scene, but you don't have to fire it. Start, Stone: "Your agent informs me you have certain reservations about my scenario." End, Stone: "I hope you take this job. Good day."

ENEMY OF THE PEOPLE, AN
by Henrik Ibsen (adapted by Arthur Miller, Dramatists Play Service)

Drama: Act I, Scene 2, pp. 28–32, Peter (30s) and Thomas (30s)
Peter is convinced that his brother's discovery of local water pollution will lead their small city into financial ruin, carrying him and his political opportunities along with it. In this very excellent scene, Peter orders Thomas to publicly disavow the scientific reports. Thomas refuses, reacting first with surprise and then with fury to his brother's request. Eliminate Catherine's line at the beginning of the scene. Start, Peter: "I received your thesis about the condition of the Springs yesterday." End, Peter: "I forbid you as your superior, and when I give orders you obey."

Drama: Act III, pp. 65–68, Peter (30s) and Thomas (30s)
Peter has succeeded in turning the town against his brother, but he wants to ensure that Thomas doesn't go somewhere else in Norway to publicize his charges of water pollution and corrupt local politics. Peter outlines possible criminal charges that can be brought against Thomas if he goes public anywhere at all. Start, Thomas: "Keep your hat on if you like, it's a little draughty in here today." End, Thomas: "Oh, we do, Peter!"

FAR COUNTRY, A
by Henry Denker (Samuel French)
Drama: Act II, Scene 1, pp. 43–51, Freud (37) and Breuer (35–45)

Freud is convinced there are significant similarities between his patient, Elizabeth, and one being treated by Dr. Breuer. Freud gets his reluctant friend to fill in the blanks that are missing from his final case report. Breuer is nervous that Freud, already controversial for his hypnotism experiments, will jump to conclusions, go public with them, and discredit both men. Breuer is full of guilt over this particular case because he fell in love with the patient. You'll have to cut and paste a bit at the end, eliminating Martha. Start, Freud: "A Schnapps?" End, Freud: "Agreed."

FENCES
by August Wilson (Samuel French)
Drama: Act I, Scene 3, pp. 33–40, Troy (53) and Cory (17)

Troy tells his son, Cory, why he doesn't want him to go to college on a football scholarship, why it is better for him to stay away from sports. Cory, of course, disagrees. Start, Troy: "You just now coming in here from leaving this morning?" End, Troy: "Then get the hell out of my face, and get on down to that A&P."

FOOL FOR LOVE
by Sam Shepard (Dramatists Play Service)
Comedy-Drama: One-act play, pp. 28–34, Eddie (late 30s) and Martin (mid-30s)

May goes into the bathroom to get dressed for her date with Martin, leaving Eddie and Martin alone. Eddie shocks Martin by telling him that May is his half-sister and that they've fooled around. Start, Martin: "She's not made or anything, is she?" Eliminate all the Old Man's lines. End, Eddie: "But the second we saw each other, that very second, we knew we'd never stop being in love."

GENIUSES
by Jonathan Reynolds (Samuel French)
Comedy: Act I, pp. 10–16, Jocko (33) and Bart (57)

Bart, the makeup man who is a dead ringer for Ernest Hemingway, pines for the long-gone simple days of movie-making, when men were men and the titles made sense. He thinks he could do a better job than Jocko, the screenwriter, is doing. Start, Jocko: "Started without us, I see." End, Bart: "There's your ending. How about this? He lives…but with a big wound."

Comedy: Act III, pp. 61–67, Jocko (33) and Milo (32)

Milo tells Jocko, the screenwriter, about the frustrations of being a star movie director. You'll have to cut and paste a bit. After Milo's line, "Well, we have two choices. Talk her out of pressing charges, or kill her. Just kidding, Jocko." Cut to Milo, continuing with: "God, I hate this picture." Then start, Milo: "Now that's what I like to see!" End, Milo: "Which is almost as much fun as making money."

GLENGARRY GLEN ROSS
by David Mamet (Samuel French)
Drama: Act I, Scene 1, pp. 7–15, Williamson (40s) and Levene (50s)

Levene's sales are slumping, so he is trying to get Williamson to give him some hot leads. He offers a bribe, which Williamson takes. Start, Levene: "John…John…John.

Okay, John. John." End, Levene: "Good. Mmm…I, you know, I left my wallet back at the hotel."

Comedy-Drama: Act I, Scene 2, pp. 15–27, Moss (50s) and Aaronow (50s)

Moss tries to con Aaronow, another salesman, into robbing the company office. Long scene, but David Mamet's dialogue moves quickly. Start, Moss: "Polacks and deadbeats." End, Moss: "Because you listened." For a shorter version, start, Moss: "Look at Jerry Graff. He's clean." Continue to the same ending.

GOAT, THE (OR, WHO IS SYLVIA?)
by Edward Albee (Dramatists Play Service)

Comedy-Drama: Scene 1, pp. 12–23, Martin (50) and Ross (50s)

The occasion is Martin's fiftieth birthday. His friend Ross is a TV producer who decides to do an interview with Martin, not only because of his fiftieth birthday but because he recently won the Pritzker Prize, architecture's equivalent of the Nobel Prize. Martin is puzzlingly ill at ease during the interview. Finally he admits to Ross that he has fallen in love—with a goat. Start, Ross: "OK? Ready? Ready Martin; here we go; just…be yourself." Go to the end of Scene 1.

Drama: Scene 3, pp. 44–50, Martin (50) and Billy (17)

Martin's gay son, Billy, simply cannot come to grips with the news that his father is in love with—and having sex with—a goat. This is an extremely difficult scene for both actors but is particularly difficult for the actor playing the son because of the required emotional range—from outrage, fury, grief, crying, to full-tilt mouth-to-mouth kiss. It is definitely not a good choice for novice actors. Start at the top of Scene 3. Billy: "Wow!" Go through the kiss on page 50. End, Martin: "No; it's all right. Here; let me hold you."

GOOSE AND TOMTOM
by David Rabe (Samuel French)

Drama: Act I, pp. 10–18, Goose (30s) and Tomtom (40s)

When Goose arrives, his friend Tomtom is happy to see him. They show each other their guns, tell each other their nightmares, and talk about Bingo's sister. At this point, the audience doesn't know that she is, in fact, being held captive in a back room. These characters are violent and dangerous, at times acting more like animals than humans. For experienced actors only. Start, Goose: "Hey." End, Tomtom: "Hey! How you? 'At's what I been waitin' for. I been onna edge a my chair."

Drama: Act I, pp. 50–56, Goose (30s) and Tomtom (40s)

Lorraine has discovered that the jewels have been stolen, and she is very angry. In this scene, Goose and Tomtom develop a plan to steal some money and buy more jewels in order to make Lorraine happy again. Start, Tomtom: "We gonna make a plan!" End, Tomtom: "We thought it was ghosts stealin' our secrets, but it was really Bingo stealin' our treasure."

HOOTERS
by Ted Tally (Dramatists Play Service)

Comedy: Act I, Scene 1, pp. 7–12, Ricky (19) and Clint (19)

Clint is home from college on a break, so he and his old high-school buddy Ricky have come to Cape Cod for some hell-raising. In this scene, they're settling into their motel room while they talk about hot babes in very graphic terms. Ricky is excited because he thinks he saw a "Ten" in the parking lot. Start, Ricky: "Did you see that?" End, Ricky: "An Ab-so-lute Ten."

Comedy: Act I, Scene 4, pp. 28–31, Ricky (19) and Clint (19)

Clint and Ricky have hooked up with a couple of older women and have invited them out to dinner. Back in the motel room, the guys are working on a game plan to get the women into bed. Basically, the plan amounts to "surprise, beer, dirty talk, divide and conquer." Start, Clint: "You piece of grunt." End, Clint: "Which one of us is going to walk the dog?"

HURLYBURLY
by David Rabe (Samuel French)

Comedy-Drama: Act I, Scene 1, pp. 9–19, Phil (mid-30s) and Eddie (mid-30s)

Phil arrives to tell a very hungover Eddie that he has had a terrible fight with his wife, during which he hit her with his fist. David Rabe has specific ideas about how this ten-page scene should be played: "It is important to note that there is an element of play in this whole scene…; on some level, it is a game, a riff." Start, Phil: "Eddie." End, Eddie: "I wouldn't piss on her if the flames were about to engulf her goddamn, you know, central nervous system!"

Comedy-Drama: Act I, Scene 1, pp. 27–33, Eddie (mid-30s) and Mickey (mid-30s)

Eddie is distressed because Mickey made an apparently successful play for his new girlfriend yesterday. Also, his ex-wife called again, which always puts him in a foul mood. Start, Mickey: "Do you realize, Eddie, that you are not toking up at eight fifty-eight in the morning on top of the shit you already put up your nose?" End, Eddie: "What do you want me to do, abandon my kid in her hands and with no other hope? Forget about it!"

Comedy-Drama: Act I, Scene 3, pp. 61–69, Phil (mid-30s) and Eddie (mid-30s)

When he arrives at the house, Phil is full of manic energy. He tells Eddie that he is returning to his wife because he is lost without her. He also admits that he has been taking some kind of poison in order to sabotage his sperm count. Eddie is alternately sympathetic and shocked. Start, Phil: "So, guess what?" End, Phil: "I come here to tell you. I got to stay married. I'm lost without her."

I HATE HAMLET
by Paul Rudnick (Dramatists Play Service)

Comedy: Act I, Scene 1, pp. 23–29, Andrew (27–33) and Barrymore (45–50)

Andrew's temporary New York apartment turns out to be haunted by John Barrymore's ghost, who moves in and out of the proceedings. The ghost tries to help Andrew prepare for the daunting task of playing the title role in *Hamlet*. In this scene, Barrymore gives Andrew some advice on acting and romance. Start, Barrymore: "Dear fellow…May I?" End, Barrymore: "You would prefer, perhaps, some form of therapy? Continued discussion? What is the present-day epithet—'communication'?"

IMMIGRANT, THE
by Mark Harelik (Broadway Play Publishing)

Comedy-Drama: Act I, Scene 5, Haskell (20s) and Milton (30)

Haskell Harelik has lived in an upstairs room in Ida and Milton Perry's house for six weeks, paying his way as a banana peddler. In this funny scene, Milton summons Haskell to his office at the bank and advises him on ways to expand his business, including the notion of buying a horse. Milton offers to finance the purchase for Haskell. The language barrier is what makes this dialogue funny. Haskell speaks, at best, broken English with a heavy Russian accent, and Milton is a no-nonsense Texan. The year is 1909. Start, Haskell: "Mr. Perry?" End, Haskell: "At home, yes. You draw very good!"

I NEVER SANG FOR MY FATHER
by Robert Anderson (Dramatists Play Service)
Drama: Act II, pp. 55–62, Gene (40) and Tom (late 70s)

Gene has decided that he wants to remarry and move to California, where his soon-to-be wife already lives and has a medical practice. In doing so, however, he'll be leaving his elderly father, Tom, alone in New York to fend for himself. In this climactic scene, the last one in a remarkable script, Gene tells his father about his decision and asks him to move to California, too. Tom won't hear of it, accusing his son of abandoning him and of being ungrateful. Powerful, primal material. Start, Gene: "You ready to be tucked in?" End, Tom: "Go to hell!"

K2
by Patrick Meyers (Dramatists Play Service)
Drama: One-act play, pp. 17–23, Harold (mid-30s) and Taylor (38)

Two mountain climbers are trying to escape from an ice ledge on the side of one of the world's highest mountains. Most of the time, Taylor is in the process of climbing up and down ropes, thereby rendering scenework impractical. In this excerpt, however, both men are at rest. It captures the basic relationship between them and also highlights their philosophical differences. Harold is a political liberal given to existential explorations, while Taylor is conservative and pragmatic. Start, Harold: "Taylor…I've got an idea." End, Taylor: "Now if you have any helpful suggestions…just…fucking…say…so!"

KILLER JOE
by Tracy Letts (Samuel French)
Comedy-Drama: Act I, Scene 1, pp. 13–17, Chris (22) and Ansel (38)

Chris has gotten into debt because of his involvement in the drug scene and approaches his father, Ansel, for a loan. Ansel has no money at all and, in fact, lives in a run-down house trailer outside of Dallas. Chris then proposes to Ansel that the two of them hire an assassin to kill Chris's mother (Ansel's ex-wife) so that they can collect on her insurance policy. Start, Ansel: "Now look what you did. I'm in the doghouse." End, Chris: "…they'll be considered accomplices."

LARGO DESOLATO
by Václav Havel (translated by Tom Stoppard, Grove Weidenfeld)
Comedy-Drama: Scene 4, Bertram (35–45) and Leopold (45–50)

Bertram is an emissary for unnamed intellectuals. He has come to Leopold's flat to see about his mental health and to encourage him to continue to defy the government. Cut Lucy's offstage lines and Leopold's responses. Start, Bertram: "How long is it since you went out?" End, Bertram: "So, I beg you—Be again that brilliant Leopold Nettles whom everybody held on high!"

LAST YANKEE, THE
by Arthur Miller (Dramatists Play Service)
Drama: One-act play, pp. 5–14, Leroy (48) and Frick (60)
Two men meet for the first time in the waiting room of a New York state mental hospital where both of their wives are being treated for depression. Frick is upscale, has money, and is impressed by appearances. Leroy, though a direct descendant of Alexander Hamilton and the son of a lawyer, is a carpenter by trade and cares nothing about appearances. Frick's pretentiousness makes Leroy angry, and this emotion confuses Frick. Do the entire play, which is only nine pages long.

LIE OF THE MIND, A
by Sam Shepard (Dramatists Play Service)
Comedy-Drama: Act I, Scene 3, pp. 13–18, Jake (28–35) and Frankie (late 20s)
Jake has beaten up his wife again. This time, however, he thinks that he has killed her, so he heads south. In this scene, Jake is holed up in a shabby motel in southern California with Frankie, his younger brother, while he tries to clear his head and consider his options. Start, Jake: "I don't want any goddamn ice! It's cold!" End, Frankie: "I won't."

LIFE AND LIMB
by Keith Reddin (Dramatists Play Service)
Drama: Act I, Scene 8, pp. 27–31, Franklin (mid-to-late 20s) and Tod (mid-to-late 20s)
Franklin applies for a job at Tod Cartmell's prosthetic-device factory. Tod is sadistic, and this very difficult material involves sexual humiliation and isn't for novice actors. Start, Tod: "How you all doing?" End, Tod: "You got the job."

LISBON TRAVIATA, THE
by Terrence McNally (Dramatists Play Service)
Comedy: Act I, pp. 30–38, Mendy (35–45) and Stephen (25–35)
The entire act is a two-character scene between two gay men in which they discuss their love for opera and their various romantic involvements. You'll need a telephone that rings. For scene-study purposes, begin about halfway through the act. Start, Mendy: "There is only one Tosca." Continue to the end of the act.

LITTLE FOXES, THE
by Lillian Hellman (Dramatists Play Service)
Drama: Act II, pp. 31–34, Oscar (late 40s) and Leo (20)
Father and son test the waters to determine precisely how dishonest each is. When Oscar learns that Leo, his son, has been snooping in his employer's safe-deposit box down at the bank, Oscar raises the prospect of "borrowing" the $80,000 worth of Union-Pacific bonds kept there. Start, Leo: "The boys in the bank don't know a thing. They haven't had any message." End, Oscar: "People ought to help other people. But that's not always the way it happens. And so sometimes you got to think of yourself."

LOBBY HERO
by Kenneth Lonergan (Dramatists Play Service)
Comedy-Drama: Act II, Scene 1, pp. 42–47, William (late 20s) and Jeff (27)
William's younger brother is in deep trouble with the police, accused of participating in a group-rape and murder. In Act I, William told Jeff that he was considering whether to provide a false alibi for his brother, saying that he was leaning
against it. He wouldn't want to do anything dishonest. In this scene, Jeff asks how
things are going with the brother and learns that William has shifted his position
radically. He has gone to the police and provided the alibi. Jeff is stunned because
he admires William and really did not expect him to do something unethical,
even to help his own brother. This is a strong scene with a nice transition in the
middle and plenty of negotiations. Start, Jeff: "Does it ever strike you as stupid
that you're 'The Captain'?" End, William: "…I still need a little time to try to find
him a decent lawyer, so at least he has a chance."

LONELY IMPULSE OF DELIGHT, A
by John Patrick Shanley (*Welcome to the Moon and Other Plays*, Dramatists Play Service; *13 by Shanley*, Applause Books)
Comedy: One-act play, Dramatists Play Service pp. 35–37, Walter (25–35) and Jim (25–35)
Walter is in love with a mermaid who lives in New York City's Central Park
Reservoir, and he brings his friend Jim to see her. Jim, understandably, doesn't
think it is smart to be in Central Park in the middle of the night, especially since
he was enjoying himself at a good party. Sally the Mermaid doesn't appear, and
Jim, who has run out of patience, leaves. Walter then sends some more secret sig-
nals out across the lake and Sally shows up. Or does she? An offstage actress will
have to read one line at the very end. Start, Jim: "What are we doing out here,
Walter?" End, Walter: "And I you. My solitary, unprovable, deepest only love."

LONG DAY'S JOURNEY INTO NIGHT
by Eugene O'Neill (Yale University Press)
Drama: Act I, James Tyrone (65) and Jamie (33)
Father and son thrust and parry. James accuses Jamie of spending all his money
on whores and liquor and of being a bad influence on his brother, Edmund. Jamie
accuses his father of being a miser. Both agree to keep wife/mother Mary calm,
hoping she won't start with morphine again—but knowing that she already has.
Start, Tyrone: "You're a fine lunkhead!" End, Jamie: "Well, if we're going to cut the
front hedge today, we'd better go to work."
Drama: Act II, Scene 1, Jamie (33) and Edmund (23)
After Jamie catches Edmund having a drink, the brothers have a heated discussion about their mother, Mary. This scene exposes the nature of Jamie and
Edmund's relationship. Start, Jamie: "Sneaking one, eh?" End, Jamie: "Damn! I
wish I'd grabbed another drink."

LUV
by Murray Schisgal (Dramatists Play Service)
Comedy: Act I, pp. 10–17, Milt (late 30s) and Harry (late 30s)
Milt discovers his old college chum Harry trying to commit suicide by jumping
off a bridge. Milt talks him out of it and then discovers that Harry is struggling

with existential angst. They wind up dueling about who had the worst childhood. The dark humor in this seven-page scene is very funny stuff. Start, Milt: "Is it…No, Harry Berlin!" End, Harry: "They were cinnamon donuts!"

MAN FOR ALL SEASONS, A
by Robert Bolt (Samuel French)
Drama: Act I, pp. 45–50, Henry VIII (25–35) and Thomas More (late 40s)
Henry VIII is searching for a legal, Church-approved way to divorce his queen, Catherine, so he can marry Anne Boleyn, with whom he hopes to produce a male heir to the throne. In his effort to influence the Catholic hierarchy, he seeks the support of his Lord Chancellor, Sir Thomas More. More is a very respected and influential man, but so far has diplomatically resisted the king's entreaties. In this scene, Henry tries once again. Start, Henry: "Listen to this, Thomas. Do you know it?" End, Henry: "I must catch the tide or I'll not get back to Richmond till…No, don't come. Tell Norfolk."

Drama: Act I, pp. 60–65, Richard Rich (early 30s) and Thomas Cromwell (late 30s)
Thomas Cromwell, former secretary to the Lord Chancellor, Cardinal Wolsey, lost his position of influence when Wolsey fell from favor and died (or was killed). Now working as an aide to the king, Cromwell is intent on increasing his influence by toppling Sir Thomas More, the new Lord Chancellor. In this scene, Cromwell bribes Richard Rich, Secretary/Librarian to the Duke of Norfolk and a confidante of More, trading a favored post for incriminating information. Start, Cromwell: "Come on. Yes, it may be that I am a little intoxicated." End, Rich: "You enjoyed that! You enjoyed that! You enjoyed it!"

MISTER ROBERTS
by Thomas Heggen and Joshua Logan (Dramatists Play Service)
Drama: Act I, Scene 1, pp. 6–9, Roberts (25–32) and Doc (35–40)
While on watch last night, Roberts saw a convoy of American battleships heading for battle, and the sight made him long all the more to get into the action. In this scene, he shows Doc his latest request for a transfer, but Doc tells him that it is futile—that he is going to succeed only in making the captain angrier. Start, Doc: "That you, Doug?" End, Doc: "I wish you hadn't seen that task force, Doug. Well, I've got to go down to my hypochondriacs."

Drama: Act I, Scene 6, pp. 39–42, Roberts (25–32) and the Captain (40–50)
Roberts reluctantly strikes a deal with the Captain in which Roberts agrees to stop being a troublemaker in exchange for a shore leave for his crew. Start, Captain: "Come in, Mister Roberts." End, Roberts: "Listen to those crazy bastards out there. Listen to them."

MODIGLIANI
by Dennis McIntyre (Samuel French)
Drama: Act I, Scene 3, pp. 18–25, Modigliani (31) and Zborowski (30s)
Modigliani's agent, Zborowski, tells Modigliani that he is going to show his work to a prominent gallery owner. Modigliani, however, has his mind on escaping the police who are after him for breaking a restaurant window. Start, Modigliani: "Zbo? Zborowski?…Zbo—be home." End, Zborowski: "He'll buy faces."

Drama: Act II, Scene 1, pp. 36–43, Modigliani (31) and Utrillo (33)

Modigliani, on the run from the law, goes to Utrillo to see if he can borrow some money. He discovers that Utrillo, who is always drunk, has signed up to join the army and plans to leave the following morning. But this is an impossible plan because Utrillo is frail and physically unfit. Start, Modigliani: "Maumau?" End, Modigliani: "I won't let you do it! I won't let you ruin it! There's nobody left after Cheron. I won't let you ruin it!"

MURDER AT THE HOWARD JOHNSON'S
by Ron Clark and Sam Bobrick (Samuel French)
Comedy: Act II, pp. 46–54, Paul (40–45) and Mitchell (36)

Arlene has abandoned both Paul and Mitchell in favor of a relationship with her guru. The men are waiting in a room at the Howard Johnson's Motel for her to arrive so that they can kill her. They plan to hang Arlene and have a scaffold built in the hotel room. You'll have to be inventive to approximate this set piece. Fortunately, it doesn't have to be practical or workable. Start, Paul: "You know, I've got six towels from this place already. How are you doing?" End, Paul: "Oh, it's going to be good with her out of the way."

NERD, THE
by Larry Shue (Dramatists Play Service)
Comedy: Act II, Scene 1, pp. 53–57, Willum (34) and Rick (30s)

Willum has tried to tell his unwelcome houseguest, Rick, that he should leave but has been unsuccessful. Begin the scene as Willum rehearses what he is going to say to Rick when he arrives. Start, Willum: "Now, Rick. Rick, sit down…Put down your tambourine." End, Rick: "Sit there, now—and don't move. I'll be in here heating up the salt!"

NUMBER, A
by Caryl Churchill (Theatre Communications Group)
Drama: Scene 1, pp. 10–21, Salter (early 60s) and Bernard aka B2 (35)

Bernard has recently learned that he may well be the result of a cloning experiment. He confronts his father about it but receives very few satisfactory answers. Start, Bernard: "A number." End, Bernard: "Probably."

Drama: Scene 2, pp. 24–34, Salter (early 60s) and Bernard aka B1 (40)

This Bernard (B1) is the actual son from which the others were cloned. His temperament, due to childhood abuse, is quite different from the Bernard we met in Scene 1. He is more aggressive and has a lot more inner rage. Salter continues to be evasive and difficult, but we in the audience are gradually filling in the blanks of these complicated relationships. Start, Salter: "So they stole—don't look at me—they stole your genetic material…" End, Bernard: "No, look in my eyes. No, keep looking. Look."

Drama: Scene 3, pp. 36–46, Salter (early 60s) and Bernard aka B2 (35)

Bernard (B2) reports back to his father after an encounter with Bernard (B1). Salter finally admits that his wife did not die in a car crash. She committed suicide by jumping in front of a train. We learn more about Salter's motives for agreeing to the cloning. Bernard (B2) says he is afraid of the other Bernard (B1) and intends to leave the country. Start, Bernard: "Not like me at all." End, Bernard: "Also, I'm afraid he'll kill me."

Drama: Scene 5, pp. 54–62, Salter (early 60s) and Michael Black (35)

By this point in time, Bernard (B1) has murdered Bernard (B2) and subsequently committed suicide. Salter has made it a priority to go ahead and meet some of the other clones. Here he tries to get to know Michael Black. The interesting thing is that the apple/clone has evidently fallen a bit farther from the tree, and these two men have very little in common. Salter becomes quite frustrated when he can't seem to learn anything significantly personal about this new "son" in his life. Start, Michael: "Have you met the others?" End, Michael: "I do yes, sorry."

ODD COUPLE, THE (MALE VERSION)
by Neil Simon (Samuel French)

Comedy: Act I, pp. 30–40, Oscar (43) and Felix (44)

In the name of friendship, Oscar invites Felix, his fastidious friend who is suffering over the breakup of his marriage, to move in with him. In this scene, the audience learns how very different the men are. Oscar and Felix's interactions are quite funny, but there isn't a great deal of overt conflict in this particular scene. It is simply good situational comedy. You'll need a telephone that rings and as much room clutter as you can manage. Start, Oscar: "Ohh, Felix, Felix, Felix, Felix!" Continue to the end of Act I. End, Felix: "Good night, Frances."

Comedy: Act II, Scene 1, pp. 47–55, Oscar (43) and Felix (44)

Felix and Oscar have been living together for two weeks, and already Felix is driving Oscar crazy with his fanatical and obsessive cleanliness. Here, Felix reluctantly agrees to a double date with the Pigeon sisters who live in an upstairs apartment. Start, Oscar: "I'd be immensely grateful to you, Felix, if you didn't clean up just now." End, Felix: "Frances. I want to get her recipe for London broil. The girls'll be crazy about it."

Comedy: Act II, Scene 2, pp. 56–59, Oscar (43) and Felix (44)

In this hysterically funny scene, the men await the arrival of their dates. Felix becomes apoplectic because the gourmet meal he has prepared is ruined by Oscar's cavalier attention to a dinner schedule. Start, Oscar: "I'm home, dear!" End, Oscar: "Then smile."

Comedy: Act III, pp. 73–82, Oscar (43) and Felix (44)

This scene has the most head-to-head conflict and is, arguably, the most difficult one to play. It takes place the day after the disastrous date with the Pigeon sisters, and Oscar seems bent on getting Felix to move out. Felix is playing the part of the wounded bird. At the end, Felix takes his suitcase and leaves—and moves in with the Pigeon sisters upstairs. You'll need a vacuum cleaner, a plate of pasta, and an offstage arrangement that will allow you to toss the pasta against the kitchen wall. Begin at the top of Act III. Start, Felix: "All right, how much longer is this gonna go on?" End, Felix: "Oh, come on, Oscar. You're not really interested, are you?"

OF MICE AND MEN
by John Steinbeck (Dramatists Play Service)

Drama: Act I, Scene 1, pp. 7–16, George (30–40) and Lennie (30–40)

In this scene George and his mentally slow sidekick Lennie pitch camp by a river, and audience members get their first glimpse into the men's relationship. We learn that they had to flee from northern California because Lennie was falsely accused of rape, that George is the smarter of the two, and that Lennie is physically powerful but mentally childlike. They talk about the farm they hope to have one day. This fifteen-minute scene can run half an hour if you aren't careful. Start, George: "Lennie, for God's sake, don't drink so much." End, Lennie: "I'm shutting up, George."

ON GOLDEN POND
by Ernest Thompson (Dramatists Play Service)
Drama: Act I, Scene 3, pp. 39–46, Norman (79) and Bill (45)
Bill has his first encounter with Norman, his lover Chelsea's crotchety dad. The two men discuss the generational morality of premarital sex and define the bottom line of their newly established relationship. Start, Bill: "So, you're a baseball fan, huh?" End, Norman: "Yes! Please do! Just don't let Ethel catch you."

ON THE OPEN ROAD
by Steve Tesich (Samuel French)
Comedy-Drama: Act I, Scene 4, pp. 23–29, Al (20–35) and Angel (20–35)
This very dark satire is set on the burned-out landscape of some future, post–civil war epoch. Angel and his mentor, Al, have been gathering art treasures from gutted museums and churches, hoping to barter their way into the Land of the Free. In this physical and emotionally demanding scene, they are in a church when Angel erupts, attacking Al. Angel demands that Al "open up" and behave in an intimate fashion. Al then pulls a knife, holding Angel at bay. They finally settle down and agree to resume their journey.

As written, Al actually cuts Angel with the knife, drawing blood. The threat will suffice for workshop presentation. You don't have to fool around with fake blood. Also, the scene calls for Al to play the piano a little bit, but you can easily work around that. Start, Angel: "Do you think this was once a church?" End, Al: "You can love a man, a woman, a child or all of mankind in less than five minutes, and then have the rest of the day to do the things you really like to do. Shall we?"

Comedy-Drama: Act II, Scene 2, pp. 46–50, Al (20–35) and Angel (20–35)
Al and Angel have been captured by soldiers of the provisional government and sentenced to die. Al is then led away for a conference, during which he strikes a deal with the captors: he and Angel will be given their freedom in exchange for carrying out a murder. They have to kill Jesus Christ, who is currently on earth during his Second Coming. In this remarkable scene, Al returns to Angel, cuts the ropes that restrain him, and explains the deal. Angel is horrified, but he agrees to join with Al because it is either that or face certain death. Start, Angel: "What's going on?" End, Angel: "To the Land of the Free, right?" Al: "Right." Angel: "Right."

ORPHANS
by Lyle Kessler (Samuel French)
Drama: Act I, Scene 3, pp. 26–34, Phillip (early 20s) and Harold (40–50)
Phillip's older brother, Treat, brought Harold home to their North Philadelphia row house last night after having met him in a bar. Deciding to hold the drunk man hostage, Treat tied Harold to a chair and gagged him. Now Phillip is alone with Harold who, after a fashion, frees himself and befriends the younger man.

Begin at the top of Act I, Scene 3. Start, Phillip: "Here comes somebody! Here comes an old man with a cane, got a newspaper under this arm...." End, Harold: "Ahhh, ya mutter! Little Dead End Kid!"

Drama: Act II, Scene 1, pp. 45–50, Harold (40–50) and Treat (late 20s)

Harold arrived as Treat's hostage two weeks ago, but in the interim has befriended him and his younger brother, lavishly spending money on them. Now Treat has fancy clothes and is enjoying his new status; however, he still doesn't understand where Harold comes from or how he makes so much money. Begin at the top of Act II, Scene 1. Harold enters singing. Start, Harold: "If I had the wings of an angel...." End, Harold: "You know who you remind me of, Treat? Fred. He didn't believe in moderation either."

OTHERWISE ENGAGED
by Simon Gray (Samuel French)

Comedy: Act I, pp. 19–25, Simon (39) and Wood (40s)

Bernard Wood drops by Simon's house to find out if Simon has, in fact, seduced his daughter. As the scene unfolds, Simon learns that Wood is really an old schoolmate from years ago, a fellow he slept with during his sexual-experimentation period, and the daughter in question is actually Wood's fiancée. Simon's visitor is a sad, rather desperate man, which gives the comedy a mean-spirited edge, particularly when the audience learns that Simon did indeed seduce the daughter. Written in the British vernacular. The entire scene runs about twenty minutes and covers an act break, so you may not want to do it in its entirety. For a shorter version, stop a couple of pages into Act II. End, Simon: "Is it worth my saying sorry over again, or will my earlier apologies serve?" You can also end, Wood: "I'd like to kill you, Hench. Yes—kill you!"

PILLOWMAN, THE
by Martin McDonagh (Faber and Faber)

Drama: pp. 14–23, Katurian (30s) and Tupolski (30s)

Tupolski interrogates Katurian, trying to link up the stories he has written to a series of what appear to be copycat crimes. Start after Ariel's exit. Katurian: "My brother's at school." End, Katurian: "...It was the children he was after in the first place."

Drama: pp. 37–43, Michal (30s) and Katurian (30s)

After being tortured, Katurian is tossed into the room with his dim-witted brother, Michal. In this scene, Katurian discovers that, contrary to what the interrogators told him, Michal has not been tortured. Katurian tries to get Michal to tell him precisely what it is he told the interrogators. Start, Michal: "Hiya. What are you doing?" End, Katurian: "...He was about nine feet tall."

Drama: pp. 47–51, Michal (30s) and Katurian (30s)

Michal confesses to his brother that he did indeed commit some of the child murders. Start, Michal: "I like The Pillowman. He's my favorite." End, Michal: "Well, I know *now*."

Drama: pp. 51–58, Michal (30s) and Katurian (30s)

Michal expands on the details of the murders and what he has told the police. Start, Katurian: "What did you tell them?" End, Michael: "...I am never never going to speak to you ever again."

P.S. YOUR CAT IS DEAD
by James Kirkwood (revised edition, Samuel French)
Comedy: Act I, Scene 2, pp. 34–43, Jimmy (38) and Vito (27)

Jimmy has managed to overpower Vito, the prowler, and has tied him up. Vito is trying to figure out a way to get loose, and Jimmy is getting to know his unwanted guest. This excerpt includes the first time that Vito comes on to Jimmy sexually. Begin after Jimmy's wild telephone conversation with Kate. Start, Jimmy: "Vito Antonucci. Hmmm, I never did trust Germans." End, Jimmy: "I'm going to put on my thinkin' cap!"

ROAD TO NIRVANA
by Arthur Kopit (Samuel French)
Comedy-Drama: Act I, Al (35–45) and Jerry (35–45)

This entire act is essentially one prolonged scene, about forty pages in length, between Al and Jerry. Al's sexy partner/lover, Lou, makes occasional interruptions. Al has summoned his former partner Jerry, who is now producing educational films back East, to his Hollywood home. He wants to entice Jerry into a new partnership to produce the filmed autobiography of rock's biggest female star, Nirvana.

Three excerpts are particularly good for scenework. **The first option is to begin after Lou's initial exit (pp. 15–22).** Start, Al: "Lou's got like enormous untapped talent." End, Jerry: "To better times." **Another choice is the part of the act where Jerry is told about Nirvana's involvement in the deal, and that her autobiography is an erotic version of Herman Melville's** *Moby Dick* **(pp. 48–57).** Start, Al: You do want in?" End, Al: "Now you're coming through." **The third option is to begin at the same place as the second excerpt and to continue to the end of Act I (pp. 48–63).** Start, Al: "You do want in?" End, Al: "One spoon or you're out."

ROSENCRANTZ AND GUILDENSTERN ARE DEAD
by Tom Stoppard (Samuel French)
Comedy: Act I, pp. 29–34, Rosencrantz (20–30) and Guildenstern (20–30)

Two minor players in Shakespeare's *Hamlet* are the stars in this comedy. In this scene, Hamlet, Ophelia, Gertrude, and Claudius have just appeared on stage and exited, leaving Rosencrantz and Guildenstern more baffled than before. Rosencrantz has had enough and wants to turn back but, of course, they don't know where they came from; they know only that they were "sent for." Stylistically, this scene feels a great deal like those in *Waiting for Godot.* Start, Rosencrantz: "I want to go home." Begin the dialogue at the point where Rosencrantz says this for the first time. End, Guildenstern: "What are the rules?"

Comedy: Act II, pp. 43–47, Rosencrantz (20–30) and Guildenstern (20–30)

By now, Rosencrantz and Guildenstern are at the castle and still don't understand the purpose of their visit. Rosencrantz would still very much like to return home, but Guildenstern feels they have a duty to perform as requested—that is, if they could figure out precisely what is being requested of them. Start, Guildenstern: "Hm?" End, Rosencrantz: "No. Double bluff!"

SEXUAL PERVERSITY IN CHICAGO
by David Mamet (Samuel French)
Comedy: One-act play, pp. 7–14, Danny (28) and Bernard (30–35)
While sitting in a singles bar, Bernard tells Danny about his night of outrageous sexual adventure with a young woman he picked up in a pancake restaurant. Start, Danny: "So how'd you do last night?" End, Bernard: "Well, alright, then. I'll tell you one thing…she knew all the pro moves."
Comedy: One-act play, pp. 49–55, Danny (28) and Bernard (30–35)
In this scene, Danny and Bernard sit on the beach, eyeing the women and discussing them in a vulgar way. Start, Bernard: "Lookit this." End, Bernard: "…with tits like that…who needs anything?"

SHAPE OF THINGS, THE
by Neil Labute (Faber and Faber)
Drama: "A Lawn," pp. 72–89, Adam (early 20s) and Phillip (early 20s)
Adam and Phillip are good friends who have not talked for a while. There has been a lot of water under the bridge since they last met. Adam has fallen under the influence of Evelyn and is being made over by her—unbeknownst to either Adam or Phillip. Adam has lost some weight, is working out, and has had a nose job. Also since the last time Adam and Phillip met, Adam has had a romantic moment with Phillip's fiancée, Jenny. In this scene, Phillip tells Adam he knows about the thing with Jenny because she told him. He also expresses amazement and disapproval about the way Adam is changing. Start, Phillip: "I'm serious, it looks good…" End, Phillip: "So long, matey." For a shorter version, end on page 85. Adam: "You got it."

SIGHT UNSEEN
by Donald Margulies (Dramatists Play Service)
Drama: Act I, Scene 1, pp. 20–24, Jonathan (35–45) and Nick (40s)
Nick's wife, Patricia, has gone outside to get vegetables for dinner, leaving him alone with her former lover and current houseguest, Jonathan Waxman. Nick doesn't like this man at all, neither personally nor professionally. Furthermore, Nick is jealous of Jonathan's relationship with Patricia. Nick is English and, though an educated man, he comes from a rural blue-collar background, and his accent should reflect those origins. This scene is a tense one, the kind that causes nervous laughter in the audience. Start, Nick: "Oops. You've spotted your painting." End, Nick: "Here we hold on to our overcoats."

SORROWS OF STEPHEN
by Peter Parnell (Samuel French)
Comedy: Act II, Scene 3, pp. 61–66, William (mid-20s) and Stephen (mid-20s)
William is convinced that his fiancée is having an affair, but he never suspects that it is with his best friend, Stephen. That is why he turns to Stephen for advice about what to do. The scene takes place in a restaurant. Eliminate the waitress's lines. Start, William: "I think she's having an affair." End, Stephen: "Yes."

SPEED-THE-PLOW
by David Mamet (Samuel French)
Comedy-Drama: Act I, pp. 17–26, Fox (40s) and Gould (40s)

Fox pitches a movie project to his friend, Gould, a high-powered Hollywood studio executive. This project will star Doug Brown and is guaranteed to make a great deal of money. Fox is almost beside himself as he smells success. Start, Gould: "I know what you wanted to say, and you're right. I know what you're going to ask." End, Gould: "But it ain't crowded."

Comedy-Drama: Act III, pp. 59–67, Fox (40s) and Gould (40s)

Gould slept with his sexy temp, Karen, last night and has decided, on her recommendation, to give the green light to a movie project based on a gloomy book about the perils of radiation. Fox enters the scene thinking that the Doug Brown project is still a "go" and is shocked to learn that Gould is putting it on the back burner in favor of the new project. Fox and Gould end up having a fistfight in the office. For scene-study purposes, start, Fox: "I'm not upset with you…Alright." End, Gould: "Alright—ask it."

SPLENDOR IN THE GRASS
by William Inge (adapted from the screenplay by F. Andrew Leslie, Dramatists Play Service)
Drama: Act II, Scene 2, pp. 51–54, Bud (18) and Ace (50)

The stock market is crashing, people are jumping out of windows in New York City, and Ace's son is flunking out of Yale. In this brief, multilayered scene, the overbearing, self-made father attempts to understand his drifting and increasingly defiant son, in order to justify all the meddling he has done in the young man's life and affairs. But there is no understanding, and they end up further apart than when they began. Start, Ace: "Sell out! What do you mean, sell out?" End, Bud: "I've got to get back to school, Dad. I'll…see you later."

SPLIT SECOND
by Dennis McIntyre (Samuel French)
Drama: Act I, Scene 1, pp. 7–16, Val (28–35) and Willis (25–35)

Willis, a white car thief, is captured and handcuffed by Val, an African-American New York City cop. When the prisoner begins to spew racial epithets, the officer loses his temper and shoots Willis right through the heart. Then, realizing what he has done, Val restages the crime scene to make it look like a case of self-defense. This is an extremely difficult scene involving violence and overt racism of the vilest nature. Definitely not for novice actors. The scene calls for a handgun that shoots blanks, so you'll have to figure out some way to approximate the sound of a gunshot. Also, you'll need a pair of handcuffs. Start, Val: "Freeze, motherfucker! Freeze it!" Continue through the end of Act I, Scene 1. End, Willis: "No difference, man! Get it?!"

Drama: Act I, Scene 2, pp. 17–28, Val (28–35) and Parker (35–45)

Parker interrogates Val about the killing that took place earlier in the evening. Val is lying about the true events, claiming he shot the criminal as an act of self-defense. Actually, Val killed Willis in cold blood. Parker smells a lie, but can't prove it. To play the entire scene, start, Parker: "Nice. Real clean. I'd say just about textbook." End, Parker: "I hope so, Johnson. Unless you get nicked in the line of duty, you're gong to be around for a long time." For a shorter version, cut from "wife, two kids and a Buick" to "You didn't happen to shoot it out." Continue to the same end.

STRANGE SNOW
by Steve Metcalfe (Samuel French)
Drama: Act I, Scene 1, pp. 23–28, Megs (late 30s) and Dave (late 30s)
The deeply buried shame of cowardice under fire is made fresh for Dave when his old Vietnam War buddy Megs unexpectedly shows up. Dave is hungover and, at any rate, doesn't seem too happy to see Megs. (Note: you can probably update this play by changing the war from Vietnam to one of the Gulf Wars. The situation could just as easily have happened there.) Start, Megs: "She's great, your sister, I like her." End, Dave: "Yeah, this trout fishing is a great time."

SUBJECT WAS ROSES, THE
by Frank D. Gilroy (Samuel French)
Drama: Act I, Scene 2, pp. 20–28, John (50) and Timmy (21)
Timmy is home from World War II, and his father has taken him to a baseball game. Back in their Bronx apartment, they share a few beers and try to get to know one another. This is the kind of relationship in which neither father nor son has ever expressed his love. Despite a surface appearance of closeness and camaraderie, there is a deep chasm between the two men. Start, John: "I haven't told that one in years." End, John: "My family called her The Lady. To their minds it was an insult. How did we get on this?"
Drama: Act II, Scene 2, pp. 52–59, John (50) and Timmy (21)
It is 10 P.M., and Nettie has mysteriously and uncharacteristically been gone all day. As John and Timmy wait for her and contemplate calling the police, their conversation turns into a session of truth-telling. Timmy recalls how, as a sickly child, he lay in bed at night and dreaded the fights that took place if his father came home. Start, Timmy: "I remember sitting here like this the night she went to have John." End, Timmy: "You pig."

SUMMER BRAVE
by William Inge (Dramatists Play Service)
Drama: Act I, pp. 22–25, Alan (early 20s) and Hal (early 20s)
Alan is surprised when Hal shows up looking for work. He hasn't seen Hal since college, when Hal borrowed his car and took off for California. Now Hal reports that things didn't go so well in Hollywood and, even though he managed to get a screen test, he has given up on becoming a movie star. What Hal wants is earnest work, preferably something in management. At first, Alan balks and wants as little contact as possible with Hal. But when Hal becomes emotional and asks for a chance to prove himself, Alan says that he'll get Hal a job. Start, Alan: "Hal! Hal! Come on over." End, Hal: "Yah. That's something I gotta learn…patience!"

SWEET BIRD OF YOUTH
by Tennessee Williams (Dramatists Play Service)
Drama: Act I, Scene 1, pp. 7–10, Chance (29) and Dr. Scudder (36)
Dr. Scudder, one of Boss Finley's underlings, tells Chance to get out of town before he gets hurt. Chance is determined not to leave St. Cloud without taking

Heavenly Finley with him. Start, Chance: "How did you know I was here?" End, Dr. Scudder: "Heavenly and I are going to be married next month."

TAKE ME OUT
by Richard Greenberg (Dramatists Play Service)
Comedy-Drama: Act I, pp. 20–24, Mason (30–50) and Darren (20s)
Darren Lemming is one of the most highly paid young professional ballplayers, with a contract for $106 million. He has also recently announced to the public that he is gay. In this scene, he meets his new financial advisor for the first time. Mason is an emotionally constricted man, also gay but not very demonstrative about it. He has a little bit of hero worship for Darren even though he is not a big baseball fan. Start, Mason: "Mr. Lemming—Mason Marzac: a pleasure to meet you!" End, Darren: "Well, that's got to be a sign, too, right?"
Comedy-Drama: Act II, pp. 42–45, Mason (30–50) and Darren (20s)
Darren is demoralized by the reaction to his announcement about being gay. In this scene, he talks to his financial advisor about his options should he announce retirement from baseball tomorrow. Start, Mason: "…You nodded to me." End, Darren: "Day after maybe."
Comedy-Drama: Act III, pp. 54–56, Darren (20) and Davey (20)
Darren and Davey have been best friends, playing for opposing baseball teams. Davey is a family man, a religious type with conservative values. This scene is the first confrontation between the men after Darren publicly announces he is gay. It is the end of the friendship. Start, Darren: "I…uh…we haven't talked…" End, Darren: "…so let me just put it this way, Davey: Drop dead."

TOPDOG/UNDERDOG
by Suzan-Lori Parks (Theatre Communications Group)
Comedy-Drama: Scene 1, pp. 9–21, Lincoln (mid-20s) and Booth (mid-20s)
Though there are other scenes for Lincoln and Booth in this play, this is my favorite. We get to see them together for the first time and to sense the tensions that exist in their brotherly rivalry. I'm suggesting that you start on page 9 because that is when Lincoln takes off his whiteface makeup. You can start at the top of the act if you want to work with the Lincoln costume and whiteface. And I'm suggesting that you stop on page 21 because that is when Lincoln picks up the guitar and starts singing. If you are an actor that can sing and play a guitar, then continue on to the end of the act. Start, Lincoln: "I was riding the bus. Really, I only had a minute to make my bus.…" End, Booth: "Good."

TRIBUTE
by Bernard Slade (Samuel French)
Comedy-Drama: Act I, pp. 36–40, Scottie (51) and Jud (20)
Scottie, having been diagnosed with leukemia, is trying to establish a closer relationship with his son, Jud, who doesn't yet know that his father is sick. As written, Scottie enters wearing a full-body chicken suit, in an attempt to make Jud laugh. Actors doing classwork will somehow have to approximate this or figure out a substitute costume. Start, Scottie: "Well, it's good to see you can still laugh." End, Scottie: "So do I, son. So do I."

TRUE WEST
by Sam Shepard (Samuel French)

Comedy-Drama: Act I, Scene 4, pp. 25–33, Austin (early 30s) and Lee (early 40s)
Lee proudly dictates his movie scenario to his brother, Austin, who types it up. As a professional screenwriter, Austin can't believe how outrageously bad Lee's story is, but he has promised producer Saul Kimmer that he'll help Austin prepare it. There is an underlying air of tension and competitiveness between the brothers. Start, Lee: "All right, now read it back to me." End, Lee: "And the one who's been chased doesn't know where he's going."

Comedy-Drama: Act II, Scene 5, pp. 34–39, Austin (early 30s) and Lee (early 40s)
Lee returns from his golf game with Saul Kimmer to report that the producer has given him an advance and made a firm commitment to produce his movie idea. Austin is flabbergasted by this turn of events, especially when he learns that Saul is putting everything—including his own movie project—on the back burner so that he can devote all his energy to selling Lee's idea. You'll need a golf club for this scene. Start, Austin: "He really liked it, huh?" End, Lee: "Relax. We're partners now."

Comedy-Drama: Act II, Scene 7, pp. 43–51, Austin (early 30s) and Lee (early 40s)
Austin, who is drunk and here waxing philosophical, watches Lee sitting at the kitchen table trying to type a screenplay, which he doesn't know how to do. Lee asks for Austin's professional help, but all Austin wants to do now is give it all up, wander in the desert, and perhaps engage in petty thievery—just like Lee does. Austin thinks that if Hollywood will buy a story as bad as Lee's, nothing makes sense any more. After a while, the brothers start talking about their reclusive, drunken father, who also lives in the desert. Start, Austin: "Red sails in the sunset." End, Austin: "Now that's a true story. True to life."

VIEUX CARRÉ
by Tennessee Williams (New Directions)

Drama: Part I, Scene 2, Writer (28) and Nightingale (50s)
This poignant scene begins with sobs and ends with a caress. Nightingale, a tubercular sketch artist, hears the younger man crying in his rooming-house cubicle and comes to comfort him. They speak of "the sound of loneliness," human sorrow, death, and love. The writer tells Nightingale about a recent homosexual encounter, his first, and Nightingale begins to gently pull back the bed sheets. The entire scene runs ten pages and is appropriate for experienced actors. Start, Nightingale: "I want to ask you something." End, Nightingale: "Shh, walls have ears! Lie back and imagine the paratrooper."

VIEW FROM THE BRIDGE, A
by Arthur Miller (Dramatists Play Service)

Drama: Act I, pp. 33–37, Eddie (40) and Alfieri (50s)
Eddie has come to Alfieri, a lawyer, hoping that something can be done to head off the developing romance between his niece Catherine and the illegal immigrant Rodolpho. Alfieri quickly recognizes that Eddie has more than parental interest in the young woman and advises him to let the lovers be. Start, Alfieri: "I

don't quite understand what I can do for you. Is there a question of law some-where?" End, Eddie: "I'll see you around."

VISIT, THE: A TRAGI-COMEDY
by Friedrich Durrenmatt (translated by Patrick Bowles, Grove Press)
Comedy-Drama: Act II, Alfred Ill (64) and Policeman (any age)
Claire Zachanassian, the richest woman in the world, has arrived in her poverty-stricken hometown after a forty-five-year absence. She then offers a million pounds to the residents if they'll murder Alfred Ill, the man who done her wrong all those years ago. The offer alone causes a rise in prosperity because local citi-zens begin to purchase goods on credit. Of course, the only way they'll be able to pay these bills when they come due is to commit murder. In this scene, Alfred Ill tries to have Zachanassian arrested for threatening his life, but the police officer won't comply with his request. In fact, the cop is wearing a new pair of shoes. Omit Zachanassian's interruptions. Also, you'll need a rifle or pistol. Start, Policeman: "Ill. What can I do for you? Take a seat. You're trembling." End, Alfred: "It's me you're hunting down."

WHO'S AFRAID OF VIRGINIA WOOLF?
by Edward Albee (Dramatists Play Service)
Drama: Act I, pp. 17–22, George (46) and Nick (30)
George and Nick, who have been drinking heavily, get to know one another as Martha shows Honey where the bathroom is. Nick isn't accustomed to George's game-playing and becomes defensive as the older man talks about his relation-ship with his wife, Martha, as well as of politics at the college. At one point, Nick threatens to take his wife and leave. Begin after Martha and Honey exit. Start, George: "So, what'll it be?" End, George: "You asked me if I knew women…Well, one of the things I do not know about them is what they talk about while the men are talking. I must find out some time."
Drama: Act II, pp. 50–55, George (46) and Nick (30)
Martha is in the kitchen nursing Honey. George and Nick talk about how much money their wives had when they married them. George tells Nick that he'll have to sleep with plenty of faculty wives if he wants to climb the ladder. This excerpt is ideal for workshop use. Begin as Martha leaves the room. Start, George: "No, Martha, I did not clean up the mess I made. I've been trying for years to clean up the mess I made." End, George: "No, baby…you almost think you're serious, and it scares the hell out of you."

WHOSE LIFE IS IT ANYWAY?
by Brian Clark (Dramatists Publishing Company)
Drama: Act II, Ken Harrison (35–45) and Dr. Travers (40–55)
After learning that Ken wants to commit suicide, Dr. Travers, the hospital psychi-atrist, pays him a visit. The doctor, however, is already predisposed to diagnose Ken as irrational. In this scene, Ken pins Dr. Travers to the wall, philosophically speaking. Start, Dr. Travers: "Mr. Harrison?" End, Dr. Travers: "I'm sorry if I upset you, Mr. Harrison."

ZOO STORY, THE
by Edward Albee (Dramatists Play Service)
Drama: One-act play, pp. 5–15, Jerry (late 30s) and Peter (early 40s)

The Zoo Story is a medium-length, one-act play that is too long for most workshops. As such, you'll have to decide whether to work on the first or second half. Keep in mind, however, that the second part is very physical and violent. The opening moments of the play contain a more interesting game of cat-and-mouse. In this scene, Peter is sitting on a bench in New York City's Central Park, enjoying a free afternoon, when a strange man approaches and strikes up a conversation. Start, Jerry: "I've been to the zoo." End, Jerry: "You do? Good."

FEMALE/FEMALE SCENES

ABSENT FRIENDS
by Alan Ayckbourn (Samuel French)
Comedy: Act I, pp. 11–13, Marge (30s) and Evelyn (30s)
Marge asks her friend Evelyn if it is true that she is having a love affair with Diana's husband, Paul. Evelyn says she isn't, which relieves Marge, but then admits that she and Paul "did it in the back of his car the other afternoon." This is a funny scene because Evelyn then starts elaborating on what a terrible lover the man is, and the women begin to directly insult each other. Start, Marge: "Evelyn, could I have a word with you?" End, Evelyn: "Yes."

AGNES OF GOD
by John Pielmeier (Samuel French)
Drama: Act I, Scene 7, pp. 30–34, Dr. Livingstone (30s) and Agnes (21)
Dr. Livingstone, a court-appointed psychiatrist, probes to see precisely how much Agnes understands about the process of childbearing. Agnes avoids answering directly and steers the conversation toward religion. Start, Agnes: "Yes, Doctor?" End, Agnes: "You should be ashamed! They should lock you up. People like you!"
Drama: Act I, Scene 10, pp. 43–48, Dr. Livingstone (30s) and Mother Superior (50s)
Dr. Livingstone is surprised to learn that the Mother Superior is, in fact, Agnes's aunt. The argument over the young woman's welfare heats up when Livingstone says that she intends to hypnotize Agnes. The conversation then turns into a debate about Catholicism and the doctor's personal background as a lapsed Catholic. A good, tense scene. Start, Dr. Livingstone: "What did you find?" End, Doctor: "That's also why I hate nuns." With a bit of cutting and pasting, you can extend this scene to the end of Act I. Eliminate Agnes's offstage singing and the references to it.
Drama: Act II, Scene 2, pp. 59–64, Dr. Livingstone (30s) and Mother Superior (50s)
Under hypnosis, Agnes has remembered the night she gave birth. With her out of

the room, Dr. Livingstone and Mother Superior lock horns over the possibility of an immaculate conception. Mother Superior wants to believe in miracles, but the doctor believes that Agnes is the sum of her psychological parts. At the end, the older nun says that she is going back to court to ask that Dr. Livingstone be taken off the case. Start, Mother Superior: "You've formed your opinion about her, haven't you?" End, Mother Superior: "Good-bye, Doctor. Oh, and as for that miracle you wanted, it has happened. It's a very small one, but you'll notice it soon enough."

ALL MY SONS
by Arthur Miller (Dramatists Play Service)
Drama: Act II, pp. 36–38, Ann (26) and Sue (40)
Sue, Ann's next-door neighbor, is supposedly looking for her husband when she and Ann start talking in the yard. The women's exchange is very friendly until Sue gets to the reason for the conversation and makes her point: She would appreciate it if, when Ann and Chris get married, they would go live someplace else. Start, Sue: "Is my husband…?" End, Sue: "…and I'm at the end of my rope on it!"

ANASTASIA
by Marcelle Maurette (adapted by Guy Bolton, Samuel French)
Drama: Act II, pp. 59–65, Dowager Empress (79) and Anna (20s)
The Dowager Empress interviews a young woman who claims to be Princess Anastasia, the only surviving daughter of the late Russian tsar Nicholas II. Because a huge fortune is at stake if Anastasia's identity is verified, the Empress is skeptical of any claims. As the interview progresses, however, Anna shares many private memories with the older woman, and the Empress finally believes her. Start, Dowager Empress: "Yes, I can see why the others have believed, especially my romantic-minded nephew." End, Dowager Empress: "Good night, Anastasia—and please—if it should not be you—don't ever tell me."

AUTUMN GARDEN, THE
by Lillian Hellman (Dramatists Play Service)
Drama: Act III, pp. 85–88, Sophie (17) and Nina (40)
Sophie, who is seventeen years old, wants enough money to pay for a return trip to her childhood home in France and to repay her mother's debts. Lacking other choices, she opts for blackmail after Nick Denery makes a drunken, fumbling attempt to seduce her. In this scene, she tries to get Nick's wife, Nina, to pay her $5,000, a tidy sum in 1949. For reasons of her own, Nina is willing to give Sophie the money but wants to call it a "gift," not "blackmail." An excellent scene, with plenty of subtext. The actress playing Sophie should affect a slight French accent. Start, Sophie: "You are a pretty woman, Mrs. Denery, when your face is happy." End, Nina: "How would—how shall we make the arrangements?"

BABY DANCE, THE
by Jane Anderson (Samuel French)
Comedy: Act I, Scene 2, pp. 9–27, Wanda (late 20s) and Rachel (30s)
Rachel and her husband are movie-industry executives who have agreed to purchase the as-yet-unborn baby that Wanda is carrying. This eighteen-page scene, which takes place in Wanda's Louisiana trailer home, is the first face-to-face meeting between Rachel and the birth mother. Here, Hollywood meets Louisiana, and

education meets ignorance. Start, Wanda: "Hello!" End, Rachel: "Sure." For a shorter, eleven-page version, begin at the same place and end as Wanda gets the peaches. End, Rachel: "You know what? You don't have to do that. I'll have the Jello." You can try another eleven-page option as well. Start, Rachel: "Is everything all right? Did our lawyer send you the check for the air conditioner?" Continue to Al's entrance.

BABY WITH THE BATHWATER
by Christopher Durang (Dramatists Play Service)
Comedy: Act II, Scene 3, pp. 32–35, Principal (35–50) and Miss Pringle (25–35)
Miss Pringle is concerned about the mental stability of her student Daisy, who is actually a boy, but the audience doesn't know that in this scene. Miss Pringle rushes into the principal's office for guidance, but the principal is off on a weird tangent of her own. This is very surreal, black comedy, wonderfully illogical. Actresses should read Christopher Durang's instructions on pp. 60–61; he comments specifically on how to play this scene. Start, Principal: "You can send Miss Pringle in now, Henry." End, Principal: "Who cares if she's dead as long as she publishes? Now, get out of here."

BAD HABITS
by Terrence McNally (1990 revised edition, Dramatists Play Service)
Comedy: "Ravenswood," pp. 65–70, Benson (late 20s) and Hedges (late 20s)
The broad comedy in this delicious scene between two nurses at a sanitarium demands bold acting choices. Hedges has a giant inferiority complex, and Benson only appears to be the picture of physical and mental health. Start, Hedges: "I admire you so much." End, Hedges: "If you say so, Ruth."

BAREFOOT IN THE PARK
by Neil Simon (Samuel French)
Comedy: Act I, pp. 26–30, Corie (early 20s) and Mrs. Banks (her mother, 50s)
During this short scene, Corie's mom visits her new apartment for the first time. Much is made out of the fact that you have to climb five flights of stairs to get there. Once she catches her breath, they get to the meat of the visit. Mom is being a fussy and busy overseer to her newlywed daughter, bringing housewarming gifts and expressing nonverbal concern about the small and yet unfurnished living quarters. Corie is mainly interested in getting her mom more involved in life, maybe (hopefully) even in a new love. Start, Corie: "Well?" End, Corie: "I'll be the judge of who's happy."

BELL, BOOK AND CANDLE
by John Van Druten (Dramatists Play Service)
Comedy: Act I, Scene 1, pp. 10–14, Gillian (27) and Miss Holroyd (45–55)
Gillian and her aunt, Miss Holroyd, are honest-to-goodness witches who live in New York City. In this scene, Gillian reprimands Miss Holroyd for using her powers to pester the handsome publisher who lives upstairs and makes her promise not to cast spells and the like in the building anymore. Gillian also confesses that she has a longing to be "normal," to stop being a witch. Start, Miss Holroyd: "So you've met him, after all? Do you still think he's attractive?" End, Gillian: "No. I don't say I wouldn't be tempted, but if I've got a week—I'd like to see how good I am, the other way."

BETWEEN DAYLIGHT AND BOONVILLE
by Matt Williams (Samuel French)
Drama: Act II, pp. 71–76, Carla (26) and Marlene (30s)
Marlene gives Carla some advice she doesn't like, so Carla tells Marlene that her husband, Big Jim, is sleeping with Wanda, the town slut. Marlene, who up to this point has spoken of Big Jim as if he were the perfect man, confesses that she has known about the affair all along and didn't say anything because she is afraid of losing him. You may want to update the reference to Burt Reynolds's love life. Start, Marlene: "You think the ghost of Elvis really talked to this woman?" End, Marlene: "Just let me alone."

CHILDREN'S HOUR, THE
by Lillian Hellman (Dramatists Play Service)
Drama: Act I, pp. 18–21, Martha (28) and Lily Mortar (45)
Martha doesn't believe that Lily Mortar is qualified to teach at the school, so she tries to get rid of her gently. Martha suggests that Lily take a nice, long ocean cruise. Lily responds angrily, accusing Martha of having unnatural feelings for her niece, Karen, and taking her frustrations out on a blameless aunt. This is a very significant scene because Lily's petulant accusations are overheard by two young girls, one of whom proceeds to spread a rumor that Martha and Karen are lesbians. Start, Mrs. Mortar: "I was asked to leave the room." End, Martha: "I want you to leave. And now. I don't wish any delay about it."
Drama: Act III, pp. 64–67, Karen (28) and Martha (28)
Martha enters this scene with a sense of relief, believing that she, Karen, and Karen's fiancé, Joe, will soon escape local scrutiny and gossip by moving to Vienna. Karen breaks Martha's happy mood by telling her that Joe, like everyone else in this small community, has come to believe they are, in fact, lesbians. Stunned by this final betrayal, Martha becomes gloomy and deeply introspective. She tells Karen that perhaps everyone else is right—perhaps she does love Karen in an unnatural way. When Karen dismisses this as craziness, Martha walks zombie-like into the next room and shoots herself. Start, Martha: "It gets dark so early now. Cooking always makes me feel better." Stop with Martha's exit. End, Karen: "Don't bring me any tea. Thank you. Good night, darling."

CLOSER
by Patrick Marber (Dramatists Play Service)
Drama: Act II, Scene 9, pp. 88–93, Anna (early 30s) and Alice (24)
This entire drama involves musical beds and rotating relationships. At this point in time, Larry is sleeping with Alice and has just moments ago signed divorce papers with Anna. This is a showdown scene between the two women. It takes place in a museum. Start, Anna: "How did you get so brutal?" End, Alice: "Do the right thing, Anna."

COMANCHE CAFÉ
by William Hauptman (Samuel French)
Comedy: One-act play, pp. 5–13, Mattie (40s) and Ronnie (20s)
Ronnie has never traveled far from her hometown in southern Oklahoma, but she has big dreams—and a number of misconceptions—about what is out there. Mattie, Ronnie's older co-worker at the Comanche Café, is relatively worldlier,

having been in love once or twice. They peel potatoes and talk about life in this charming and textured scene. Start, Ronnie: "I don't see why we've got to work on Sunday." End, Ronnie: "And I'm going to see them all. Just let me go anyplace but here—in Oklahoma."

COME BACK TO THE FIVE AND DIME, JIMMY DEAN, JIMMY DEAN
by Ed Graczyk (Samuel French)

Comedy-Drama: Act I, pp. 25–29, Mona (30s, playing late teens) and Sissy (30s, playing late teens)

Mona has unexpectedly returned home, opting not to go to college after all because of her "asthma." In this four-page flashback scene, she and Sissy, a girl-friend who is fixated on her large bosom and its effect on boys, talk about Joe, who recently disappeared after being fired from his job at the five-and-dime store. Sissy doesn't know that Mona is pregnant with Joe's child. This scene is interesting to work on mainly for its character development and subtext. Start, Sissy: "Me an' Joe was gonna get Stella Mae to take your place doin' the McGuire Sisters, but she wouldn't have been as good as you." End, Mona: "It's just 'deceivin' to the eye,' that's all."

COUPLA WHITE CHICKS SITTING AROUND TALKING, A
by John Ford Noonan (Samuel French)

Comedy: Act I, Scene 3, pp. 21–28, Maude (30s) and Hannah Mae (30s)

Maude, overcome with guilt, confesses that she made love with Hannah Mae's husband, Carl Joe, a short time earlier. Surprisingly, Hannah Mae seems to take this news in stride, contending that this just makes their friendship stronger. Maude becomes increasingly exasperated with Hannah Mae's illogical response. Start, Hannah Mae: "A red rose of apology." End, Maude: "Get out!"

CRIMES OF THE HEART
by Beth Henley (Dramatists Play Service)

Comedy-Drama: Act I, pp. 29–32, Meg (27) and Babe (24)

Meg talks to her sister Babe, trying to find out what happened on the day she shot her abusive husband, Zachary. Babe tells Meg about the very satisfying affair she has been having with Willy Jay, a black boy. Start, Meg: "What did Zachary do to you?" End, Meg: "…see, 'cause he's gonna be on your side."

DARK AT THE TOP OF THE STAIRS, THE
by William Inge (Dramatists Play Service)

Drama: Act II, pp. 52–57, Cora (34) and Lottie (38)

Lottie tells her sister, Cora, why Cora and her children can't come live with her and Morris; she confesses that they, too, have an unhappy home. Morris hasn't made love to Lottie for three years and has become distant and nervous, occasionally seeking psychotherapy. (Seeking psychological help was a big deal during the 1920s.) In addition, Lottie says that she never enjoyed sex in the first place. Start, Lottie: "My God, Cora, we can't stay here all night." End, Lottie: "So, don't come to me for sympathy, Cora. I'm not the person to give it to you."

DELICATE BALANCE, A
by Edward Albee (Samuel French)
Drama: Act II, Scene 1, pp. 33–36, Agnes (late 50s) and Julia (36)
This scene is a brief, hostile confrontation between a mother and her adult daughter. Their relationship, which is ordinarily tense, is stretched to the breaking point by the strange presence of Harry and Edna, family friends, who have moved into the daughter's upstairs bedroom. Start, Julia: "Do you think I like it? Do you?" End, Julia: "You go straight to hell."

DINNER WITH FRIENDS
by Donald Margulies (Theatre Communications Group)
Comedy-Drama: Act II, Scene 2, pp. 52–59, Beth (40s) and Karen (40s)
Beth has been separated from her husband for five months and has met another man. She is having lunch with her friend Karen to share the good news. Karen, however, is not happy to hear about Beth's good fortune, and the conversation turns bitter, a reevaluation of their friendship. This is an excellent scene because of the subtext and the way it leads to a moment of rare self-realization and clarity. Karen is something of a perfectionist and control freak and, though she would never say so out loud, it is important to her sense of self-worth that Beth continue to be unhappy and to rely on her for support. Start, Beth: "When you promise your little girl you're gonna call at eight o'clock and eight o'clock comes and goes..." End, Karen: "We're good. We're fine."

DOLL'S HOUSE, A
by Henrik Ibsen, Adapted by Frank McGuinness (Dramatists Play Service)
Drama: Act I, pp. 11–17, Nora (25–35) and Mrs. Linde (30–35)
When Nora's old school friend, Mrs. Kristine Linde, shows up unexpectedly on the day before Christmas, she finds Nora in an ecstatic mood because her husband, Torvald Helmer, has recently been appointed manager of Joint Stock Bank, a politically influential position that carries with it the promise of financial security. This good fortune means even more to Nora because, with the prospect of a hefty increase in family income, she'll be able to pay off a burdensome—and illegal—personal loan that her husband knows nothing about. Mrs. Linde tells Nora that she is a widow now and is close to being destitute. Perhaps Nora could speak to Torvald about a job at his bank? Nora agrees immediately and then confides in Mrs. Linde about her fraudulent loan and how happy she is that it will soon be paid off. Start, Mrs. Linde: "Nora, hello." End, Nora: "Stay, please. I'm not expecting anybody. It'll be for Torvald."

DOUBT—A PARABLE
by John Patrick Shanley (Theatre Communications Group)
Drama: Scene 4, pp. 17–24, Sister James (20s) and Sister Aloysius (50s–60s)
Sister James tells Sister Aloysius that the parish priest has taken an interest in one of the young male students. Under Aloysius's encouragement, she says that she saw the priest take the boy into the rectory privately and, when the boy returned to the classroom, he smelled of alcohol. That is all the evidence Aloysius needs, even though we later get a completely plausible explanation for the smell of alcohol. As far as Aloysius is concerned, Father Flynn is guilty as suspected. Start,

Sister James: "Good afternoon, Sister." End, Sister Aloysius: "Go then. Take them. I will be talking to you."

Drama: Scene VIII, pp. 42–50, Sister Aloysius (50s–60s) and Mrs. Muller (30s, African-American)

Sister Aloysius has summoned the mother of a boy she believes has been sexually molested by the parish priest. The mother's reaction is surprising, mainly because the boy's home life is so bad. His father beats him, and the only encouraging male companionship the boy is getting is from the priest. The mother says that, even if the priest made an advance, the boy is better off staying in school until graduation—and that she is grateful for the attention the priest has shown her son. Start, Sister Aloysius: "Mrs. Muller?" End with Mrs. Muller's exit. "...I'll be standing with my son and those who are good with my son. It'd be nice to see you there. Nice talking with you, Sister. Good morning."

EFFECT OF GAMMA RAYS ON MAN-IN-THE-MOON MARIGOLDS
by Paul Zindel (Bantam)

Drama: Act I, Beatrice (30s) and Ruth (16)

Beatrice calms her daughter, Ruth, after another violent nightmare, evidently brought on by memories of an elderly boarder who once roomed with them. This is a very interesting, complex scene because Beatrice and Ruth relate not only as mother and daughter, but also as two emotionally troubled souls. Start, Beatrice: "There, now, nobody's after you. Nice and easy. Breathe deeply....Did the big bad man come after my little girl?" End, Beatrice: "What's left for me?"

EVERYTHING IN THE GARDEN
by Edward Albee (adapted from the play by Giles Cooper, Dramatists Play Service)

Drama: Act I, Scene 1, pp. 20–24, Jenny (late 30s) and Mrs. Toothe (50)

Mrs. Toothe, a mysterious English lady, knocks on the door of Jenny's home, which is located in a fashionable neighborhood. Within minutes, Mrs. Toothe solicits Jenny for a prostitution ring. Jenny is outraged at the proposition, threatens to call the police, and kicks Mrs. Toothe out. After the lady is gone, however, the audience sees that Jenny may very well accept the offer because she and her husband could certainly use the money. Begin after Jack, the flirtatious neighbor, exits. Start, Jenny: "You mustn't believe a thing Jack says, Mrs...." End, Mrs. Toothe: "What a lovely garden. Do you have a greenhouse?"

FALLEN ANGELS
by Noel Coward (Samuel French)

Comedy: Act II, pp. 36–43, Julia (late 20s) and Jane (late 20s)

Jane and Julia are preparing to entertain their mutual former lover, Maurice, who is a handsome Frenchman. To calm their anxiety, the women drink martinis—and then champagne. As the liquor takes effect, their friendship gives way to competitiveness and, finally, to an all-out argument. Jane storms out. Actresses will need someone offstage to ring a telephone several times on cue. Also, Saunders, the maid, moves in and out of the scene, but it is easy to work around her if necessary. Start, Jane: "Julia, what a pretty girl Saunders is." Continue to the end of

Act II. End, Jane: "It's true. And I shall go away with him at once, and you and Fred and Willy can go to hell, the whole lot of you!"

FATHER'S DAY
by Oliver Hailey (Dramatists Play Service)
Comedy-Drama: Act I, pp. 25–29, Louise (30–35) and Marian (30–35)

Estelle has just gone inside to prepare lunch, leaving Louise and Marian alone for a moment on the patio. Suddenly, Louise turns uncustomarily serious about her divorce and discloses that her seven-year-old son has chosen to go live with his father in the Midwest. Start, Louise: "I don't like her gazpacho either." End, Marian: "…no child should be permitted to."

FOX, THE
by Allan Miller (based on D. H. Lawrence's short novel, Samuel French)
Drama: Act II, Scene 2, pp. 42–46, Jill (29) and Nellie (29)

Jill and Nellie invited a young soldier who was passing by to stay with them a few days on their farm, which is in much need of a man's strong back. Within days, it becomes clear to Jill that the soldier isn't so innocent; in fact, he is trying to take over the place and to have his way with Nellie. In this scene, Jill tells Nellie that she wants the soldier to leave, but Nellie defends him. Written in the British vernacular. Start, Jill: "Well I can't wait any more." End, Nellie: "Leaving you would be like leaving half my life, how could I do that? Go on up, Jill. Go on."

GETTING OUT
by Marsha Norman (Dramatists Play Service)
Drama: Act II, pp. 46–51, Arlene (early 20s) and Ruby (40s)

Arlene has been out of jail for only a couple of days and is trying to find her way. In this scene, she meets her upstairs neighbor, Ruby, a tough woman who also happens to be an ex-convict. They establish an immediate bond, and Arlene is impressed by the fact that Ruby has made a successful transition to life outside prison, and is now working as a waitress. Both roles are appropriate for advanced actresses. Start, Ruby: "Candy, I gotta have my five dollars back." End, Ruby: "Mine's the one with the little picture of Johnny Cash on the door."

GINGERBREAD LADY, THE
by Neil Simon (Samuel French)
Comedy-Drama: Act I, pp. 23–29, Evy (43) and Polly (17)

Polly welcomes her mother, Evy, home from ten weeks of drying out in a sanitarium by announcing that she is moving in with her. Start, Polly: "I don't want to get your hopes up, but I have reason to believe I'm your daughter." End, Polly: "Some people have it all."

Comedy-Drama: Act III, pp. 64–69, Evy (43) and Toby (40)

Evy returns home with a black eye after a drunken night with her old abusive lover, Lou. Her friend Toby is waiting for her. Start, Toby: "Well, good morning." Stop just before Polly's entrance. End, Toby: "I have to stop off first and blow up my beauty parlor."

GIRL ON THE VIA FLAMINIA, THE
by Alfred Hayes (Samuel French)
Drama: Act I, pp. 15–18, Lisa (early 20s) and Nina (early 20s)

Facing dire economic circumstances in war-ravaged 1944 Rome, Lisa has agreed to take the same route that many other Italian women have taken. She agrees to be "kept" by an American soldier, one of the country's liberators. In this three-page scene, Lisa has just arrived at the house where she'll be living with the man, but she is desperately unhappy with the prospect facing her. Nina, who arranged the deal for Lisa, is pragmatic, contending that a sexual trade is the best option available. Nina tries to prepare Lisa for the imminent arrival of her "husband," but Lisa feels like a prostitute. Both women are Italian, so slight Italian accents are appropriate. Start, Nina: "I'm exhausted. Such a day. Such excitement." End, Nina: "Would you like to bet?"

HEDDA GABLER
by Henrik Ibsen, Adapted by Jon Robin Baitz (Grove Press)
Drama: Act I, pp. 19–25, Hedda (25–35) and Mrs. Elvsted (25–35)

Mrs. Elvsted drops by Hedda's house unexpectedly to ask for a favor. Hedda remembers Mrs. Elvsted very well from their old school days and was, in fact, something of a competitor in the social department. Now Mrs Elvsted is asking that Hedda and her husband "look after" Eilert Lovborg, who also happens to be in town. Hedda does not tell Mrs. Elvsted that Eilert is an old flame but is overcome with feelings of jealousy when Mrs. Elvsted reveals that she has left her husband to follow Eilert. The wonderful thing about this scene for actresses is that everything is left unsaid. Both women are careful about how much intimacy they reveal. Start after Tesman leaves the room. Hedda: "Now then. Here we are…" End, Mrs. Elvsted: "Yes! My God! Of course!"

HOOTERS
by Ted Tally (Dramatists Play Service)
Comedy: Act I, Scene 2, pp. 13–17, Ronda (22) and Cheryl (25)

Cheryl, facing some serious life decisions, has brought Ronda to Cape Cod for a weekend of sun and quiet girl talk. As they check into their motel room, however, they meet a couple of wild-and-crazy nineteen-year-old post-adolescents. In this scene, the women are watching the guys, who are peering at them through binoculars. You'll need a bed for this scene. Start, Ronda: "I think they're in that last room on the other wing. There's a light on." End, Cheryl: "Good night, Ron."

Comedy: Act I, Scene 5, pp. 31–35, Ronda (22) and Cheryl (25)

To Ronda's dismay, Cheryl has played along with Clint and Ricky, a couple of teenage guys who are obviously interested in little more than getting laid. Cheryl has accepted a dinner date with them, and the women are getting dressed in their motel room. Ronda tells Cheryl she should start acting her age. Start, Ronda: "Where's my bracelet?" End, Ronda: "Right."

IMMIGRANT, THE
by Mark Harelik (Broadway Play Publishing)
Comedy-Drama: Act II, Scene 1, Ima (30s) and Leah (20s)

Leah, who is nine months pregnant, is still worried that she is living too far from her Russian-Jewish roots and that the future is too uncertain. In this amusing scene, she and Ima prepare vegetables for a stew and share their respective superstitions. Superstitions are the same the world over, it seems. At the end of the scene, Leah sings a verse of a Russian song in Yiddish as the women dance around the kitchen. She then goes into labor. Start, Ima: "Oh! Leah! You scared me! What is it? Are you feeling all right?" End, Ima: "Well, honey, it's about time."

IMPORTANCE OF BEING EARNEST, THE
by Oscar Wilde (Samuel French)
Comedy: Act II, pp. 58–64, Gwendolen Fairfax (20) and Cecily Cardew (18)
Gwendolen Fairfax has traveled to Mr. Worthing's country home where she unexpectedly meets his pretty young ward, Cecily Cardew. Both women mistakenly believe that they're engaged to marry the same man, whose name is Earnest. Gwendolen and Cecily's proverbial claws come out when they share a very proper tea in this very famous scene. (Virtually every young actress will work on this scene at one time or another.) For scene-study purposes, cut Merriman's entrance, lines, and actions. Eliminate the need for a butler by having Cecily serve the tea. Although this may not reflect the propriety of the day, it increases the comic tension between the women. Start, Cecily: "Pray let me introduce myself to you." End, Cecily: "It seems to me, Miss Fairfax, that I am trespassing on your valuable time."

INDEPENDENCE
by Lee Blessing (Dramatists Play Service)
Comedy-Drama: Act I, Scene 1, pp. 14–18, Evelyn (53) and Kess (33)
When Kess, Evelyn's oldest daughter, goes home for the first time in four years, they feel each other out. Evelyn wants to know if Tess is "still homosexual," and Tess tries to determine if Evelyn has recovered from her nervous breakdown. Start, Evelyn: "Have a seat." End, Evelyn: "But it's not true! I am perfectly capable of functioning in a warm and loving universe. Which I try constantly to create!"
Drama: Act I, Scene 3, pp. 26–32, Evelyn (53) and Jo (25)
Evelyn tells Jo, her out-of-wedlock pregnant daughter, that she intends to give Tess a much-fought-over family heirloom. Then Evelyn really puts the pressure on Jo to live at home after her baby is born. Start, Evelyn: "That takes care of that." End, Evelyn: "It will be a lovely gesture. From the both of us."

IN THE BOOM BOOM ROOM
by David Rabe (Samuel French)
Drama: Act II, pp. 66–73, Chrissy (early 20s) and Susan (25–35)
Susan, who is a lesbian as well as a hardened survivor of strip-club joints, wants to make love to Chrissy, who is unsophisticated, and tells her so. Chrissy does her best to decline gracefully. Start, Chrissy: "You never been interested in astrology, huh?" End, Susan: "No."
Drama: Act II, pp. 78–82, Chrissy (early 20s) and Helen (mid 40s)
Chrissy accuses her mother of not wanting her to be born; she thinks that Helen wishes she'd had an abortion. This very emotional scene ends with Chrissy sobbing on the floor. Omit Harold's line at the beginning of the scene. Start, Helen: "You been over here talkin' to your father." End, Chrissy: "I gotta stop. I gotta. I'm gonna stop."

ISN'T IT ROMANTIC?
by Wendy Wasserstein (Dramatists Play Service)

Comedy: Act II, Scene 1, pp. 34–37, Lillian (50s) and Tasha Blumberg (50s)

Tasha is the original Jewish mother, and Lillian is her very Waspy counterpart. They meet through the friendship of their daughters. Lillian and Tasha talk about the travails of motherhood and then agree to have lunch together. In this gently humorous scene, two cultures look at each other, finding common ground. Start, Lillian: "Mrs. Blumberg?" End, Tasha: "That's why we put out such nice products."

Comedy: Act II, Scene 3, pp. 43–47, Harriet (28) and Lillian (50s)

Mother and daughter have lunch at the posh Four Seasons restaurant in New York City. Harriet asks Lillian for motherly advice on career and family issues, but her successful business-executive mother's answers are unsatisfactory. Start, Lillian: "Everything all right with you?" End, Lillian: "Lovely lunch, Tom. Thank you."

Comedy: Act II, Scene 5, pp. 52–55, Janie (28) and Harriet (28)

Harriet has just surprised everyone by announcing that she is marrying a man she has known for only two weeks. When these two friends are alone, Janie lets Harriet know that she is frustrated with and feels betrayed by this simplistic solution to the career/family puzzle. Janie feels particularly vulnerable because she has just broken up with Paul, the doctor everyone thought was Mr. Right. Start, Janie: "She's in a good mood." End, Janie: "Do you really think anyone ever met someone throwing out the garbage?"

JAR THE FLOOR
by Cheryl West (Dramatists Play Service)

Comedy-Drama: Act II, Madear (90) and Raisa (28)

Raisa is an unusual visitor in this African-American household. In this funny and touching scene, she makes the acquaintance of Viola Dawkins, better known as Madear, whose ninetieth birthday is today. Madear is senile but uncommonly wise and a real character. Raisa shows the oldster her mastectomy scar, and Madear shows the younger woman her childbirth stretch marks. They have more in common: the internal scars shared by all women. Start, Raisa: "Where's everybody?" End, Raisa: "You got me on the ropes. And she's down…1-2-3…Wait a minute…Wait a minute…Slowly but surely, she's getting up…up…she's up. And the senior Dawkins kicker strikes again…Down for the count.…"

Drama Act II, Scene 4, Vinnie (27) and Maydee (47)

Maydee has sacrificed a great deal to see her daughter, Vinnie, graduate from college, but it isn't going to happen. In this emotional scene, mother and daughter finally have it out over Vinnie's aspirations to be a singer. Start, Vinnie: "So. I thought you said all you had to say earlier." End, Maydee: "Well good. Maybe her liking will transport the both of you wherever you plan to go."

JOINED AT THE HEAD
by Catherine Butterfield (Dramatists Play Service) (*Women Playwrights: The Best Plays of 1992*, Smith & Kraus)

Comedy-Drama: Act I, Dramatists Play Service pp. 26–31, Maggy (30s) and Maggie (30s)

Jim has taken his wife, Maggy, and his former high-school lover, Maggie, to dinner in a nice restaurant. By now, Maggie knows that Maggy has cancer, and she is determined to write, in book form, the story of her courageous struggle against the disease. As Maggy and Jim share a romantic moment, Maggie gets up from the table and addresses the audience, sharing her reactions to what has happened. Then, a shock: Maggy gets up and also begins to address the audience! Since all of this is happening in Maggie's imagination, Maggy's intrusion is discombobulating. In addition, Maggy is annoyed that Maggie's version of her story is too maudlin. Embarrassed because the enterprise is getting out of her artistic control, Maggie tries to get Maggy to go back and sit down. They wind up debating the merits of the story, with the theater audience judging who is right. This is a good scene to work on because of the way it breaks down and reestablishes the "fourth wall." The scene works best when an actor sits silently as Jim, but you can do it without him. Start, Maggie: "We looked at our menus. I don't know why, but I was feeling very happy." End, Maggie: "We finished dinner, and Jim went to get the car."

Drama: Act II, Dramatists Play Service pp. 60–65, Maggy (30s) and Maggie (30s)

Maggy is in the hospital for chemotherapy, and everyone—including her—knows that she is going to die soon. Maggie visits her. As always, Maggy has a great sense of humor. Start, Maggie: "Maggy?" End, Maggy: "My friend, you absolutely will. 'Bye."

KATHY AND MO SHOW, THE: PARALLEL LIVES
by Mo Gaffney and Kathy Najimy (Dramatists Play Service)
Comedy: Kathy (22–35) and Mo (22–35)

The challenge in performing the fourteen comedy sketches that comprise this wonderful play is the need to make quick shifts into radically differing characterizations. In various scenes, the two actresses are called upon to play males, young girls at church, or a couple of angels. None of these scenes is heavyweight, just fun sketch comedy. Five sketches are particularly humorous. In "Period Piece," a menstruating migrant farm worker talks about Lilac Spring Tampons (pp. 25–27). Then two modern women talk about the monthly "curse," theorizing what life would be like if men menstruated. Then they become the men. All this takes place in two pages. "God" features Teri and Tina, who are five and six years old, respectively (pp. 71–80). The two little girls are in church trying to figure out God, religion, etc.

Some of the sketches focus on the nature of romance. In "Kris and Jeff," a jock takes his girlfriend to a gay hangout for an after-movie snack (pp. 17–22). You may also want to work on "Futon Talk" (pp. 91–94). Here, Jeanine and Bill lie in bed and kick around their relationship. Bill wants to know if sex with him is better than with Jack "Jackhammer," and Jeanine wants to know if she is keeping Bill from moving to Oregon. Another hilarious scene is "Hank and Karen Sue" (pp. 97–103). In a country-and-western bar, Hank puts his regular moves on Karen Sue, assuring her about fifteen times that she is "very very pretty tonight, darlin'." But he is all hot air, and finally Karen Sue goes home to her children. Play each of the sketches in its entirety.

KEELY AND DU
by Jane Martin (Samuel French)
Drama: One-act play, Scene 15, pp. 44–54, Du (65) and Keely (early 30s)

Keely has been held captive for several months by a radical Christian anti-abortion group that is intent on preventing her from terminating her pregnancy, which resulted from a rape (her husband). She has formed a bond with Du, the woman assigned to be her companion and nurse. Just moments ago, Du's boss, a pastor named Walter, visited Keely for more anti-abortion indoctrination. She spit in his face, an act that she and Du simultaneously found very funny. They broke into uncontrolled laughter, and Walter made as dignified an exit as possible.

In this twenty-minute scene, the women get to know one another on a deeper level. The scene is interesting not for the overt conflict, but for the way Keely and Du edge toward each other despite their prisoner/guard roles, finding things in common. Begin after Walter exits. Start, Du: "Oh, my." End, Du (singing): "*K-K-K-Katy...beautiful lady...you're the only g-g-girl that I adore....*"

LAST SUMMER AT BLUEFISH COVE
by Jane Chambers (JH Press)
Comedy-Drama: Act I, Eva (early 30s) and Lil (early 30s)

Lil has just told Eva that because of an error made by the rental agent, she is the only straight woman living in Bluefish Cove, which is a lesbian enclave. Eva considers leaving but, frankly, she is enjoying Lil's company. Furthermore, she has no place else to go since her marriage broke up. Start, Lil: "...and to the left, that's the yacht basin. July 4th, they'll race." End, Lil: "Eva, I am your friend, everything's going to be just fine, you'll see. Now, go on. It's freezing out here. Good night."

Comedy-Drama: Act I, Eva (early 30s) and Lil (early 30s)

In this sweet, quiet scene, Eva awkwardly acknowledges being romantically attracted to Lil, who is bemused by the whole situation. Start, Lil: "Who is it?" End, Lil: "This is the first time I've ever taken her advice. Goodnight. Goodnight, Eva."

Comedy-Drama: Act II, Eva (early 30s) and Lil (early 30s)

Eva and Lil have spent the last glorious month together and are planning to share an apartment when they return to New York City. However, Lil still hasn't told Eva that she has inoperable cancer. As a result, Eva doesn't understand Lil's reticence. Start, Eva: "How big is your dining room?" End, Lil: "All right, you asked for it."

LATER
by Corinne Jacker (Dramatists Play Service)
Drama: Act I, Scene 1, pp. 5–13, Molly (55–65) and Kate (37–40)

Kate suggests that her mother, Molly, sell the summer place now that her father is dead. She thinks that it is too full of memories. Molly, however, has no intention of listening to her daughter's advice. Start, Kate: "I don't know what I meant." End, Molly: "We saw the sailboats. They were beautiful. Now. Let's go home."

Drama: Act I, Scene 1, pp. 20–24, Kate (37–40) and Laurie (35)

Sisters Kate and Laurie talk about their sibling rivalry, bicker, laugh, and try to figure out what to do about their mother now that their father is dead. Start, Laurie: "Have you ever had an abortion?" End, Laurie: "Well, you're gonna tell her it's gone, not me."

LIE OF THE MIND, A
by Sam Shepard (Dramatists Play Service)
Comedy-Drama: Act III, Scene 1, pp. 64–72, Lorraine (50s) and Sally (early-to-mid-20s)

In this eight-page scene, Sally comforts her distressed mother. Lorraine has taken to bed because Sally's brother, Jake, has apparently gone to Montana. He wants to see his wife after beating her up pretty badly recently. Lorraine and Sally talk about the bizarre events surrounding Sally's father's death in Mexico years ago. You'll probably want to use a bed here. Start, Sally: "Rise and shine! It's coffee time!" End, Lorraine: "Pure blue. Pure, pure blue. Wouldn't that be nice?"

LIFE AND LIMB
by Keith Reddin (Dramatists Play Service)
Drama: Act I, Scene 7, pp. 24–26, Effie (20s) and Doina (20s)
Effie tells Doina, her best friend, that she is having an affair but she doesn't love the man. Doina is all for it. You'll need a Christmas tree; a miniature one will do. Also, Doina has a pretty strong New Jersey accent. Start, Doina: "So a very merry Christmas." End, Doina: "You bet."

LOST IN YONKERS
by Neil Simon (Samuel French)
Comedy-Drama: Act II, Scene 3, pp. 88–93, Bella (35) and Grandma (mid-70s)
Bella returns home after a two-day absence and has it out once and for all with her mother, who is known in the play as Grandma. Bella tells Grandma how horrible it was to be raised in a home where no one expressed their love. She then stuns the older woman by admitting that she has slept with a great many boys and men in her life, all because she craves love. This is a beauty of a scene for the right actresses. Grandma has a heavy German accent, and Bella has an unnamed learning disability, making her childlike in some respects. Start, Bella: "Hello, Momma…Would you like some tea?" End, Bella: "I think we've both said enough for today…don't you?"

LUDLOW FAIR
by Lanford Wilson (*Balm in Gilead and Other Plays by Lanford Wilson*, Hill & Wang/Noonday)
Comedy-Drama: Rachel (20s) and Agnes (20s)
Rachel is worried that she might have done the wrong thing by turning her boyfriend in to the authorities for stealing money from her and Agnes. Agnes thinks that Rachel is overreacting and that the guy had it coming. But all Agnes really wants to do is get over her cold so she can face the awful lunch she is supposed to have with her boss's son tomorrow. Start, Agnes: "Are you going to take a bath or what?" End, Agnes: "Me? I'm always nursing someone else's broken heart. Just once I'd like a broken heart of my own."
Comedy-Drama: Rachael (20s) and Agnes (20s)
This scene starts precisely where the preceding one left off and continues to the end of the play—if the actress playing Agnes wants to tackle a two-page monologue. Start, Rachel: "You're great." End, Agnes: "I snore actually. Why don't you go to bed?" For a shorter version, end, Agnes: "No lie, I can't wait till summer to see what kind of sunglasses he's going to pop into the office with. Probably those World's Fair charmers. A double unisphere. Are you going to sleep?…Well, crap."

MIDDLE OF THE NIGHT, THE
by Paddy Chayefsky (Samuel French)

Drama: Act II, Scene 1, pp. 32–35, Betty/The Girl (23) and Marilyn/The Girl Friend (early 20s)

Betty's friend Marilyn tries to talk her out of the relationship she has started with a man who is twice her age. Start, The Girl: "Would you close the door please, Marilyn?" End, The Girl Friend: "Yes I do."

MRS. WARREN'S PROFESSION
by George Bernard Shaw (Signet Classic)

Drama: Act IV, Mrs. Warren (40–50) and Vivie (20)

Vivie banishes her mother from her life forever after discovering that she continues to operate a chain of brothels on the Continent. Mrs. Warren then challenges the value of Vivie's university education if it has brought her to a place where she can disown her mother, who has worked very hard all of her life to improve her circumstances. Start, Mrs. Warren: "Well, Vivie, what did you go away like that for without saying a word to me? How could you do such a thing?" End, Vivie: "Good-bye…and Good-bye, Frank."

'NIGHT, MOTHER
by Marsha Norman (Dramatists Play Service)

Drama: One-act play, Jessie (late 30s) and Mama (late 50s to early 60s)

In this two-character, one-act, real-time drama, the tension builds steadily until, in the final moments, the daughter commits suicide. The scenes become increasingly difficult to play as the action progresses. Attempting scenes that begin after the play's midpoint is the acting equivalent of trying to jump onto a rapidly moving train. Two early scenes capture the situation, the mother/daughter relationship, establish conflict, and are accessible.

The first option begins at the top of the play and continues through the references to Jesus committing suicide (pp. 9–17). This section includes the first suggestion that Jessie intends to kill herself, as well as Mama's reaction to the comment. Start, Mama: "Jessie, it's the last snowfall, sugar. Put it on the list." End, Mama: "You'll go to hell just for saying that, Jessie!" Jessie: "I didn't know I thought that." The second scene starts a couple of pages after the first excerpt ends (pp. 18–23). The stakes are getting higher, and Mama begins to realize that Jessie is quite serious. Start, Mama: "What's this all about, Jessie?" End, Mama: "We've got a good life here!"

NIGHT OF THE IGUANA, THE
by Tennessee Williams (Dramatists Play Service)

Drama: Act I, Scene 2, pp. 24–27, Maxine Jelkes (40s) and Hannah (39)

Hannah and her ninety-seven-year-old grandfather are flat broke, but they still have their pride. As she helps Maxine set the tables for dinner on the verandah, Hannah attempts to barter with her for food and lodging. Maxine, however, wants cash up front. This is a quiet, short, tense scene. Each woman is desperate in her own way. The surface conflict is minimal and is only a mask. Begin at the top of Act II. Start, Maxine: "Miss Jelkes?" End, Maxine: "I do. It gives me the shivers."

NORMAN CONQUESTS, THE—TABLE MANNERS
by Alan Ayckbourn (Samuel French)
Comedy: Act I, Scene 1, pp. 1–7, Sarah (30s) and Annie (30s)
Sarah arrives at the country house to relieve Annie of her mother-nursing duties so that she can take a romantic holiday, presumably with her longtime friend, Tom. However, Annie admits that she is planning to travel with her romantic, charming, very-much-married brother-in-law, Norman. This rich, comic scene has plenty of texture. Written in the British vernacular. Start, Sarah: "Hallo! We're here." End, Sarah: "What you need is a rest."

ODD COUPLE, THE (FEMALE VERSION)
by Neil Simon (Samuel French)
Comedy: Act II, Scene 1, pp. 47–53, Florence (35–45) and Olive (35–45)
Olive's hormones are raging, so she arranges a double date for herself and Florence with the Spanish men who live upstairs. But Florence, who has been separated from Sidney for only three weeks, isn't in the mood. Start, Florence: "That's something, isn't it, Olive? They think we're lucky." End, Florence: "You didn't tell me his name was Jesus....I'll make something simpler. Fish and loaves or something."
Comedy: Act II, Scene 2, pp. 54–57, Florence (35–45) and Olive (35–45)
For tonight's double date with the Spanish guys, Florence has prepared a gourmet meal. No one shows up on time, however, throwing Florence into a compulsive snit. Start, Olive: "Oh God, it's gorgeous…it looks like a Noel Coward play." End, Florence: "I am through."
Comedy: Act II, Scene 3, pp. 73–79, Florence (35–45) and Olive (35–45)
Olive is fed up with Florence after eight months of her compulsive cleanliness and neurotic worrying. The fight in this scene occurs because Florence ruined last night's double date with their upstairs neighbors. This is the most difficult scene in the play because the conflict is more oblique here. Start, Florence: "Alright, how much longer is this going to go on?" End, Olive: "Okay…I tried."

ON GOLDEN POND
by Ernest Thompson (Dramatists Play Service)
Drama: Act II, Scene 1, pp. 56–60, Ethel (69) and Chelsea (42)
Chelsea surprises her mother by announcing that she married Bill during her European vacation. In this scene, Ethel and Chelsea also try, unsuccessfully, to discuss the always-strained relationship between Chelsea and her father, Norman. Start, Chelsea: "How." End, Ethel: "Well he's afraid of you. You should get along fine."

OTHER PEOPLE'S MONEY
by Jerry Sterner (Samuel French)
Drama: Act I, pp. 44–46, Kate (35) and Bea (early 60s)
Bea convinces Kate, her daughter, who is a bright and successful investment banker, to work on behalf of her company in its fight against an attempted corporate takeover. Start, Bea: "How dare you talk to him that way?" End, Kate: "Mom, don't push it."

PIZZA MAN
by Darlene Craviotto (Samuel French)
Comedy: Act I, pp. 31–43, Julie (late 20s) and Alice (mid-20s)
Acting on impulse and unfocused anger at men in general, Julie and Alice agree
to pick a man, any man, and rape him. In this somewhat lengthy act, the
women make this decision and begin their search. You'll need some dishes to
break during this scene (some actors use empty soda pop cans), as well as a
telephone. Start, Julie: "We shouldn't have to go through any of this. Me getting drunk. You getting fat." End, Julie: "That was not the point of the phone
call."

PROOF
by David Auburn (Dramatists Play Service)
Drama: Act I, Scene 4, pp. 35–40, Claire (29) and Catherine (25)
It is the morning after a big party. Catherine is in a good mood because she slept
with Hal for the first time, who is at this moment upstairs fetching some papers
from a desk. Catherine's sister, Claire, is hungover but has something on her
mind as she enters the scene. She tells Catherine that she is selling the family
house and strongly urges her to come to New York and live. Catherine wants no
part of it and is furious. Start, Catherine: "Good morning." Claire: "Don't yell
please. Calm down."

SCENES FROM AMERICAN LIFE
by A. R. Gurney, Jr. (Samuel French)
Comedy-Drama: Act II, pp. 44–48, Mother (40ish) and Daughter (17)
Here, a mother takes her daughter to a fancy New York City restaurant to feel the
young woman out as to whether she wants to have an expensive coming-out party
when she graduates from high school—or go to college. The father won't pay for
both. The daughter prefers college, much to her mother's utter disappointment.
The playwright envisions actresses playing broad age ranges in this play so, for
example, actresses in their twenties could play both of these roles. As written, a
waiter moves in and out of the scene but has only one line. If you can't arrange
for an actor to play that part, simply eliminate him. Start, Daughter: "Oh,
Mummy! Thank you, thank you, thank you for the tennis dress, and the bathing
suit, and the Bermuda shorts. They're just yummy, Mummy." End, Mother: "Now
eat up, or we'll be late for *Kiss Me, Kate*."

SPOILS OF WAR
by Michael Weller (Samuel French)
Drama: Act II, pp. 47–53, Emma (late 30s) and Elise (mid-30s)
Elise and Emma are best friends and dedicated "leftists," politically committed
since they lived together in a commune in the 1930s. In the mid-1950s, Emma
and Elise are still raising their voices in a world that won't listen. Tonight, Elise is
going to a party where she'll see her estranged husband. This meeting has been
engineered by her sixteen-year-old son. Emma is upset that Elise is trying to take
her new flame, Lew, away from her. A very good scene. Eliminate Lew's lines.
Start, Emma: "My God, Elise, you look gorgeous! Why? I mean, what are you
doing here?" End, Emma: "Next week? Same time? Same place?"

STEEL MAGNOLIAS
by Robert Harling (Dramatists Play Service)
Drama: Act I, Scene 2, pp. 32–35, Shelby (25) and M'Lynn (50)
Shelby happily tells her mother that she is pregnant. But M'Lynn knows that the doctors have advised Shelby not to become pregnant because she has diabetes, and reacts to the news with anger rather than delight. Start, M'Lynn: "Shelby!" End, Shelby: "Please don't tell anybody yet. I want to tell daddy first."

STREETCAR NAMED DESIRE, A
by Tennessee Williams (Dramatists Play Service)
Drama: Act I, Scene 1, pp. 9–16, Blanche (early 30s) and Stella (late 20s)
Blanche unexpectedly arrives at Stella's New Orleans apartment. This is basically an expository scene, a setup for what is to come. The audience is made aware of the sisters' differences, but the scene doesn't contain a lot of overt conflict. Blanche is in conflict with her situation. Start, Stella: "Blanche! Blanche!" End, Blanche: "Oh, Stella, Stella, you're crying!"
Drama: Act I, Scene 4, pp. 43–51, Blanche (early 30s) and Stella (late 20s)
Last night, Stella and Stanley had a knock-down, drag-out fight, then reconciled and made passionate love. Blanche anxiously watched all of this, and now in this excellent scene tries to convince Stella to leave her husband. Stella won't hear of it. Begin at the top of Act I, Scene 4. Start, Blanche: "Stella?" End, Blanche: "Don't hang back with the brutes!"

SUMMER AND SMOKE
by Tennessee Williams (Dramatists Play Service)
Drama: Part II, Scene 4, pp. 66–69, Alma (25–29) and Nellie (18–22)
Nellie, Alma's longtime music student, gives her a Christmas gift and a card signed by Nellie and John, Alma's lifelong love. This is the first time that Alma realizes that John has become serious about someone else. It is important that Alma appear to be at least eight years older than Nellie. One of the points of the scene is that time has passed, and Nellie has grown up. Start, Nellie: "Here you are!" End, Nellie: "Goodbye, Miss Alma."

TASTE OF HONEY, A
by Shelagh Delaney (Grove Press)
Drama: Act I, Scene 2, Jo (17) and Helen (40)
Jo's bar-hopping, sluttish mother is moving out of their flat to marry a young boyfriend. As Helen packs, she discovers that Jo has been given an engagement ring. After the mother and daughter argue about Jo's readiness for marriage, the conversation then turns on the identity of Jo's natural father. Helen says that he was a half-wit she picked up in a bar, a man with "strange eyes." This six-page scene is excellent. Written in the British vernacular. Start, Helen: "Jo! Jo! Come on. Be sharp now." End, Jo: "Good luck, Helen."

TOP GIRLS
by Caryl Churchill (Samuel French)
Comedy-Drama: Act II, Scene 2, pp. 88–98, Marlene (30s) and Joyce (30s)
In the final scene, which clarifies everything that has taken place so far, the audience

learns that Marlene gave up her daughter sixteen years ago to pursue success in the competitive business world. Marlene's sister, Joyce, has reared the rather slow-witted child. This is the sisters' first visit in six years. During this time, Marlene has acquired all the worst traits of successful businesspeople and is a philosophical conservative, while Joyce is still a country person at heart. The sisters argue about class differences, business philosophy, and family loyalty. Written in the British vernacular. Start, Joyce: "So what's the secret?" End, Joyce: "No, pet. Sorry."

TOYS IN THE ATTIC
by Lillian Hellman (Dramatists Play Service)
Drama: Act II, pp. 39–45, Lily (21) and Albertine (45)
Lily, who is frail, needy, and uncertain, is worried that she is losing her husband, Julian, to another woman. Here, she asks her mother, Albertine, if the real reason Julian married her in the first place was because he was paid to. Start, Albertine: "How are you, Lily? I haven't seen you in a whole year." End, Albertine: "Then be very careful. Same thing as loving it."

TWO ROOMS
by Lee Blessing (Dramatists Play Service)
Drama: Act I, Scene 3, pp. 21–24, Lainie (30s) and Ellen (40s)
Ellen, a government official, tells Lainie that Walker Harris intends to publish an unauthorized article on the kidnapping of her husband in Beirut and her subsequent vigil. Ellen implores Lainie to publicly disavow the article so that it won't impede the efforts of the U.S. State Department to free the hostages. Start, Ellen: "I got a call today." End, Lainie: "Mine was. Now offer me hope."

VIEW FROM THE BRIDGE, A
by Arthur Miller (Dramatists Play Service)
Drama: Act I, pp. 31–33, Beatrice (40) and Catherine (17)
Beatrice has seen the depth of her husband's anguish over the romance developing between Catherine and Rodolpho and is starting to become a bit jealous of the younger woman. In this scene, Beatrice advises Catherine that if she wants Eddie to stop treating her like a child, she must stop acting like one. For example, Catherine should stop sitting on the edge of the tub to talk to Eddie while he is shaving in his underwear, and should stop letting him see her in her slip. Start, Beatrice: "Listen, Catherine. What are you going to do with yourself?" End, Catherine: "Okay."

WAITING FOR THE PARADE
by John Murrell (Talonbooks, Canada)
Drama: Scene 9, Janet (late 30s) and Marta (30s)
Janet, the self-appointed and sanctimonious monitor of local patriotism, pays Marta an unannounced visit at her father's small tailoring shop. Janet is upset because Marta plays recordings of German love songs too loudly in the store. In addition, Marta's father is currently being imprisoned as a suspected Nazi sympathizer. When Janet strongly suggests that Marta herself is a Nazi, Marta almost bodily tosses her out of the shop. Marta has a slight German accent. Start, Janet:

"Good afternoon. I rang the bell on the counter, but nobody came." End, Marta: "Get out of my shop."

WHAT I DID LAST SUMMER
by A. R. Gurney, Jr. (Dramatists Play Service)
Drama: Act II, pp. 45–51, Anna (60s) and Grace (30)
Grace is worried about the growing influence that Anna "the Pig Woman" has over her fourteen-year-old son, Charlie. In this showdown, Grace demands that Charlie be made to return home. Anna responds with good humor and a firm commitment to let Charlie decide for himself. It turns out Grace was once one of Anna's "students." Start, Grace: "Anna!" End, Grace: "Good night, Anna."

WIT
by Margaret Edson (Dramatists Play Service)
Drama: One-act play, pp. 51–56, Vivian (50) and Susie (28)
The relationship between Vivian and Susie Monahan, the primary nurse in the cancer unit, is the most textured in the play. Susie empathizes with Vivian in a way that the more clinical doctors do not, so it is with her that Vivian occasionally drops her guard. In this scene, Vivian admits that she is in terrible pain, mainly due to the chemo treatments. Start, Vivian: "…It was late at night, the graveyard shift. Susie was on." End, Susie: "…It's very simple, and it's up to you."

WOMEN, THE
by Clare Boothe Luce (Dramatists Play Service)
Comedy: Act I, Scene 2, pp. 18–20, Mary (mid-30s) and Olga (any age)
Olga, the gossipy manicurist at Michael's Salon, tells Mary all about Mr. Stephen Haines and his affair with Crystal Allen. Unbeknownst to Olga, however, Mary happens to be Mrs. Stephen Haines. When Olga discovers this, she is mortified. Start, Olga: "Funny, isn't she?" Continue through Mary's exit at the end of the scene. End, Mary: "Thank you. Good day."

Comedy: Act I, Scene 3, pp. 24–26, Mrs. Morehead (55–60) and Mary (mid-30s)
Mary's wealthy husband is having an affair with a young store clerk, and she doesn't know what to do about it. In this scene, Mrs. Morehead, her colorful mother who has been successfully around the male/female track a couple of times and understands all there is to know about men, counsels Mary. Start, Mary: "Mother, Dear!" Continue to the end of the scene, stopping just before Jane enters. End, Mary (on the telephone): "…No dear—I won't wait up—Stephen. I love—"

Comedy-Drama: Act I, Scene 4, pp. 34–36, Mary (mid-30s) and Crystal (early 20s)
Mary gets her nerve up and confronts "the other woman." This short, classic showdown takes place in the dressing room of a clothing store. Start, Crystal: "Come in!" End, Crystal: "Oh, what the hell!"

PART SIX

MALE/FEMALE SCENES

AFTER THE FALL
by Arthur Miller (Dramatists Play Service)

Drama: Act I, pp. 28–30, Quentin (40s) and Louise (35)

Quentin and Louise, two complex, sophisticated people, debate the true meaning of a mature relationship in this three-page scene. Start, Louise: "Quentin, I'm trying to understand why you got so angry with me at the party the other night." End, Louise: "Good God! What an idiot!"

Drama: Act I, pp. 36–40, Quentin (40s) and Louise (35)

Quentin has innocently met and spent a little time in the park with Maggie, the switchboard operator in his business firm. When he arrives home, Louise, his wife, reminds him that he has missed an important business meeting. Quentin tells her about Maggie, and they fight. Start, Quentin: "Hi…What's the matter?…Well, what's the matter?" End, Louise: "It's all it's been about the last three years. You don't want me." For a longer version, end with Quentin's line, "God! Can that be true?"

Drama: Act II, pp. 47–52, Quentin (40s) and Maggie (25–30)

Quentin visits Maggie in her apartment. This is their first face-to-face meeting since they met in a park two years ago. Since then, she has become a celebrity singer, and he has followed her progress. Maggie is based on Marilyn Monroe, to whom playwright Arthur Miller was briefly married. Omit Louise and Mother's lines. Start, Maggie: "I can't hardly believe you came! Can you stay five minutes?" End, Quentin: "Not yet, dear; but I intend to try. Don't be afraid to call me if you need any help."

AH, WILDERNESS!
by Eugene O'Neill (Samuel French)

Comedy: Act II, Scene 1, pp. 66–71, Belle (20) and Richard (16)

Determined to teach his steady girlfriend a lesson, Richard accepts a blind date with a young woman who has loose morals and, as he is to learn, charges for her services. Despite all of Richard's big talk, he is still a kid; as such, when Belle and Richard meet in a seedy bar, he is thoroughly intimidated. The peroxide blonde is as worldly as he is innocent. Cut the bartender's interruption of the scene. Start, Belle: "You shouldn't be so generous, Dearie. Gets him in bad habits." End, Belle: "And don't want to. Shut up about her, can't you?"

Comedy: Act III, Scene 2, pp. 108–117, Muriel (15) and Richard (16)
Shades of *Romeo and Juliet* circa 1906. Richard and Muriel, two young lovers, sneak out of their respective homes, defying specific parental edicts, and rendezvous on a nearby moonlit beach. They quarrel and spoon and kiss, the very vision of innocent romance. Start, Muriel: "Oh, Dick." End, Muriel: "That'll be wonderful, won't it?"

ALL MY SONS
by Arthur Miller (Dramatists Play Service)
Drama: Act I, pp. 29–31, Chris (32) and Annie (26)
Chris has secretly been in love with Annie for a long time, even though she was the girlfriend of his late brother, Larry, who died in World War II. Judging that enough time has gone by, Chris decides to declare his love. When the moment arrives, however, he finds that he is still standing in his brother's shadow. Start, Annie: "It's lovely here. The air is sweet." End, Chris: "Oh, Annie, Annie…I'm going to make a fortune for you!"

AMADEUS
by Peter Shaffer (Samuel French)
Drama: Act I, pp. 54–59, Salieri (35–45) and Constanze (20s)
Mozart is attracting attention, but little money. Salieri, his more financially successful competitor, is jealous of the younger man's talent and attempts to injure him by seducing his wife, Constanze. Salieri offers to intercede on Mozart's behalf with the Emperor if she'll sleep with him. Though she wants to help her husband, she refuses to cooperate. Start, Salieri: "If she did, how would I behave? I had no idea of that either." End, Salieri: "I will study them overnight—and you will study my proposal. Not to be vague, that is my price. Good afternoon."

AMEN CORNER, THE
by James Baldwin (Samuel French)
Drama: Act II, pp. 66–71, Margaret (35–45) and Luke (40–50)
Luke is dying. He is spending his last days with his ex-wife, Margaret, who, ten years ago, took their infant son and left him. Now she is the pastor of a small Harlem church, having buried the pain of her marriage in courtship to the Lord. The prospect of death, however, presents an opportunity for reassessment. Margaret and Luke talk about the joys and challenges of their marriage, as well as of how she struggled with their poverty and his love of music, which caused him to be away from home so much. Start, Margaret: "Luke, ain't you never going to learn to do right?" End, Margaret: "You're going to die, Luke."

Drama: Act III, pp. 84–89, Margaret (35–45) and David (18)
David has made his choice: he'll leave home and pursue a life as a professional musician. More important, however, is his determination to be his own man, not a puppet of his mother's religious teachings. In this scene, David has been out all night and comes home with a hangover. Margaret recognizes his sad state and slaps

him in the face—hard. He lifts his head, and she slaps him again. It is a moment of truth for mother and son. Both characters have excellent monologues. You'll have to cut and paste, eliminating Odessa's lines. Start, Margaret: "Where you been until this time in the morning, son?" End, David: "No, Mama. I ain't hungry now."

AMERI/CAIN GOTHIC
by Paul Carter Harrison (*Totem Voices, Plays from the Black World Repertory*, edited by Paul Carter Harrison, Grove Press)
Drama: Act II, Harper (mid-30s) and Cass (30s)
As Harper and Cass talk about life and fears, he keeps an eye on the motel across the street, the one Martin Luther King will soon stay in. Start, Harper: "That creep is on the prowl again!" End, Cass: "I don't believe you, Harper."

AMERICAN PLAN, THE
by Richard Greenberg (Dramatists Play Service)
Comedy-Drama: Act I, Scene 1, pp. 5–12, Lili (20) and Nick (20s)
This scene isn't what it appears to be. On the surface, it is a boy-meets-girl-in-the-Catskills scene. But what the audience doesn't know is that Nick is actually gay, and Lili has serious emotional problems. Challenging work for resourceful actors. Start, Nick: "Oh…Hi!" End, Lili: "I don't think so."
Comedy-Drama: Act I, Scene 3, pp. 19–24, Lili (20) and Nick (20s)
Lili has started a rumor that Nick has a venereal disease, causing the young woman he has been dating all summer to panic and very abruptly leave the Catskills with her family. In this scene, Nick confronts Lili and demands an explanation for her actions. Then he stays for tea. Start, Lili: "Bobby Darin." End, Nick: "All these words!"
Drama: Act I, Scene 6, pp. 32–36, Eva (40s) and Nick (20s)
Eva has investigated Nick's background and discovered that almost everything he has told her daughter about himself is a lie. In this tense scene, Eva confronts him, and he explains. At least the audience and Eva *think* he explains—but he isn't telling the whole story. Start, Eva: "It has warmed my heart to see the change in Lili over these last weeks." End, Eva: "That is no longer either here or there."

ANASTASIA
by Marcelle Maurette (adapted by Guy Bolton, Samuel French)
Drama: Act II, pp. 56–59, Empress (79) and Paul (25–30)
Paul is apparently convinced that Anna is the real Anastasia, the only surviving daughter of the Russian Tsar Nicholas II, and he has brought his aunt, the Dowager Empress, to see for herself. It is February 1926, and the Empress has met many pretenders since the royal family was assassinated in 1918, so she is inclined to be skeptical. After all, where would a real princess have hidden for so many years? Paul urges the Empress to keep an open mind. Start, Paul: "Does Anastasia know you are here?" End, Empress: "Leave them. Leave them wrapped in the dignity of death."
Drama: Act III, pp. 77–79, Empress (79) and Bounine (40s)
A woman believed to be the real Princess Anastasia, the only surviving daughter of the last Russian Tsar Nicholas II, is about to be presented to the press. If all goes well, Bounine and his cohorts, the group that discovered the young woman, will come into their share of the heiress's huge fortune tomorrow. In this scene, the Dowager Empress, evidently convinced that Anna is the real Anastasia, surprises

Bounine by announcing that she knows the whole plan is a scam. Cornered, he at first denies the charge but then caves in, blaming everything on Anna. When the Empress doesn't go for that, he switches gears again, urging her to go ahead with a public endorsement of the young woman so that they can all gain access to the fortune. This short scene is interesting for its many twists and turns. Start, Bounine: "I assume from Your Majesty's attitude that the—the Princess has told you certain things?" End, Empress: "The audience is over. I am through with you, Arcade Arcadievitch Bounine."

Drama: Act III, pp. 81–83, Anna (20s) and Dr. Serensky (25–35)

Anna's former lover, Dr. Serensky, has shown up on the day she is to be presented to the world as the real Princess Anastasia. He knows it isn't true. As the scene progresses, however, it is clear that Anna can pass, whether it is true or not, and she is going for the gold. All Dr. Serensky has to offer is love and a struggling medical practice. Start, Serensky: "How lovely you look. And how well." End, Anna: "If we are parting, Michael."

ANGELS IN AMERICA: A GAY FANTASIA ON NATIONAL THEMES, PART I: MILLENNIUM APPROACHES
by Tony Kushner (Theatre Communications Group)

Drama: Act I, Scene 5, Harper (early 30s) and Joe (early 30s)

Joe tells his wife, Harper, that he wants to accept a political position and move from Brooklyn to Washington, DC. Harper, an agoraphobe and a borderline Valium addict, is terrified of such a move. Disregard Louis and the Rabbi's appearance in this split scene. Start, Harper: "Washington?" End, Harper: "…skin burns, birds go blind, icebergs melt. The world's coming to an end."

Drama: Act I, Scene 7, Harper (early 30s) and Prior (30)

In this sequence, Harper and Prior appear in one another's dreams. She is an agoraphobe and dependent on Valium; he is gay, flamboyant, and dying of AIDS. They meet here for the first time but, because it is a dream, they already seem to know a lot about each other. The whole scene is slightly disconnected from reality. Start, Prior: "I'm ready for my close-up, Mr. DeMille." End, Prior: "People come and go so strangely here. I don't think there's any uninfected part of me. My heart is pumping polluted blood. I feel dirty."

Drama: Act I, Scene 8, Harper (early 30s) and Joe (early 30s)

Harper and her husband, Joe, have a troubled marriage. She is addicted to various prescription drugs, and since they stopped having sex regularly, Joe has stayed out much later at night, and his business trips seem longer. Sensing some kind of fundamental change in the man, she hysterically confronts him in this scene, asking whether he is homosexual. Joe doesn't provide a straightforward answer to the question; instead, he suggests that they pray more and ask God for guidance. This only serves to infuriate Harper. Simultaneous scenes are being played on stage here, so disregard Louis and Prior. Start, Harper: "Where were you?" End, Harper: "No. Yes. No. Yes. Get away from me. Now we both have a secret."

ANNA CHRISTIE
by Eugene O'Neill (Vintage Books)

Drama: Act II, Anna (20) and Mat Burke (30)

For the past ten days, Anna has been living happily on her father's coal barge, relishing the fresh sea air. Then a group of shipwrecked sailors come on board, and

Anna is swept off her feet by one of them, an Irishman named Mat Burke. Fifteen minutes after he meets her, he asks her to marry him. Mat has a slight Irish accent. Start, Anna: "Here you are. Here's a drink for you. You need it, I guess." End, Burke: "I'm telling you there's the will of God in it that brought me safe through the storm and fog to the wan spot in the world where you was!"

Drama: Act IV, Anna (20) and Chris (50)

After her father, Chris, and Mat react so strongly to Anna's disclosure that she's been a prostitute, Anna decides to return to the streets. She is packed to leave when her father returns from his drunken binge, asks her forgiveness for having been a bad parent all her life, and announces that he is shipping out to Cape Town. The role of Chris requires a heavy Swedish accent, and O'Neill has written it with those inflections. The scene calls for a revolver, but it is never fired. Begin at the top of Act IV. Start, Anna: "Come in." End, Anna: "Good night."

Drama: Act IV, Anna (20) and Burke (30)

Mat has decided that despite Anna's sordid past, he loves her and again asks her to marry him. She accepts this time. Mat has a slight Irish accent. Also, the scene calls for a revolver that does not get fired. Start, Anna: "What are you doing here?" End, Mat: "We'll be happy now, the two of us, in spite of the divil."

ANOTHER ANTIGONE
by A. R. Gurney, Jr. (Dramatists Play Service)

Comedy-Drama: One-act play, pp. 10–14, Judy Miller (early 20s) and Dave (early 20s)

Judy Miller has written a modern, antiwar adaptation of the Greek classic *Antigone* and, now that her Greek drama teacher has refused to give her a passing grade for the effort, she has become defiant; she is determined to mount a university production of her play. In this scene, Judy tries to enlist her boyfriend, Dave, to play Antigone's sister, a character she has changed into Antigone's lover. He isn't excited by the prospect. Begin as Dave reads aloud from the script. Start, Dave: "No, Antigone, no. Please reconsider. Do not take on this dangerous enterprise. The risks are too great, the payoff insignificant." End, Dave: "No. Antigone, no. Please reconsider."

Comedy-Drama: One-act play, pp. 14–23, Diana (35–45) and Henry (40–50)

Diana, the dean of Humane Studies, has been caught up in the growing conflict between Henry Harper and his defiant student, Judy Miller. Diana visits Henry's office and asks him to back off, but he won't consider it. Then she tells him that campus whispers portray him as anti-Semitic. Start, Diana: "Henry?" End, Diana: "Now where did she get an idea like that?"

Comedy-Drama: One-act play, pp. 41–47, Diana (35–45) and Henry (40–50)

In this gripping scene, Diana delivers the news that Henry is being granted a year off with full pay so he can visit Greece and do some research. He refuses the offer, however, because his wife has left him and because Diana shows no interest in accompanying him on the trip and beginning a romance. Then she levels him by reporting that there are practically no pre-enrollments for his course next year, and that the college is, in fact, laying him off for a while. Henry leaves their meeting determined to drum up some enrollments. Start, Henry: "Woman at her work. I am reminded of Penelope at her loom." End, Henry: "Then I'll have to get them, won't I?"

Drama: One-act play, pp. 49–55, Judy (early 20s) and Henry (40–50)
In this final scene between Judy and her teacher, he offers an olive branch if she'll help him get some students in his next semester's class. Judy doesn't need Henry anymore, however, because another teacher—significantly, a Jewish teacher—has agreed to give her an A on the project that Henry dismissed. Excellent scene illustrating a power struggle. Start, Judy: "You wanted to see me, Professor Harper?" End, Henry: "Good God. What have I done?"

AUTUMN GARDEN, THE
by Lillian Hellman (Dramatists Play Service)
Drama: Act II, Scene 1, pp. 49–52, Rose (43) and Mr. Griggs (53)
Rose is desperately trying to save her twenty-five-year marriage, which is in shambles. Her husband, however, is intent on divorce, wants to start a new life for himself, and is unmoved even when she tells him that another man may be standing in the wings. Start, Rose: "Nasty old thing. I'm driving over to see him." End, Rose: "I am going to try, dear. Really I am. It's evidently important to you."
Drama: Act II, Scene 2, pp. 68–70, Sophie (17) and Nick (45)
The oh-so-continental Nick has had far too much to drink and is feeling lonely and full of self-pity when he discovers Sophie preparing her bed in the living room. He makes a fumbling attempt at seducing her, but his efforts disgust her, and he falls asleep. Sophie has a slight French accent. Start, Nick: "Constance! What is this—A boys' school with lights out at eleven!" End, Nick: "Have a little pity. I am old and sick."
Drama: Act III, pp. 78–82, Nina (40) and Nick (45)
Stung by Nick's drunken insults last night, Nina, his wife, has packed to leave. When he realizes that she is serious about separation, he begs forgiveness. She relents, sending him on ahead to Mobile, Alabama, to wait for her while she tries to clean up the human mess he has left in his wake. This is an excellent scene in which two adults redefine the terms of their relationship, essentially lowering their expectations. Start, Nick: "Nina, I just want to say before you go that they're making an awful row about nothing." End, Nina: "You love me and I love you and that's that and always will be."

BAD HABITS
by Terrence McNally (1990 revised edition, Dramatists Play Service)
Comedy: "Dunelawn," pp. 46–48, April (late 20s) and Roy (30s)
April and Roy are professional actors who have been married only three months and can't get along because they are so competitive. Here, they lounge in the sunshine and tear each other to shreds. Start, Roy: "Honey! You're blocking my sun." End, April: "Give him skin cancer, God, give him skin cancer, please!"
Comedy: "Dunelawn," pp. 27–32, Dolly (late 20s) and Harry (30s)
Dolly arrives for a visit and discovers that after three months of treatment, her husband, Harry, is a changed man. Now he drinks, smokes, dances, sings, and sculpts. In this scene, they talk about why they've tried so often to kill each other, and he tells her how great he's doing. Eliminate Dr. Pepper in the beginning of the scene, and the interruptions of the public-address system. Start, Harry: "You look wonderful, Dolly." End, Dolly: "Doctor!…What have you done to him?"

Comedy: "Ravenswood," pp. 83–90, Ruth Benson (late 20s) and Hugh Gumbs (30s)

Hugh Gumbs was the love of Ruth's life until he ran off with Mildred Canby five years ago. To win him back, Ruth has remade herself, giving up smoking and drinking, and losing a great deal of weight. Now she is an attractive nurse employed at Ravenswood. Unexpectedly, Hugh checks in for treatment, a man in the gutter, an alcoholic loser. When she reveals her new identity to him, he still rejects her, this time because she is too good for him. Eliminate Dr. Toynbee. Also, the scene calls for Hugh to be in a wheelchair and, though that is ideal, you can work without it. Start, Hugh: "Aaaaaaaaaa!" End, Benson: "All right, Hugh, and remember, you asked for it."

BAREFOOT IN THE PARK
by Neil Simon (Samuel French)
Comedy: Act II, Scene 2, pp. 60–69, Corie (early 20s) and Paul (early 20's)

This is the first newlywed argument and, of course, it takes only a short while for the "divorce" word to come up. We know all along that there isn't going to be any divorce but, to these new lovers, the entire world is at stake. Physical comedy, innocent and fun. Start, Paul: "What a rotten thing to do…to your own mother." End, Paul: "Six days does not a week make."

THE BEAR
by Anton Chekhov (*The Sneeze, Plays and Stories by Anton Chekhov*; translated and adapted by Michael Frayn, Dramatists Play Service)
Comedy: One-act play, pp. 47–55, Smirnov (45–55) and Popova (45–55)

Smirnov has arrived at the widow Popova's home to collect a debt owed by her late husband. When she can't pay immediately, Smirnov refuses to leave, staging a kind of sit-in. Within fifteen minutes, his anger has turned to lust and he declares his love for her. For workshop purposes, eliminate Popova's servant completely. You'll have to do a bit of editing, but it is well worth the effort. Start, Smirnov: "Smirnov, Grigory Stepanovich Smirnov, landowner and lieutenant of artillery, retired." End, Popova: "I've no desire to converse with impertinent hobbledehoys! Kindly get out of here!" Or, you can continue through their kiss.

BEAU JEST
by James Sherman (Samuel French)
Comedy: Act II, Scene 2, pp. 60–68, Sarah (20s) and Bob (20s)

In order to fool her parents into thinking she has a nice Jewish boyfriend, Sarah called an escort service, asked for a Jewish date for the evening, and arranged a dinner with the folks. It turns out, however, that Bob, the escort, isn't Jewish at all. Fortunately, he is a charming actor and manages to play his role beautifully, winning over Sarah's parents. In this scene, which takes place immediately after the second visit with the parents, Bob and Sarah relax together at her place. They're clicking for real, an erotic buzz is in the air, and love is blooming. He massages her shoulders, they talk, he gets up to leave, and they kiss. They kiss again. He stays. Start, Bob: "You got anything to drink in this place? Besides wine?" End, Sarah: "You're not Jewish! Oy!"

BEAUTY QUEEN OF LEENANE, THE
by Martin McDonagh (Dramatists Play Service)
Drama: Act I, Scene 3, pp. 19–24, Maureen (40) and Pato (40s)

Pato brings Maureen home after a party. They've both had maybe a little too much to drink, and Pato is being amorous. At forty years of age, Maureen is still a virgin, but it is clear that tonight may be the night. This scene is for advanced actors who are comfortable with an Irish accent and Irish ways. Start, Pato (singing) "*...the Cadillac stood by the house...*" End, Maureen: "...Go lower...lower."

BELL, BOOK AND CANDLE
by John Van Druten (Dramatists Play Service)
Comedy: Act I, Scene 2, pp. 21–26, Gillian (27) and Shep (35)

Gillian is an honest-to-goodness witch who is smitten with Shep, the handsome publisher who lives upstairs. Afraid that she is about to lose him, she casts a spell to guarantee his affections. It works well, and he falls immediately and passionately into her arms. Three hours later, in the afterglow of lovemaking, Gillian and Shep discuss the future. He is just about ready for marriage, but she wants their romance to continue on for a while. Anyway, unbeknownst to Shep, witches can't really fall in love. If they do, they lose their powers. Start, Shep: "Say something." End, Gillian: "Soon."

Comedy: Act II, pp. 43–47, Gillian (27) and Shep (35)

At the risk of losing Shep, Gillian confesses that she is a witch and that she used a spell to get him to fall in love with her. He, of course, does not believe in witches and so doesn't accept a word of what she is saying. Start, Shep: "Is anything the matter?" End, Shep: "I believe you cast an absolutely wonderful spell on me, and I'm crazy about it."

Comedy: Act III, Scene 2, pp. 65–70, Gillian (27) and Shep (35)

In the very last scene, Shep has come to say good-bye but, in the process, discovers that Gillian has truly fallen in love with him and that she has lost her magical powers. They fall into one another's arms, presumably to live happily ever after. Start, Shep: "This isn't a friendly visit." End, Gillian: "I'm only human."

BETRAYAL
by Harold Pinter (Dramatists Play Service)
Drama: Scene 1 (1977), pp. 7–12, Emma (30s) and Jerry (30s)

After learning that her husband, Robert, has been carrying on romantic affairs for years, Emma wants to talk to her former lover, Jerry. In this restaurant conversation, the first face-to-face meeting they've had since they broke up two years ago, Emma and Jerry discuss their respective families and reminisce about the glory days of their seven-year romance. She tells him that she and Robert plan to separate. Start, Jerry: "Well." End, Emma: "It's all over."

Drama: Scene 3 (1975), pp. 17–19, Emma (30s) and Jerry (30s)

Emma and Jerry agree to end their seven-year affair. They discuss what to do with their apartment and joint possessions. This scene has an important subtext: Emma long ago told her husband, who is Jerry's best friend, about their affair, but Jerry doesn't know this. Start, Jerry: "What do you want to do then?" End, Emma: "Listen. I think we've made absolutely the right decision."

Drama: Scene 5 (1973), pp. 24–27, Emma (30s) and Robert (30s)
While on holiday in Venice, Emma tells Robert that she has been carrying on a longtime affair with his best friend, Jerry. Start, Emma: "It's Torcello tomorrow, isn't it?" End, Robert: "Tell me, are you looking forward to our trip to Torcello?"

Drama: Scene 8 (1971), pp. 35–38, Emma (30s) and Jerry (30s)
Their affair still young and exciting, Emma prepares lunch for Jerry in the flat they secretly maintain. At the end of the scene, she tells him that she is pregnant with her husband's child. Start, Jerry: "Hullo." End, Jerry: "Yes. Yes, of course. I'm very happy for you."

BETWEEN DAYLIGHT AND BOONVILLE
By Matt Williams (Samuel French)

Comedy-Drama: Act I, pp. 12–19, Carla (26) and Cyril (30s)
Carla, discontent with her coal-miner husband, Larry, and their dreary trailer-park existence, plans to escape. In this scene, she asks Cyril, a miner who is out of work because of a hand injury, to give her and her child a lift to the bus station. Cyril is a jokester and a flirt, but he wouldn't really play around with his friend's wife. He also isn't crazy about the idea of helping Carla run away from Larry. You'll have to cut and paste a bit, eliminating Jimmy. Start, Cyril: "Waaaah!" End, Cyril: "Please don't tickle. I'm goin' to pee in my pants."

BEYOND THERAPY
by Christopher Durang (Samuel French)

Comedy: Act I, Scene 1, pp. 7–13, Prudence (29–32) and Bruce (30–34)
Prudence and Bruce meet through a personal ad, but the date is disastrous. It turns out that he has a male lover. Start, Prudence: "Hello." End, Prudence: "Absolutely nothing seems to get that waiter's attention, does it?"

Comedy: Act I, Scene 2, pp. 14–18, Prudence (29–32) and Dr. Stuart Framingham (35–45)
Prudence tells Dr. Framingham, her psychotherapist, about her disastrous date with Bruce, but all the therapist wants to talk about is his own masculinity and his sexual relationship with Prudence. Start, Dr. Framingham: "You can send the next patient in now, Betty." End, Prudence: "Please, don't you talk either."

Comedy: Act I, Scene 3, pp. 18–23, Charlotte Wallace (45–55) and Bruce (30–34)
Bruce tells Charlotte Wallace, his therapist, about his disastrous date with Prudence. The psychologist, however, doesn't think it sounds bad at all. Influenced by *Equus,* she thinks it is better to be outrageous and impulsive than to be boring. Start, Charlotte: "You may send in the next patient, Marcia." End, Charlotte: "Marcia, I'll buzz back when I think of it."

Comedy: Act I, Scene 4, pp. 24–33, Prudence (29–32) and Bruce (30–34)
At the insistence of his therapist, Bruce has placed another personal ad, this time completely exaggerating his physical assets and intellectual accomplishments. Of course, Prudence has responded to it and shows up at the appointed meeting place expecting to meet Mr. Tall, Dark, and Handsome. Instead, she finds Bruce. To their mutual surprise, however, this time they click. This scene isn't nearly as wild and crazy as was their first encounter, but it is just as interesting for scenework because they must find honest values in one another. Start, Prudence: "Oh." End, Prudence: "…but there was something about the texture of vanilla ice cream."

Comedy: Act I, Scene 5, pp. 33–38, Prudence (29–32) and Dr. Stuart Framingham (35–45)
Prudence tells her therapist that her relationship with Bruce is progressing nicely, that she likes him after all, and that they've slept together. Responding as a man and not as a doctor, Dr. Framingham is completely threatened by this news. Start, Dr. Framingham: "Hiya, babe, it's me." End, Prudence: "I don't think you do either."

BIRDBATH
by Leonard Melfi (*Encounters, Six One-Act Plays,* by Leonard Melfi, Samuel French)
Drama: One-act play, pp. 12–22, Velma (26) and Frankie (late 20s)
Although Velma and Frankie have been working side by side at the cafeteria, this is the first time they speak. Before the night is out, they'll go back to his place, but they won't make love. Try combining the first part of the play, which takes place in the cafeteria, and the second part, which takes place on the street outside the cafeteria. Start, Velma: "Hi." End, Velma: "You know, Frankie, maybe instead of the coffee I'd better have hot tea instead."
Drama: One-act play, pp. 30–42, Velma (26) and Frankie (late 20s)
After Frankie and Velma go to his apartment and the liquor starts to take effect, he tries to get a little closer to her. She becomes increasingly agitated, however, and finally turns on him with a knife. Start, Frankie: "Relax, Velma." Continue to the end of the play. End, Frankie: "I have a treat for you in the morning, Velma. I've just written you…a valentine."

BITTER SAUCE
by Eric Bogosian (*Love's Fire—Seven New Plays Inspired by Seven Shakespearean Sonnets,* William Morrow, 1998)
Comedy: One-act play, Rengin (a bride, 20s) and Herman (her fiancé, 20s)
Rengin is getting married in the morning, but tonight she's drunk. When we first see her in her living room, she is sloppily clad in her wedding dress and trying to figure out what to do about Red, the biker with whom she has been having hot sex. Red is scheduled to arrive momentarily for a little pre-wedding roll in the hay. Before Red gets there, however, Rengin's hapless and unsuspecting fiancé, Herman, arrives. He immediately sets about sobering her up, during which he learns all about Red. End the scene when Red knocks on the door. I suggest you start at the top of the play but skip Herman's first speech, which is actually supposed to come out of an answering machine. Start, Rengin: "What is this I'm wearing? A white dress." End, Herman: "Go."

BLUE WINDOW
by Craig Lucas (Samuel French)
Comedy-Drama: Scene 2, pp. 44–346, Libby (33) and Griever (35–40)
Libby is hosting her first dinner party since her husband's death. She is embarrassed because a cap on her missing front tooth fell off and, anyway, it is "too soon" for her to be trying to give a party. She fears the evening isn't going well. Griever, her friend and sometimes lover, comforts and consoles her. Start, Griever: "Congratulations, it's going great, don't you think?" End, Libby: "Go!"

BORN YESTERDAY
by Garson Kanin (Dramatists Play Service)

Comedy: Act I, pp. 39–42, Billie Dawn (29) and Paul Verrall (30s)

Harry Brock, a corrupt, self-made millionaire, has hired Paul Verrall, a serious-minded journalist to tutor his dumb but beautiful girlfriend, Billie Dawn. Harry is worried that Billie, an ex-chorine, will be inept in social situations as he attempts to influence the movers and shakers in Washington, DC, so he wants Paul to educate her. In this first meeting between the tutor and his charge, sparks of attraction fill the room. Start, Paul: "Your—friend Mr. Brock has an idea he'd like us to spend a little time together. You and me, that is." End, Billy: "Or the night!"

Comedy: Act I, pp. 43–46, Billie Dawn (29) and Harry Brock (40s)

Toward the end of Act I, Harry and Billie are alone onstage together for the first time, and the audience gets its first look at their relationship, seeing how they communicate in private. Beginning with a silent gin game that Billie readily wins and ending with Harry's attempt to draw Billie into the upstairs bedroom, this three-page scene illuminates a fascinating status/power struggle. Start, Billy (singing): "…*Anything Goes (tata tata—tata tata—tzing!)*" End, Billie: "Good authors too, who once—"

Comedy: Act II, pp. 54–59, Billie Dawn (290) and Paul Verrall (30s)

Paul has been tutoring Billie for two months, and she is thriving on the newfound knowledge. To her confusion, however, he hasn't tried to sleep with her—and she's up for it. The entire scene runs about fifteen pages. For a shorter version, start, Billie: "Oh, and you know that thing you gave me about Napoleon?" End, Paul: "I know. He's got a brain of gold."

BOSOMS AND NEGLECT
by John Guare (Dramatists Play Service, revised edition)

Comedy-Drama: Act I, pp. 31–34, Deirdre (20s–30s) and Scooper (late 30s)

Things heat up here when they almost kiss. After that event, we have more subtext going on, adding increased substance to the always-witty dialogue. Start just after the failed kiss. Deirdre: "I'm not married." End, Deirdre: "What Beethoven is to the sonata, I am to the couch."

BOYS' LIFE
by Howard Korder (Dramatists Play Service)

Comedy: Scene 3, pp. 14–19, Maggie (late 20s) and Jack (late 20s)

Jack and Maggie meet at a children's playground. He tries to pick her up but bombs out. Both get progressively stoned from marijuana. Start, Maggie (out of breath from running): "Oh God. Oh God." End, Jack: "One…Two…Three…Four…All right, that's it. I'm calling mommy!"

BREAKING THE CODE
by Hugh Whitemore (Samuel French)

Drama: Act I, Scene 7, pp. 48–54, Pat (early 30s) and Alan Turing (39)

Pat Green is a cryptanalyst working at the Government Code and Cipher School during World War II. Assigned to work with Alan Turing on the German code project, she falls in love with him. In this scene at his mother's home, Pat and Turing are left alone. She declares her feelings for him but, as she suspected might be the case, he tells her that he is a homosexual. Start, Pat: "She's quite right, you know." End, Turing: "It would stop me making love to you. I don't want that sort of life and I don't think you do either."

Drama: Act II, Scene 3, pp. 72–76, Sara (60) and Alan Turing (39)

Alan Turing tells Sara, his mother, that he is homosexual and will have to stand trial for his "crime." She is shocked to learn about her son's sexual orientation, having long presumed his lack of interest in women was because he was bookish. This is a very touching scene. Start, Sara: "Alan, my dear, you are so silly!" End, Sara: "Do come and look at the guest room. I'm so pleased with it."

BROOKLYN BOY
by Donald Margulies (Theatre Communications Group)

Drama: Act I, Scene 3, pp. 40–50, Eric (40s) and Nina (40s)

Eric comes by the apartment he used to share with Nina to pick up what remains of his belongings. After a trial two-month separation, he would really like to fire the relationship back up, but Nina is committed to moving on. The marriage is officially coming to an end. Nevertheless, these two people clearly still love one another, which gives the scene a very nice kick. Start, Nina: "What's the matter, you don't believe in doorbells?" End, Nina: "This is it, bubbie. It's over. This is what the end looks like."

Drama: Act I, scene 4, pp. 58–66, Eric (40s) and Allison (20s)

Eric has been signing copies of his novel, *Brooklyn Boy*, at Book Soup on Sunset Boulevard in Los Angeles. He picks up a young fan and brings her back to his hotel room. For sex? Maybe. For company? Hard to tell. What she doesn't know is that he received word earlier today that his father had died. He is reaching out for human contact. The generation gap between them is what fuels the scene. The full Act I, Scene 4, takes up thirteen pages, too long for most acting workshop purposes. I suggest a cut that starts several pages in. Start, Alison: "What do people call you? Continue to the end of Scene 4, after Eric autographs her copy of his novel. End, Eric: "My pleasure."

BURN THIS
by Lanford Wilson (Hill & Wang/Noonday; HarperCollins Canada Ltd.)

Comedy-Drama: Act II, Anna (32) and Pale (36)

Anna tells Pale not to mistake their two nights of passion for something permanent. Start, Anna: "Pale, would you do me a favor?" End, Pale: "What's that mean—truculent?" For scene-study purposes, you can play this with Larry onstage or omit his presence altogether. To eliminate him, cut from Pale's line, "Hawaii, Brazil. See places" to Anna's line, "Pale, I don't even know how this nonsense started; it never should have." Cut Larry's lines, too. This will get around the problem of Pale having to leave and change clothes.

CANDIDA
by George Bernard Shaw (Signet)

Comedy-Drama: Act II, Prosperine (30) and Eugene Marchbanks (18)

Eugene accuses Prosperine, Morell's secretary, of not being honest about her romantic longings. He manages to elicit something of a confession that she secretly loves Morell, a fact that depresses Eugene because he is convinced that

Morell is unlovable. Start, Prosperine: "Bother! You've been meddling with my typewriter." End, Prosperine: "Yes."

CAT ON A HOT TIN ROOF
by Tennessee Williams (Dramatists Play Service)
Drama: Act I, pp. 10–16, Margaret (early 20s) and Brick (27)
Margaret, who is also called Maggie, is dressing for Big Daddy's party as she and her husband, Brick, bicker and then argue more violently about their nonexistent sex life, his alcoholism, his curious relationship with Skipper, and Big Daddy's fatal disease. Start, Maggie: "Y'know—your brother Gooper still cherishes the illusion he took a giant step up on the social ladder when he married Miss Mae Flynn of the Memphis Flynns." End, Margaret: "They're impossible conditions!"

CHAPTER TWO
by Neil Simon (Samuel French)
Comedy: Act I, Scene 6, pp. 40–49, Jennie (32) and George (42)
Actress Jennie Malone, newly divorced after a six-year marriage, meets novelist George Schneider, whose wife of fourteen years recently died. The sparks fly in this scene, which is full of wit, embarrassment, and awkwardness. Start, Jennie: "Hello?…Faye, I can't talk to you now." End, George: "I can't believe you're from the same man who gave us Bambi and Vilma."
Comedy: Act II, Scene 5, pp. 93–104, Jennie (32) and George (42)
George and Jennie had an awful time on their honeymoon. Having just walked into George's apartment with their luggage, they think they may have made a big mistake by marrying. Play entire scene. Start, Jennie: "That was fun! Three days of rain and two days of diarrhea." End, George: "We got, as they say in the trade, problems, kid."
Comedy: Act II, Scene 6, pp. 105–114, Faye (35) and Leo (40)
George's brother, Leo, and Jennie's friend, Faye, are launching an affair, using Jennie's old apartment for a clandestine meeting. However, Faye is guilt-ridden, and Leo wants only sex, no romance, so the liaison isn't working out. Start, Leo: "I'm sorry." End, Leo: "Hold on to your sheet, kid, kissing is my main thing."

CHASE, THE
by Horton Foote (Dramatists Play Service)
Drama: Act I, Scene 3, pp. 26–29, Mrs. Reeves (60ish) and Sheriff Hawes (38–45)
Mrs. Reeves tries to bribe Sheriff Hawes not to kill her son, who is an escaped convict. The scene gets pretty emotional as Mrs. Reeves begs for her son's life. As such, the role of the mother is best suited for an experienced actress. The play is set in Texas, so southern accents are appropriate. Start, Sheriff Hawes: "Mrs. Reeves, where have you been?" End, Mrs. Reeves: "I hope your child is hunted and killed some day. I hope it is. I hope it is."

CHEATERS
by Michael Jacobs (Samuel French)
Comedy: Act I, Scene 3, pp. 20–25, Michelle (20s) and Allen (20s)
Allen and Michelle have been living together for eighteen months and are returning to their apartment tonight after attending a friend's wedding. Michelle is mortified because Allen caught the bridal bouquet—and tossed it back. She

presses him to make a commitment to marry her. When he balks, she walks out on him. This is a delightful scene for which you'll need a bed or futon. The characters often dress and undress (no nudity) and get into and out of bed as they fight with and try to seduce one another. Start, Michelle: "I want to thank you for the most embarrassing night of my life!" End, Allen: "I really showed her."

CHILDREN OF A LESSER GOD
by Mark Medoff (Dramatists Play Service)
Drama: Act I, pp. 23–25, Sarah (mid-20s) and James (30)
Because Sarah, who is deaf, refuses to speak, preferring to sign, she has been in conflict with James, who is supposed to teach her to speak. But something else is going on. The teacher/student relationship is turning romantic, although neither Sarah nor James has acknowledged this yet. In this short scene, which takes place at a duck pond, Sarah gets jealous of James's relationship with another student, and her jealousy makes him angry. Then they kiss. Start, James: "Well, at last. 'Dear Sarah, please meet me at the duck pond after dinner. I'll bring the stale bread. James Leeds.'" End, James: "It's always worked before. See, when I get in trouble, I kiss the girl and make everything better. (She exits) Oh, come on, Sarah!…Sarah!"

Drama: Act I, pp. 27–28, Sarah (mid-20s) and James (30)
James meets Sarah while she is working at her regular job as a maid in a school for the deaf. After discovering that she was considered retarded until she was twelve years old, he confronts her. James wants to know if this is why she hates hearing-people, or whether she hates herself. Sarah then accuses him of wanting to teach her the joys of sex with a hearing man and tells him that she was quite promiscuous in her teens. Start, James: "Hello. I left you a note. It said: 'Please see me this afternoon. I'll bring the boxing gloves.' You didn't come so I ate all the gloves myself. I'm sorry to interrupt your work." End, James: "Your secret. No hearing person has ever gotten in there to find out…No person, period."

Drama: Act I, pp. 32–34, Sarah (mid-20s) and James (30)
In this scene, James and Sarah talk about marriage and the prospect of having deaf children. Start, James: "Sorry I'm late. I got held up." End, James: "I know you want to, but we can't. The point is, it's all possible. And you know it. Say it. Say: 'I know it's possible.'"

Drama: Act I, pp. 36–38, Sarah (mid-20s) and James (30)
A lovely scene that takes place in Sarah's childhood bedroom. James tells her about his mother's suicide, and they cling to each other. Start, Sarah: "My room." End, Sarah: "You and me. Joined."

Drama: Act II, pp. 64–68, Sarah (mid-20s) and James (30)
Sarah is going to make a speech before the Equal Employment Opportunity Commission, asking that the school for the deaf be forced to hire more deaf people. She offends James by telling him that she wants Orin, a hearing-impaired person, not James, to translate for her. Their conversation escalates into a big argument, during which James accuses Sarah of refusing to speak just so she can control people. He holds her arms when she tries to sign and, for the first time in the play, she speaks. It isn't really clear speech, but an expression of passion and frustration. This is an extremely powerful scene. Start, James: "You're home from work." Sarah: "It's exciting to feel I have a job." End, Sarah: "Me have nothing. Me

deafy. Speech inept. Intelligence—tiny block-head. English—blow away. Left one you. Depend—no. Think myself enough. Join. Unjoined."

THE CHILDREN'S HOUR
by Lillian Hellman (Dramatists Play Service)
Drama: Act III, pp. 61–54, Karen (28) and Dr. Joseph Cardin (35)

Karen's fiancé, Dr. Joseph Cardin, guiltily asks her if the allegations about her being a lesbian are true. Deeply hurt, she assures him that they are not and then gives him the opportunity to back out of their relationship with grace. Excellent scene. Begin after Martha's exit. Start, Cardin: "You'll like Jake and he'll like you." End, Karen: "I don't think so."

CLOSER
by Patrick Marber (Dramatists Play Service)
Drama: Act I, Scene 1, pp. 1–12, Alice (24) and Dan (35)

Alice was hit by the taxi in which Dan was a passenger. Hers isn't a major injury—a cut on the leg—but he escorted her to the hospital emergency room anyway. They get to know one another while waiting for a doctor to see her. He is an aspiring novelist who is working as an obit writer on a newspaper; she is more mysterious, a bit of a drifter, living out of her knapsack. Sparks fly between them. (Note: Larry the doctor briefly interrupts the scene. The actors can easily eliminate him, though.) Start at top of Act I, with Alice fishing in Dan's briefcase. End, Alice: "Alice. My name is Alice Ayres."

Drama: Act I, Scene 2, pp. 12–19, Anna (early 30s) and Dan (35)

This scene takes place in a photography studio a year after the first scene. By now, Dan is living with Alice and, inspired by her, has written a novel that is soon to be published. Anna has been hired to photograph Dan for the cover of the book. As was the case in the first scene, an erotic charge permeates the room. Dan learns that Anna is married but separated, and Anna learns about Alice. There is a ten-second kiss late in the scene. (Note: Anna is a photographer and snaps shots of Dan throughout the scene. You'll need a camera, preferably hooked up to a flash.) Start at top of Scene 2. Anna: "Good." End, Anna: "Dan…Your shirt."

Drama: Act I, Scene 4, pp. 28–33, Anna (early 30s) and Larry (mid-30s)

Anna is passing time watching fish in the city aquarium. Larry walks up and introduces himself, erroneously presuming that she is the hot babe he met on the Internet. He thinks he is in for a wild afternoon fling in a motel, and she thinks he is a bit nuts. When they straighten things out, they realize that Larry was tricked by Dan. This isn't a long scene, but it is fun to play and has many transitions. Start, Larry: "Anna?" End, Larry: "Happy Birthday."

Drama: Act I, Scene 5, pp. 40–43, Anna (early 30s) and Dan (35)

Anna, who has been going with Larry for the past four months, is having a photography exhibit. Dan shows up and tries to talk her back into his life. A few sparks remain, but she's not budging. Start Anna: "I can't talk for long." End, Dan: "…I'm begging you…I'm your stranger…jump."

Drama: Act I, Scene 6, pp. 54–61, Anna (early 30s) and Larry (mid-30s)

We are in Larry and Anna's apartment. He first tells her that he had sex with a whore in Manhattan, expecting her to be furious. Instead of that, she tells him that she is leaving him because she is again involved with Dan. Larry flies into a jealous rage. He wants to know the raw details of her most recent tryst with Dan.

Very graphic language. Start, Anna: "Why are you dressed?" Go to the end of Act I. End, Larry: "Now fuck off and die. You fucked-up slag."

Drama: Act II, Scene 11, pp. 102–111, Alice (24) and Dan (35)

Larry has told Dan that he slept with Alice. In this scene, Dan tests Alice to see if that is true. When he does so, she decides she no longer loves him. She hates being in a position where she doesn't want to lie and can't tell the truth. The scene ends cruelly, when Dan hits her. Raw stuff. Actors will chew the scenery with it. Start, Alice: "Show me the sneer." End, Alice: "Do you have a single original thought in your head?"

COASTAL DISTURBANCES
by Tina Howe (Samuel French)

Comedy-Drama: Act I, Scene 2, pp. 20–24, Leo (28) and Holly (24)

Holly arrives at the beach to take some photographs. Leo, the lifeguard, helps her unfold her tripod, and a relationship begins. Start, Leo: "Well, well, long time, no see." End, Holly: "Or at least take some pictures of other people for a change— widen my focus for God's sake."

Comedy-Drama: Act II, Scene 4, pp. 73–81, Holly (24) and Andre (49)

Andre, Holly's lover for the last three years, arrives at the resort for a weekend visit, hoping to patch up their relationship. Elegant and European born, Andre is the owner of an art gallery. The scene requires a tall lifeguard stand. If you can't believably and safely simulate the structure in class, just omit the references to it and work around it. Start, Holly: "Well, here we are again…the little beach where I spent all my summers as a child. It doesn't have anywhere near the sweep of Crane's where I took you yesterday, but…Are you OK?" End, Holly: "I just…can't."

COME BACK, LITTLE SHEBA
by William Inge (Samuel French)

Drama: Act I, Scene 2, pp. 33–38, Lola (39) and Doc (mid-40s)

In this short scene, Lola wants to talk about the early years of their relationship, but Doc, her husband, doesn't. Start, Lola: "I love to watch you shuffle cards, Daddy. You use your hands so gracefully. Do me one of your card tricks." End, Lola: "What are we sitting round here so serious for?…Let's have some music."

Drama: Act II, Scene 3, pp. 60–63, Lola (39) and Doc (mid-40s)

Doc comes home drunk and abusive. He verbally destroys Lola and then threatens her with a hatchet. Start, Lola: "Mr. Anderson? Mr. Anderson, this is Mrs. Delaney again." End, Doc: "Lola…my pretty Lola."

Drama: Act II, Scene 4, pp. 73–76, Lola (39) and Doc (mid-40s)

Doc arrives home after drying out, humbled and quiet. His long-suffering wife, Lola, does her best to affect an air of normality; she tells him about her dream last night and fixes him dinner. Everything is in the subtext. Start, Lola: "Docky!" End, Lola: "I'll fix your eggs."

CRIMES OF THE HEART
by Beth Henley (Dramatists Play Service)

Comedy-Drama: Act I, pp. 26–29, Barnett (26) and Meg (27)

Barnett meets Babe's older sister, Meg, for the first time. Meg is concerned about his qualifications to defend Babe. Barnett then tells Meg that he excelled in law school; furthermore, he has a personal vendetta against Zachary, the man Babe shot. Start, Barnett: "How do you do?" End, Barnett: "Goodbye."

Comedy-Drama: Act II, pp. 34–38, Babe (24) and Barnett (26)

This is the first in-depth interview between lawyer and client. Barnett has a secret crush on Babe. Start, Barnett: "Mmmm-huh! Yes! I see, I see!" End, Babe: "Goodbye, Barnett."

Comedy-Drama: Act II, pp. 49–51, Meg (27) and Doc (early 30s)

Meg meets her former flame again, and that old feeling still exists. This scene contains plenty of subtext. Start, Meg: "I feel like hell." End, Meg: "Yeah—forget the glasses. Forget the goddam glasses."

CROSSING DELANCEY
by Susan Sandler (Samuel French)

Comedy: Act II, pp. 39–43, Bubbie (80s) and Sam (early 30s)

Bubbie is a Jewish grandmother with one foot still in the old country. She has employed a matchmaker to cook up a romance for her unmarried granddaughter, Isabelle, but the young woman isn't interested. Bubbie tells the matchmaker's choice, Sam, that he is going to have to pursue Isabelle with more fervor if he wants to win her heart. Sam is more than willing. Start, Bubbie: "In that corner." End, Bubbie: "Who invited her?"

Comedy: Act II, pp. 60–63, Isabelle (late 20s) and Tyler (early 40s)

Isabelle has become infatuated with Tyler, a romantic novelist who frequents the bookstore where she works. In some fairly unsubtle ways, she has let him know that she is interested in him. In this scene, Isabelle and Tyler are alone for the first time in a romantic setting. She quickly discovers that he primarily wants to go to bed with her, that he is a smooth-talking fast mover. She then tells him to kiss off. Start, Isabelle: "You put on a new hat, you become a new person." End, Isabelle: "There's an old Yiddish expression my Bubbie taught me—quite appropriate here—*kush mir in tuchas.*"

Comedy: Act II, pp. 63–68, Isabelle (late 20s) and Sam (early 30s)

Sam and Isabelle's introduction was arranged by a matchmaker, but she has resisted such an old-world custom. Even though Sam has charmingly pursued her, Isabelle has had her sights fixed on a romantic novelist who frequents the bookstore where she works. Earlier this evening, Isabelle stood Sam up, opting for dinner with the novelist, a date that turned into disaster when he was too sexually aggressive. Now, hat in hand, Isabelle returns to her grandmother's apartment and discovers that Sam has been waiting for her all this time. By the end of the scene, love blooms, and they are in each other's arms. A very sweet and romantic five-page scene. Start, Isabelle: "I didn't think you'd still be here." End, Isabelle: "It's all right."

CRUCIBLE, THE
by Arthur Miller (Dramatists Play Service)

Drama: Act I, Scene 2, pp. 27–31, Elizabeth Proctor (25–32) and John Proctor (mid-30s)

At first, this appears to be a scene of domestic tranquility in the Puritan community, but it turns out that John committed adultery with young Abigail Williams several months ago and, although he has confessed and asked for forgiveness, Elizabeth is still madly jealous. Abigail and a group of other young women and girls have accused some local citizens of being witches, and trials are under way in Salem. Elizabeth wants John to go to Salem and discredit Abigail, which he could easily do, but he resists because he doesn't want his adultery to become public knowledge. From Elizabeth's perspective, of course, it appears that John is still lusting after Abigail and simply doesn't want to hurt her. Start, Elizabeth: "What keeps you so late? It's almost dark." End, Proctor: "Oh, Elizabeth, your justice would freeze beer."

Drama: Act II, Scene 1, pp. 48–51, Abigail Williams (17) and John Proctor (mid-30s)

It is the night before Elizabeth Proctor's trial for the charge of practicing witchcraft. Here in the woods near Salem, John Proctor is meeting urgently with Abigail Williams, his former lover and the young woman who is responsible for Elizabeth's arrest. He warns Abigail that if she doesn't recant, he is prepared to announce publicly in court that they've been lovers and that she is motivated by jealousy. Furthermore, John claims to have documented evidence that Abigail knew all along that Elizabeth isn't a witch; he is ready to present this in court, too. Abigail, reacting with furious defiance, challenges him to carry out his threat. Start, Proctor: "I must speak with you, Abigail." End, Abigail: "…From yourself I will save you."

Drama: Act II, Scene 3, pp. 84–86, Elizabeth Proctor (25–32) and John Proctor (mid-30s)

John is sentenced to hanging for being a witch. He can save his own life only by admitting that he is under control of the devil. In this short, emotional scene, he tells his pregnant wife, Elizabeth, that he has decided to confess and tell the judges what they want to hear so that he can live. She responds by saying that whatever be his choice, she can't be his judge because she too has sinned. Had she been a good and loving wife in the first place, John wouldn't have been literally on the gallows steps. Start, Elizabeth: "You have been chained?" End, Proctor: "…Good then, it is evil, and I do it!"

DANNY AND THE DEEP BLUE SEA
by John Patrick Shanley (Dramatists Play Service) (*13 by Shanley*, Applause Books)

Drama: Scene 1, Dramatists Play Service pp. 12–19, Roberta (31) and Danny (29)

Danny and Roberta meet in a Bronx bar and, despite their hostile, defensive facades, are attracted to one another. They talk across the room, she moves to his table, they talk some more and, finally, they go to her place for the night. Danny tells Roberta that he thinks he killed a man, and she confesses to him that she had sex with her father when she was a child. This is a difficult scene because the characters are alternately vile and kind to one another. Start, Roberta: "You ever been in jail?" End, Roberta: "Come on. Let's get outta here. Let's go home."

Drama: Scene 2, Dramatists Play Service pp. 23–32, Roberta (31) and Danny (29)

After Danny and Roberta make love, their defenses slowly begin to crumble. It is hard, very hard, for Roberta and Danny to accept love or kindness. He asks her to marry him. Start, Roberta: "I went to the deli this mornin' to get a roll. Chinese guy put it in the bag." End, Danny: "Are you asleep? I love you."

Drama: Scene 3, Dramatists Play Service pp. 32–39, Roberta (31) and Danny (29)

In the cold light of day, the tenderness of the night before embarrasses Roberta, and she climbs back inside herself, trying to reject Danny. He refuses to be unkind, saying he meant everything he said last night and still wants to marry her.

Finally, Roberta moves toward Danny. Start, Roberta: "Tag!" End, Danny: "Yeah. I do. I definitely definitely think I do."

DARK AT THE TOP OF THE STAIRS, THE
by William Inge (Dramatists Play Service)
Drama: Act I, pp. 22–28, Rubin (36) and Cora (34)
This scene features an emotionally and physically abusive fight between a husband and a wife. Rubin, struggling to make financial ends meet, is furious when he discovers that Cora has secretly bought an expensive party dress for their daughter, Reenie. The argument escalates when Cora accuses him of fooling around with other women during his business trips. Rubin slaps her and storms out. Omit Reenie's brief interruption of their fight. Start, Rubin: "What the hell's been goin' on behind my back?" End, Cora: "I'll never forget what you've said. Never! Don't you ever come back in this house again!"

DAYS OF WINE AND ROSES
by J. P. Miller (Dramatists Play Service)
Drama: Act III, pp. 45–48, Joe (36) and Kristen (30)
Joe has been sober for almost a year, has a steady job, and is pulling himself and Debbie, his young daughter, out of the gutter. His wife, Kristen, unexpectedly appears at the apartment one night when Debbie is asleep; Kristen asks Joe to take her back, telling him that she hasn't had a drink in two days. Although he longs for her, he realizes that, as long as she is in denial about her alcoholism, the relationship will be impossible. He refuses. Start, Kristen: "Debbie asleep?" Continue to the end of the play. End, Joe: "God—grant me the serenity to accept the things I cannot change."

DEATH AND THE MAIDEN
by Ariel Dorfman (Penguin)
Drama: Act II, Scene 1, Paulina (40) and Gerardo (45)
Paulina is convinced that Roberto is her former torturer. She tells her husband, Gerardo, that she intends to put the man, who is tied up in the living room, "on trial." Eliminate the short section where Paulina goes to Roberto, tightens his bonds, and speaks to him. Start, Gerardo: "What are you trying to do? What are you trying to do, woman, with these insane acts?" End, Gerardo: "No need to smile at him but basically yes, that is what we have to do. And start to live, yes."
Drama: Act III, Scene 1, Paulina (40) and Gerardo (45)
Paulina agrees to tell Gerardo the truth about the details of her captivity and torture fifteen years ago if he'll tell her the truth about a woman she found in his bed. Start, Paulina: "I don't understand why." End, Paulina: "That's when I met Doctor Miranda."

DEATH OF BESSIE SMITH, THE
by Edward Albee (Plume)
Drama: Scene 2, Nurse (26) and Father (55)
Both father and daughter are southern racists. They argue about who is going to have use of the car. The daughter, who is a nurse, wants to use it to drive to work, and the father wants to use it to go down to the Democratic Club and hang out with the other politicos. A nasty duo. Start, Father: "Stop it! Stop it! Stop it!" End,

Father: "And don't you stay out there all night in his car, when you get back. You hear me? You hear me?"

Drama: Scene 4, Nurse (26) and Orderly (28)

The white nurse is a racist, and the African-American orderly is trying to improve himself. In this rough scene, he talks about what he hopes to do in life, and she shoots him down, accusing him of bleaching his skin so that he'll be more acceptable to whites. The nurse has a very foul mouth. Start, Orderly: "The mayor of Memphis! I went into his room and there he was, the mayor of Memphis." End, Nurse: "Yes'm...yes'm...ha, ha, ha! You white niggers kill me."

Drama: Scene 6, Nurse (26) and Intern (30)

The intern has been trying unsuccessfully for some time to get the nurse into bed, but she continues to tease him. In this scene, he presses his case, and she cruelly reminds him that he can't afford her on an intern's salary. They argue about politics, she insults him again, and he remarks that he is probably the only under-sixty white man in the vicinity who hasn't had sex with her. After the nurse threatens to have the intern fired, she backs off, instructing him instead to court her. This difficult scene is appropriate for experienced actors. Start, Nurse: "Well, how is the Great White Doctor this evening?" End, Intern: "You impress me. No matter what else, I have to admit that."

DELICATE BALANCE, A
by Edward Albee (Samuel French)

Drama: Act II, Scene 1, pp. 36–39, Julia (36) and Tobias (early 60s)

Julia's fourth marriage is on the rocks, and she has returned to her parents' home. Tensions that usually run high here are exacerbated by the strange presence of family friends Harry and Edna in the upstairs bedroom. Like a couple of adversarial and wary woods animals, Julia and Tobias, her father, talk about these events. Start, Tobias: "What was that...all about?" End, Tobias: "Your brother would not have grown up to be a fag."

Drama: Act III, pp. 68–73, Agnes (late 50s) and Tobias (early 60s)

Because all the guest bedrooms are full of visitors, both welcome and unwelcome, Tobias had to sleep with his wife, Agnes, last night. This morning, they discuss the implications, and Agnes presses Tobias to make a decision regarding the guests. Begin at the top of Act III. Start, Agnes: "Ah, there you are." End, Agnes: "I don't know. I'm listening."

Drama: Act III, pp. 73–76, Agnes (late 50s) and Tobias (early 60s)

In this continuation of the preceding scene, Agnes and Tobias talk about the death of their infant son thirty-four years ago and how the event altered their sex life. Start, Agnes: "Well, isn't that nice that Julia's making coffee? No?" End, Agnes: "Whatever you like. Naturally."

DINNER WITH FRIENDS
by Donald Margulies (Theatre Communications Group)

Comedy-Drama: Act I, Scene 2, pp. 19–27, Beth (40s) and Tom (40s)

This is a crackerjack marriage-on-the-rocks scene. Tom has told Beth that, after twelve years together, he doesn't love her any more and in fact is in love with a travel agent. Earlier this evening, Beth had dinner with their best friends, Karen and Gabe, and told them that the marriage has fallen apart. As we enter this scene,

Beth is back at home and has put the two children to bed. Tom is supposed to be in Washington, DC, on a business trip. As Beth gets ready for bed herself, Tom suddenly appears in the bedroom doorway, having been snowed out at the airport. Their bickering accusations escalate into a flat-out fight. The tension builds, turns into a wrestling match on the bed and, in the final moments, erupts into raw sexuality. Start with Tom's entrance. Beth: "Tom! Jesus…" Go through the end of the scene. It is important that the actors include the nonverbal sexuality at the end, as the lights dim.

DIVISION STREET
by Steve Tesich (Samuel French)
Comedy: Act I, pp. 23–27, Sal (30s) and Dianah (30s)
Sal is Dianah's nebbish Legal Aid Society lawyer. An unassertive man most people ignore, Sal is desperately in love with Dianah, but she still has eyes only for her estranged husband, Chris. Here, Sal declares his undying love while Dianah carries on about Chris and how great their life was during the 1960s radical movement. Both characters have good comic monologues in this scene. Start, Dianah: "Chris! Chris! Chris!" End, Sal: "Hurt me! I don't care!"
Comedy: Act I, pp. 39–43, Chris (37) and Nadja (19)
Nadja the slut shows up at Chris's apartment, mistaking him for a john. They share their stories and are attracted to each other. You'll need an actor to play dead on the floor the whole time. Start, Chris: "I'm coming." End, Nadja: "Well, I will not be a whore. I'm a slut."

DOES A TIGER WEAR A NECKTIE?
by Don Petersen (Dramatists Play Service)
Drama: Act I, Scene 2, pp. 34–42, Linda (18) and Conrad (20)
Linda and Conrad have just finished having sex in a midnight session on the floor of Mr. Winter's office. In this postcoital scene, they talk about the future. Conrad hopes to kick his drug habit, but Linda is more cynical, looking at a short life as a junkie hooker. As the scene progresses, they become more polarized while, at the same time, they experience a true "connection." Eliminate Tonto's interruption. Start, Conrad: "Baby, if old Pete could see us now, he'd flip." End, Linda: "You keep 'em! The trick was on the house. I don't want your cigarettes…or nothing else you got!"

DOLL'S HOUSE, A
by Henrik Ibsen, Adapted by Frank McGuinness (Dramatists Play Service)
Drama: Act I, pp. 22–27, Krogstad (30s–40s) and Nora (25–35)
Krogstad threatens to blackmail Nora with the forged loan document. Start, Krogstad: "I beg your pardon, Mrs. Helmer—" End, Krogstad: "…If I am hurled back into the gutter a second time, I will take you with me."
Drama: Act II, pp. 37–40, Dr. Rank (58–65) and Nora (25–35)
Nora is going to ask longtime family friend, Doctor Rank, for a secret loan so that she can pay off her blackmailer. Before she can ask, however, Doctor Rank tells her that he has always loved her. With that knowledge, she can't ask for the money. Start, Nora: "Dr. Rank, it's you. Don't go into Torvald yet. I believe he is busy." End, Nora: "…But you can imagine being with Torvald is a little bit like being with Papa."

Drama: Act II, pp. 41–43, Krogstad (30s–40s) and Nora (25–35)

Krogstad, now formally fired from the bank, is bent on revenge and determined to follow through with his blackmail threat unless Nora intercedes immediately on his behalf with her husband. Start, Nora: "…Keep your voice down. My husband's at home." End, Krogstad: "…I will never forgive him for that. Goodbye, Mrs. Helmer."

Drama: Act III, pp. 48–51, Mrs. Linde (30–35) and Krogstad (30s-40s)

This is a late, surprise development in the story. Up until now, the audience has not known that Mrs. Linde and Krogstad were anything more than acquaintances. It turns out that they were once romantically involved, and Mrs. Linde dropped him for another man. In this scene, she proposes a new romance to him and, after a bit of negotiation, he accepts. Start, Mrs. Linde: "Come in, no one's here." End, Mrs. Linde: "It's happened. It's actually happened. Someone to work for, someone to live for. A home to bring joy to. I'll make it so comfortable."

Drama: Act III, pp. 61–67, Helmer (40s) and Nora (25–35)

This is the famous climax of the play, in which Nora stands up to her husband and, in the end, walks out the door into a life of her own. I have decided to begin the scene selection after Nora has returned from the bedroom and has changed into her day clothes. When she reenters, Helmer is surprised by what he sees. Start, Helmer: "…What's this? I thought you had gone to bed. Have you changed?" End with Nora's exit. Nora: "That our marriage could become a life together. Goodbye." You can, if you want, end on Helmer's last line after Nora has departed.

DOUBT—A PARABLE

by John Patrick Shanley (Theatre Communications Group)

Drama: Scene VII, pp. 38–42, Father Flynn (30s) and Sister James (20s)

In the garden, Sister James tells Father Flynn that she does not believe he molested a student at the school. She acknowledges that all her original suspicions can be tracked back to conversations with Sister Aloysius. She is torn between loyalty to her superior and her priest. Start, Flynn: "Good afternoon, Sister James." End, Flynn: "…That's a great relief to me. Thank you very much."

Drama: pp. 50–56, Father Flynn (30s) and Sister Aloysius (50s–60s)

Fireworks go off during this scene between two strong-willed people. Sister Aloysius tells Flynn directly that she wants him to resign, that he doesn't belong in the priesthood given his behavior with a young male student. However, such alleged behavior is total speculation on the part of Aloysius. Finally, Flynn implores her not to do this, that it would ruin his career. It falls on deaf ears. Start, Flynn: "May I come in." End, Flynn: "…I need to make an appointment to see the bishop."

DRAMA

by Anton Chekhov (*The Sneeze: Plays and Stories by Anton Chekhov*, translated and adapted by Michael Frayn, Samuel French)

Comedy: One-act play, pp. 22–30, Pavel Vasilyevich (35–50) and Murashkina (25–50)

In this eight-page play, Pavel Vasilyevich wants to be nice to the woman who shows up on his doorstep because, after all, she is an avid admirer of his writing. But Murashkina has written a drama and wants his feedback on its merits. Refusing to leave it for him to read later, she begins to read it aloud. At first Pavel is patient, but when she continues to read the quite awful material, he becomes increasingly distraught. Finally, when Murashkina won't stop, he takes out a knife and kills her. Start, Murashkina: "Such an admirer! Every book, every play! Such a talent!" End, Pavel: "Nice twist at the end, though."

DREAM GIRL
by Elmer Rice (Dramatists Play Service)
Comedy: Act I, pp. 25–30, Georgina Allerton (23) and Clark Redfield (28)
Clark Redfield sells a few review copies of some books to Georgina Allerton at the Mermaid Bookshop. She is both attracted to and repelled by him; eventually, however, her hate-at-first-sight turns into love. Clark says that he has finished reading the novel she wrote, and it is awful. This criticism outrages her. Omit the telephone call Georgina places to her mother. Start, Clark: "Good morning, Miss Allerton." End, Georgina: "You great big ape!"

DRESSER, THE
by Ronald Harwood (Samuel French)
Drama: Act II, pp. 60–63, Sir (about 60) and Her Ladyship (50s)
Between acts of *King Lear,* Her Ladyship talks to Sir in his dingy dressing room. She implores the increasingly frail man to retire and to make the announcement after that night's performance, but he won't entertain the notion. They speak of their relationship, having lived together for years as husband and wife without benefit of marriage. In fact, Sir has never obtained a divorce from his first wife, probably because he didn't want to jeopardize his chances for a knighthood. Start, Sir: "Is it my cue?" End, Sir: "I shall never forgive them for what they wrote about me."

DUET FOR ONE
by Tom Kempinski (Samuel French)
Drama: Act I, Session 1, pp. 1–8, Stephanie Abrahams (33) and Dr. Feldmann (45–60)
World-famous violinist Stephanie Abrahams was diagnosed with multiple sclerosis seven months ago. Now deprived of her life's defining skill, she has become depressed and suicidal. Here, Stephanie meets Dr. Feldmann, a psychiatrist, and tries to cover over her pain with airs, humor, and other diversions. But he isn't fooled. Dr. Feldmann has a slight German accent. Stephanie is in a wheelchair almost all the time so, unless you can find a real wheelchair, you'll have to fake it for scenework. Written in the British vernacular, Stephanie can be portrayed with a standard American accent. Start, Feldmann: (offstage) "Mrs. Liebermann." End, Stephanie: "Well, good-bye, and thank you."

DYLAN
by Sidney Michaels (Samuel French)
Drama: Act I, pp. 11–20, Caitlin (mid-30s) and Dylan (38)
Caitlin doesn't want Dylan to go on the scheduled lecture tour of the United States. She is afraid he'll spend his money on liquor and his time with other women, and that he'll burn out as an artist. What is worse, she'll be left in Wales to care for their three young children—with no money. Dylan speaks with a Welsh accent, while Caitlin has an Irish accent. Start, Caitlin: "So here you are, you scum." End, Caitlin: "Oh, Dylan, Dylan—Hurry up!"
Drama: Act II, pp. 52–59, Meg (mid-20s) and Dylan (38)
Meg is educated, responsible, attractive, and not the least charmed by Dylan's lit-

tle-boy-lost persona. Or is she? In this scene, which takes place at 4:30 A.M. in Meg's Greenwich Village apartment, she tends to a quite-drunk Dylan. He is bloodied from a random fight, looks sloppy, and is soaking wet from standing in the rain. As Meg undresses Dylan, he makes haphazard romantic passes. As he sobers up a bit, they discuss his sad financial status, the unhappy state of his marriage, and his lack of artistic output. She gives him some hard-nosed advice. Then they go to bed together. The scene calls for a practical bathtub. You can get around that by eliminating reference to it and simply having Meg undress Dylan to dry his clothes. Also, you'll need an offstage telephone to ring. Start, Dylan: "The sky's divorced! The weather's go boom. What are we doing? Who am I?" End, Meg: "There are needs in this world that have nothing to do with love, and marriages that never get recorded in a court house. Happy birthday, Dylan."

ECCENTRICITES OF A NIGHTINGALE, THE
by Tennessee Williams (Dramatists Play Service)
Drama: Act I, Scene 1, pp. 11–13, Alma Winemiller (25–29) and John Buchanan (25–29)
This later version of *Summer and Smoke* takes place during a Fourth of July celebration in Glorious Hill, Mississippi, just before World War I. Alma, the high-strung daughter of the local Episcopal minister, has just performed a song before the celebratory crowd. What is really on her mind, however, is seeing John, the next-door boy she has loved from afar all these years. In this scene, Alma and John sit near the fountain and catch up. He has finished medical school and will soon leave for Cuba on a grand adventure to fight some mysterious epidemic—and to meet some senoritas, the "caviar among females." Start, John: "Hello, Miss Alma." End, Alma: "Be careful you don't get caught. They say that the tropics are a perfect quagmire. People go there and never are heard of again."
Drama: Act I, Scene 2, pp. 15–20, Alma Winemiller (25–29) and Rev. Winemiller (60s)
Rev. Winemiller, Alma's father, is concerned about his daughter's ever-more-apparent eccentricities, and urges her to control them. Start, Rev. Winemiller: "Actually, we have about the same number of communicants we've had for the past ten years." End, Alma: "I can't breathe!" For a shorter version, start Rev. Winemiller: "Alma. Sit down for a moment. There's something I want to talk to you about." Continue to the same end.
Drama: Act II, Scene 1, pp. 29–32, Mrs. Buchanan (50–60) and John Buchanan (25–29)
Mrs. Buchanan, John's doting mother, tries to steer him away from any involvement with Alma, warning him that she is an eccentric—one of those odd people you'll find in almost any southern town. Start, Mrs. Buchanan: "Son?" End, Mrs. Buchanan: "Heavens, yes, that's a story, but it's too long for bedtime. Good night, my precious! Sleep tight!"
Drama: Act II, Scene 3, pp. 38–43, Alma Winemiller (25–29) and John Buchanan (25–29)
Alma is having a panic attack and goes next door to John's house at 2 A.M. to get some medicine. He lowers the lights and gives her some brandy, and she settles down. He unbuttons her blouse to listen to her heart and diagnoses her as "lonely." This makes her angry, and she tells him off for being condescending. John then invites Alma to go to the movies the next day. This is a pretty intense

scene for Alma, and it ends with an oblique hint of future sexual activity between them. Eliminate Mrs. Buchanan's lines. Start, John: "Why, it's you, Miss Alma!" End, John: "I'll take you to see Mary Pickford at the Delta Brilliant tomorrow."

Drama: Act III, Scene 1, pp. 44–49, Alma Winemiller (25–29) and John Buchanan (25–29)

Alma behaves in a fashion she never would have in *Summer and Smoke*. She is quite sexually aggressive with John, openly inviting him to go to a hotel room that is rented by the hour. Start, Alma: "God." End, Alma: "Give me something to guarantee your return!"

Drama: Act III, Scene 2, pp. 49–53, Alma Winemiller (25–29) and John Buchanan (25–29)

A terrific scene that takes place on New Year's Eve in a cheap hotel room. At first, the fireplace won't light, and the romantic adventure seems to be a flop. Then the fire springs to life, and the scene ends with Alma and John moving toward the bed. Start, John: "Here it is, the room is cold." End, John: "No one has ever been able to answer that question."

ECHOES
by N. Richard Nash (Samuel French)
Drama: Sam (25–35) and Tilda (20–25)

Echoes is a two-act, two-character drama that takes place in a single room in a mental institution where the characters are under constant surveillance through surrounding two-way mirrors. Sam and Tilda move continually in and out of reality, playing pretend games and fighting pretend enemies. Editing this material for scenework is challenging but worthwhile. **For a six-page scene, begin at the top of Act I (pp. 5–11).** Here, Sam and Tilda wake up in the morning and decorate an imaginary Christmas tree. Tilda talks to herself, a problem that they discuss, and Sam hears someone call him a name. Start, Tilda: "Sam!... Sammy!...Sa-mu-el! Sammy—please—wake up!" End, Sam: "There are only two of us! Who the hell can I blame? I don't know his name any better than I know my own."

For another six-page excerpt, begin shortly after the preceding dialogue ends (pp. 11–17). After Sam and Tilda talk about names, she wants to play teacher. He resists because he is a real teacher. Then Tilda tries to break the imaginary window in which she sees her unwanted reflection. Next, they play imaginary baseball. Start, Tilda: "I wish we didn't have any fixed names." End, Tilda: "There's still nobody there...except me."

Another option is to begin in Act I where Tilda sings "Take Me Out to the Ballgame" and climbs to place the angel on top of the imaginary tree (pp. 35–41). Once there, she becomes transfixed. Start, Tilda: "Is she on all right?" End, Sam: "Help me! Hey, you—Person!" This excerpt runs about six pages, and **the following scene from Act II runs about seven pages long. Begin at the top of the act as Tilda tries to wake up Sam (pp. 43–50).** She pretends to take off her clothes, and he touches her cheek in a gentle moment. Tilda then tells Sam about her bad dream, in which he was talking to "The Person" (the doctor)—but it wasn't a dream at all. Sam and Tilda then talk of death and the illusion of communication, as well as play with echoes. Sam is beginning to have real difficulty staying with Tilda in the "pretend" world. Start, Tilda: "Good morning! Good morning, Sammy!" End, Tilda: "I'm sorry, Sam."

Act II provides other opportunities. In a five-page dialogue, Sam has heard the doctor call a name and is trying to figure out what it means (pp. 50–55). Tilda is increasingly desperate to keep Sam in their "pretend" world, but he is having trouble staying there. She pretends to watch television, but he doesn't. Start, Sam: "Jess!" End, Sam: "I don't know."

A longer, seven-page scene in Act II is another choice (pp. 61–68). Here, Sam has just finished talking to the doctor again and is reporting what he said to Tilda. The doctor told Sam about his wife and three-year-old son and said he'll soon be allowed to visit with them. More than anything, Tilda doesn't want Sam to leave her, but that is exactly what happens as the curtain falls. Start, Sam: "You were right. He didn't answer any of the big questions. About God." End, Tilda: "…Mama!…Ma-ma!…Ma-ma!"

EDUCATING RITA
by Willy Russell (Samuel French)
Comedy: Act I, Scene 5, pp. 22–27, Rita (26) and Frank (50s)
This is the first major transition in the play. Last night, when Rita's husband discovered that she has been secretly going to school, he burned her books. She arrives this morning for her regular tutorial session with Frank, and they connect on a deeper level than before. She talks him into going with her to a movie. Written in the British vernacular. Start, Frank: "You know, this is getting to be a bit wearisome." End, Rita: "Don't go spoilin' it for me."

Comedy: Act II, Scene 7, pp. 50–52, Rita (26) and Frank (50s)
Almost a year has gone by since Rita began studying with Frank, and they know each other pretty well, though not romantically. Because of his drinking, he is being exiled to the university system in Australia and, as the two-page final scene begins, is packing his stuff. Rita arrives to tell Frank that she has developed a deeper appreciation for him and his values. He invites her to go to Australia with him. Maybe she will, and maybe she won't. Before she does anything else, she gives him a symbolic (as in a quick surface change) haircut. He sits down, and she begins. Written in the British vernacular. Start, Rita: "Merry Christmas, Frank. Have they sacked y'?" End, Frank: "Ouch!"

EMPRESS OF CHINA
by Ruth Wolff (Broadway Play Publishing)
Drama: Act I, Tzu-Hsi (60s) and Jung Lu (60s)
Tzu-Hsi's long-banished former lover, soldier Jung Lu, has returned to warn the empress about a spirit of rebellion in the land and urges her to stop it. Start, Jung Lu: "Empress." End, Jung Lu: "The day you cease to be in power will be the day you cease to live."

Drama: Act I, Tzu-Hsi (60s) and Kwang Yu-Wei (30s)
Kuang-Hsu, the ineffectual Emperor, has issued a series of edicts that are heavily influenced by his activist tutor, Kwang Yu-Wei. When Tzu-Hsi reads them, she flies into a rage, not only because this was done behind her back, but because the clear intent of the rulings is to embrace western culture. She summons the tutor and, in this scene, they battle over the wisdom of the papers. Finally, Tzu-Hsi signs an order banishing Kwang Yu-Wei from the country. Start, Tzu-Hsi: "I have read—the Emperor's—new edicts. They are immensely edifying." End, Tzu-Hsi: "From the moment you leave my sight, your life is in peril! Go!"

ENTER LAUGHING
by Joseph Stein (Samuel French)
Comedy: Act I, Scene 5, pp. 24–28, David (20) and Angela (28–32)
David is definitely smelling the greasepaint and anticipating the roar of the crowd when he comes to sexy Angela's theater dressing room to rehearse their big scene. He is dazzled by her relaxed sensuality and jaded glamour while she is bemused by his youth and innocence. He is a very young twenty, while she is a fully seasoned twenty-eight. An extremely funny scene. Start, Angela: "Enter!" End, David: "You're a better man than I am, Gunga Din!"

EVERYTHING IN THE GARDEN
by Edward Albee (adapted from the play by Giles Cooper, Dramatists Play Service)
Drama: Act I, Scene 2, pp. 28–35, Jenny (late 30s) and Richard (43)
Unbeknownst to her husband, Richard, Jenny has secretly begun working as a high-priced prostitute and is making good money. She mails a bundle of cash to him at home from an "anonymous" donor. He is shocked by this blessing from heaven but, with her encouragement, agrees to keep the money and not take it to the police. Begin at the top of Act I, Scene 2. Start, Jenny: "Hello." End, Jenny: "Call it five thousand even; sounds so much nicer."
Drama: Act I, Scene 2, pp. 41–47, Jenny (late 30s) and Richard (43)
Richard discovers that Jenny, his very respectable wife, is working as a high-priced call girl. This powerful scene provides plenty of fun for actors who want to chew the scenery. Begin after Jack's exit. Start, Jenny: "Is Jack gone?" End, Richard: "…men kill their wives for this sort of thing." Jenny: "Oh, darling."

EXTREMITIES
by William Mastrosimone (Samuel French)
Drama: Act I, Scene 1, pp. 8–15, Marjorie (25–30) and Raul (30–45)
This very physical scene centers on an attempted rape, which begins with a psychological cat-and-mouse–style pursuit and then turns violent. At the last minute, when Raul has Marjorie pinned to the floor, she gets the upper hand, sprays poison in his face, and then ties him up. Actors need to be careful with blocking. It is easy to injure yourself when enacting a physical fight like this. Start, Raul: "Joe? Hey, Joe? It's me. How ya doin'? Joe in?" Stop when Marjorie sprays insecticide in his face. End, Marjorie: "Just for you!"
Drama: Act I, Scene 3, pp. 18–24, Marjorie (25–30) and Raul (30–45)
Raul is tied up in the fireplace, blindfolded, and in pain from the insecticide Marjorie sprayed in his eyes when he tried to rape her. She tries to find out how he knows her name and so many details of her life. She becomes increasingly violent toward him. Here, the victim becomes the victimizer. Start, Raul: "Where am I? Marjorie? Where am I?" End, Marjorie: "Talk again and I smash you like a fuckin' bug!"

FALLEN ANGELS
by Noel Coward (Samuel French)
Comedy: Act III, pp. 46–51, Julia (late 20s) and Willy (30s)
When Willy returns from his golf weekend, he discovers that his wife, Jane, isn't at home, so he goes to see if she is with her friend Julia. Julia and Jane had a ter-

rible fight last night, however, and Julia is jealous and convinced that Jane is somewhere with Maurice, the handsome Frenchman. Julia tells Willy everything about the women's respective prenuptial romances with Maurice. Willy is stunned to learn that his wife might be having an affair at this very moment. Start, Willy: "Good morning, Julia." End, Julia: "I don't care if she's feeling heavenly, she won't be when I'm finished with her."

FAR COUNTRY, A
by Henry Denker (Samuel French)
Drama: Act II, Scene 2, pp. 61–66, Elizabeth (20s) and Freud (37)
Under Freud's insistent encouragement, his patient Elizabeth recalls painful childhood events surrounding her father's illness and death. She goes from being flirtatiously happy to sobbing and dissolving into anguished hysteria. Start, Freud: "Elizabeth." End, Elizabeth: "Dead? Oh! No! Oh! No!"

Drama: Act III, pp. 71–84, Elizabeth (20s) and Freud (37)
Freud has determined that the mysterious pain and paralysis in Elizabeth's legs has been caused by guilt over her love for Frederick, her brother-in-law. In this very emotional scene, she reluctantly acknowledges that she has been in love with Frederick and that she was, in fact, happy to see her sister, Charlotte, die. The guilt resulting from these feelings led to Elizabeth's phantom leg pain and made her an invalid. As Freud points out to her, the pain ensured that people would think of her as "poor Elizabeth" rather than "terrible Elizabeth."

As these thoughts surface, Elizabeth cries out in anguish and discovers that she can once again walk. Begin as Freud enters his office to greet Elizabeth. Simply ignore the argument between Martha and Frederick that takes place simultaneously outside Freud's office. Start, Freud: "Good morning, Lisl—how to you feel today? No crutches today?" Stop as Elizabeth walks toward the door. End, Elizabeth: "No, let me! I've never opened that door myself." This scene runs thirteen pages. For a shorter, eight-page version, begin immediately after the Martha/Frederick argument outside the door. Start, Freud: "Elizabeth! Right now—do you have a pain?" Continue to the same end.

FATHER'S DAY
by Oliver Hailey (Dramatists Play Service)
Drama: Act II, pp. 46–50, Louise (30–35) and Tom (32–38)
Louise is distraught because her seven-year-old son has chosen to live with his father in the Midwest. She makes one last futile—and pathetic—attempt to reconstruct the ideal family that never was. When Louise asks Tom to divorce his present wife and remarry her, he refuses. Start, Louise: "…what are you smirking about?" End, Louise: "Admitted!"

FENCES
by August Wilson (Samuel French)
Drama: Act II, Scene 1, pp. 62–68, Troy (53) and Rose (43)
Troy tells Rose, his wife, that he is going to have a child by another woman. She isn't happy to hear this. For scene-study purposes, omit Gabriel's interruption and few lines. Start, Rose: "What they say down there? What's happening with Gabe?" End, Troy: "Don't you tell that lie on me!"

FIRST BREEZE OF SUMMER, THE
by Leslie Lee (Samuel French) (*Black Thunder: An Anthology of Contemporary African American Drama*, Mentor/Penguin)

Drama: Act I, Samuel French pp. 15–23, Lucretia (17) and Sam (20)

This flashback sequence takes place during the late 1920s or early 1930s in the Deep South. Sam, who is African-American, got into an altercation with a white customer at the train station when he defended an elderly porter who had dropped some baggage. Instead of being grateful to Sam, the old fellow apologized to the white man, humiliating Sam. Determined now to move on to the next town, he bought his girlfriend, Lucretia, a strand of imitation pearls as a going-away present. When Sam tells her he is leaving, she flies into a rage and calls him names, and he slaps her. Then they reconcile and, as the scene ends, move to the bed to make love. What he doesn't know is that she is already pregnant. Start, Lucretia: "Oh, Sam, those are lovely!—They really are!" End, Lucretia: "Sam?…Sam, I—I want to talk to you about…something."

Drama: Act I, pp. 27–29, Lucretia (17) and Sam (20)

Sam is packed to leave and is standing at the door. When Lucretia tells him that she is pregnant, he isn't happy to hear the news. He says that he'll send her his address and that when the baby comes, she should contact him. They both know, however, that this is the last time they'll see each other. This short scene is filled with emotion. Start, Lucretia: "Are you leaving now, Sam?" End, Lucretia: "Sam, I'm scared…all of a sudden I'm scared!"

Drama: Act I, pp. 32–35, Lucretia (18) and Briton (early 20s)

Lucretia and her child live with the southern white family she works for as a domestic. Briton, the family's adopted son, lusts for Lucretia and aggressively pursues her. She doesn't really love him; she longs to be held, even if it is by "Mr. Briton." In this scene, he pursues, and she resists. Finally, he grabs her, kisses her, and she responds. Then she pulls away as she hears the family coming home downstairs. Start, Lucretia: "Mr. Briton, I—I haven't finished my cleaning, and I got cooking to do." End, Briton: "Tomorrow, Lucretia, do you hear?… Lucretia?…Tomorrow! We're outcasts—okay?"

Drama: Act I, pp. 42–47, Lucretia (18) and Briton (early 20s)

When Lucretia tells Briton that she is pregnant, suddenly he isn't so affectionate with his favorite "negra." Start, Briton: "I've decided, goddammit, Lucretia! Just now, laying here with you! I'm not going back to school!" End, Lucretia: "Briton…don't…don't say no more, please!"

Drama: Act II, pp. 62–66, Lucretia (20s) and Harper (30s)

Lucretia now has two illegitimate children and is trying to get a husband. She has her eye set on Harper Edwards, a very shy and sexually inexperienced miner who is studying for the ministry. In this scene of chaste courtship, it is clear that she has told him she is a widow, and he is already planning on having her in his future. Start, Lucretia: "You have to go now, Harper?" End, Lucretia: "Your hat, Harper, don't forget it!"

Drama: Act II, pp. 71–73, Lucretia (20s) and Harper (30s)

In this short scene, Lucretia's lie about being a widow is about to catch up with her. On Harper's first day of preaching, a man in the congregation tells Harper that he recognized Lucretia's child. When Harper confronts her, Lucretia lies again, claiming that she has never been in Roanoke. Still trusting her, Harper plans to marry her soon. Start, Lucretia: "I keep saying to myself: That's Reverend Edwards—Reverend Edwards!" End, Lucretia: "Never been to Roanoke in my life—not even near it…wouldn't know it if I stumbled over it!"

FOB
by David Henry Hwang (Dramatists Play Service)
Comedy: Act I, Scene 1, pp. 14–19, Grace (20) and Steve (late 20s)
Grace is alone at her parents' Chinese restaurant when Steve enters, declaring that he is Gwan Gung, the Chinese god of warriors, writers, and prostitutes. To Steve's dismay, Grace seems unimpressed and sends him outside to see if anyone recognizes him. Start, Grace: "Aaaai-ya!" End, Steve: "Very well. You will learn—learn not to test the spirit of Gwan Gung."

FOOL FOR LOVE
by Sam Shepard (Dramatists Play Service)
Comedy-Drama: One-act play, pp. 8–13, May (early 30s) and Eddie (late 30s)
Eddie has found his half-sister/lover in a motel on the edge of the Mojave Desert and intends to take her back to their trailer home. This is the opening scene of the play, and the fact that May and Eddie are related hasn't been revealed yet. Start, Eddie: "May, look. May? I'm not goin' anywhere. See?" End, May: "You can take it, right? You're a stuntman."

FRANKIE AND JOHNNY IN THE CLAIR DE LUNE
by Terrence McNally (Dramatists Play Service)
Comedy-Drama: Act I, Frankie (40) and Johnny (40)
Frankie and Johnny, co-workers in a greasy-spoon restaurant, have just made love for the first time. Although this two-act, two-character play has potential male/female excerpts throughout, the scenes in Act I are more appropriate for scene-study purposes simply because they involve fewer props. **One option is to begin as Frankie enters from the bathroom, having changed into a brightly colored kimono (pp. 14–21).** During this scene, she good-naturedly tries to edge Johnny out the door, but he angles to stay all night. You'll need the makings of a meatloaf sandwich. Start, Frankie: "Hello." End, Johnny: "There you go."

   In the next scene, Johnny bandages Frankie's finger (pp. 21–27). They're getting to know each other a little better, and they've started exchanging private information. But Frankie still wants Johnny to leave, and he is still scheming to stay. Start, Johnny: "There you go." End, Johnny: "It was a crime of passion. They were the last of the red hot lovers. We're the next."

   Another good scene to work on involves a revelation (pp. 27–33). Here, Johnny tells Frankie that he loves her, and she responds by trying to reject him. Start, Frankie: "You're not from Brooklyn." End, Frankie: "Did anyone ever tell you you talk too much?"

GENIUSES
by Jonathan Reynolds (Samuel French)
Comedy: Act II, pp. 53–55, Jocko (33) and Skye (early 20s)
Skye, a former Playmate of the Year, has decided that Jocko's hostility toward her is actually veiled lust and agrees to go to bed with him even though he hasn't

asked her. Jocko appreciates the gesture but declines on the grounds that she has the runs. Start, Skye: "You win. Let's go." End, Jocko: "Good night and so forth."

GINGERBREAD LADY, THE
by Neil Simon (Samuel French)
Comedy-Drama: Act I, pp. 31–36, Evy (43) and Lou (33)
Evy dried out for ten weeks in a Long Island sanitarium and has been back in her apartment for just a few moments when Lou Tanner, her former lover, shows up and asks if he can move back in. Although he still pushes her buttons, Evy can't stand the thought of returning to a relationship in which she is the caretaker of this younger, rootless, needy man who is inclined to chase other women and beat her up occasionally. Evy's better judgment rules the day, she refuses his appeal, and Lou beats a petulant retreat. Cut and paste around Polly's slight interruption at the top of the scene. Start, Lou: "Hello, Evy." Stop with Lou's exit. End, Lou: "Probably not."

Comedy-Drama: Act II, pp. 44–49, Evy (43) and Jimmy (40)
Jimmy, Evy's flamboyant actor/friend, is morose, having just been fired from a play. Evy consoles him and pours champagne. He is horrified to see her drinking since she only recently returned home from drying out. You'll have to cut and paste a bit. Omit Jimmy's line, "Ten thousand kids a month getting drafted and they leave this one behind to produce my show." Start, Evy: "No kiss?…No hello?" End, Jimmy: "Some mood I'm in for a party. Christ!"

GIRL ON THE VIA FLAMINIA, THE
by Alfred Hayes (Samuel French)
Drama: Act I, pp. 27–31, Lisa (early 20s) and Robert (early 20s)
Facing dire economic prospects in war-ravaged 1944 Rome, Lisa has agreed to be "kept" by Robert, an American occupation soldier. This kind of arrangement was quite common at the time, but Lisa feels cheapened by it nonetheless. In this scene, Robert and Lisa are alone in their bedroom for the first time. She explodes with indignation, telling him how awful Americans are, to which he responds by reminding her that her country has lost the war. She slaps him, and he slaps her back. After they calm down, Robert apologizes, and they settle into bed, presumably to consummate their union. Lisa is Italian, so a slight accent is appropriate. Start, Robert: "It's cold. There's a big villa at Anzio. In the pine wood." Continue to the end of Act I. End, Robert: "It came all the way from America."

Drama: Act II, Scene 1, pp. 26–42, Lisa (early 20s) and Robert (early 20s)
It is the day after the "honeymoon" night, and Lisa is disgusted with herself; she is ashamed that she has sold herself so cheaply. Robert enjoyed the sex, but is still lonely because he knows that Lisa didn't really want to sleep with him. In this scene, they're still trying to establish the terms of their relationship, but their conversation is colored now by their forced intimacy. Start, Robert: "I bought a clock so Adele won't have to knock on the door in the morning. See? That looks almost matrimonial, doesn't it—the clock and the bed?" End, Robert: "All right. I'll go smoke a cigarette."

Drama: Act II, Scene 2, pp. 51–56, Lisa (early 20s) and Robert (early 20s)
This classic love/hate scene takes place on New Year's Eve, a night for lovers and celebration. It is clear by this point in the play that, under different circumstances, Lisa and Robert might have made a good couple, but that it is never to be. Here, they talk about how they got together in the first place and what the future holds.

Start, Robert: "Would you like some cognac? Ugo thinks I was overcharged for it."
End, Robert: "I ought to kiss somebody a Happy New Year's."
Drama: Act III, pp. 77–81, Lisa (early 20s) and Robert (early 20s)
Unable to produce marriage documents, Lisa has been officially designated a prostitute by the Italian government and issued a yellow identification card so that she can work the streets. Robert feels bad about his part in bringing about her dilemma, but there is nothing he can do about it now. In what is probably the most powerful scene between them, Lisa and Robert act out the fantasy of what their lives would be like if they'd met under different circumstances and were free to be in love. He tears up Lisa's identification card. Start, Robert: "Lisa—If there was anything I could have done, I'd have done it." End, Robert: "Then kiss him. He just came home from a tough day in the office. Kiss him."

GLASS MENAGERIE, THE
by Tennessee Williams (Dramatists Play Service)
Drama: Act I, Scene 5, pp. 28–32, Amanda (40s) and Tom (21)
Amanda tries to enlist Tom's help in finding a gentleman caller for his sister, Laura. This scene highlights the conflict between mother and son. Tom is late for work, but Amanda wants to talk. Start, Tom: "I'm sorry mother. I'm sorry for all those things I said. I didn't mean it. I apologize." Stop with Tom's exit. End, Tom: "Yes!"
Drama: Act II, Scene 7, pp. 54–64, Laura (23) and Jim (23)
At his mother's insistence, Tom invited his co-worker Jim home for dinner. Unbeknownst to Tom, however, Amanda has made elaborate preparations for the event, seeing this as an opportunity to fix up her shy daughter, Laura, with a gentleman caller. When Jim arrives, Laura is embarrassed to recognize him as the high-school hero she long ago had a secret crush on.

After dinner, Laura and Jim are finally alone in the parlor and, for a while, it is a very sweet meeting as the two of them replay the good old days and wax ecstatic about what a swell and talented fellow Jim was. Soon, however, he figures out that Laura is looking for a potential mate and awkwardly explains that he is engaged. Laura is mortified, but she covers her discomfort in ladylike fashion. This scene runs about fifteen to twenty minutes and is difficult to cut down. Start, Jim: "How are you feeling now? Any better?" End, Laura: "A—souvenir."

GOAT, THE (OR, WHO IS SYLVIA?)
by Edward Albee (Dramatists Play Service)
Comedy-Drama: Scene 2, pp. 26–33, Martin (50) and Stevie (40–50)
Stevie learned moments ago that her husband, Martin, is having an affair with a goat. In this scene, she demands that he tell her all about it. And he does. Start after Billy's exit on page 26. Stevie: "…Well; now; just you and me." End, just before Billy reenters on page 33. Stevie: "Jesus!"

GOLDEN BOY
by Clifford Odets (Dramatists Play Service)
Drama: Act I, Scene 4, pp. 27–31, Lorna Moon (20–25) and Joe Bonaparte (22)
Joe Bonaparte is an exciting young boxer with a great deal of potential, but he is pulling his punches in the ring, trying to protect hands that also play the violin. His fight manager and promoters are stymied as well as frustrated because they can't get Joe to give 100 percent. Lorna Moon, the promoter's sexy, streetwise girl-

friend, volunteers to help. She intends to use her feminine wiles to convince Joe to fight. Start, Lorna: "Success and fame! Or just a lousy living." End, Joe: "I know."
Drama: Act II, Scene 2, pp. 44–48, Lorna (20–25) and Joe (22)
Joe has fallen in love with Lorna and tries to convince her to leave Tom Moody. Although she has fallen in love with Joe, her allegiance is to Moody because he got her out of the gutter. Start, Joe: "Some nights I wake up—my heart's beating a mile a minute!" End, Joe: "Poor Lorna!"

HATFUL OF RAIN, A
by Michael Vincente Gazzo (Samuel French)
Drama: Act I, Scene 1, pp. 20–26, Celia (early 20s) and Johnny (27)
Unaware that her husband has become a drug addict and fearful that he is having an affair on the nights when he isn't at home, Celia presses Johnny for an explanation about his increasingly withdrawn and erratic behavior. The truth is that he is roaming the streets at night trying to get a fix. Start, Celia: "There's no hot water, is there?" End, Celia: "The rain's stopped. I think I'd better open the windows. Everything's so damp in here."
Drama: Act I, Scene 2, pp. 30–36, Celia (early 20s) and Polo (mid-20s)
Johnny's brother, Polo, is drunk and unable to sleep. He stumbles into the kitchen to get some water. Celia is also restless because her husband is out on the street somewhere. She hears the noise in the kitchen and joins Polo. They talk about their mutual attraction for each other, and she tells him that he had better move out of the apartment before they get into trouble. Start, Celia: "Don't do that, Polo! You'll give yourself a stomach cramp." End, Polo: "I'm not Johnny, I'm Polo."
Drama: Act II, Scene 3, pp. 57–61, Celia (early 20s) and Johnny (27)
Johnny can't bring himself to confess his drug addiction to his wife, Celia. Instead, he tries to revive their relationship by surprising her with flowers and a clean apartment when she gets home from work. Celia, however, is convinced that their relationship is damaged beyond repair and that Johnny must be having an affair. She wants to separate from him even though she is pregnant. Start, Celia: "Polo." End, Celia: "No, Johnny, I'm gonna get an apron."

HEDDA GABLER
by Henrik Ibsen (adapted by Jon Robin Baiz, Grove Press)
Drama: Act II, pp. 33–38, Judge Brack (40–50) and Hedda (25–35)
Judge Brack is a confirmed bachelor, part of a rather wild social scene. He and Hedda engage in some cat-and-mouse verbal exchanges about the kind of relationship he wants to have with her now that she is married to the very boring and academic George Tesman. The negotiation is sexual, but not overt. Start at the top of Act II if you can find a prop pistol for Hedda. Otherwise, begin the scene just after the bit with the gun. End, Hedda: "Yes. That would be a huge relief."

HEIDI CHRONICLES, THE
by Wendy Wasserstein (Dramatists Play Service)
Comedy: Act I, Scene 2, pp. 13–18 (1968); Heidi (age changes from 16 to 40) and Scoop (from 16 to 40)
Heidi, a nineteen-year-old volunteer for the Eugene McCarthy presidential campaign, meets Scoop Rosenbaum at a dance in New Hampshire. The Princeton dropout and underground newspaper publisher is about the same age. When Scoop

puts some intense, highly philosophical moves on her and challenges her intellectual independence, sparks fly. Heidi and Scoop leave the dance to go have sex. Actors play a wide age range, from sixteen to forty, because the play spans twenty-four years. Start, Scoop: "Are you guarding the chips?" End, Scoop: "No. I trust them."

Comedy: Act I, Scene 5, pp. 35–40 (1977); Heidi (27ish) and Scoop (27ish)
After being involved with Heidi sexually and otherwise off and on for ten years, Scoop is settling down and marrying Lisa. This scene takes place at their wedding reception, where Heidi and Scoop find a moment alone, and he confides that despite the fact that they'll never marry, he'll always love her. Heidi suffers a great deal from the loss, but she knows that their lives are taking different paths. You'll need someone offstage to announce a song and play it on a tape recorder. Start, Heidi: "Did she just say 'shake your booties,' doctor?" Continue through the end of the act. As the lights fade, Heidi and Scoop are romantically dancing to a Sam Cooke recording of "You Send Me." End, Scoop: "*Honest you do. Honest you do.*"

Comedy: Act II, Scene 5, pp. 63–68 (1987); Heidi (late 30s) and Peter (late 30s)
Peter is "the best pediatrician under forty" in New York City and is running a hospital clinic for children. Heidi, his lifelong friend, pays a midnight visit to drop off a box of Christmas gifts for the young patients before leaving for Minnesota to write and teach. Peter behaves strangely, acting cold and aloof. Finally, he admits that his former lover has AIDS. Peter and Heidi talk about the value of friendship and the point of work. She then decides to stay in New York. Start, Heidi: "He seems very nice." End, Heidi: "Merry Christmas, Peter."

Comedy: Act II, Scene 6, pp. 68–75 (1989); Heidi (40) and Scoop (40)
The final scene in the play provides a summing up. Scoop sold his magazine for millions two hours ago and has dropped by Heidi's new apartment with a gift for the baby she has adopted. They discuss where they've been in their lives, where they are going, and shifting values. You'll need a baby carriage, preferably, or a bassinet. Start, Scoop: "Hello. Hello." End, Heidi: "*Honest you do, honest you do, honest you do.*"

HELLO AND GOODBYE
by Athol Fugard (Samuel French)

Drama: Johnny (late 20s) and Hester (late 30s)
This two-character, two-act drama between a brother and a sister contains many possible scenes that expose interesting character points and contain tension. Both characters are Afrikaner, so accents would be appropriate. **You'll find a good scene in Act I (pp. 18–25).** Here, Johnny picks up a packet of unopened mail to look for a letter from his sister, Hester. After a moment, she reenters. It becomes clear that Johnny has given up his dreams of a career and is tending to their father, who is evidently dying in the next room. Start, Hester: "What you up to?" End, Johnny: "None of you know me and you went for good. What is it this time? Why have you come back?"

Another potential scene immediately follows (pp. 25–33). In this excerpt, Johnny learns that Hester is a prostitute and that she has come home to collect her share of their father's insurance money. Start, Hester: "Must I have a reason to visit my own home?" End, Hester: "I've got a funny feeling." An excerpt in the second act doesn't contain as much hysterical and dramatic revelation as those in the last part of the play, but it is arguably better for scenework because **Hester is opening boxes that contain remnants of her childhood and her family history (pp. 34–45).** The revelations are more subtle and personal. If you decide to work on this scene, keep in mind that you'll have to accumulate all of those remnants: newspapers, photographs, old dresses, shoes, and plenty of boxes and twine. Start, Hester: "Frickie—Frickie who—Must have been a relative!—Who's she?" End, Johnny: "Dear God, please let Hester find the money!…Any luck?"

In a later excerpt from Act II, Johnny learns that Hester has had abortions, a fact that wounds his religious sensibility even more than learning that she is a prostitute (pp. 45–52). And Hester learns that Johnny applied to railroad school, was accepted, and just didn't go. Start, Johnny: "All those in favor of sleep hold up their hands!" End, Hester: "I couldn't stop hating and it hurts, it hurts."

HELLO OUT THERE
by William Saroyan (Samuel French)
Drama: One-act play, pp. 5–28; Young Man (25–30) and The Girl (17)
A drifter wakes up in jail after being falsely accused of rape. He then begins a relationship with the unsophisticated teenager who cooks and cleans there. Although doing the entire scene is best, you can shorten it slightly for scene purposes by eliminating all the young woman's offstage dialogue and beginning with her entrance. Start, Young Man: "I'm lonesome. I'm as lonesome as a coyote. Hello— out there!" End, Young Man: "Now hurry. And don't forget, if I'm not here when you come back, I'll meet you in San Francisco."

HERE WE ARE
by Dorothy Parker (*24 Favorite One Act Plays*, edited by Bennett Cerf and Van H. Cartmell, Doubleday/Main Street)
Comedy: He (early 20s) and She (18–23)
This 1931 one-act comedy is only ten pages long. Young newlyweds are on the train en route to their New York City honeymoon. He is eager to consummate the union, while she is just a little nervous about the prospect. They banter, argue, hedge, and hug, talking about everything except what is really on their minds. A cute and fun scene. Were people ever really this innocent? Start, He: "Well!" End, She: "Yes, here we are, aren't we?"

HOOTERS
by Ted Tally (Dramatists Play Service)
Comedy-Drama: Act II, Scene 3, pp. 58–61, Ronda (22) and Ricky (19)
Ronda and Ricky's friends have returned to the motel to have sex, leaving them alone on the beach. At first, they were very hostile to one another because Ronda didn't want to party in the first place, and Ricky is jealous that his buddy is scoring with Ronda's prettier friend. But as Ricky and Ronda talk, mutual respect evolves. Start, Ronda: "See that buoy out there?" End, Ricky: "Whatever that is in Spanish."

HOUSE OF BLUE LEAVES, THE
by John Guare (Samuel French)
Comedy: Act I, pp. 9–15, Artie (45) and Bunny (late 30s)
Bunny excitedly bursts into Artie's apartment at 4:45 A.M., rousing him to go see the Pope pass by in a parade. Artie is depressed because his songs bombed during amateur night at the El Dorado Bar & Grill last night. Both actors need to have a good feel for New York regional speech patterns. Start, Bunny: "You know what your trouble is? You got no sense of history." End, Bunny: "And I'm sorry last night went sour."

HOUSE OF RAMON IGLESIA, THE
by José Rivera (Samuel French)

Drama: Act II, Scene 1, pp. 57–61, Javier (22) and Caroline (28)
Now that Javier is a college graduate and is about to pursue the American Dream, he intends to leave his Puerto Rican background behind him—and this includes his old girlfriend, Caroline. In this scene, he tells her about his decision, hurting her deeply. Start, Caroline: "Hi." End, Javier: "Here I come Dad—again!"

HOW I LEARNED TO DRIVE
by Paula Vogel (Dramatists Play Service)

Comedy-Drama: pp. 49–54, Uncle Peck (45) and Li'l Bit (playing 18, but can be older)
You'll have to cut and paste just a bit to make this scene work for class, but it's worth the trouble. The scene takes place in an upscale hotel room and is basically a thwarted scene of seduction. Here's the cut to make: throughout the play, the playwright uses the theatrical device of a Greek chorus, and the chorus makes an appearance toward the end of this scene. You need to eliminate the chorus and Li'l Bit's two or three lines that fit into the chorus. The part that should be cut begins toward the top of page 53 in the Dramatists Play Service acting edition, and ends at the top of page 54. In other words, you want this scene to be exclusively between Uncle Peck and Li'l Bit, with no chorus. Start, Peck: "Why don't you sit?" End, Peck: "I'm fine. I just think—I need a real drink."

HURLYBURLY
by David Rabe (Samuel French)

Drama: Act II, Scene 1, pp. 104–111, Bonnie (late 30s) and Eddie (mid-30s)
Eddie fixed Bonnie up with Phil, who just signed his divorce papers today, thinking that the two of them would happily go have sex. Once out in the car, however, Phil exploded and shoved Bonnie out of the moving vehicle. Furious and bruised, Bonnie storms back to tell off Eddie for putting her in such jeopardy. Eddie, already drunk, is unfazed by her dilemma. This is a full-throttle, brakes-off scene for Bonnie. Start, Bonnie: "You know, Eddie, how come you gotta put me at the mercy of such a creep for?" End, Eddie: "For myself."

Drama: Act III, Scene 1, pp. 128–137, Darlene (30s) and Eddie (mid-30s)
Darlene tells Eddie about an abortion she had seven years ago, and how she didn't know which of two men had gotten her pregnant. Eddie, who is already upset, is further depressed by this news and is soon talking about how his sadistic minister father beat him as a child. At the end of the scene, Eddie receives word that his best friend, Phil, has been killed in a car crash on Mulholland Drive. Start, Eddie: "Let's just hang around a little in case he calls." End, Eddie: "What?"

HUSBANDRY
by Patrick Tovatt (Samuel French)

Drama: Scene 2, pp. 21–29, Harry (37) and Dee (55)
Dee gets a little drunk and tells her son, Harry, how rough it has been to keep the family farm going. She hints that he should take it over. Start, Harry: "Hey, what are you doin' up at this hour?" End, Harry: "I'll go down there, Ma, and you go up…and sleep well…I love you, Ma…even when I don't know what the dickens to do."

Drama: Scene 2, pp. 46–52, Harry (37) and Bev (34)
Bev argues with her husband, Harry, about the wisdom of taking over his parents' farm. She wants to get back to New York City immediately because she just found out that their daughter, Sadie, has gotten sick. Start, Bev: "Why didn't you get me up?" End, Bev: "If you can't understand why I have to go…I'll go without you. I'm going up."

I AM A CAMERA
by John Van Druten (Dramatists Play Service)
Drama: Act II, Scene 1, pp. 40–42, Sally (20s) and Christopher (20s)
Sally is recovering from the abortion she had. Christopher is bemoaning his aimless summer, and the fact that he isn't writing enough. They take stock of their poverty, sort out their lives, and declare their friendship. Start, Christopher: "This awful, obscene laziness! I ought to be flogged." End, Sally: "So do I."
Drama: Act II, Scene 2, pp. 58–63, Sally (20s) and Christopher (20s)
Sally has just received a note from her rich American friend, Clive, saying that the world cruise he promised is off. On an impulse, he has departed for America. Since Sally and Christopher are already packed to leave on the cruise, they greet the news with shock and disappointment. After they calm down, they decide to turn over a new leaf, get jobs, and lead responsible lives for a change. Then, just as abruptly, Sally changes her mind, deciding to throw herself back into the party scene. You'll have to cut and paste, eliminating Fraulein Schneider's lines. Start, Christopher: "Really, Sally, that was a little cruel. Fritz really is in trouble." Then, cut from Sally's line: "We could ask Fraulein Schneider to phone" to Christopher's line: "You know he's gone, don't you?" Next, cut from Sally's line: "I don't think we're much good as gold-diggers, are we, darling?" to Christopher's line: "Do you want to come out and have some lunch?" Continue to the end of Act II. End, Sally: "Can't you laugh now? Come on."
Drama: Act III, Scene 1, pp. 64–69, Sally (20s) and Christopher (20s)
Sally is hungover and has been "away" for the past couple of days. She and Christopher exchange some low-key pleasantries and, when he asks how she likes the article he has written, she dismisses it as dull. In fact, Sally explains, she has asked someone else to write the article. His artistic pride wounded, Christopher rages at her. She rages back and then storms out, promising to move out altogether. As he mutters to himself about how awful she is, Sally bursts in again to say that her mother is in town unexpectedly and is coming up the stairs! She asks Christopher to masquerade as her fiancé because that is what her mother thinks he is to Sally. Before Christopher can protest, Sally's mother enters. This is a good scene on account of its unexpected emotional twists and turns. Start, Christopher: "I haven't seen you for a day and a half." End, Sally: "Don't believe everything I said at first. She isn't easy. Please, darling. Please!"

I HATE HAMLET
by Paul Rudnick (Dramatists Play Service)
Comedy: Act II, Scene 1, pp. 54–57, Lillian Troy (70s) and John Barrymore (45–50)
This is a magical scene in which Lillian Troy, now in her 70s, reminisces with her old sweetheart, John Barrymore, who is actually a ghost. He would be in his 70s, too, but he stopped aging when he died twenty years ago. At any rate, Lillian is

older than John, and they dance and laugh and talk about how lovely it was back then. Start, Lillian: "You. You look terrible." End, Lillian: "Surprise me."

IMMIGRANT, THE
by Mark Harelik (Broadway Play Publishing)
Drama: Act I, Scene 9, Leah (20s) and Haskell (20s)

Leah is distressed because she and Haskell have settled in Texas, far from their Russian Jewish roots, and because there are no other Jews anywhere nearby. She is also upset that they don't eat kosher or pray at sundown. He thinks that this is all part of becoming American and says that he has no intentions of abandoning his Jewish faith. Then Leah tells Haskell that she is pregnant. At the top of the scene, Leah speaks Russian; at the end, Haskell sings a verse from a Yiddish song. Leah: "*Ach, mei Gott, siz ah meshugenneh velt.*" End, Haskell (singing): "*Fraylich lustik iz gevain ihr meene Ot axoy grevain is mein kusine.*"

IMPASSIONED EMBRACES
by John Pielmeier (Dramatists Play Service)
Comedy: "An Intellectual Discussion (or The Poor Man's Samuel Beckett)," pp. 71–73, He (20–35) and She (20–35)

In this sketch, which takes place at a kitchen table, the dialogue is in the spirit of the Abbott and Costello "Who's on First?" routine, full of double negatives and confusing context. The scene ends with a modified food fight. Start, He: "You're wrong." End, She: "Forget it."

Comedy: "Goober's Descent," pp. 87–93, He (30–45) and She (25–40)

He is a business executive looking for a new position, and She is interviewing him. In this reverse sexual-harassment scene, the woman gets the man stripped down to his underpants and then reminds him that she worked briefly as his secretary years ago. She was the one who wouldn't have sex with him and who quit when he started coming on to her. Revenge is sweet. Start, He: "Hi there." End, She: "Zilla, you can start sending in the next year."

I NEVER SANG FOR MY FATHER
by Robert Anderson (Dramatists Play Service)
Drama: Act II, pp. 51–54, Gene (40) and Alice (early 40s)

Alice traveled from Chicago to Long Island to help her brother, Gene, with family arrangements after their mother's death. The most pressing issue is what to do with their father, who is now almost eighty and increasingly frail. Gene and Alice have just had a very tense discussion with him, in which he became furious at Alice's suggestion that he hire a live-in housekeeper. Ideally, the father wants Gene to remain close at hand, but Gene wants to move to California to remarry. Overcome with guilt, Gene suddenly tells his father that he'll stay, at least for a while. When the older man stalks off, Alice yells at Gene for not standing his ground, for giving in to his father, for not being a man. Start, Gene: "For God's sake, Alice." End, Alice: "Suddenly I miss Mother so."

IN THE BOOM BOOM ROOM
by David Rabe (Samuel French)
Drama: Act II, pp. 73–77, Chrissy (early 20s) and Harold (50s)

Chrissy talks to Harold, her alcoholic father, about the abuse she suffered as a child. She asks him why he once put vodka in her baby bottle, causing her to be hospitalized, as well as why he is still with Helen, her mother, who has shown in many ways that she wishes her daughter were dead. Harold is remorseful about what happened years ago but makes excuses; he says he was just kidding around at the time. An excellent, low-key scene. Start, Chrissy: "Hi, Pop." End, Harold: "Here comes your mother. She's been shopping at the store."

Drama: Act II, pp. 82–87, Chrissy (early 20s) and Eric (mid-20s)

Eric loves Chrissy. She wants his help with her astrology chart while he wants to talk about how much he loves her and how wonderful their life could be together. Chrissy gets progressively frustrated with him. Start, Eric: "Come in!" End, Eric: "Don't worry. Just call. Just call."

I OUGHT TO BE IN PICTURES
by Neil Simon (Samuel French)

Comedy: Act I, Scene1, pp. 14–24, Libby (19) and Herb (45)

Herb wakes up one morning in Hollywood to discover that his daughter, whom he hasn't seen since she was a small child, is sitting in his living room. If you have access to a telephone that rings, begin the scene when Libby answers the phone. If not, begin with Herb's entrance. Start, Herb: "I didn't hear you get up." End, Libby: "Hello."

Comedy: Act II, Scene 2, pp. 50–57, Steffy (39) and Herb (45)

Steffy tells Herb that, after a two-year relationship, it is time for him to make a deeper commitment to her. His response is typical of many men. Start, Steffy: "It's okay. I know how you feel." End, Herb: "You're just dumb when it comes to picking men."

IT HAD TO BE YOU
by Renée Taylor and Joseph Bologna (Samuel French)

Comedy: Act I, pp. 26–36, Theda (28–35) and Vito (40)

Theda and Vito came back to her place, spent the night, and this morning Vito is beginning to grasp just how eccentric this woman is. He has discovered that she eats health food and has been writing a perfectly awful play for herself for the past three years. Just a minute ago, Theda hid his clothes all over her small apartment, including in the freezer. Vito tries to make a graceful exit, chalking this one up to experience. However, the door seems to be locked, so he can't get out. Furthermore, it is snowing hard, and he may have to stay longer. Start, Vito: "The door seems to be stuck. Would you please open it?" End, Theda: "I know it doesn't look good for my love story but I had one thing going in my favor. He was still here!" This excerpt includes a great deal of physical comedy. For a longer version start, Vito: "Uh…look, I've got to be going, I'm all disoriented." Continue to the same end.

Comedy: Act II, pp. 37–43, Theda (28–35) and Vito (40)

Vito tries to help Theda write her one-woman play, wanting to add rubber-chicken jokes and such to her very Russian plotline. It doesn't work. Begin at the top of Act II as Theda reads her play-in-progress aloud. Start, Theda: "In the name of Mother Russia, stop the torturing." End, Theda: "Well they should have! Now I want another idea for my play! And this time I want a good one!"

JOINED AT THE HEAD
by Catherine Butterfield (Dramatists Play Service) (*Women Playwrights: The Best Plays of 1992*, Smith & Kraus)

Comedy-Drama: Act II, Dramatists Play Service pp. 53–57, Maggie (late 30s) and Jim (late 30s)

Maggie and her former high-school lover, Jim, spend an evening together at his place while his wife undergoes chemotherapy at the hospital. After dinner, he plays snippets from a couple of songs on the piano. This leads to a discussion about who-left-whom at the high-school prom twenty years ago, which, in turn, leads to talk about whether or not Maggie is being honest in her best-selling book about a father/daughter relationship. Jim's piano playing is a very important part of the scene. If you don't have access to a piano, you probably shouldn't attempt the scene. Start, Maggie (to audience): "I went to dinner at Jim's that night. I'll make this quick, then we'll move on to other things." End, Maggie: "You didn't screw it up, Jim. You did just fine."

KEY EXCHANGE
by Kevin Wade (Dramatists Play Service)

Comedy: Scene 4, pp. 19–23, Lisa (late 20s) and Philip (about 30)

Lisa wants to deepen the level of commitment in her relationship with Philip, which is signified by the exchanging of apartment keys. Philip, however, doesn't want to be fenced in. A good short scene. Start, Philip: "So great. So we get keys made for each other's apartments." End, Lisa: "Please. Go."

Comedy: Scene 6, pp. 26–31, Lisa (late 20s) and Philip (about 30)

When Lisa invites Philip to meet her father, he hedges because he doesn't want to be pushed too fast in their relationship. She gets angry, and the confrontation ends with the couple breaking up. Begin at the top of Scene 6. Cut Michael's appearance in the scene. Start, Philip: "Yes." End, Lisa: "No. You're getting what you want. I won't push you anymore. You win. I don't want to play anymore."

LANDSCAPE OF THE BODY
by John Guare (Dramatists Play Service)

Drama: Act I, pp. 9–16, Capt. Holohan (40–45) and Betty (36)

Captain Holohan interrogates Betty at the police station. He is convinced that she murdered her fourteen-year-old-son, but the truth is that she didn't. Omit Raulito and Rosalie's brief interruptions. Start, Betty: "I don't see how you can ask me these questions." End, Betty: "I can look you right in the eye. I didn't throw up. I won."

Comedy-Drama: Act I, pp. 23–27, Betty (36) and Raulito (35–45)

Betty takes over her deceased sister's old job at Dawn's Promising Star Travel Agency in New York City. Raulito, the owner/operator, is a flamboyant Cuban refugee whose modus operandi is scamming newlyweds into buying honeymoon vacations. In this scene, after he shows Betty the ropes and describes his colorful background, she gives scamming a try. The scene calls for a cassette recording of audience cheers and applause, but this isn't absolutely essential. Start, Raulito: "You take the *Daily News*. You take the *Sunday Times*." End, Betty: "I'm me. I can't do the job. I don't want the job."

LARGO DESOLATO
by Václav Havel (translated by Tom Stoppard, Grove Weidenfeld)
Comedy-Drama: Scene 6, Marguerite (early 20s) and Leopold (45–50)
Marguerite, a university philosophy student, comes to Leopold's flat, declares her intellectual indebtedness to him and, when she recognizes his despair, decides to rescue him with affection. Start, Marguerite: "Good evening." End, Marguerite: "…and now, I'll awaken love in you!"

LARK, THE
by Jean Anouilh (adapted by Lillian Hellman, Dramatists Play Service)
Drama: Act I, pp. 15–18, Joan of Arc (18) and Sire de Beaudricourt (40–50)
After listening to the "voices" of God for three years, Joan of Arc accepts her calling and prepares to raise an army and march on Orléans to repel the British. As a first step, she has come to the manor of the Sire de Beaudricourt to ask for an armed escort and a horse. Initially, he toys with the idea of a sexual trade with the young woman, but because she appeals to his intelligence, he gives her what she wants. Start, Sire de Beaudricourt: "What's the matter with you, young woman? You've been carrying on like a bad girl. I've heard about you standing outside the doors ragging at the sentries until they fall asleep." End, Joan: "Good. Now that we have got that out of the way, let's pretend that you've given me the clothes of a boy and we're sitting here like two comrades talking good sense."

LAST OF THE RED HOT LOVERS
by Neil Simon (Samuel French)
Comedy: Act II, pp. 41–51, Barney (47) and Bobbi (27)
Barney entices Bobbi, a pretty singer/actress, up to his mother's apartment for a tryst. Bobbi turns out to be a dingbat, and Barney winds up smoking his first marijuana cigarette. This scene fills the entire twenty pages of Act II. For scene-study purposes, begin halfway through the act. Start, Bobbi: "Are you married?" Continue to the end of the act. End, Bobbie: "…That's the only thing that there's just too little of…"
Comedy: Act III, pp. 54–63, Barney (47) and Jeanette (39)
Jeanette is a longtime friend of Barney and his wife. He brings her to his mother's apartment for a tryst. She turns out to be quite depressed and pops tranquilizers. Start, Jeanette: "Why am I here, Barney?" End, Jeanette: "You actually found three people who you consider gentle, loving and decent. I congratulate you."

LES LIAISONS DANGEREUSES
by Christopher Hampton (based on Pierre Choderlos de Laclos's novel of the same name, Samuel French)
Drama: Act I, Scene 1, pp. 16–22, Madame Merteuil (25–35) and Valmont (28–35)
Madame Merteuil's lover, Gercourt, has jilted her and is now planning to marry Cécile, the young virgin. Bent on revenge, Madame Merteuil tries to convince her sometime-lover Valmont to seduce the young woman before her wedding night, just to teach Gercourt a lesson. Valmont refuses because he doesn't see much sport in seducing a fifteen-year-old. Furthermore, he is in pursuit of a much bigger prize, the very married, very religious, and very straight-laced Madame de Tourvel. Madame Merteuil is skeptical of Valmont's ability to bed

Madame de Tourvel, so she challenges him to a bet with a sexual payoff if he can deliver proof of his seduction. Start, Merteuil: "Your aunt?" End, Merteuil: "Good night, Vicomte."

Drama: Act I, Scene 2, pp. 28–32, Madame de Tourvel (22) and Valmont (28–35)
Valmont is determined to seduce Madame de Tourvel because she is such an unwilling victim. Start, de Tourvel: "I can't understand how someone whose instincts are so generous could lead such a dissolute life." End, Valmont: "I only want to say what I hardly thought it would be possible for me to say to you: Goodbye…I'll write soon."

Drama: Act I, Scene 5, pp. 51–55, Madame de Tourvel (22) and Valmont (28–35)
Although Madame de Tourvel has strongly rebuffed Valmont, her heart is beating with desire. In this short scene, he raises the stakes and increases the tempo of his pursuit. Begin as de Tourvel reenters after her walk in the garden. Start, Valmont: "I trust you're feeling a little better, Madame." Continue to the end of the scene. End, Valmont: "Nothing."

Drama: Act II, Scene 2, pp. 83–86, Madame de Tourvel (22) and Valmont (28–35)
Valmont succeeds in his seduction of Madame de Tourvel. She has literally been driven to the edge of emotional collapse with sexual desire and internal conflict. The only blemish on Valmont's otherwise perfect seduction is that he has made the mortal error of actually falling in love with the woman. This short, intense scene ends with de Tourvel succumbing to his passion. Start, Valmont: "I understand Father Anselme has explained to you the reasons for my visit." End, de Tourvel: "Yes. You're right. I can't live either unless I make you happy. So I promise. No more refusals and no more regrets."

Drama: Act II, Scene 3, pp. 86–91, Madame Merteuil (25–35) and Valmont (28–35)
Unbeknownst to Valmont, Madame Merteuil has taken young Danceny as her lover. Her passion for this dalliance, however, has been dulled by her discovery that Valmont has fallen in love with Madame de Tourvel and impregnated fifteen-year-old Cécile. These games of cruel seduction aren't supposed to involve true emotion or weaknesses. In this scene, Madame Merteuil and Valmont take stock of their feelings for each other. Start, Valmont: "Success." End, Merteuil: "Goodbye."

LIE OF THE MIND, A
by Sam Shepard (Dramatists Play Service)

Comedy-Drama: Act II, Scene 3, pp. 54–60, Beth (early-to-mid-20s) and Frankie (late 20s)
In order to find out if Jake has murdered his wife Beth, Frankie has traveled to her parents' place in Billings, Montana. Beth's father mistook Frankie for a deer and shot him in the leg. Now he is recuperating right alongside Beth, who suffered brain damage from Jake's violent beating. Here, Beth tends to Frankie's wound by taking off her shirt and wrapping it around his leg. Then, because her brain still isn't working right, she starts to fantasize about how it would be if Frankie were a gentler version of Jake. Beth comes on to Frankie, but he doesn't want to get involved with his brother's wife. Start, Frankie: "Un—look—Beth—Don't you think you oughta put your shirt back on?" End, Beth: "Then why is this so empty? So empty now. Everything. Gone. A hole."

LIFE AND LIMB
by Keith Reddin (Dramatists Play Service)

Drama: Act I, Scene 3, pp. 13–16, Franklin (mid-to-late 20s) and Effie (mid-to-late 20s)

Franklin and his wife, Effie, have an awkward reunion. This is the first time they've seen each other since he lost his arm in the Korean War. Start, Effie: "Hi, Franklin!" End, Effie: "Sure."

Drama: Act I, Scene 5, pp. 19–21, Franklin (mid-to-late 20s) and Effie (mid-to-late 20s)

Franklin is deeply depressed about his injury and inability to land a job, and he is taking it out on Effie, who is doing the best she can to be a good wife. In this tense scene, Franklin seems to pick a fight with Effie for no reason at all. Start, Franklin: "Take your coat off." End, Franklin: "No shit."

Drama: Act II, Scene 6, pp. 45–48, Franklin (mid-to-late 20s) and Effie (mid-to-late 20s)

Effie was killed in a freak accident at the movie theater and, in this fantasy sequence, she returns from the dead to tell Franklin about the affair she had. He tells her how much he misses her. A lovely scene. Start, Franklin: "Effie, is that you?" End, Effie: "I miss you. I miss you and the movies."

LION IN WINTER, THE
by James Goldman (Samuel French)

Drama: Act I, Scene 2, pp. 16–20, Eleanor of Aquitaine (61) and Henry II (50)

Henry II and Eleanor of Aquitaine have become loving and comfortable adversaries. In this scene, they argue about which of their sons will be the heir to the English throne. Start, Eleanor: "Henry, I have a confession." End, Eleanor: "Good. That will make this pleasanter."

Drama: Act I, Scene 4, pp. 33–37, Eleanor of Aquitaine (61) and Henry II (50)

Henry and Eleanor strike a deal: her freedom in exchange for her endorsement of their youngest son John getting the Aquitaine. This would be a major capitulation for Eleanor because she is in favor of their oldest son, Richard Lionheart, ascending to the throne. Start, Henry: "Well, how'd you do with Richard? Did you break his heart?" End, Henry: "Where's a priest? I'll do it. I'll show you. By Christ, I will."

Drama: Act II, Scene 1, pp. 61–70, Eleanor of Aquitaine (61) and Henry II (50)

Henry tells his wife that he wants their marriage annulled. Eleanor refuses, threatening open war if he tries to have it done against her will. Their dispute takes a nasty, even more personal turn when she claims to have slept with Henry's father. Shortening this scene without disrupting the flow and tension is difficult. Start, Eleanor: "I'm rather proud; I taught her all the rhetoric she knows." End, Eleanor: "It's cold. I can't feel anything. Not anything at all. We couldn't go back, could we, Henry?"

Drama: Act II, Scene 2, pp. 70–73, Alais (23) and Henry III (50)

Henry tells his mistress, Alais, that they're going to Rome to have his marriage annulled; he'll then be able to marry her. Before Alais will accept Henry's proposal, she wants him to promise to keep his sons got by Eleanor locked in a dungeon forever. Alais believes that if Henry's plan succeeds and his sons were free, they would band together to wage war against him and, in time, probably kill him. This short scene has interesting dynamics and a great deal of subtext. Start, Henry: "Get up, wake up, it's morning." End, Henry: "I shall have to, shan't I?"

LITTLE FOXES, THE
by Lillian Hellman (Dramatists Play Service)
Drama: Act II, pp. 41–44, Regina (40) and Horace (45)
Regina is more interested in her husband Horace's money than in the fact that he is dying from a heart ailment. She lured Horace home from the hospital under the pretense that she has decided to be romantic. Regina and Horace haven't had sex for ten years. But all she really wants to do is get $75,000 from him to seal a business arrangement with her unethical brothers. Start, Regina: "Well. Here we are. It's been a long time." End, Regina: "You will see what I've done while you've been away. How I watched your interests."

Drama: Act III, pp. 62–66, Regina (40) and Horace (45)
Horace tells his wife that her brothers and nephew have conspired to steal $80,000 from him, that he considers her to be part of the same pack of dogs, and that he intends to punish her—and them—in his will. Regina responds by telling Horace how much she has always hated him. As their tempers and tensions rise, he suddenly suffers another major heart attack. Regina watches dispassionately as he dies, not even moving to get his medicine for him. Start, Regina: "We had agreed that you were to stay in your part of this house and I in mine." End, Regina: "Horace. Horace. Addie! Cal! Come in here!"

LOBBY HERO
by Kenneth Lonergan (Dramatists Play Service)
Comedy-Drama: Act I, Scene 2, pp. 16–19, Bill (30) and Dawn (early 20s)
Dawn, a rookie New York City cop, is nervous because she struck a rampaging drunk too hard with her nightstick, and he might be seriously hurt. Her seasoned partner, Bill, is playing the big shot and assures her he'll see to it that nothing comes of the incident. There are a couple of interesting negotiations in this scene: First, Dawn and Bill are romantically involved, so there is an implied sexual element somewhere in the transaction; second, Dawn seriously admires Bill as a policeman and as a person, considering him to be her mentor in the police department. She does not realize at this point that he is an opportunistic liar who is right now preparing to go up to apartment 22J to sleep with the "actress" that lives there. Start, Bill: "Take it easy, will you? Just take it easy." End, Dawn, "I'll try."

Comedy-Drama: Act I, Scene 2, pp. 24–29, Jeff (27) and Dawn (early 20s)
Bill is up in apartment 22J making love to Mrs. Heinvald, the "actress" that lives there. Jeff and Dawn are talking in the lobby, during which Jeff finds Dawn very attractive. In the four pages leading up to this excerpt, Jeff has been telling Dawn all about himself and generally trying to get closer to her. Sensing that she has a thing for Bill, he tells her that Mrs. Heinvald in fact has a lot of "friends." Dawn is shocked and dismayed to learn that Bill is double-timing her. Start, Jeff: "…So what's he doin' up there anyway? Investigatin' a crime or somethin'?" End, Jeff: "You know what? You're damned right."

Comedy-Drama: Act I, Scene 2, pp. 38–41, Bill (30) and Dawn (early 20s)
Note: You'll need someone to enter the scene midway and deliver two lines, as the character Jeff. Bill returns to the lobby, unaware that Dawn knows he has been upstairs having sex with Mrs. Heinvald. She confronts him and he tries to lie his way out of it. Then Jeff comes in and says that Mrs. Heinvald called to say Bill left his hat in the apartment. The cat is now out of the bag, and so Bill changes tactics with Dawn. Very good scene because of the transitions. Start, Dawn: "You

have a good time?" End, Bill: "…You're never going to be anything. So go ahead. Take off."

Comedy-Drama: Act II, Scene 1, pp. 57–64, Jeff (27) and Dawn (early 20s)

The essential transaction in this excellent scene takes place when Jeff tells Dawn the truth. His boss, William, whose brother is in deep legal trouble, has provided a false alibi to the police. In order to get the most juice out of the scene, it is essential that actors carefully study the pages that precede it (pp. 48–55). The scene will be too long for classwork if you include all of those pages in a workshop presentation, but the subtext contained there is critical. Start, Jeff: "So listen: I have a hypothetical situation I want to ask you about." End on page 64, as Bill enters. Dawn: "OK. Great.…"

LONG DAY'S JOURNEY INTO NIGHT
by Eugene O'Neill (Yale University Press)

Drama: Act I, Mary (54) and Edmund (23)

Edmund tells his mother Mary that he is afraid she is lapsing back into morphine addiction. Although this accusation is true, Mary is angry and defensive about it. Edmund then agrees not to spy on her further. The scene begins late in Act I and continues to the end of the act. Start, Mary: "Here you are. I was just going upstairs to look for you." End, Edmund: "…I'll go down and help Jamie bear up. I love to lie in the shade and watch him work."

LOOK HOMEWARD, ANGEL
by Ketti Frings (based on the novel of the same name by Thomas Wolfe, Samuel French)

Drama: Act I, Scene 2, pp. 32–37, Laura (23) and Eugene (17)

Eugene talks quietly on the porch with Laura, the new boarder. Even though they both realize that he is too young for her, there is an immediate and profound attraction between them. Eugene tells Laura about his dreams in this lovely scene. What he doesn't know is that she is engaged. Omit Jack Clatt's interruption. Start, Laura: "Good evening." End, Laura: "Gene, if we keep rushing together like this, we're going to have a collision."

Drama, Act I, Scene 2, pp. 37–40, Eliza (57) and W. O. Gant (60)

After a drunken uproar, Gant, Eliza's husband, is sleeping it off when she enters his bedroom. He lurches awake, mistakenly thinking that his daughter, Helen, has come to take care of him. Eliza, furious earlier, soothes him now and seems to be genuinely concerned about the old man's well-being. The truth is that she wants to pressure him to sell the valuable property on which his business is located. You'll need a bed for this scene. Start, Gant: "Helen?" End, Gant: "Have mercy and pity upon me. Give me another chance in Jesus' name…Oh-h-h!"

Drama: Act III, pp. 76–78, Laura (23) and Eugene (17)

For reasons of her own, Laura hasn't told Eugene that she is engaged to a man in another town; instead, she lets this new romance blossom. Now deeply in love, Eugene asks Laura to marry him in a very brief, very tender, lovely scene. It is best to have a bed for this scene, but you can get away without using one. Start, Laura: "Gene? What was that?" End, Laura: "Eugene…I will love you always…Gene!"

Drama: Act III, pp. 83–85, Eliza (57) and Eugene (17)

Now that Laura is gone, Eugene knows that his dreams of romance with her were empty. Suddenly, he realizes he must leave this place and, in this dynamic climax, he and Eliza, his domineering mother, finally come to terms. Start, Eliza: "Gene. You know what I'd do if I were you? I'd just show her I was a good sport, that's what!" End, Eugene: "Ah, you were not looking, were you? I've already gone."

LOSS OF ROSES, A
by William Inge (Dramatists Play Service)
Drama: Act I, Scene 1, pp. 10–17, Kenny (21) and Helen (mid-40s)
Kenny discovers that he is being temporarily moved out of his bedroom to make space for houseguest Lila Green. He and Helen, his mother, argue about this and about his unwillingness to move out of the house altogether. Kenny is, after all, twenty-one years old. Start, Kenny: "All right. How long's she gonna stay?" End, Helen: "All right, Kenny! All right."

Drama: Act II, Scene 1, pp. 44–49, Kenny (21) and Lila (32)
Lila has been living with Kenny and his mother for a month and is comfortable with the situation. This afternoon, Kenny comes home from his job at the gas station to find Lila on the front steps. A mild flirtation turns lustful, and Lila reluctantly pushes Kenny away. Start, Lila: "Good evening, Mr. Kenny Baird." End, Lila: "Yes you are. I can tell. Oh, sometimes I wish I'd never been born."

LOU GEHRIG DID NOT DIE OF CANCER
by Jason Miller (*Three One-Act Plays,* by Jason Miller, Dramatists Play Service)
Drama: One-act play, pp. 43–50, Barbara (28) and Victor (32)
Barbara and Victor are a husband and wife on the verge of separating. This scene is tense, biting, and honest. Miller describes Barbara as "lean, tanned, large-breasted," and you should make an effort to cast a physically appropriate actress. Barbara's body is a point of reference when Victor makes comments to hurt her. Similarly, Miller describes Victor as "a sad little clown underneath a coarse and sometimes volatile temperament." Find a suitable actor. Start, Barbara: "Barbara speaking!…No, Mr. Toomey, my husband is not here." End, Victor: "Have a nice time."

Drama: One-act play, pp. 51–57, Helen (mid-30s) and Victor (32)
Helen Martin comes to Victor's home to talk about her shy son, a bench-warming player on the little-league team that Victor coaches. Because he just got fired from his coaching position, their meeting turns into an introspective and, ultimately, poignant event during which Victor gives Helen a present for her son; the gift, his prized possession, is a baseball personally autographed by Lou Gehrig. Start, Victor: "Who are…don't tell me, I know. I have it. You are Mrs. Martin." Continue to the end of the play. End, Victor: "One cream and two sugars."

LOVER, THE
by Harold Pinter (Dramatists Play Service)
Drama: One-act play, pp. 20–26, Sarah (30–35) and Richard (30–40)
Sarah is having an affair with her "pretend" lover, who is actually her own husband, Richard. He decides to call off the whole arrangement because he is getting jealous of her relationship with this other self. But it is too late because they're both addicted to the game. This scene, the last one in the play, is appropriate for advanced actors. Written in the British vernacular, but you can play it with standard American speech. Start, Richard: "Hello." End, Richard: "You lovely whore."

LOVERS AND OTHER STRANGERS
by Renée Taylor and Joseph Bologna (Samuel French)
Comedy: "Brenda and Jerry," pp. 5–12, Brenda (20s) and Jerry (20s)

Jerry and Brenda met thirty minutes ago at Maxwell's Plum, and Jerry manages to get her up to his apartment after they leave the restaurant. He tries to seduce her, she resists, and then she gives in. The scene is funnier than it sounds. Start, Jerry: "My apartment is right over here." End, Brenda: "Oh, Jerry! Aren't you glad we waited?"

Comedy: "Hal and Cathy," pp. 12A-12F, Hal (48–52) and Cathy (30s)

Cathy wants Hal to divorce his wife of thirty-two years, but he keeps dragging his feet. She threatens to marry another man if he won't come round. They resolve nothing by the end of the scene, and continue their affair as before. As written, this scene takes place in a small bathroom while a party is going on in another part of Hal's house. If this setting isn't practical for classwork, simply change the setting to a guest room. Start, Hal: "Cathy? Are you in there, Cathy?" End, Hal: "Then the responsibility rests not with me, not with you, Cathy, not with Bernice…but with Phil!"

Comedy: "Johnny and Wilma," pp. 13–22, Johnny (40s) and Wilma (30s)

Wilma wants to make love tonight, but Johnny wants to go to sleep, so they fight, verbally and physically. They argue about male/female relationships, submissive versus dominant roles, and lovemaking frequency. Johnny finally confesses that he has had a bad day at work and has lost a big account, so he needs her to be submissive. Wilma complies. Wilma and Johnny move around a great deal here; they are in and out of bed, and in and out of the bathroom. Start, Wilma: "Are you going to make love to me, or not?" End, Wilma: "Are you going to let me surrender to you, or not?"

LUV
by Murray Schisgal (Dramatists Play Service)
Comedy: Act I, pp. 32–38, Harry (late 30s) and Ellen (mid-30s)

Harry has been swept up in Ellen's hysteria and pain as she talks about her failed marriage to Milt. She pulls out the knife she was going to use to kill Milt and, in an emotional fit, almost kills Harry. Begin the scene as Ellen and Harry regain their composure. Start, Ellen: "I've been a great deal of trouble to you." End, Ellen: "I love you! I love you!"

Comedy: Act II, pp. 42–48, Milt (late 30s) and Ellen (mid-30s)

Milt's recent marriage to Linda hasn't been working out. In fact, Linda has maintained a dirty house, let her underarm hair grow, and quit her job. Even worse, she left Milt three days ago; now he is in despair, longing to reconcile with Ellen, his former wife. As it happens, Ellen's recent marriage to Harry Berlin has also been rocky; he has taken to lying in a corner of the living room with a paper bag over his head, moaning. As Act II evolves, Milt and Ellen finally do get back together, but this six-page excerpt ends before that happens. Start, Milt: "El? Ellen? Is that you?" End, Ellen: "The door is closed, Milt."

MATCHMAKER, THE
by Thornton Wilder (Samuel French)
Comedy: Act I, pp. 24–29, Mrs. Dolly Levi (40–50) and Horace Vandergelder (60)

Dolly Levi intends to marry Horace Vandergelder, but he doesn't know it yet. In this fun and innocent scene, she double-talks him into believing that she is going to fix him up with a seventeen-year-old who has secretly fallen in love with him. Later on, he'll get even more confused and wind up marrying Dolly! Start, Mrs. Levi: "Oh, Mr. Vandergelder, how handsome you look! You take my breath away!" End, Mrs. Levi: "…very well; I'll meet you on one of those benches in front of Mrs. Molloy's hat store at four thirty, as usual." For a longer version, eliminate Cornelius's lines. End, Mrs. Levi: "…and the only way you can save yourself now is to be married to somebody by the end of next week. So think that over!"

M. BUTTERFLY
by David Henry Hwang (Dramatists Play Service)
Drama: Act II, Scene 6, pp. 41–44, Gallimard (30s) and Renee (late teens)
Gallimard, a French diplomat, begins an affair with Renee, a bored American university student he meets at a party in the Austrian embassy. The first part of the scene takes place in the embassy, the second in a bedroom. Renee, who is always perky, shares her theories on the correlation between penis size and world wars with the diplomat. Start, Gallimard: "1963. A party at the Austrian embassy." End, Gallimard: "This was simply not acceptable."

MIDDLE AGES, THE
by A. R. Gurney, Jr. (Dramatists Play Service)
Comedy-Drama: Act I, pp. 5–10, Eleanor (playing 40s) and Barney (playing 40s)
Eleanor tries to talk Barney out of making an embarrassing speech at his father's memorial service. Unbeknownst to her, he has purchased the private men's club that has figured so significantly in all of their lives and in which the service is taking place. Start, Eleanor: "I knew you'd be in here." End, Eleanor: "Nuts to you, Barney. Just—nuts to you."
Comedy: Act I, pp. 21–28, Eleanor (playing late teens) and Barney (playing late teens)
Barney is madly in love with Eleanor, but she is leaning toward his younger brother, Billy. In this very physical scene, Barney makes a hopelessly romantic, virginally awkward play for her in the trophy room of the men's club. He wants to have sex with her tonight, right here, right now. If Eleanor goes on that Bermuda trip tomorrow with Billy, it will be too late. To play this properly, you'll need dressy clothes, a man's robe, the makings of a picnic, and someone to operate offstage music to simulate the dance party going on in the next room. Begin as Eleanor and Barney dance into the trophy room, as the action shifts from the 1940s to the 1950s. Start, Eleanor: "Hey!" End, Barney: "Not at all. I'll be right back."

MIDDLE OF THE NIGHT
by Paddy Chayefsky (Samuel French)
Drama: Act II, Scene 2, pp. 40–44, The Manufacturer (53) and The Girl (23)
After an unsatisfactory attempt at lovemaking, The Manufacturer feels awful that he wasn't able to perform sexually. The Girl is very understanding. He asks her to marry him. Start, The Manufacturer: "I'm sorry, Betty." End, The Manufacturer: "Oh, my sweet girl, I love you so much you don't know. If you change your mind tomorrow, I won't be angry with you. I won't lie to you, Betty. I'm afraid."
Drama: Act III, Scene 1, pp. 65–68, The Girl (23) and The Husband (late 20s)
The Girl sent The Husband a letter asking for a divorce. He flew in from Las Vegas

to try to talk her out of it. But The Girl is determined; anyway, she is in love with The Manufacturer. Start, The Girl: "George, I'd like to know why you came back. I mean it really." End, The Husband: "I swear I won't do it again."

MISS JULIE
by August Strindberg (*Six Plays of Strindberg,* translated by Elizabeth Sprigge, Doubleday/Anchor)
Drama: One-act play, Julie (25) and Jean (30)
This ninety-minute, one-act play is divided into two parts: a seduction scene between Miss Julie and her father's valet, Jean, and the consequences of their passion. In this scene, Kristin, a minor character, has conveniently fallen asleep. Julie invites Jean to go outside into the night and pick lilacs. As they prepare to leave, Jean gets something in his eye, which Julie tends to. As she does, she becomes more sexually provocative. This is fairly outrageous behavior for a woman of that era, particularly with a man from a lower class. The tempo of the dance between Jean and Julie increases until they go into Jean's room, presumably to make love, as a group of party revelers approaches. Start, Julie: "Now come out and pick some lilac for me." End, Jean: "I swear."

Drama: Julie (25) and Jean (30)
Julie and Jean emerge from his bedroom, having just made love. She is agitated, trying to determine what to do now that she has violated class lines and made herself submissive to a lowly valet. She decides to run away and attempts to get Jean to accompany her. Perhaps they'll run a hotel somewhere. For Jean's part, their lovemaking has transformed him into someone cruelly dominant. In fact, Jean insults Julie now that she is "his." Start, Jean: "Now you see! And you heard, didn't you? Do you still think it is possible for us to stay here?" End, Jean: "Orders always sound unkind. Now you know. Now you know."

MISS LONELYHEARTS
by Howard Teichmann (adapted from Nathanael West's novel, Dramatists Play Service)
Drama: Act I, Scene 4, pp. 24–27, Betty (early 20s) and Miss Lonelyhearts (26)
Betty's fiancé hasn't been around for three weeks, ever since he started writing a daily lovelorn advice column for the newspaper. The newspaper readers know him now as "Miss Lonelyhearts." In this short, intense scene, he appears unexpectedly at Betty's apartment, and she can tell right away that he has changed in some negative way. No longer quite as glib and cynical, he seems more introspective and disturbed. Start, Betty: "God only knows about men, too. Women don't." End, Betty: "Why don't you let me alone? I felt swell before you came, and now I feel rotten. Go away. Please, go away!"

Drama: Act I, Scene 8, pp. 42–45, Fay (30s) and Miss Lonelyhearts (26)
Miss Lonelyhearts has agreed to a face-to-face meeting with a troubled reader who wrote to him for advice. Fay, a sad, physically strong woman, comes to his apartment. As she shares her terrible story, the sexual tension between them increases. Within minutes, they head for the bedroom. This scene is best for experienced actors. Start, Lonelyhearts: "Come in…Want to give me your coat?" End, Fay: "Oh, honey, turn off the light."

Drama: Act II, Scene 1, pp. 51–54, Betty (early 20s) and Miss Lonelyhearts (26)
Concerned about Miss Lonelyhearts's mental and physical health, Betty has

brought him to the country for some rest and relaxation. After four days, however, he is more troubled than ever, and he has made no effort at all to sleep with her. In this scene, Betty lets Miss Lonelyhearts know that she is ready to go to bed with him, but he refuses, explaining that he has decided to give himself to all people, not just one special woman. The scene calls for a telephone that rings, but they don't answer it. You can easily omit the references to it if you want. Start, Miss Lonelyhearts: "Hullo." End, Betty: "That's not for us either. Good night."

MODIGLIANI
by Dennis McIntyre (Samuel French)
Drama: Act I, Scene 4, pp. 26–34, Modigliani (31) and Bea (late 20s)
Modigliani's girlfriend, Bea, tries to make him work, but he is demoralized, sick, hungry, and a bit manic. At one point in this scene, she challenges him to paint by stripping off her clothes and posing. You can easily adjust this moment to stop short of full nudity. Start, Modigliani: "A day-and-a-half!" End, Bea: "I know. Sleep."

MONDAY AFTER THE MIRACLE
by William Gibson (Dramatists Play Service)
Drama: Act I, pp. 15–17, Annie (35) and John (26)
This short scene begins with John trying to convince an angry Annie to help him with the book he is writing about Helen Keller. Annie is tired of living in Helen's shadow and wants to be appreciated for herself. Then, suddenly, the action turns romantic when Annie tries to make a dramatic exit. John grabs her, and they roll on the ground and kiss. At age thirty-five, Annie has had no experience with romance. Start, John: "My, you're a contrary type. If you ever drown, I'll look for you upstream." End, Annie: "It—deserves its reputation."
Drama: Act I, pp. 20–22, Annie (35) and John (26)
Annie and John are hiding from Helen because she doesn't know they're romantically involved. They want each other, and John asks Annie to marry him. Annie is excited by the proposal but doesn't accept for two reasons. John is younger than she is, and the latter feels that she is already married—to Helen Keller. Start, Annie: "She's gone." End, John: "How many children are you planning on?"
Drama: Act II, pp. 51–54, Annie (35, playing 40) and John (26, playing 31)
Annie came home to find John kissing Helen by the fireplace, and this scene is the fallout. He tells Annie that he feels he is married to Siamese twins, Annie and Helen, that he has neither wife nor child, and that he feels unfulfilled. Annie damns him for taking advantage of Helen and for not appreciating all her own hard work. Start, John: "Kissed the girls and made them cry." End, John: "She makes me feel tender. You don't."

MOON FOR THE MISBEGOTTEN, A
by Eugene O'Neill (Samuel French)
Drama: Act III, Josie (28) and Tyrone (early 40s)
Josie and Tyrone are alone in the moonlight. She longs for romance but discovers that he wants only forgiveness for the sins he committed while accompanying his mother's body cross-country last year. Actors who try this material should pay particular attention to the very specific casting guidelines playwright Eugene O'Neill demanded for Josie: "She should be a big woman, perhaps 5 feet 11 inches, weighing maybe 180 pounds, full-breasted, not mannish."

The material, which takes up all of Act III, is dense, rich, and demanding. As such, it is much too long for most workshops. You can divide it into two sections. **For the first excerpt, begin with Josie's entrance at the top of Act II (pp. 66–78).** Start, Josie: "You'd think I'd been gone years." End, Tyrone: "Thanks, Josie." **The second scene begins where the first excerpt ends (pp. 78–93).** Start, Tyrone: "Why did you say a while ago I'd be leaving for New York soon." End, Josie: "God forgive me, it's a fine end to all my scheming, to sit here with the dead hugged to my breast, and the silly mug of a moon grinning down, enjoying the joke!"

MRS. DALLY HAS A LOVER
by William Hanley (Dramatists Play Service)
Drama: Mrs. Dally (38) and Frankie (18)
This two-character, one-act play presents several possibilities for scenework. **In one seven-page scene, it is late afternoon, and Mrs. Dally and Frankie are organizing themselves after what was apparently a very passionate lovemaking session (pp. 45–52).** Start, Frankie: "What happened to my…?" End, Mrs. Dally: "Wait a sec."

In the second excerpt, Mrs. Dally tells Frankie that she'd like to go out in public with him, to visit museums and such (pp. 59–68). They talk about what makes them happy, the differences in their ages, and religious guilt. Start, Mrs. Dally: "I'd like to go for a walk. Down by the river, maybe." End, Mrs. Dally: "Well…you'll understand soon enough."

Yet another choice for scenework overlaps the preceding excerpt (pp. 66–75). Here, Mrs. Dally tells Frankie about her show-business career and plays the trombone a tiny bit, after which they discuss John Donne's poetry. If you don't want to attempt playing the trombone, simply eliminate all mention of it. Start, Mrs. Dally: "Frankie…did you ever wonder if I did this before?" Continue to the end of the play. End, Mrs. Dally: "Just remember what I said: listen to the sweet music…and pass it on."

MURDER AT THE HOWARD JOHNSON'S
by Ron Clark and Sam Bobrick (Samuel French)
Comedy: Act I, Scene 1, pp. 8–11, Arlene (38) and Mitchell (36)
Arlene and her dentist/lover, Mitchell, wait in a room at the Howard Johnson's hotel for her husband, Paul. She intends to ask him for a divorce. If he balks, she and Mitchell plan to murder him. The closer they get to the moment of truth, the more sexually turned on they get. Start, Mitchell: "Well, the bathtub is ready." End, Mitchell: "Think positive."
Comedy: Act I, Scene 2, pp. 27–32, Arlene (38) and Paul (40–45)
Arlene has discovered that Mitchell is having an affair with his dental assistant, and she is bent on revenge. Faking a suicide attempt, she tricks her ex-husband, Paul, into rescuing her and then enlists his assistance in killing Mitchell. Start, Arlene: "Hello, Mitchell. This is Arlene." End, Paul: "Who needs a hundred per-cent? Don't do it!"

NIGHT OF THE IGUANA, THE
by Tennessee Williams (Dramatists Play Service)
Drama: Act II, pp. 49–52, Maxine (40s) and Shannon (35)
Shannon is struggling with inner demons, trying to choose between returning as a priest to a hypocritical church he despises, or committing suicide. Here, he com-

poses a letter to the dean of the divinity school at Sewanee as the lusty Maxine, recently widowed, presses him to forget all that and move in with her. Begin at the top of Act II. Start, Maxine: "Workin' on your sermon for next Sunday, Rev'rend?" End, Shannon: "I'll handle it myself and you keep out of it, please."

NORMAN CONQUESTS, THE—TABLE MANNERS
by Alan Ayckbourn (Samuel French)
Comedy: Act I, Scene 2, pp. 23–27, Ruth (30s) and Norman (30s)
Sarah has summoned Ruth, Norman's wife, to the country house for the weekend because it has come to light that Norman has been planning a romantic holiday with Ruth's sister, Annie, who is also in residence. In this scene, which takes place at breakfast time, Ruth has just arrived. After a few moments, Norman tells her outright that he is planning to go away with Annie. Ruth just laughs in his face. You'll need some breakfast cereal, bowls, and utensils. Written in the British vernacular. Start, Ruth: "Oh, Reg, how are you? I've been meaning to ring you, but I haven't had a minute." End, Ruth (laughing uncontrollably): "I never heard anything so funny."

NOT ENOUGH ROPE
by Elaine May (Samuel French)
Comedy: One-act play, pp. 5–8, Edith (25–35) and Claude (25–35)
Edith wants to borrow some rope from the new man moving in across the hall so she can hang herself. He has only some packing twine. Begin at the top of the play, and continue until Edith's exit back into her own apartment. Start, Edith: "Hi, there! I'm your neighbor from across the hall…" End, Claude: "You're welcome…Oh God…"

OF MICE AND MEN
by John Steinbeck (Dramatists Play Service)
Drama: Act III, Scene 1, pp. 59–63, Lennie (30–40) and Curley's wife (20s)
Curley's pretty wife has decided to leave her jealous husband and run away to Hollywood to pursue a career in the movies. As she hides her suitcase in the barn for tonight's escape, she encounters Lennie, who is sadly hiding there because he has accidentally killed his new puppy. Lennie tells her about the farm he and George are going to have someday, and she tells him about how she is really cut out to be an actress. Then she places his hand on her hair so he can feel how soft it is. When Lennie innocently grasps her hair too hard, she panics and tries to get away from him. Then Lennie, a physically powerful man, accidentally breaks her neck, killing her. Start, Curley's wife: "What—what you doin' here?" End, Lennie: "I'll throw him away. It's bad enough like it is."

OH DAD, POOR DAD, MAMMA'S HUNG YOU IN THE CLOSET AND I'M FEELIN' SO SAD
by Arthur Kopit (Samuel French)
Comedy: Act I, Scene 2, pp. 16–24, Rosalie (20–25) and Jonathan (18–25)
Rosalie babysits for the absentee couple in the penthouse across the way and comes to visit Jonathan, who has recently arrived in this Caribbean resort with his mother. In this comically wild first meeting, Rosalie learns that Jonathan's mother has completely shielded him from the outside world. As a result, he has no social skills or experience with the opposite sex, and devotes all his energy to his hob-

bies: coin and stamp collecting. Toward the end of the scene, Rosalie turns seductive; this behavior stumps Jonathan. You'll need the sound of an offstage cuckoo
clock that gets progressively louder. Start, Rosalie: "But if you've been here two
weeks, why haven't I seen you?" End, Jonathan: "I—I—I lllove you. I love you. I
love you. I love you. I…"

OLD TIMES
by Harold Pinter (Grove Press)
Drama: Act I, Keeley (40s) and Kate (40s)
As Kate and Keeley wait at home for her friend's arrival, they discuss Anna, whom
Kate hasn't seen for twenty years. Actually, Anna is standing onstage during all of
this, but she hasn't entered the scene. Start, Kate: "Dark." End, Keeley: "Anyway,
none of this matters."
Drama: Act II, Deeley (40s) and Anna (40s)
Kate is in the bathroom. Deeley and Anna talk. Did Deeley and Anna know each
other before Deeley married Kate? Were Anna and Kate lovers? Only playwright
Harold Pinter knows for sure. Start, Deeley: "Here we are. Good and hot." End,
Deeley: "If I walked into The Wayfarers Tavern now, and saw you sitting in the
corner, I wouldn't recognize you."

OLEANNA
by David Mamet (Dramatists Play Service)
Drama: Act II, pp. 30–36, John (35–45) and Carol (20)
John's tenure was derailed because of the sexual harassment accusations one of
his students filed. In this fifteen-page act, he has summoned Carol to his office to
try to resolve the issue before more damage is done. There is, however, no rea-
soning with her. You'll need a telephone that rings. Start, John: "You see, I love to
teach. And I flatter myself I am skilled at it." End, Carol: "Let me go. Let me go.
Would somebody help me please?" For a shorter excerpt, start, Carol: "Whatever
you have done to me—to the extend that you've done it to me, do you know,
rather than to me as a student." Continue to the same end.

ONLY GAME IN TOWN, THE
by Frank D. Gilroy (Samuel French)
Drama: Act I, Scene 7, pp. 37–47, Fran Walker (28) and Thomas Lockwood (52)
Tom Lockwood, Fran Walker's longtime lover, shows up unexpectedly at her Las
Vegas apartment and lets himself in while she is at work. Fran walks in at 2 A.M.
with Joe Grady, who lives with her and is stunned to discover Tom sitting in the
living room. Joe leaves them alone, and Tom tells her that he has obtained a
divorce at last and wants her to marry him. Initially ecstatic, Fran suddenly realizes that she can't go through with it. She tells Tom that she isn't going with him
and that she has fallen in love with Joe. Start, Fran: "I've been living with him."
End, Fran: "You too, Mister."
Drama: Act II, Scene 2, pp. 60–71, Fran Walker (28) and Joe Grady (30–35)
Joe Grady and Fran Walker have had a relationship-of-convenience for two years,
neither having spoken the words, "I love you." After a traumatic day and night
during which Joe gambles away all his money—and then wins it back—he realizes his love for Fran is important. He returns to the apartment, declares his feelings, and asks her to marry him. Fran is still afraid of deep emotional

commitment and resists at first. Then she agrees. This is the final scene of the play. Start, Joe: "Top of the morning." End, Joe: "One…two…three."

OPEN ADMISSIONS
by Shirley Lauro (Samuel French)
Drama: Act I, pp. 50–60, Ginny (30s) and Calvin (18)
Calvin realizes that his grades in the New York State university system mean nothing. He has been getting Bs but doesn't understand ten percent of the subject matter covered. Here, Calvin confronts Ginny, one of his teachers, as she is leaving for the day. This is a very powerful, sometimes physical scene. For a lengthy excerpt, you can begin with Ginny's telephone call, which establishes her personal problems. End, Calvin: "Burn it! Bullshittin Image bitch!!! Burn it, burn it, down, down down!!!" For a shorter version, begin as Ginny starts to leave the room and discovers Calvin. "OOOHH!! You scared me!" Continue to the same end.
Drama: Act II, pp. 70–75, Salina (20s) and Calvin (18)
When Calvin arrived home, he was still upset by the confrontation with his teacher, and slapped his seven-year-old niece. Now he is overcome with guilt. Calvin's sister, Salina, tries to figure out what is going on with him, and when she realizes that he intends to quit school, she is infuriated. Eliminate the niece's line, and roll up some blankets to serve as the child onstage. Start, Salina: "Calvin!…Calvin!" End, Salina: "Oh Lord God, where you goin? Come back! Don't do nothin' crazy, hear? Calvin?!?!? Oh God!"
Drama: Act II, pp. 80–87, Ginny (30s) and Calvin (18)
In the final scene, Calvin and his teacher come to terms with each other, and Ginny agrees to actually teach him something rather than give him Bs and walk him through the classes. This dynamic scene is very physical at times and quite emotional. Start, Ginny: "Oh! My God! Calvin! You scared me!" Continue to the end of the play. End, Calvin: "Asking…asking…asking…asking…"

OTHER PEOPLE'S MONEY
by Jerry Sterner (Samuel French)
Comedy-Drama: Act I, pp. 46–50, Garfinkle (40–45) and Kate (35)
Kate and Garfinkle, two bright, aggressive people, talk business. But there is an erotic subtext, which is sometimes overt. Start, Garfinkle: "You know what kills me? I've done maybe seven—eight deals like this." End, Garfinkle: "I think I'm falling in love."
Comedy-Drama: Act II, pp. 75–78, Garfinkle (40–45) and Bea (early 60s)
Kate's mother, Bea, tries to give Garfinkle money from her personal stock holdings in exchange for him stopping his efforts to take over the company she works for. Start, Bea: "Good afternoon, Mr. Garfinkle." End, Bea: "I hope you choke on your money and die!"

OTHERWISE ENGAGED
by Simon Gray (Samuel French)
Comedy-Drama: Act II, pp. 31–36, Simon (39) and Beth (30s)
Simon has suspected for months that his wife, Beth, is having an affair but has chosen to say nothing about it. Simon himself isn't altogether sexually faithful. In this comically tense scene, Beth returns from a supposed business trip, which was actually a tryst, and all the cards are laid on the table. Written in the British

vernacular. Begin after Stephen exits. Start, Beth: "What did he say?" Stop just before Dave's entrance. End, Beth: "Because I hate you."

PHILADELPHIA STORY, THE
by Philip Barry (Samuel French)
Comedy: Act II, Scene 2, pp. 76–82, Tracy Lord (24) and Mike Connor (30)
Mike Connor and a female photographer are on assignment for a gossip magazine, reporting on the wedding of wealthy socialite Tracy Lord to successful, self-made businessman George Kittredge. One thing has led to another and, in this scene, Tracy and Mike find themselves in a romantic embrace. It is almost dawn, and both of them have had a bit too much to drink. Start, Tracy: "Hello you." End, Tracy: "Not me—oh, not me! Put me in your pocket, Mike."

PIANO LESSON, THE
by August Wilson (Plume Drama)
Comedy-Drama: Act II, Scene 2, Avery (38) and Berniece (35)
Avery tries to get Berniece to marry him, telling her that she can use the piano in his new church. But she doesn't want to get married. Start, Berniece: "Who is it?" End, Avery: "God says He will soothe the troubled waters. I'll come by tomorrow and bless the house."

PICNIC
by William Inge (Dramatists Play Service)
Drama: Act II, pp. 54–56, Madge (18) and Hal (early 20s)
Everyone except Madge and Hal have departed for the picnic. Hal is trying to sort out his feelings from an earlier confrontation with Rosemary Sidney, who accused him of being a bum and a fraud. Madge and Hal talk and kiss, and at scene's end, walk off hand in hand, presumably to make love. Start, Madge: "Don't feel bad. Women like Miss Sidney make me disgusted with the whole female sex." End, Hal: "Do we? There's other places…with not so many people."
Drama: Act III, Scene 1, pp. 57–60, Rosemary Sidney (about 40) and Howard (42)
After making love with Rosemary Sidney, Howard brings her home. She is depressed and shaken. As he turns to leave, she suddenly and forcefully demands that he marry her. But he, being a confirmed bachelor, hedges. Start, Howard: "Here we are, honey." End, Howard: "Good night."

PLAY MEMORY
by Joanna M. Glass (Samuel French)
Drama: Act II, pp. 59–62, Jean MacMillan (20s, playing early teens) and Cam (late 50s)
Jean MacMillan comes home from school and, as usual, finds Cam, her father, sitting alone, immersed in self-pity. She tells him how much she longs for a "normal" family, and he launches into a speech about how despicable "normal" is. Jean is frustrated and sad that she can't seem to inspire her father to get his act together. Cam knows how his behavior appears to others, but he is evidently unable to change. His is a slow, steady descent into alcoholism and poverty. Start, Cam: "Hello…May I deduce that things did not go well at school today?" End, Cam: "I can see you need to—change your clothes."

Drama: Act II, pp. 68–72, Ruth (50s) and Cam (late 50s)

After Cam swapped his twelve-year-old daughter's beautiful carved closet door for some liquor, she stopped talking. She hasn't made a sound for two weeks. This scene begins as Ruth, Cam's wife, comes in, having spoken to the school counselor about options. The counselor has suggested that mother and daughter move out of this home and has arranged a place for them to go. But Ruth wants more than anything to hold the family together, even in the face of its poverty and alcoholism. Cam, however, knows that the situation has gone too far, and he encourages Ruth to take the girl and leave him. He insists and, finally, Ruth agrees. A very touching, intense scene. Start, Ruth: "Any change in Jean?" End, Cam: "Should have paid more attention since he's now to be the—steward of my family."

PORCH
by Jeffrey Sweet (Samuel French)

Drama: One-act play, pp. 8–14, Amy (early 30s) and Ernest Herbert (early 60s)

Ernest Herbert is a widower, facing exploratory surgery tomorrow. In this scene, he presses Amy, his daughter and only surviving child, to marry and have a family, to give him grandchildren. Start, Herbert: "So tell me." End, Herbert: "No, you're not."

Drama: One-act play, pp. 21–31, Amy (early 30s) and Sam (early 30s)

Amy is visiting with her father when her old high-school boyfriend, Sam, shows up. Amy's father told Sam that she was in town, hoping that sparks would fly again between these two lovers, who haven't seen each other for eleven years. Begin after Herbert leaves them alone on the porch. Start, Amy: "Subtle, isn't he?" End, Amy: "Yup."

Drama: One-act play, pp. 30–39, Amy (early 30s) and Sam (early 30s)

Amy still believes that the decision she made years ago to abort her pregnancy by Sam was the right one. Though she hasn't seen him or answered his letters for eleven years, some of those old sparks are still glowing. In this excerpt, Sam and Amy talk about what might have been, but she refuses to rekindle their romance. Start, Sam: "You ever wonder what would have happened if we'd gone through with it? Gotten married, had the kid?" Stop with Sam's exit. End, Amy: "Yuh."

PRELUDE TO A KISS
by Craig Lucas (Broadway Play Publishing)

Comedy: Act I, Rita (mid-to-late 20s) and Peter (mid-to-late 20s)

Because most scenes in this play are quite short, you'll probably want to combine two. In this excerpt, the first part takes place in Rita's apartment. After Peter and Rita make love, they talk about sexual fantasies, whether or not to have children, and political preferences—the kinds of topics you would expect new lovers to talk about. In the second part, which takes place in Rita's apartment six weeks later, Peter asks Rita to marry him. As written, the scenes are intended to be played back-to-back. Start, Peter: "Christ!" End, Rita: "Uh huh."

PRISONER OF SECOND AVENUE, THE
by Neil Simon (Samuel French)

Comedy: Act I, Scene 2, pp. 18–29, Mel (46) and Edna (early 40s)

Mel is in a bad enough mood because he lost his job. Then he comes home to discover his apartment has been robbed. The thieves even took his dental floss. This rather long scene moves fast. You'll need props that suggest the apartment has been ransacked. Start, Edna: "Edison…Mrs. Edna Edison…I've just been robbed." End, Mel: "Because it's not a heart attack. It's pains in my chest."

PRIVATE LIVES
by Noel Coward (Samuel French)
Comedy: Act I, pp. 10–12, Sybil (23) and Elyot (30)

The setting: the terrace of Elyot and Sybil's honeymoon suite on a romantic, moonlit night in the south of France. Sybil went inside to dress for dinner and, as she returns, is shocked to hear an inexplicably rattled Elyot announce that he wants to leave the hotel immediately. His insistence leads to an argument when she balks. What Sybil doesn't realize, however, is that Elyot discovered only a few moments ago that his ex-wife, Amanda, is honeymooning with her new husband in the adjacent suite! Start, Sybil: "Cocktail, please." End, Sybil: "Oh, Elli, Elli, Elli."

Comedy: Act I, pp. 13–15, Amanda (late 20s) and Victor (35)

The setting: the balcony of Amanda and Victor's honeymoon suite on the same romantic, moonlit night in the south of France. Victor went inside to dress for dinner and, as he returns, is shocked to hear an inexplicably rattled Amanda announce that she wants to leave the hotel immediately. Her insistence leads to an argument when he balks. What he doesn't realize, however, is that Amanda discovered only a few moments ago that her ex-husband, Elyot, is honeymooning with his new wife in the adjacent suite! Start, Victor: "You were certainly right when you said you weren't normal." End, Amanda: "Go away, go away, go away."

Comedy: Act I, pp. 15–22, Amanda (late 20s) and Elyot (30)

Amanda and Elyot's new spouses have left their respective hotel suites in anger, and Amanda and Elyot confront each other on their respective terraces. Still madly in love, the formerly married couple soon decides to abandon their new spouses, cast caution to the wind, and run away together to Paris. The characters refer to offstage music at key points in this scene. If you don't use music, omit the corresponding references. Start, Amanda: "Thoughtful of them to play that, wasn't it?" End, Elyot: "Solomon Issacs." For an alternative, shorter excerpt that doesn't require smoking, start, Amanda: "I'm in such a rage." Continue to the same end.

Comedy: Act II, pp. 24–29, Amanda (late 20s) and Elyot (30)

Act II is a prolonged scene between Amanda and Elyot in her Paris flat. The scene begins very romantically and ends with the couple literally rolling on the floor fighting, obviously on the road to breaking up again. Start, Amanda: "I'm glad we let Louise go." End, Elyot: "I think I love you more than ever before. Isn't it ridiculous? Put your feet up."

PROOF
by David Auburn (Dramatists Play Service)
Drama: Act I, Scene 1, pp. 5–12, Robert (50s) and Catherine (25)

This is actually a dream sequence because Catherine's father, Robert, died a week ago. She is disheveled, deep in thought on the back porch of the house she shared with her dad. He enters and they talk about whether or not she has inherited his mental instability. The scene is fueled by both love and loss. Start, Robert: "Can't sleep?" End, Robert: "For you, Catherine, my daughter—who I love very much—it could be a bad sign."

Drama: Act 1, Scene 1, pp. 12–20, Hal (28) and Catherine (25)
Hal has been upstairs riffling through Catherine's late father's journals, hoping that they contain as-yet-unfound insights of genius into mathematics. He comes downstairs, heading for the front door, when this scene takes place. Catherine correctly guesses that Hal is stealing one of her dad's journals. Later in the play, these two characters become lovers, so there should be a spark. Start with Hal's entrance on page 5. Catherine: "What?" End, Catherine: "Shit!"

PROPOSAL, THE

by Anton Chekhov (*The Sneeze: Plays and Stories by Anton Chekhov*, translated and adapted by Michael Frayn, Samuel French)

Comedy: One-act play, pp. 84–89, Natalya Stepanovna (25) and Lomov (35)
Lomov has finally gotten up the nerve to ask Natalya Stepanova to marry him. But before he can get to the important part of his proposal, the exchange degenerates into an argument about whether her family or his owns a nearby parcel of land, Ox Lea Meadows. Start, Natalya: "Oh, good Lord, it's you!" End, Lomov: "They're mine!"

P.S. YOUR CAT IS DEAD

by James Kirkwood (revised edition, Samuel French)

Comedy: Act I, Scene 1, pp. 15–23, Jimmy (38) and Kate (32)
Kate has chosen New Year's Eve to break off her live-in relationship with Jimmy. While he is out of their apartment, she is packing her stuff. Jimmy comes home unexpectedly, and he and Kate have a breakup scene. Start, Kate: "Oh—Jimmy." End, Kate: "Enchanting!…Good-bye!"

RAINMAKER, THE

by N. Richard Nash (Samuel French)

Drama: Act II, pp. 64–70, Lizzie (27) and File (late 30s)
File has allegedly traveled to the Curry place to apologize for hitting Lizzie's brother Jim earlier in the day. The truth is that File wants to see Lizzie. They're attracted to each other, but neither is comfortable with the opposite sex. This charming scene is frequently overlooked because everyone wants to do the Lizzie/Starbuck scenes. Eliminate Noah's brief interruption. Start, Lizzie: "How about a cup of coffee?" End, File: "Don't be so damn ridiculous. Be yourself!"

Drama: Act II, pp. 75–79, Lizzie (27) and Starbuck (30s)
Lizzie was humiliated by her brother Noah when he called her an old maid and suggested that she get used to the idea that she is, in fact, plain, not pretty. Distraught, she ran from the room, picking up Starbuck's bed linen on the way. She came directly to the barn where he is spending the night, intent on delivering the linen to him. During the scene, Starbuck tells Lizzie that she is pretty. They kiss. Start, Starbuck: "Who's that?…Who's there?" Continue to the end of the act. End, Lizzie: "Oh, is it me? Is it really me?!"

Drama: Act III, pp. 88–90, Lizzie (27) and Starbuck (30s)
In the afterglow of lovemaking, Starbuck confesses to Lizzie that he is a fraud and a dreamer, and that, contrary to his claims, he has never made it rain. Start, Starbuck: "And I always walk so fast and ride so far I never have time to stop and ask myself no question." End, Lizzie: "And then one night you look down—and there it is—shining in your hand!"

RAISIN IN THE SUN, A
by Lorraine Hansberry (Samuel French)
Drama: Act III, Beneatha (20) and Asagai (mid-20s)
Beneatha's older brother, Walter Lee, has foolishly entrusted the family nest egg to a would-be business partner, who promptly stole it. Now facing a future with no funds for medical school, Beneatha is growing more embittered about the sorry state of humanity. When Asagai, her Nigerian friend and fellow student, arrives, they have a full-force philosophical disagreement over these matters. Then Asagai asks Beneatha to marry him, go live in Nigeria, and rediscover her African roots. Start, Asagai: "I came over…I had some free time." End, Asagai: "How often I have looked at you and said, 'ah—so this is what the New World hath finally wrought.'"

RED COAT, THE
by John Patrick Shanley (*Welcome to the Moon and Other Plays*, Dramatists Play Service; *13 by Shanley*, Applause)
Comedy: One-act play, Dramatists Play Service pp. 9–12, Mary (16) and John (17)
In this short play, John is at a festive party but still feels lonely, so he goes outside to sit in the light of the full moon. When Mary, who is on her way to the same party, arrives, they talk. Their conversation quickly becomes an exultant declaration of mutual love and understanding. Start, John: "Hi, Mary." End, John: "I know. I can feel them shining."

REUNION
by David Mamet (*Reunion and Dark Pony*, Grove Press)
Drama: One-act play, Carol (24) and Bernie (53)
The subject of this one-act play is the reunion of a father and daughter after a twenty-year separation. Just twenty-three pages long, the play is divided into fourteen brief scenes that take place during a single conversation. **One option is to perform scenes 1, 2, and 3 without interruption; together, they contain plenty of subtext (pp. 9–16).** This excerpt includes the opening moments of Carol and her father Bernie's meeting. They're trying to figure out how to talk to one another and are feeling their way in the dark. Start, Bernie: "I would have recognized you anywhere. It is you, isn't it?" End, Bernie: "I'll be goddamned if I don't feel like I'm gonna bust out crying. And I almost did."

A second option is to perform scenes 10, 11, 12, 13, and 14 without interruption for an excerpt that runs about five-and-a-half pages (pp. 27–32). In the final moments of the play, Carol tells her father that she looked him up because she simply "felt lonely…I never had a father." He gives her a gift, a gold bracelet he had specially inscribed to mark the occasion. Start, Bernie: "But I can't work for the phone company anymore. When they finally pulled my license, that was it." End, Bernie: "Thank you."

ROAD TO NIRVANA
by Arthur Kopit (Samuel French)
Comedy: Act II, pp. 79–89, Jerry (30s to 40s) and Nirvana (late 20s)
Nirvana, rock's biggest female star, and Jerry spend their first moments alone next to her massive swimming pool. They talk about reincarnation, loyalty, and movie deals. What Jerry doesn't know is that Nirvana is sizing him up and, very soon,

will ask for his testicles—or at least one of them—as proof of his loyalty to her and the price of her participation in the movie project he is producing. Start, Nirvana: "Have you any coke?" End, Nirvana: "You're my protector now."

SCENES AND REVELATIONS
by Elan Garonzik (Samuel French)

Comedy-Drama: Scene 6, pp. 20–24, Millie (23, playing teens) and Dennis (20s, playing teens)

Millie dreams of being a famous painter. In this flashback scene, she paints a portrait of Dennis, the young man from the farm next door. He is feeling his oats and wants her to be the first one he kisses, so after a while they go ahead and do it. Dennis discovers that kissing Millie "ain't like kissin' old Aunt Eleanor or huggin' my horse." Start, Millie: "Dennis Houser, how could you speak such an awful lie? Why, you make me just indignant!" End, Millie: "Oh, Dennis Houser, eat your raspberries."

Drama: Scene 10, pp. 32–37, Helena (25) and Samuel (27)

The year is 1893, and Samuel, the manager of Helena's Pennsylvania farm, is trying to save up enough money to head west. But he and Helena have known one another for a few weeks, and romance is in the air. In this five-page scene, which takes place in a ripe raspberry patch, they dance around the issues of commitment and marriage. In a nice monologue, Helena tells Samuel about her first true love and how it evaporated. Then they kiss. Start, Samuel: "And we spent seven dollars on new planking for the barn." End, Samuel: "Wanting so much. Desiring so much."

Comedy-Drama: Scene 12, pp. 40–46, Millie (21) and Dennis (21)

It is Dennis's birthday, and Millie has bought him a pipe. They smoke the pipe together as they talk about the future. She admits that she has always loved him, that she knows he loves her, and that she expects them to marry. Dennis then tells Millie that he has been courting another woman. Millie may be crushed, but she takes the high road, wishing him all the luck in the world. Then they go skinny-dipping. Start, Millie: "Dennis! Deeennnniss! Hurry up! Or the moon'll go down and we won't see a thing." End, Millie: "Anyway, Dennis Houser, this is 1893. And that's not the Middle Ages!"

SEAGULL, THE
by Anton Chekhov (a new version by Jean-Claude Van Itallie, Dramatists Play Service)

Drama: Act IV, pp. 49–53, Nina (21) and Treplev (27)

Two years ago, Nina left her father's comfortable home outside Moscow, moved to the big city to become an actress, and began an affair with Trigorin, a famous novelist much older than she. The affair resulted in a child who died, and ultimately, Trigorin abandoned her. Nina's acting career has been mediocre, but since being disowned by her father, she has been forced to make her meager living from the stage.

In this scene, Nina appears unexpectedly one night in Treplev's studio. He is ecstatic to see her since he has loved her madly for years. He again declares his undying love; she, in turn, tells him she still loves Trigorin even though the man has treated her badly. As quickly as Nina appeared, she bids farewell to Treplev, leaving for a winter acting engagement in a distant province. After her departure, Treplev is in despair over this life that will never be fulfilled, and takes his own. Start, Treplev: "I've talked a lot about new forms." End, Treplev: "I hope no one sees her in the garden and tells Mamma. Mamma would be upset."

SEA HORSE, THE
by Edward J. Moore (Samuel French)

Drama: Act I, pp. 11–19, Gertrude (late 30s) and Harry (late 30s)

This two-character play examines the relationship between a strong, independent woman and the sailor who has come to love her. There are a number of possibilities for scenework. In one scene, which is filled with conflict, Harry tells Gertrude about his plans to buy a fishing boat and marry her. She doesn't like the idea because she can't accept that kind of intimacy. They argue, and then make up. If you decide to use this play for scene study, keep in mind that Moore specified an important casting consideration: Gertrude is described as a "big woman" and should be overweight. Start, Gertrude: "This run was a lot longer, wasn't it?" End, Gertrude: "Yeah, I think you better tell me about it now!"

Drama: Act II, pp. 33–41, Gertrude (late 30s) and Harry (late 30s)

Gertrude wakes up to find Harry fixing breakfast for her and trying to make amends for the fight they had last night. Still unwilling to accept this kind of intimacy, she gets angry. Start, Harry: "Oh…morning…Wow!" End, Harry: "Yeah, yeah, yeah, yeah!"

SEXUAL PERVERSITY IN CHICAGO
by David Mamet (Samuel French)

Comedy: One-act play, pp. 14–17, Bernard (30–35) and Joan (about 25)

In this short scene, Bernard tries to pick Joan up in a singles bar. He is arrogant, crude, dishonest, and insulting. It is unclear why Joan is in a singles bar in the first place. Start, Bernard: "Evening. Good evening." End, Bernard: "You got a lot of fuckin' nerve."

SHADOW BOX, THE
by Michael Cristofer (Samuel French)

Drama: Act I, pp. 13–18, Joe (48–55) and Maggie (38–45)

Joe hasn't seen his wife, Maggie, and their young son for six months. During his time here in the hospital, he has come to terms with his prognosis of terminal cancer, but she is still in denial. Maggie continues to put on a happy face, hoping everything will turn out okay. During this scene, Maggie tries to get Joe to come back home and talks about plans for the future. But Joe resists. He insists that she realize how very much he loves her even though he is dying. In the end, the reality of the situation drags Maggie into despair. Start, Maggie: "End of line." End, Maggie: "I knew it. I knew it."

Drama: Act I, pp. 22–27, Beverly (mid-30s) and Mark (25–30)

Beverly has come to the hospital to visit her ex-husband, Brian, who is dying of cancer. She drinks herself into a party mood, and when she happily bursts into his room, she is surprised to find herself face-to-face with his male lover, Mark, who is not at all happy to see her. Start, Beverly: "Surprise!" End, Beverly: "Hey!"

Drama: Act I, pp. 37–41, Brian (mid-40s) and Beverly (mid-30s)

Now that he is dying, Beverly gets reacquainted with Brian, her ex-husband. They talk about their feelings and come to terms with his prognosis. Laughter through tears. No longer married, they are still good friends. Start, Beverly: "Caro! Caro! You old fart!" End, Beverly: "Yes. But why it is I always seem to end up in Naples?"

Drama: Act II, pp. 76–80, Joe (48–55) and Maggie (38–45)

Here, Joe and Maggie talk about the farm they never had and their life together, and Maggie begins to accept the fact that Joe is going to die from cancer. Start, Joe: "It would have been nice." End, Maggie: "I can't. I can't."

SHAPE OF THINGS, THE
by Neil Labute (Faber and Faber)

Drama: "A Park," pp. 46–58, Adam (early 20s) and Jenny (early 20s)

Jenny is engaged to marry Phillip, and Adam is involved with another woman. They meet in a park just to catch up on things and wind up sharing a totally unexpected romantic kiss. Could this be a relationship that might have been? Start, Adam: "…hey." End, Jenny: "Come on. We should go bury this. Out in the woods…"

Drama: "An Exhibition Gallery," pp. 123–137, Adam (early 20s) and Evelyn (early 20s)

This is the final scene in the play and presents considerable acting challenges. Moments before the scene begins, Adam learns that he has been the object of an elaborate hoax perpetuated by Evelyn. He thought the two of them were in love, but she was in fact "sculpting" him, making him over as a living art project. He has just learned that she really only objectifies him. In this complex emotional scene, he confronts her. Start, Adam: "…not a big 'modern art' crowd, I guess, huh?" End, Adam: "…oh."

SIGHT UNSEEN
by Donald Margulies (Dramatists Play Service)

Drama: Act I, Scene 1, pp. 9–20, Patricia (35–45) and Jonathan (35–45)

During the years following the failure of Jonathan and Patricia's love affair, he has become a celebrated and financially successful painter. On the occasion of his first major exhibit outside North America, he looks Patricia up. She is now married to an archaeologist and living on a farm in Norfolk, England. Start, Jonathan: "You look beautiful." End, Patricia: "You aren't invited. You're cold. I think it actually is warmer inside."

Drama: Act I, Scene 4, pp. 32–36, Patricia (35–45) and Jonathan (35–45)

In this flashback scene that takes place shortly after Jonathan's mother's death, he tells Patricia, who has come to console him, that he no longer loves her. Start, Patricia: "Jonathan!" End, Jonathan: "I don't love you, Patty."

SILENT NIGHT, LONELY NIGHT
by Robert Anderson (Samuel French)

Drama: Act I, Scene 2, pp. 33–43, Katherine (mid-30s) and John (40)

John and Katherine occupy adjoining rooms in a New England inn this Christmas Eve. The only other guests in the inn are the honeymooners upstairs. After meeting for the first time a few hours ago, Katherine and John go to a movie and have drinks with the other couple afterward in Katherine's room. Alone again now, with dawn approaching, the prospect of whether or not to go to bed together hangs in the air.

Katherine says that it isn't going to happen, and then tells John about the trouble she is having with her husband. He, in turn, tells her about other Christmases abroad. Both of them need to be close to someone tonight, so rather than return to his room, John sleeps on the sofa. Start, Katherine: "Maybe I'd better say something. It may sound ridiculous, but…Oh, no, it is ridiculous." End,

John: "Christmas Eve is Hell, isn't it? The Fourth of July is much easier." For a five-page version of this scene, start, Katherine: "What are you doing here alone in a God-forsaken spot on Christmas Eve?" Continue to the same end.

Drama: Act II, Scene 2, pp. 57–62, Katherine (mid-30s) and John (40)
This scene is filled to the brim with subtext. John and Katherine have bared their souls and finally slept together only a few hours ago. Now they're going their separate ways with no regrets, certain that the experience was significant, important, and perhaps even lifesaving. John enters into Katherine's room as she is packing. You'll need a telephone to ring. Start, John: "Good morning." End, Katherine: "I have nothing either....(reaches in her pocket) a handkerchief."

SNOWANGEL
by Lewis John Carline (*Cages*, Dramatists Play Service)
Drama: One-act play, John (40s) and Connie (35–45)
This nineteen-page one-act play centers on a 4 A.M. meeting between a prostitute and a john (customer). Several excerpts capture the essence of Connie and John's complicated involvement. **One option is to begin at the top of the play and continue through to John's suggestion that Connie reenact the first meeting he had with his first love (pp. 7–15).** Connie responds with outrage and telephones her pimp, who tells her that she has to do it. Start, John: "Connie?...Connie?" End, Connie: "You got your way! Now what'a ya want me to do?"

The second scene choice begins where the first excerpt ends and continues to the end of the play (pp. 15–26). This excerpt is far more physically and emotionally demanding than the first one. Connie gets progressively drunk while she attempts to act out John's fantasy, and he is frustrated with her inability to reenact it as he remembers it. Finally, he slaps her. When Connie recovers, they begin to act out *her* first-love fantasy. Start, John: "Your dresses in here?" End, Connie: "A dark angel...it's me. Me!"

SOCIAL EVENT, A
by William Inge (*Eleven Short Plays by William Inge*, Dramatists Play Service)
Comedy: One-act play, pp. 30–35, Randy (25–30) and Carole (25–30)
In this rare comedy from William Inge, Randy and Carole are two Hollywood actors on the make. They're trying to get an invitation to the funeral of a prominent actor they cared little about. All that matters to them is being "seen" at this social event. Start, Randy: "Muriel? We're getting up now. Bring up the usual breakfast." End, Randy: "Just a slight case so you could tell them with a straight face."

SORROWS OF STEPHEN
by Peter Parnell (Samuel French)
Comedy: Act I, Scene 2, pp. 11–17, Stephen (mid-20s) and Liz (mid-20s)
When Stephen arrives at the apartment he shares with Liz, he is stunned to discover her packing to leave him. He tries to talk her out of it while she packs. They discuss the situation in a civil and enlightened way, they kiss and hug, and then she leaves. Start, Stephen: "I don't believe it." Stop with Liz's exit, or continue to the end of the scene and end, Stephen: "...Sorry. I'm sorry to disturb you...I must have copied the wrong...number...."

Comedy: Act II, Scene 2, pp. 53–61, Stephen (mid-20s) and Christine (mid-20s)
Christine loves William, but she has begun an affair with his best friend, Stephen.

Both Stephen and Christine feel conflicted about this romantic triangle, but they kiss and hug a great deal. Start, Christine (reading): "As you know me, you will understand only too clearly what attracts me." End, Stephen: "Let me embrace you. Let me make you feel safe."

Comedy: Act II, Scene 5, pp. 69–75, William (mid-20s) and Christine (mid-20s)
William has booked a lovely suite at the Plaza Hotel for Christine and himself. He is still apologizing for last night's mix-up at the opera when he punched the man he erroneously suspected was having an affair with her. William has been drinking champagne and is now tipsy. When he asks Christine to marry him, she agrees even though she also secretly loves Stephen. You'll need a bed for the scene. Start, Christine (reading): "Lotte had slept little that night." End, Christine: "The Yanamam. Yes."

Comedy: Act II, Scene 7, pp. 77–83, Stephen (mid-20s) and Christine (mid-20s)
On a romantic, rainy afternoon in the sculpture garden at New York's Museum of Modern Art, Stephen asks Christine to marry him. She refuses, explaining that she is going to marry Stephen's best friend, William. She then says that she and Stephen have to end their affair. This is a meaty scene because Christine legitimately loves both men. Start, Christine: "It's nice out here, isn't it?" End, Stephen: "Christine, please! Go!"

SPEED-THE-PLOW
by David Mamet (Samuel French)

Comedy: Act I, pp. 37–44, Karen (20s) and Gould (35–45)
This is a choice scene in which studio executive Gould has most of the lines. He is "teaching" Karen, his sexy temp secretary, about the movie system before assigning her a boring book on radiation to read. Gould is actually after a roll in the hay with Karen. She is less naive than she appears. Start, Karen: "Mr. Gould." End, Gould: "And tell him that he owes me five hundred bucks."

Comedy: Act II, pp. 45–55, Karen (20s) and Gould (35–45)
Karen, the sexy office temp, has read the boring radiation book and is pushing it for movie development. Gould wants to get her into bed. Start, Karen: "He puts his hand on the child's door." End, Karen: "You asked me to come. Here I am." For a shorter version, start, Gould: "You've done a fantastic job." Continue to the same end.

SPINNING INTO BUTTER
by Rebecca Gilman (Dramatic Publishing)

Drama: Act I, Scene 2, pp. 9–15, Sarah (mid-to-late 30s) and Ross (mid-to-late 30s)
Ross and Sarah, both members of the Belmont College faculty, have been having a sexual relationship. In this scene, Ross tells Sarah that his previous girlfriend, Petra, has returned from her sabbatical and that he is resuming his relationship with her. He wants to "just be friends" with Sarah. By the end of the scene, she accepts that relationship. Start, Ross: "Have you got a second?" End, Sarah: "Okay. Next?"

Drama: Act I, Scene 6, pp. 45–49, Sarah (mid-to-late 30s) and Patrick (19)
Patrick has written an editorial in the school newspaper, accusing school administrators of racial "tokenism." Sarah correctly recognizes herself as the unnamed administrator and tries to talk it out with the student. The more she tries to explain herself, however, the worse it gets. Start, Sarah: "…Sorry about the wait. Did you get a letter from financial aid?" End, Sarah: "Patrick. I'm sorry."

Drama: Act II, Scene 1, pp. 50–54, Sarah (mid-to-late 30s) and Ross (mid-to-late 30s)

Sarah attempts to convince Ross that he is guilty of "idealizing" people that are different from him, thereby prohibiting them from being his true equal. Ross denies it. Start, Ross: "You know, I grew up on a farm." End, Ross: "…You're equivocating."

Drama: Act II, Scene 3, pp. 58–71, Sarah (mid-to-late 30s) and Ross (mid-to-late 30s)

This is a difficult scene to play, for several reasons. Basically, the playwright is laying out the philosophical underpinnings of the entire play as Sarah cleanses herself by admitting to being a closet racist. Ross is appalled. The challenge for the actors is to find the real negotiations in the scene and to avoid a one-note rant. Start, Sarah: "Who is it?" End, Sarah: "I know, I know, I know."

SPLIT SECOND
by Dennis McIntyre (Samuel French)

Drama: Act I, Scene 4, pp. 33–41, Alea (28–35) and Val (28–35)

Val is an African-American New York City cop who, a few hours ago, lost his temper and killed a racist Caucasian car thief he'd taken into custody. After shooting the thief, Val restaged the crime scene to make it look like a case of self-defense. It is now 4:30 A.M., and he is arriving home where his wife, Alea, has fallen asleep on the sofa. At first Val lies about what happened earlier, but then he tells Alea the truth. Her reaction is to tell him he made the right choice by officially altering the facts. Start, Alea: "What time is it?" End, Val: "No."

Drama: Act II, Scene 4, pp. 65–69, Alea (28–35) and Rusty (55–60)

Alea and her father-in-law, Rusty, both know what actually happened when Val shot and killed a car thief who was already handcuffed and in custody. Rusty, a retired cop, is ashamed of his son's actions and the subsequent lie he told to cover up the crime. Alea thinks that expediency was the best choice, that it was better for Val to distort the truth than to risk going to jail. In this tense, four-page scene, Alea tries to get Rusty to change his position to one of support for his son. Start, Rusty: "We could have talked about it over the phone." End, Alea: "As long as he's here, that's all that counts."

SPOILS OF WAR
by Michael Weller (Samuel French)

Drama: Act I, pp. 7–16, Elise (mid-30s) and Martin (16)

Martin comes home from boarding school to find the electricity turned off in his mother's small Greenwich Village apartment. Elise doesn't realize that he has been seeing her estranged husband on the sly, planning to engineer a reconciliation between them. An interesting scene because of the age differences between the characters and their complex relationship. Elise is quite the bohemian. Start, Martin: "Mom!" End, Elise: "Angel!"

Drama: Act I, pp. 39–41, Penny (20s) and Martin (16)

In this short scene, Martin talks to Penny, his father's girlfriend, and tries to convince her not to show up at the party next Sunday. Penny doesn't know that Martin is scheming to get his mother and father back together at the function. Start, Martin: "I got lost after the Sheep Meadow, sorry." End, Penny: "I know my overalls stink, but I can still smell bullshit when a truckload of it falls on my head. The answer is no, en-oh."

Drama: Act I, pp. 42–46, Elise (mid-30s) and Martin (16)

Martin finally tells his mother that he has been secretly seeing his father for some time. He then tells Elise that next Sunday he wants her to come to a party that his father will be attending. Elise resists at first but then agrees to attend. Start, Elise: "Martin, hurry up in there, what are you doing, plotting the Revolution?!" End, Elise: "After all the pains taken, how could I disappoint? We should call and warn him, it's only fair. But on the other hand, in love and war. Well? What a pair we are, you and I."

STRANGE SNOW
by Steve Metcalfe (Samuel French)

Drama: Act I, Scene 2, pp. 30–41, Megs (late 30s) and Martha (mid-30s)

Megs and Martha share a common high-school-prom fantasy that leads to a moment of true affection, but Martha resists it. The scene requires a few props: Martha fixes Megs a bowl of soup, which he eats. Stop just before Megs angrily puts his fist through a glass windowpane. Start, Megs: "Martha! Hey, Martha!?" End, Megs: "That bad a dancer, huh!" If you can figure out a way to safely break a window on stage, end, Megs: "Joseph. You're too much, Martha. M-A-R-T-H-A."

Drama: Act II, Scene 1, pp. 42–48, Dave (late 30s) and Martha (mid-30s)

Dave, who is unwilling to confront his personal demons, definitely doesn't want Megs, his old Vietnam War buddy, to come for dinner. But Martha, Dave's sister, is attracted to Megs and definitely wants him to come. Start, Dave: "Whata you mean you invited him over for dinner?" End, Dave: "Get 'm for me, huh?"

STRANGEST KIND OF ROMANCE, THE
by Tennessee Williams (*The Theater of Tennessee Williams, Volume 6*; New Directions)

Drama: Scene 2, Landlady (40) and Little Man (35–40)

Little Man has moved into this seedy rooming house and keeps to himself, becoming friends with the cat that was left behind by a former boarder. In this scene, Landlady, who is lonely, walks in on Little Man and tries to seduce him. This event only makes him more nervous and uncertain. Later in the play, Little Man has a complete nervous breakdown. This scene is appropriate for sophisticated actors. Start, Landlady: "Oh—you were playing possum." End, Landlady: "Nature says—Don't—be lonesome."

STREETCAR NAMED DESIRE, A
by Tennessee Williams (Dramatists Play Service)

Drama: Act I, Scene 2, pp. 20–24, Stanley (about 30) and Stella (late 20s)

Stanley returns to the apartment and discovers Blanche's fine clothing and jewelry lying around. He figures she bought these relatively expensive items with the money she swindled from Stella. This scene requires some specific props, including clothes and jewelry. Start, Stanley: "Hiya, sweetheart." End, Stanley: "You're damn' tootin' I'm goin' to stay here."

Drama: Act I, Scene 2, pp. 27–29, Stanley (about 30) and Blanche (early 30s)

Stanley demands that Blanche show him the documents of sale for Belle Reve,

Stella's family home. This short but powerful scene contains their first confrontation. Start, Blanche: "The poor little thing was out there listening to us." End, Blanche: "I didn't know she was going to have a baby."

Drama: Act II, Scene 2, pp. 61–68, Blanche (early 30s) and Mitch (about 30)

In this key scene, Blanche has been coming on to Mitch. Alone in the apartment after a date, they move cautiously toward a deeper relationship. He still doesn't know the truth about her sordid past. If you choose to work on this scene, keep in mind that Mitch is described in the play as six feet tall and weighing 207 pounds. There is a specific reference to his weight in this scene. Begin at the top of the scene. Start, Blanche: "Well…" End, Blanche: "Sometimes—there's God—so quickly." For a shorter version, start, Mitch: "Blanche—Blanche—guess how much I weigh?" Continue to the same end.

SUBJECT WAS ROSES, THE
by Frank D. Gilroy (Samuel French)

Drama: Act I, Scene 1, pp. 6–10, Nettie (45) and John (50)

It is 1946. Timmy has been discharged from the Army and has returned to the Bronx apartment he has always shared with his parents, Nettie and John. Last night the family celebrated, and Timmy is sleeping it off as John and Nettie talk in the kitchen. They are both grateful that he wasn't killed or injured in World War II, as so many other young men were, and they have plans to really enjoy him now. Their conversation, however, seems more like sparring than discussion, and it becomes clear that they are competing for Timmy's affections. This is the first glimpse of a tense relationship that has been sexless for many years. Start, Nettie: "It's a lovely day…Timmy still asleep?" End, John: "Did I say it wasn't? There."

Drama: Act II, Scene 1, pp. 48–51, Nettie (45) and Timmy (21)

Last night, the family ate out in a fancy restaurant and then went to a dance club. After Timmy went to bed, John tried—for the first time in a long time—to make love to Nettie and was rebuffed. This morning, he is in a foul mood and takes out his frustration on Timmy. A few moments ago, John stormed out, apparently on his way to church. In this scene Timmy blames his mother for the problems at home, says she has never really understood or been supportive of John, and has been too involved with her own mother and cousin. Nettie is stunned by the verbal assault. Start, Nettie: "Now what was that all about?" End, Nettie: "Thank you for the roses."

SUBSTANCE OF FIRE, THE
by Jon Robin Baitz (Samuel French)

Drama: Act II, pp. 48–55, Issac Geldhart (60s) and Marge Hackett (50s)

Marge Hackett, a psychiatric social worker, is sent by Issac Geldhart's children to determine whether he is competent to manage his own affairs. It turns out that Marge and Issac have much in common. Start, Marge: "We usually do this at the office. It took a bending of the rules." End, Marge: "I'm not from Sotheby and I should be here. Goodbye, Mr. Geldhart."

SUMMER AND SMOKE
by Tennessee Williams (Dramatists Play Service)

Drama: Part I, Scene 1, pp. 14–19, Alma (25–29) and John (25–29)

John teases Alma for "putting on airs," and she gets angry. Then they make up.

Start, Alma: "What book is she talking about?" End, John: "Get one!"

Drama: Part I, Scene 7, pp. 45–51, Alma (25–29) and John (25–29)

John and Alma are on a date, and he wants to go to the cockfights at the Moonlight Casino. When Alma won't hear of it, they argue and she leaves. For scene-study purposes, eliminate Dusty, the waiter. Start, John: "I don't understand why we can't go in the casino." End, Alma: "You're not a gentleman."

Drama: Part II, Scene 5, pp. 69–75, Alma (25–29) and John (25–29)

Alma comes to John's office to let him know that she loves him and is now willing to sleep with him. She discovers that he has changed his mind, however, and that it is too late. Time has passed them by. Start, Alma: "No greetings? No greetings at all?" End, John: "I'll write a prescription for you."

SURE THING

by David Ives (*All in the Timing: Six One-Act Comedies,* Dramatists Play Service)

Comedy: One-act play, pp. 13–21, Bill (mid-20s) and Betty (mid-20s)

Bill and Betty meet in a café and fall in love. What makes this scene so delicious to play is the inclusion of an offstage bell-ringer. Every time Bill or Betty make a false start, a gaffe or faux pas, the offstage bell rings. They do not acknowledge the sound of the bell, but every time it rings, it causes them to back up and start again. Everything is in the timing. Make sure you get somebody sharp to ring the bell offstage. And make sure the bell is loud enough to be heard by the audience. Keep the pace brisk. Start, Bill: "Excuse me. Is this chair taken?" End, Bill and Betty together: "Waiter!"

SWEET BIRD OF YOUTH

by Tennessee Williams (Dramatists Play Service)

Drama: Act II, Scene 2, Chance (29) and Aunt Nonnie (35–45)

Aunt Nonnie tries to get Chance to leave town before Boss Finley's henchmen hurt him. But Chance is sinking more deeply into a drug-induced haze and only wants to talk about his love for Heavenly. Start, Aunt Nonnie: "I've got just one thing to tell you, Chance. Get out of St. Cloud." End, Aunt Nonnie: "I'll write to you. Send me an address. I'll write to you." (This scene does not appear in the Dramatists Play Service acting edition, but you can find it in earlier library compilations.)

SYLVIA

by A. R. Gurney (Dramatists Play Service)

Comedy: Act I, pp. 26–30, Greg (45–55), Sylvia (a dog, 20–30)

Greg takes Sylvia for a nighttime stroll in Central Park. He speaks to her of philosophical things, which she of course does not understand. Then she sees a cat and, like dogs everywhere, wants to tear its head off. What's funny about this scene is the shift in mood from quiet philosophical conversation to the no-holds-barred profane pursuit of the cat. Start, Greg: "Know something? I'm beginning to like these late night walks, Sylvia…." End, Greg: "Surprise me, Sylvia. Surprise me."

Comedy: Act II, pp. 63–68, Greg (45–55), Sylvia (a dog, 20–30)

Greg has finally given in to his wife's demands and has arranged to give Sylvia to a family in the country. In this scene, he tells Sylvia that she has to go. Start, Greg:

"You look particularly glamorous today, Sylvia." End, Sylvia: "…After all, her majesty won't be there to object."

TAPE
by José Rivera (*Ten-Minute Plays: Volume 3 from Actors Theatre of Louisville,* Samuel French)
Comedy: One-act play, Male (any age) and Female (any age)
The setting is purgatory, a dimly lit room with nothing in it except a table, a tape recorder, a glass, and a pitcher of water. The man is there to listen to tape recordings of every lie he ever told in his life. He learns that there are ten thousand boxes of tapes. By the way, with a slight script alteration, these roles could easily be played by two actors of the same sex.

TASTE OF HONEY, A
by Shelagh Delaney (Grove Press)
Drama: Act I, Scene 1, Jo (17) and Boy (22)
Jo finds romance with a sailor. In her mind, Boy is a black prince of mysterious origins. And in Boy's mind, Jo is a delightful convenience while he is in port. They haven't been intimate yet, but they will be. A sexual charge is in the air. Written in the British vernacular. Start, Jo: "I'd better go now. Thanks for carrying my books." End, Jo: "Because you're daft."
Drama: Act II, Scene 1, Jo (17) and Geoffrey (20s)
Geoffrey, a homosexual student, has moved in with Jo to care for her during her pregnancy. As this scene begins, they've been living together for about two months, and she isn't looking forward to motherhood. Although there is no sexual attraction between Geoff and Jo, he would love to be a father. He kisses her, trying to get something started, but it is hopeless. An excellent six-page scene for two people trying to define the parameters of their relationship. Written in the British vernacular. Start, Jo: "God, it's hot." End, Jo: "I don't suppose so."
Drama: Act II, Scene 2, Jo (17) and Geoffrey (20s)
Jo, who is in her ninth month of pregnancy, is still unhappy about having a baby. Geoffrey wants to marry her, even though he is gay. Written in the British vernacular. Start, Jo: "Ninth month, everything should now be in readiness for the little stranger." End, Jo: "I think I'll give it to you, Geoff. You like babies, don't you? I might call it Number One. It'll always be number one to itself."

TENTH MAN, THE
by Paddy Chayefsky (Samuel French)
Comedy-Drama: Act III, pp. 78–82, Evelyn (18) and Arthur (30s)
As Arthur and Evelyn await final preparations for her exorcism, she tells him that she has fallen in love with him. Arthur says that this is impossible for several reasons. They've known each other for only five hours, he doesn't believe in love, and, at any rate, she is schizophrenic and doesn't know her own mind. When Evelyn insists, Arthur resists. Still, there is a very strong attraction between them. Eliminate the group of elderly Jewish men eavesdropping on this scene from an adjacent room. Start, Evelyn: "I am very frightened, Arthur." End, Evelyn: "We could be very happy if you would have faith in me."

TIME OF YOUR LIFE, THE
by William Saroyan (Samuel French)
Comedy-Drama: Act II, pp. 55–60, Joe (25–35) and Mary (25–35)
Mary is "an unhappy woman of quality and great beauty." Joe is a man trying to lead a life in which he doesn't hurt anybody. They meet in Nick's waterfront bar in 1939. Joe and Mary are attracted to one another but after this conversation in which they speak of life and philosophy, she leaves, never to return. A wonderfully poetic scene, classic Saroyan. Start, Joe: "Is it Madge—Laubowitz?" End, Joe: "Good-bye."

TOUCH OF THE POET, A
by Eugene O'Neill (Dramatists Play Service)
Drama: Act I, Nora (40) and Melody (45)
Cornelius Melody, one of Eugene O'Neill's most colorful characters, has an ambivalent relationship with Nora, his wife. He loves her deeply, but he is ashamed of her working-class roots. During this scene, Melody remembers that today is the anniversary of his war victories and decides to celebrate. Nora has a slight Irish brogue. Start, Melody: "Good morning, Nora." End, Melody: "Yes! In a while. Fifteen minutes, say. But leave me alone now."

Drama: Act I, Sara (20) and Melody (45)
Sara's contempt for her father is barely disguised when she discovers him preening in front of a mirror. She is on her way to beg Neilan the storekeeper for more credit in her father's name, resenting every moment of the humiliating task. Father and daughter discuss the possibilities of her romance with wealthy young Harford, who is recovering from an illness in an upstairs room. Melody wants them to marry so that he can get some of Harford's family money. Start, Melody: "Thank God, I still bear the unmistakable stamp of an officer and a gentleman." End, Sara: "Father! Will you never let yourself wake up—not even now when you're sober, or nearly?"

Drama: Act III, Sara (20) and Melody (45)
Still devising ways to get his hands on young Harford's family money, Melody tells Sara that he has talked to the fellow, prodding him to make a marriage commitment and a financial "settlement." Sara is, of course, outraged by this development. In this scene, Melody is supposed to be wearing his old military uniform, a garment that somewhat transforms him into the strong, daring soldier he used to be. Such a costume is rarely practical for workshops, but the actor playing this role should make some kind of appropriate substitution. Start, Sara: "You're drunk. If you think I'm going to stay here and listen to…" End, Melody: "I believe I have said all I wished to say to you. If you will excuse me, I shall join Corporal Cregan."

TOYER
by Gardner McKay (Samuel French)
This two-character, two-act drama turns on whether or not Peter is actually a serial mutilator/rapist, an actor doing a weird acting exercise, a voyeur, or all of the above. He terrorizes Maude, a psychiatrist, in her Hollywood Hills home. Peter sends her through extreme emotional peaks and valleys. First, he makes her think that she is about to die; then he tells her that he was only joking, that the

whole thing is an acting exercise, and then he seduces her. The next morning he tells her that he is in fact the real criminal after all. The later scenes are more difficult for the actress because of all the accumulating and emotionally draining transitions. Maude is alternately terrorized and relieved, to the point that she becomes disoriented.

Drama: Act I, Scene 1, pp. 14–24, Maude (30s) and Peter (20s)

Peter makes his first entrance into Maude's house. He is going to make a telephone call, and she thinks he is a strange but helpful biker who did her a favor earlier in the day. This expository scene is worth doing for the subtext it creates. Maude is wary of strangers because of the highly publicized stalker on the loose, and Peter, alias Toyer, is looking for victim number 12. Start, Peter: "This is fun." End, Maude: "I am an expert."

Drama: Act I, Scene 1, pp. 26–37, Maude (30s) and Peter (20s)

Peter has made a fake call to the police to report a voyeur. He acts as though he is going to leave and then suddenly admits that he is, in fact, the voyeur. Danger hangs in the air. Peter then tells Maude that he loves her. As a psychiatrist, Maude has firsthand knowledge of scopophilia (voyeurism), so she strikes a deal with Peter. She'll let him watch her undress if he'll leave. He agrees, and she takes off her blouse and bra, allowing him to watch in a mirror. But as Peter puts his hand on the doorknob to leave, he turns and admits that he is actually Toyer. Start, Peter: "Maybe I'd better go." End, Peter: "Yeah. Really. You sure are. Sort of."

Drama: Act II, Scene 1, pp. 37–45, Maude (30s) and Peter (20s)

This excerpt, which runs for eight pages, begins with Maude believing that Peter is Toyer. She is in fear for her life. As she emotionally collapses into tears, he jumps up gaily and says it was all a joke, that he is really only an actor doing an elaborate acting exercise. Doubtful at first, Maude slowly comes to believe him. Then, just as Peter is about to leave, he changes course again, saying that he is, after all, Toyer. Start, Peter: "I'm always touched by someone I can completely control." End, Peter: "I love you."

Drama: Act II, Scene 1, pp. 52–60, Maude (30s) and Peter (20s)

Maude has turned the lights off, grabbed a knife, and cut Peter on his arm. Suddenly, he is docile again, claiming the stunt was a joke and that he is afraid of blood. She feels sorry for him, treats his wound, and apologizes for having injured him. They drink some liquor, start dancing, undress each other, and head for the bedroom. You can eliminate the nudity from this eight-page scene. Start, Peter: "You still hate me." End, Maude (offstage): "Where are you?"

Drama: Act II, Scene 2, pp. 63–70, Maude (30s) and Peter (20s)

The next morning, Maude discovers that Peter actually is, after all, Toyer. He tries to give her an animal tranquilizer, and she pretends to drink it while she slips him some powerful tranquilizers of her own. Then she fakes the effects of the poison she supposedly ingested while he gets excited by her becoming incapacitated. As Peter starts marking Maude's neck with a magic marker, preparing to sever her spinal cord, the stuff she gave him kicks in, and he collapses. She jumps up and ties him to a chair. Now that she is utterly distraught, she decides to sever his spinal cord—just as he did to all those other women. As the curtain falls on this climactic scene, Maude is reaching for the knife. Start, Maude: "How do you like it?" End, Maude: "I'm sorry for you, Peter, dreadfully sorry for what I'm about to do."

TRIBUTE
by Bernard Slade (Samuel French)
Comedy: Act I, pp. 43–48, Maggie (mid-40s) and Scottie (51)
Scottie reluctantly shares his true feelings with Maggie, his ex-wife, about being terminally ill. She comforts him in a scene filled with laughter and tears, after which they fall into a romantic embrace. Start, Scottie: "Hello, Operator—Hi there, how are you?" End, Scottie: "Times have changed. I used to laugh you into bed."

TRIP BACK DOWN, THE
by John Bishop (Samuel French)
Drama: Act II, pp. 82–87, Bobby (37) and Barbara (39)
Depressed by the state of his life, Bobby has been driving around Mansfield. He winds up at his brother's home, where he is staying. He finds himself alone with his brother's wife, Barbara. After they commiserate, they recall how hot they used to be for each other back in their dating days. Bobby and Barbara then fall into one another's arms. At the end of the scene, it appears as if they are about to go upstairs and make love. But they don't. Start, Barbara: "What are you doing here?" End, Barbara: "Oh, Christ, I've wanted you for so long. Upstairs. All right?"

TWENTY-SEVEN WAGONS FULL OF COTTON *Volume 6*
by Tennessee Williams (*The Theater of Tennessee Williams, Volume 6*; New Directions)
Drama: Scene 2, Silva Vicarro (35–50) and Flora Meighan (35–45)
Silva Vicarro, the manager of the Syndicate Plantation, is alone on the porch with Flora Meighan, Jake's uneducated, childlike wife. She quickly lets it slip that her husband is the one who set the big fire last night, burning down Silva's cotton gin. Silva responds by cruelly seducing the woman, who behaves much like a trapped animal. The erotic buildup in this fifteen-page scene is slow and deadly, difficult to shorten, and appropriate for sophisticated actors. These characters are rural, earthy, sweaty, dusty, and raw. Start, Silva: "The good-neighbor policy!" End, Flora: "Don't follow. Please don't follow!"

TWICE AROUND THE PARK
by Murray Schisgal (Samuel French)
Comedy: "A Need for Brussels Sprouts," pp. 13–20, Margaret (40s) and Leon (50s)
Leon is a New York actor who has been practicing for an upcoming commercial audition in which he must mime an opera singer. His upstairs neighbor has complained about the volume of his opera tapes to no avail. Margaret, a police officer, knocks on the door and gives Leon a summons for disturbing the peace. It turns out that she is actually the upstairs neighbor. After the initial shock, Leon and Margaret begin to establish a relationship that, very soon, will result in true love. You'll need a recording of *Tosca* and, ideally, a recording of a dog barking. If you can't get the latter, simply omit the reference to it. Start, Margaret: "Are you the tenant of this apartment?" End, Margaret: "Margaret, Margaret Heinz."
Comedy: "A Need for Brussels Sprouts," pp. 28–33, Margaret (40s) and Leon (50s)
Margaret is role-playing with Leon. She is a judge, and he is going to testify about

his three failed marriages. Start, Leon: "Margie, all men aren't the same." End, Margaret: "If you can't stand the heat, mister, stay out of the kitchen."

Comedy: "A Need for Less Expertise," pp. 54–60, Edie (50s) and Gus (50s)

Edie and Gus have been married for twenty-six years, live on the East Side of New York, and are experiencing sexual difficulties. The main problem is that he isn't interested. Edie has been spending a great deal of money on therapy, self-help groups, and sexual-advice gurus. Today, she has convinced Gus to grudgingly follow the recorded instructions of one Dr. Oliovsky. After a while, Gus quits in disgust, and Edie begins to sulk. In this excerpt, he confronts her, and they rehash their problems. Start, Gus: "I don't know what the hell is going on. Every week, you find a reason to start a fight." End, Gus: "Be fair now, Edie. You have to be fair, too. Didn't I tell you to get a job?"

TWO ROOMS
by Lee Blessing (Dramatists Play Service)

Drama: Act I, Scene 2, pp. 16–20, Lainie Wells (30s) and Walker Harris (30s)

Walker Harris is a newspaperman who wants Lainie Wells to go public with the story of her husband's kidnapping in Beirut and her subsequent painful vigil. Although she is supposed to be showing him slides, you can substitute a photo album. Start, Lainie: "This is a hotel in Beirut near where he lives." End, Lainie: "Get out! If I want to see a scavenger, I'll go to the marsh."

TWO SMALL BODIES
by Neal Bell (Dramatists Play Service)

Drama: Act I, Scene 5, pp. 14–17, Eileen Mahoney (late 20s) and Lieutenant Brann (40s)

Lieutenant Brann has been investigating the disappearance of Eileen Mahoney's children for some time when he drops by her place for a talk. By now, she is close to the edge and fed up with his continual probing. Tension, including vaguely sexual, bristles between them. Start, Lieutenant Brann: "Nice night." End, Eileen: "Do you know what I mean?"

Drama: Act I, Scene 6, pp. 17–20, Eileen Mahoney (late 20s) and Lieutenant Brann (40s)

Lieutenant Brann changes clothes in front of Eileen Mahoney as they discuss the kidnapping of her children. This scene has more overt hostility than the previous one. You'll need a table, a tablecloth and unbreakable dishes. As written, Lieutenant Brann has to rip the tablecloth off the table, sending the dishes flying. A gun and shoulder holster would also be useful costuming. Start, Eileen: "What's that?" End, Lieutenant Brann: "That was a joke, huh? See, I'm catching on."

Drama: Act I, Scene 8, pp. 23–25, Eileen Mahoney (late 20s) and Lieutenant Brann (40s)

The investigation of her children's kidnapping is stretching Eileen Mahoney to the breaking point emotionally. Lieutenant Brann is apparently enjoying the tension. Start, Lieutenant Brann: "Let me show you something." End, Lieutenant Brann: "There are walls and walls."

Drama: Act II, Scene 1, pp. 26–39, Eileen Mahoney (late 20s) and Lieutenant Brann (40s)

Although Eileen Mahoney's lawyer advises her not to talk to Lieutenant Brann, they can't resist each other, and their relationship is becoming erotic. At one point in this scene, Eileen strips to her underwear and, at another point, she places Lieutenant Brann in handcuffs and then massages his shoulders. At the end, he tells her the police have caught her children's killer, that a man has confessed and that they have positive proof. The question is, Why doesn't Lieutenant Brann tell Eileen this at the beginning of the scene? Precisely what is the nature of their relationship? This challenging thirteen-page scene is hard to shorten because it contains transitions at several levels. It is best played by experienced actors. Start, Eileen: "Can't you knock?" End, Lieutenant Brann: "I don't know."

VALUE OF NAMES, THE
by Jeffrey Sweet (Dramatists Play Service)

Drama: One-act play, pp. 23–27, Norma Teitel (early 20s) and Leo Greshen (late 60s)

After the original director of a new play suffers a stroke, Leo Greshen replaces him. As a result, the female lead, Norma Silverman, threatens to withdraw. Leo learns that Norma is the daughter of his old crony Benny Silverman, whom he named as a communist sympathizer when testifying before the House Un-American Activities Committee during the 1950s. Leo goes to Benny's Hollywood Hills home, where Norma is staying, to convince her to remain with the production and to make up with Benny. Start, Leo: "Miss Teitel?" End, Leo: "You're a lot like him, Miss Teitel. By the way, that's a compliment."

Drama: One-act play, pp. 48–52, Norma Teitel (early 20s) and Benny Silverman (late 60s)

Norma tries to convince her father that his unwillingness to forgive Leo Greshen is self-destructive. Begin after Leo's exit. Start, Norma: "Okay, I think I've got it now." Continue to the end of the play. End, Benny: "Norma Teitel is the daughter of actor Benny Silverman."

VIEUX CARRÉ
by Tennessee Williams (New Directions)

Drama: Part II, Scene 9, Jane (20s) and Tye (25–30)

No one in the rooming house knows that Jane has leukemia, not even her lowlife lover, Tye. So when she receives word from a medical clinic that her blood count "had changed for the worse," she keeps the news to herself. In this eight-page scene, Jane orders Tye out of her life, citing two reasons. He has begun to shoot heroin again, and she has given up fashion illustration in favor of prostitution. The first reason is true, but the second one probably isn't. Jane may have toyed with the idea of prostitution, but her primary problem is the blood disease. This terrific scene, which is full of rough material and a great deal of physicality, is best suited for experienced actors. Start, Jane: "Tye, Tye, oh-Christ." End, Tye: "Yes, yes, yes, yes, yes!"

VIEW FROM THE BRIDGE, A
by Arthur Miller (Dramatists Play Service)

Drama: Act I, pp. 24–26, Eddie (40) and Beatrice (40)

Eddie is becoming increasingly jealous of the love affair that is developing between Catherine, his wife's beautiful seventeen-year-old niece, and Rodolpho, the Sicilian immigrant who is staying with the family. Since Eddie reared

Catherine from childhood, however, his relationship with her is parental, and he would never even speak of his secret lust for her. This is the first scene to expose the depth of his conflict. Eddie is so distressed by recent developments that he has stopped making love to Beatrice, his wife. She sees the situation for exactly what it is. Start, Eddie: "It's after eight." End, Eddie: "I'll be in right away. Go ahead."

Drama: Act I, pp. 29–30, Eddie (40) and Catherine (17)
Eddie finally confronts Catherine about her feelings for Rodolpho, in the course of which she admits she is in love. Eddie warns her that Rodolpho is interested in her only because, through marriage, he can become an American citizen. The truth is, however, that Eddie is jealous. Catherine begins to sob and runs into the house. Start, Catherine: "Why don't you talk to him, Eddie? He blesses you, and you don't talk to him hardly." End, Catherine: "I don't believe it and I wish to hell you'd stop it."

Drama: Act II, pp. 45–48, Catherine (17) and Rodolpho (early 20s)
Catherine and Rodolpho are very much in love, but Eddie, her guardian and surrogate father, is deeply jealous and has been trying to break them up. He warns Catherine that Rodolpho is interested in her only because, if she marries him, he'll get his U.S. citizenship. In this excellent scene, she first entertains the idea of getting married and living in Italy instead of America. When Rodolpho realizes she is questioning his love and motives, he becomes angry. Catherine knows right away that he loves her and that she was wrong to be doubtful. They fall into one another's arms and then head for the bedroom to make love for the first time. Rodolpho is an Italian immigrant, so an accent would be appropriate. Start, Catherine: "You hungry?" End, Rodolpho: "There's nobody here now. Come inside. Come…And don't cry any more."

Drama: Act II, pp. 52–54, Eddie (40) and Beatrice (40)
Eddie has made an anonymous call to the Immigration Bureau to report Rodolpho and Marco, aware that the men will be deported. It is his last resort in trying to break up the romance between Rodolpho and Catherine. Arriving home, he discovers that the lovers have moved upstairs with Mrs. Dondero. This is a disastrous development, seeing that Mrs. Dondero has two other illegal immigrants living with her, who are sure to be included in the Immigration Bureau sweep. As Eddie suffers for what he has done, Beatrice tells him that Catherine and Rodolpho are getting married right away. This news crushes Eddie even more. Start, Eddie: "Where is everybody? I says where is everybody?" End, Eddie: "I'm goin', I'm goin' for a walk."

VISIT, THE: A TRAGI-COMEDY
by Friedrich Durrenmatt (translated by Patrick Bowles, Grove Press)
Comedy-Drama: Act III, Claire (63) and Schoolmaster (40–55)
The schoolmaster tries to convince Claire to withdraw her offer of one million pounds to the citizens of the town if they'll murder Alfred Ill, the man who done her wrong many years ago. She refuses, explaining that she can make her own rules in the game of life with the money she already has. You'll have to do a little editing to make this a two-character scene. Eliminate the doctor, perhaps give his lines to the schoolmaster, and eliminate Roby and Toby. Start, Schoolmaster: "Madam." End, Claire: "Guellen for a murder, a boom for a body."

WAITING FOR LEFTY
by Clifford Odets (Dramatists Play Service)

Drama: Scene 1, "Joe and Edna," Edna (30) and Joe (30s)

In 1935, the Depression is making life tough. Joe arrives home to discover that the creditors came today and repossessed all the furniture, and that his wife is threatening to leave him for another man if he can't become a better provider for the family. The children aren't eating regularly, their shoes are worn out, and the family is about to fall two months behind in the rent. Joe argues that he is doing his best and tries to give Edna the $1.04 he earned today, but they both know it isn't enough. At the end of the scene, Joe vows to support a strike action in the hope of winning higher wages for cab drivers. Although the language is very dated now, this play is still powerful, and is unquestionably one of the most significant dramas in American theater history. Start, Joe: "Where's all the furniture, honey?" End, Joe: "I'll be back."

Drama: Scene 3, "The Young Hack and His Girl," Flor (20s) and Sid (20s)

Flor can't afford to marry Sid because he doesn't make enough as a cab driver to support them both. Furthermore, Flor's immediate family needs the nine dollars she brings home each week. Sid and Flor try to smile through their misery, but it is no use. Sid ends the scene by falling to his knees, sobbing into Flor's skirt. Start, Sid: "Hello, Florrie." End, Flor: "Hello honey. You're looking tired."

WASH, THE
by Philip Kan Gotanda (Dramatists Play Service)

Drama: Act II, Scene 8, pp. 45–47, Masi (67) and Nobu (68)

Masi and Nobu are Nisei, second-generation Japanese American, and have been married for forty-two years. But Masi left Nobu thirteen months ago, has taken up with a new man, and wants to marry him. In this excellent and tense scene, she tells Nobu that she has seen a lawyer and is filing for divorce. It is important to remember that divorce is very unusual among older-generation Nisei. Start, Masi: "I want to talk, Nobu." End, Masi: "Because I want to be happy, Nobu. I have the right to be happy."

WHO'S AFRAID OF VIRGINIA WOOLF?
by Edward Albee (Dramatists Play Service)

Drama: Act I, pp. 5–12, George (46) and Martha (52)

George and his wife, Martha, arrive home after a faculty reception and prepare to entertain Nick, the new young biology professor, and Honey, his wife, who are dropping by for late-night drinks. As the curtain goes up, George and Martha have already been drinking most of the evening and are engaged in their customary verbal sparring. This is definitely the easiest George/Martha scene for workshop use. You'll need an offstage doorbell. Begin at the top of Act I, and continue until Nick and Honey's entrance. Start, Martha: "Jesus…" End, Martha: " Screw you!"

Drama: Act II, pp. 71–75, George (46) and Martha (52)

George has completely humiliated Honey, who has once again headed for the bathroom to throw up. Nick furiously goes to comfort her, leaving George and Martha alone. The verbal warfare between the pair escalates. Begin after Nick's exit. Start, Martha: "Very good, George." George: "Thank you, Martha." Stop just before Nick reenters. End, George: "Total war?" Martha: "Total."

Drama: Act II, pp. 82–85, George (46) and Honey (26)

During the last moments of Act II, Martha humiliates George by making out with Nick in the kitchen. Honey comes out of the bathroom, weak, still drunk, and vulnerable, and George berates her. Then he gets the notion of telling Honey that his and his wife Martha's "son" has died. Begin as Honey enters, and continue to the end of the act. Start, Honey: "Bells. Ringing. I've been hearing bells." End, George: "…It's about our…son. He's dead. Can you hear me, Martha? Our boy is dead."

Drama: Act III, pp. 86–91, Martha (52) and Nick (30)

Martha took Nick to her bedroom to have sex, but he was unable to perform because he was too drunk. Now back in the living room and deep in her own alcoholic haze, Martha belittles him for his impotence and says that George is the only man who has ever made her happy. You'll need an offstage doorbell. Begin at the top of the act, and stop when George arrives with flowers. Start, Martha: "Hey, hey…Where is everybody…?" End, Nick: "Christ."

WHOSE LIFE IS IT ANYWAY?
by Brian Clark (Dramatic Publishing Company)

Drama: Act I, Ken Harrison (35–45) and Mrs. Boyle (35)

Mrs. Boyle, a medical social worker, is sent to see Ken because the hospital staff thinks he is depressed. In this first encounter between them, he tells Mrs. Boyle that he chooses not to go on living with his physical limitations. (He is paralyzed from the neck down.) Start, Mrs. Boyle: "Good morning." End, Ken: "Go…For God's sake get out…Go on…Get out…Get out."

Drama: Act I, Ken Harrison (35–45) and Dr. Scott (25–30)

Ken became angry during his meeting with the medical social worker, and the nurses had to give him oxygen to breathe. As he calms down, Dr. Scott enters to find out what is going on. During this scene, Ken tells her what it is like to still have sexual desires and not be able to act on them. Start, Dr. Scott: "And what was all the fuss about?" End, Ken: "You still have lovely breasts."

WILD HONEY
by Michael Frayn (adapted from an early, untitled play by Anton Chekhov; Samuel French)

Comedy: Act I, Scene 2, pp. 49–51, Anna Petrovna (late 20s) and Platonov (28–32)

Along with Platonov in the garden, Anna Petrovna suddenly declares her love for him. He resists, admitting his attraction to her but worried about the threat to his marriage. Start, Anna Petrovna: "And here he is. Our philosopher. Shunning us all." Stop with Platonov's exit. End, Anna Petrovna: "Intolerable man! Come back here! Misha! Misha!"

Comedy: Act II, Scene 1, pp. 61–64, Anna Petrovna (late 20s) and Platonov (28–32)

Anna Petrovna continues her attempted seduction of Platonov, and he continues to resist, although less enthusiastically now. This scene is a little stronger than their Act I encounter. Start, Anna Petrovna: "Platonov! I knew you wouldn't be asleep. How can anyone sleep on a night like this?" End, Anna Petrovna: "To the old summerhouse!" For a longer version, eliminate Sasha's offstage lines and end, Anna Petrovna: "…I'll come in and fetch you."

Comedy Act II, Scene 2, pp. 77–81, Sofya (early 20s) and Platonov (28–32)

Sofya and Platonov were lovers back in their university days but are now married to other partners. During a night of mad love and confusion three weeks ago, they started an affair. Platonov's wife, who mistakenly believes he has become involved with Anna Petrovna, left him and took the baby. Since then, he has hung around the house in something of a drunken stupor. In this scene, Sofya convinces Platonov to run away with her, an option he accepts unenthusiastically. She surprises him by saying that she has told her newlywed husband of their affair. Start, Sofya: "Platonov! Wake up!" End, Sofya: "I've got some money—we'll eat on the way. And smarten yourself up a bit for the journey!"

Comedy: Act II, Scene 2, pp. 89–95, Anna Petrovna (late 20s) and Platonov (28–32)

Anna Petrovna doesn't realize that Platonov has begun an affair with her daughter-in-law, Sofya. Anna Petrovna seeks him out, wanting to know why he hasn't been responding to her letters. Then she suggests a plan that has them running away together. Platonov, for his part, is miserable with all this romance and primarily wants to reunite with his wife. Start, Anna Petrovna: "Come here, Platonov. Why are you running away from me?" End, Anna Petrovna: "He can easily give me some of it. That's all we need, my love."

WIT
by Margaret Edson (Dramatists Play Service)

Drama: One-act play, pp. 7–12, Vivian (50) and Dr. Kelekian (50)

Begin at the very top of the play, where Vivian steps out and introduces herself to the audience. After her initial speech, we go into a flashback vignette in which Dr. Kelekian first tells Vivian that she has cancer. It is not a long scene but is worth working on because of the shock of the news and the interaction between the two. Begin, Vivian: "Hi. How are you feeling today?" End with Vivian's speech after Kelekian exits. Vivian: "That is why I chose, while a student of the great E. M. Ashford, to study Donne."

WOOLGATHERER, THE
by William Mastrosimone (Samuel French)

Comedy-Drama: Act I, pp. 5–12, Rosie (mid-20s) and Cliff (25–35)

Cliff picks up Rosie and goes back to her place, hoping for a one-night stand. The evening doesn't go as planned, however, and she turns out to be just a little bit strange. Start, Rosie: "And there was this girl…She was a poet." End, Cliff: "How would you know if the boards were up when you moved in?"

Comedy-Drama: Act I, pp. 38–45, Rosie (mid-20s) and Cliff (25–35)

Cliff gets frustrated with Rosie's avoidance of intimacy, decides that she is something of a fruit, and leaves. As he does, she asks if she can keep his sweater. Start, Cliff: "Someday I'm gonna take you cross country in my truck." End, Cliff: "Me? Cold? Hey, Rosie, you're lookin' at the only survivor of the Great Ice Age."

PART SEVEN

THREE-PERSON SCENES

ABSURD PERSON SINGULAR
by Alan Ayckbourn (Samuel French)

Comedy: Act I, pp. 29–35, Sidney (30s), Geoffrey (30s), and Ronald (40s)
On the surface, this scene is about three men in a kitchen discussing the women in the other room. It offers a kind of leering, low-ball comedy. What the scene is actually about, however, is the male pecking order. If you are careful not to underestimate playwright Alan Ayckbourn, you'll get a lot out of this material. Written in the British vernacular. Eliminate Jane's appearance at the outside window. Start, Ronald: "Ah, there you are, old chap." End, Geoffrey: "I mean face it, there's just too much good stuff wandering around simply crying out for it for you not…[Eva enters]…Anyway, I think that would be a good idea. Don't you?"

AND MISS REARDON DRINKS A LITTLE
by Paul Zindel (Dramatists Play Service)

Comedy-Drama: Act I, pp. 13–20, Anna (30s), Ceil (40s), and Catherine (40s)
Catherine and Ceil try to figure out what to do about their sister, Anna, who has had a nervous breakdown after becoming sexually involved with one of her high-school students. Anna, although distressed, frequently makes more sense than both of them. Start, Catherine: "Remember when Mama took us to St. Mary's Bazaar and we put her on that little Ferris wheel? There was only enough money for one, and Mama said she could go alone." End, Catherine: "That noise might have been just what we needed. Nowadays you need nice noises every so often—like Lebonnons Indian-wrestling under your window."

BABY DANCE, THE
by Jane Anderson (Samuel French)

Comedy: Act I, Scene 2, pp. 28–39, Rachel (30s), Wanda (late 20s), and Al (30s)
Good old boy Al returns to his trailer home to meet the Hollywood visitor he and his wife Wanda are waiting for. Rachel and her husband, Richard, have agreed to

purchase the as-yet-unborn child Wanda is carrying. The scene works on several levels: Hollywood meets Louisiana, liberalism meets bigotry, and money meets poverty. The play is billed as a drama, and the ultimate message is quite serious. The individual scenes, however, are funny. Start, Rachel: "Hello. Are you Al?" End, Rachel: "Well, Al, that's another way of looking at it."

Comedy: Act II, Scene 1, pp. 58–67, Richard (30s), Ron (30–50), and Al (30s)
Richard and his lawyer, Ron, are waiting in a Louisiana hospital for Wanda to give birth to her baby. Richard and his wife, Rachel, have agreed to purchase the child from poverty-stricken Wanda and her husband, Al. In this scene, Al arrives and tries to up the ante, asking for a new car as part of the deal. Richard balks, and a fistfight erupts. Finally, Al settles for a new set of tires. Start, Ron: "Al? Ron Davis. We talked on the phone." End, Richard: "Well, good. Thank you...Jesus, I'm exhausted."

Comedy-Drama: Act II, Scene 1, pp. 67–74, Richard (30s), Rachel (30s), and Ron (30–50)
Rachel rushes into the waiting room to announce to Richard and Ron that Wanda's baby has been born. The euphoric celebration is short-lived, however, when they learn that the baby was oxygen-deprived and may have brain damage. Rachel and Richard then decide to back out of the deal to buy the baby. Start, Richard: "Jesus, I'm exhausted." End, Richard: "Do you want to look at this?"

BABY WITH THE BATHWATER
by Christopher Durang (Dramatists Play Service)
Comedy: Act I, Scene 1, pp. 3–11, John (late 20s), Helen (late 20s), and Nanny (30–50)
John and Helen have a new baby and don't know what to do with it. In fact, they aren't even sure what gender it is. Nanny arrives from who knows where and helps out. This is outrageously surreal comedy, full of transitions that don't make much sense and wildly fluctuating emotions. Begin at the top of the scene. Start, Helen: "Hello, baby. Hello." End, Nanny: "Very well! Let's just do it in the kitchen. Come on."

BEYOND THERAPY
by Christopher Durang (Samuel French)
Comedy: Act I, Scene 6, pp. 38–53, Bruce (30–34), Bob (30–34), and Prudence (29–32)
Prudence comes to Bruce's apartment for dinner, thinking that his male lover, Bob, is out for the evening. Bob has changed his mind, however, and the romantic evening turns into a competition between Bob and Prudence for Bruce's affections, a struggle that Prudence would rather not participate in. Start, Bruce: "Hi, come on in." End, Bruce (on telephone): "Mrs. Wallace, this is Bruce, we have a bit of an emergency, I wonder if you can help...We're in desperate need of some therapy here."

BOYS' LIFE
by Howard Korder (Dramatists Play Service)
Comedy: Scene 2, pp. 8–14, Karen (late 20s), Phil (late 20s), and a Man (late 20s)
Karen and Phil unexpectedly meet at Jack's party. Phil tries to rekindle their love affair, but Karen reminds him that it was, in fact, just a one-night stand, and he hasn't called her for two months. He persists even more, inviting her to go away with him for a weekend. Karen resists at first but gradually softens. Through it all, a Man tries repeatedly to enter the bedroom where Karen and Phil are talking,

and Phil keeps shooing him out. Finally, as Karen and Phil sink onto the coats on the bed and begin some serious necking, the Man enters once again, insisting that he be allowed to retrieve his coat. Karen is suddenly embarrassed and flees from the room. Once she is gone, the Man tells Phil that he is actually Karen's date for the night. In terms of dialogue, Karen and Phil have the most, but the Man's role can be a hoot. Start, Phil: "Well, there you are." End, Man: "You want to reimburse me for cab fare or what?"

COVER
by Jeffrey Sweet with Stephen Johnson and Sandra Hastie (*25 Ten-Minute Plays from the Actors Theatre of Louisville*, Samuel French)
Comedy: One-act play, pp. 205–212, Marty (20s), Frank (20s), and Diane (20s)
Marty wants Frank to lie and tell his lady-friend Diane that the two of them were together last night, but the truth is that Marty had a date. Frank doesn't want to lie, but when Diane brings the issue up, he finds the false words coming out of his mouth. Diane sees right through him but doesn't challenge the men's story. The play, which is less than eight pages long, is interesting for the undercurrent of all the negotiations going on. Start, Marty: "Work, work, work." End, Marty: "I guess we'd better get going, hunh?"

DOUBT—A PARABLE
by John Patrick Shanley (Theatre Communications Group)
Drama: Scene 5, pp. 25–36, Sister Aloysius (50s–60s), Sister James (20s), and Father Flynn (30s)
Father Flynn comes to Sister Aloysius's office on the presumption that they are going to discuss the upcoming school Christmas pageant. Once settled in, however, the topic shifts to a charge of sexual abuse. Sister Aloysius is convinced that the priest has molested a twelve-year-old boy. Sister James herself smelled alcohol on the boy's breath after he spent time alone in the rectory with Father Flynn. Flynn is furious at the charge, which he declares false, and he provides the women with a thoroughly plausible explanation for all of that, including the alcohol smell. Sister Aloysius is hearing none of it. As far as she is concerned, he is guilty as charged. Start with Sister Aloysius on the telephone, "Hello, St. Nicholas School?…" End with Sister Aloysius on the telephone, calling the boy's parents: "…I would like you and your husband to come down here for a talk. When would be convenient?"

HEDDA GABLER
by Henrik Ibsen, Adapted by Jon Robin Baitz (Grove Press)
Drama: Act II, pp. 51–56, Hedda (25–35), George Tesman (35–45), and Eilert Lovborg (35–45)
Hedda's former lover, Eilert, arrives for a visit with Hedda and her new husband, George. Hedda and Eilert sit on a sofa and browse through photographs taken on her recent European honeymoon, but Eilert wants to talk about nothing but his feelings for her. Clearly, he hasn't gotten over her. George, meanwhile, doesn't have a clue (or maybe he does). He comes into and out of the scene serving coffee and cookies and pointing out the high points in the photographs. Start, Hedda: "Would you like to see some photographs of our trip?…" End, Hedda: "Careful! There's no point in thinking that way."

HOUSE OF RAMON IGLESIA, THE
by José Rivera (Samuel French)
Drama: Act II, Scene 1, pp. 49–57, Dolores (45), Ramon (49), and Javier (22)
The American Dream is a big bust for Dolores and Ramon, and they're trying to move back to Puerto Rico after a nineteen-year struggle in the United States. However, selling their dilapidated Long Island house involves expensive trips back and forth to Puerto Rico to untangle the title, and they are broke. In this very dynamic scene, Ramon swallows his pride and asks his eldest son, Javier, for a loan. Javier, however, is ashamed of Ramon and his peasant ways, as well as the fact that he has worked as a janitor, and refuses to help him. Start, Dolores: "I heard what he said." End, Javier: "Mom…(a knock at the door) Come in! It's open!"

MISTER ROBERTS
by Thomas Heggen and Joshua Logan (Dramatists Play Service)
Drama: Act I, Scene 2, pp. 17–25, Mister Roberts (25–32), Doc (35–40), and Ensign Pulver (20–25)
Ensign Pulver has been reading Mister Roberts's most recent request for a transfer when Roberts walks in with Doc, explaining that he just gave away their treasured bottle of scotch in an effort to have the boat ordered to a liberty port. Pulver is dismayed because he had plans for the scotch that involved a certain nurse with a red birthmark on her bottom. Doc and Roberts make a new bottle of scotch out of alcohol, Coca-Cola, and Kreml Hair Tonic. Then the conversation turns again to how much Roberts wants a transfer into battle, and Doc lights into him, explaining that he is probably already doing his best for the war effort by staying where he is. Start, Roberts: "Hey, Frank, has Dolan been in here yet with my letter?" End, Pulver: "I just threw that firecracker under your goddamn bunk."

MURDER AT THE HOWARD JOHNSON'S
by Ron Clark and Sam Bobrick (Samuel French)
Comedy: Act I, Scene 1, pp. 11–20, Arlene Miller (38), Paul Miller (40–45), and Dr. Mitchell Lovell (36)
Arlene Miller has fallen madly in love with her family dentist, Dr. Mitchell Lovell, and they have decided that she'll ask her husband, Paul, for a divorce. Anticipating that he might not give her one, however, the lovers have cooked up elaborate plans to kill him. Paul arrives at the Howard Johnson's motel room where Arlene and Mitchell are secretly waiting for him. Arlene tells him about the divorce, he refuses, and an inept attempt at murder takes place. Lots of dentist jokes and cheap laughs make this a very funny scene. Start, Paul: "Arlene!?!!" End, Arlene: "Great idea. Ever since we thought of killing you at Howard Johnson's, I've had a taste for fried clams."

ODD COUPLE, THE (MALE VERSION)
by Neil Simon (Samuel French)
Comedy: Act II, Scene 2, pp. 63–68, Cecily Pigeon (30s), Gwendolen Pigeon (30s), and Felix Unger (44)
Gwendolen and Cecily Pigeon, the British sisters who live upstairs, have come down for dinner and, maybe, some fun and games. Oscar Madison happily leaves the room to fetch some drinks, leaving his friend, Felix Unger, to momentarily

entertain Cecily and Gwendolen. Felix manages to transform a festive mood into one of utter gloom in no time at all by showing the girls pictures of his wife and children. This causes them to bemoan the loss of their own past loves. As Oscar reenters with the drinks, everybody is sitting on the sofa crying into their handkerchiefs. Start, Felix: "Er…Oscar tells me you're sisters." End, Gwendolen: "Oh dear, Oh dear, Oh dear."

OUR LADY OF THE TORTILLA
by Luis Santeiro (Dramatists Play Service)
Comedy: Act I, pp. 5–14, Aunt Dolores (50), Dahlia (49), and Nelson (early 20s)
In this scene, Nelson wants his colorful family to behave while his college girlfriend is visiting, but this is a lost cause. Aunt Dolores, who speaks with a thick Spanish accent, prays to various saints at the drop of a tortilla and maintains a working altar in the living room. Nelson's mother, Dahlia, is a flashy dresser who is currently bent on winning back her estranged husband from that "cow…with an ass that goes from here to the Lincoln Tunnel." Eliminate the radio announcer. Begin at the top of the act. Start, Dolores (singing): "Ave, Ave, Ave Maria…" End, Dahlia: "…get the pastilitos ready. I'm going to change."
Comedy: Act II, Scene 1, pp. 39–43, Dolores (50), Dahlia (49), and Eddy (mid-20s)
Aunt Dolores has discovered the face of the Virgin Mary on a tortilla shell, and now the sick, needy, and religious are crowding into the front yard wanting to share the experience. Eddie, a religious skeptic, sees a way to make a quick buck. In this scene, he tries to convince Dahlia, his mother, and his aunt, Dolores, to speak to the media. Start, Dahlia: "…get the pastilitos ready." Continue to the end of the scene. End, Eddy: "…The tortilla lady…right!"

PIZZA MAN
by Darlene Craviotto (Samuel French)
Comedy: Act II, Scene 1, pp. 46–54, Julie (late 20s), Alice (mid-20s), and Eddie (late 20s)
Eddie, the pizza-delivery man, has no idea that Julie and Alice intend to rape him. As he relaxes on the sofa, engaging in small talk, the women begin an awkward seduction—awkward because they've never done anything like this before. Start, Eddie: "So when I was in the service, I started thinking about what I wanted to do with my life." End, Eddie: "We always got extra guys to cover at night, so it's cool. I'll just drop off these two pizzas and I'll be right back."

PRELUDE TO A KISS
by Craig Lucas (Broadway Play Publishing)
Comedy: Act I, Peter (mid-20s), Rita (mid-20s), and a Waiter (any age)
Unbeknownst to Peter, his bride's body is now occupied by the soul and personality of a mysterious old man who kissed Rita at their wedding. Now on their honeymoon in Jamaica, Peter slowly realizes that something is very wrong with his bride. She suddenly can't remember the most intimate details of their lives, isn't putting salt on her food, is sleeping long hours, seems to have changed her political views, and, most significantly, has decided that she wants to have children. The role of the waiter is perfunctory but necessary to the scene. Start, Peter:

"Don't you want to try one?" End, Rita: "This is me. And maybe what you saw wasn't there at all."

Comedy: Act II, Peter (mid-20s), Rita (mid-20s), and an Old Man (70s)

In the final scene, Peter orchestrates another meeting between Rita and the Old Man in the hope that their body transformation can be reversed. He succeeds, and the play ends on a very romantic and bittersweet note. During the first part of the scene, the Old Man speaks and acts like Rita, and she like him. Midway, he begins to act like himself, and she begins to act like herself. Begin after Mrs. Boyle's exit. Start, Peter: "How've you been?" Continue to the end of the play. End, Peter: "You."

PROPOSAL, THE

by Anton Chekhov (*The Sneeze: Plays and Stories by Anton Chekhov*, translated and adapted by Michael Frayn, Samuel French)

Comedy: One-act play, pp. 93–100, Natalya Stepanovna (25), Lomov (35), and Chubukov (50s)

Lomov's marriage proposal to Natalya Stepanovna totally soured when they started arguing about whose family owns Ox Lea Meadows. He stormed out when Natalya's father, Chubukov, joined the argument, taking her side. Now everyone has calmed down, and Lomov returns to try again. Before long, however, they argue about who has the better dog. Then, overcome with anxiety, Lomov faints. In the end, though, the lovers get together. The challenge in this excerpt is to focus on the emotional roller-coaster everyone has been on just before Lomov comes back. Start, Lomov: "Terrible palpitations!…My leg's gone numb….Pain in my side…." End, Chubukov: "Champagne! Champagne! Champagne!"

RAISIN IN THE SUN, A

by Lorraine Hansberry (Samuel French)

Drama: Act I, Scene 1, pp. 20–27, Ruth (about 30), Walter (35), and Beneatha (20)

Early-morning life in this tenement apartment on Chicago's South Side is a crowded affair, especially since two families share a bathroom that is down the hall. Against the background of constant jockeying for bathroom time, Walter tells Ruth about his dream of owning a liquor store. Then Beneatha comes into the room, and they talk about her dream of being a doctor. Start, Walter: "You know what I was thinking 'bout in the bathroom this morning?" End, Ruth: "Fifty cents? Here, take a taxi."

SIGHT UNSEEN

by Donald Margulies (Dramatists Play Service)

Drama: Act II, Scene 5, pp. 37–47, Jonathan (35–45), Patricia (35–45), and Nick (40s)

Jonathan is the houseguest of his former lover and her archaeologist husband at their place in Norfolk, England. After dinner, sparks begin to fly when Nick announces that he detests Jonathan's paintings. Even worse, he considers them pornographic. Jonathan, a famous and wealthy artist, defends himself and counterattacks. Patricia, Nick's wife, is caught in the crossfire. Jonathan and Patricia are American. Nick is English and, though an educated man, comes from a rural, working-class background. His accent should reflect those origins. Start,

Jonathan: "Drive down with me tomorrow." End, Nick: "Um…shall I? Would you like me to make your bed?"

SPOILS OF WAR
by Michael Weller (Samuel French)
Drama: Act II, pp. 68–79, Elise (mid 30s), Martin (16), and Andrew (40s)

Martin has successfully engineered a meeting between Andrew and Elise, his estranged parents. However, Martin's plan turns into a disaster as they compete for his loyalty. Elise is trying to expose Andrew as the jerk she always said he was, and Andrew is trying to expose Elise as the true culprit. You'll have to cut and paste a bit, eliminating Andrew's young girlfriend, Penny, who comes in and out. Start, Andrew: "You haven't changed." End, Martin: "Everything's kind of screwy tonight. She makes you all tangled up. I know why you had to get away." For a longer version, end, Andrew: "Martin…Martin, god damn it, you're a man now, stop asking for help."

TRUE WEST
by Sam Shepard (Samuel French)
Comedy-Drama: Act I, Scene 3, pp. 19–24, Austin (early 30s), Lee (early 40s), and Saul Kimmer (late 40s)

Austin is putting the finishing touches on his deal with movie producer Saul Kimmer when his brother, Lee, comes in with a stolen television, plops it onto the kitchen counter, and proceeds to hustle Saul, wanting to pitch his own movie idea. This is a funny scene, with Lee playing out his naive idea of the Hollywood hustle while Austin is embarrassed and Saul is thrown off guard by the colorful, shabbily dressed man. Start, Saul: "Well, to tell you the truth, Austin, I have never felt so confident about a project in quite a long time." End, Austin: "Give me the keys."

PLAYS REFERENCED IN THIS BOOK

ABSENT FRIENDS (1975)
by Alan Ayckbourn

ABSURD PERSON SINGULAR (1972)
by Alan Ayckbourn

AFTER THE FALL (1964)
by Arthur Miller

AGNES OF GOD (1979)
by John Pielmeier

AH, WILDERNESS! (1933)
by Eugene O'Neill

ALL MY SONS (1947)
by Arthur Miller

AMADEUS (1979)
by Peter Shaffer

AMEN CORNER, THE (1954)
by James Baldwin

AMERI/CAIN GOTHIC (1970)
by Paul Carter Harrison

AMERICAN BUFFALO (1976)
by David Mamet

AMERICAN PLAN, THE (1990)
by Richard Greenberg

ANASTASIA (1954)
by Marcelle Maurette

ANDERSONVILLE TRIAL, THE (1959)
by Saul Levitt

AND MISS REARDON DRINKS A LITTLE (1971)
by Paul Zindel

ANGELS IN AMERICA: A GAY FANTASIA ON NATIONAL THEMES, PART I: MILLENNIUM APPROACHES (1991)
by Tony Kushner

ANNA CHRISTIE (1921)
by Eugene O'Neill

ANOTHER ANTIGONE (1988)
by A. R. Gurney, Jr.

APPROACHING ZANZIBAR (1989)
by Tina Howe

ART (1996)
by Yasmina Reza

AUTUMN GARDEN, THE (1951)
by Lillian Hellman

BABY DANCE, THE (1998)
by Jane Anderson

BABY WITH THE BATHWATER (1984)
by Christopher Durang

BAD HABITS (1971; published 1974)
by Terrence McNally

BAREFOOT IN THE PARK (1963)
by Neil Simon

BEAR, THE (1888)
by Anton Chekhov

BEAU JEST (1994)
by James Sherman

BEAUTY QUEEN OF LEENANE, THE (1996)
by Martin McDonagh

BEDROOOMS: FIVE COMEDIES (1986)
by Renée Taylor and Joseph Bologna

BELL, BOOK AND CANDLE (1951)
by John Van Druten

BENT (1978)
by Martin Sherman

BETRAYAL (1978)
by Harold Pinter

BETWEEN DAYLIGHT AND BOONVILLE (1979)
by Matt Williams

BEYOND THERAPY (1982)
by Christopher Durang

BIRDBATH (1965)
by Leonard Melfi

BIRDY (1997)
Adapted by Naomi Wallace from the 1980 William Wharton novel

BITTER SAUCE (1998)
by Eric Bogosian

BLUE WINDOW (1984)
by Craig Lucas

BORN YESTERDAY (1946)
by Garson Kanin

BOSOMS AND NEGLECT (1979)
by John Guare

BOYS' LIFE (1988)
by Howard Korder

BREAKING THE CODE (1986)
by Hugh Whitemore

BROOKLYN BOY (2004)
by Donald Margulies

BURN THIS (1987)
by Lanford Wilson

BUTLEY (1971)
by Simon Gray

CANDIDA (1903)
by George Bernard Shaw

CAT ON A HOT TIN ROOF (1955)
by Tennessee Williams

CHAPTER TWO (1977)
by Neil Simon

CHASE, THE (1952)
by Horton Foote

CHEATERS (1972)
by Michael Jacobs

CHERRY ORCHARD, THE (1904)
by Anton Chekhov

CHILDREN OF A LESSER GOD (1980)
by Mark Medoff

CHILDREN'S HOUR, THE (1934)
by Lillian Hellman

CLOSER (1997)
by Patrick Marber

COASTAL DISTURBANCES (1986)
by Tina Howe

COLORED MUSEUM, THE (1986)
by George C. Wolfe

COMANCHE CAFÉ (1976)
by William Hauptman

COME BACK, LITTLE SHEBA (1950)
by William Inge

COME BACK TO THE FIVE AND DIME, JIMMY DEAN, JIMMY DEAN (1982)
by Ed Graczyk

COUPLA WHITE CHICKS SITTING AROUND TALKING, A (1979)
by John Ford Noonan

COVER (1989)
by Jeffrey Sweet with Stephen Johnson and Sandra Hastie

CRIMES OF THE HEART (1979)
by Beth Henley

CROSSING DELANCEY (1987)
by Susan Sandler

CRUCIBLE, THE (1953)
by Arthur Miller

DANCE AND THE RAILROAD, THE (1981)
by David Henry Hwang

DANNY AND THE DEEP BLUE SEA (1983)
by John Patrick Shanley

DARK AT THE TOP OF THE STAIRS, THE (1957)
by William Inge

GETTING OUT (1977)
by Marsha Norman

GINGERBREAD LADY, THE (1970)
by Neil Simon

GIRL ON THE VIA FLAMINIA, THE (1954)
by Alfred Hayes

GLASS MENAGERIE, THE (1944)
by Tennessee Williams

GLENGARRY GLEN ROSS (1984)
by David Mamet

GOAT, THE (2000)
by Edward Albee

GOLDEN BOY (1937)
by Clifford Odets

GOOSE AND TOMTOM (1986)
by David Rabe

HATFUL OF RAIN, A (1955)
by Michael V. Gazzo

HEDDA GABLER (1890)
by Henrik Ibsen

HEIDI CHRONICLES, THE (1989)
by Wendy Wasserstein

HELLO AND GOODBYE (1965)
by Athol Fugard

HELLO OUT THERE (1941)
by William Saroyan

HERE WE ARE (1931)
by Dorothy Parker

HOOTERS (1978)
by Ted Tally

HOUSE OF BLUE LEAVES, THE (1971)
by John Guare

HOUSE OF RAMON IGLESIA, THE (1986)
by José Rivera

HOW I LEARNED TO DRIVE (1997)
by Paula Vogel

HURLYBURLY (1984)
by David Rabe

HUSBANDRY (1984)
by Patrick Tovatt

I AM A CAMERA (1951)
by John Van Druten

I HATE HAMLET (1981)
by Paul Rudnick

IMMIGRANT, THE (1990)
by Mark Harelik

IMPASSIONED EMBRACES (1989)
by John Pielmeier

IMPORTANCE OF BEING EARNEST, THE (1895)
by Oscar Wilde

INDEPENDENCE (1984)
by Lee Blessing

I NEVER SANG FOR MY FATHER (1967)
by Robert Anderson

IN THE BOOM BOOM ROOM (1973)
by David Rabe

I OUGHT TO BE IN PICTURES (1980)
by Neil Simon

ISN'T IT ROMANTIC? (1983)
by Wendy Wasserstein

I STAND BEFORE YOU NAKED (1992)
by Joyce Carol Oates

IT HAD TO BE YOU (1982)
by Renée Taylor and Joe Bologna

JAR THE FLOOR (1997)
by Cheryl West

JOE TURNER'S COME AND GONE (1986)
by August Wilson

JOINED AT THE HEAD (1992)
by Catherine Butterfield

K2 (1982)
by Patrick Meyers

KATHY AND MO SHOW, THE: PARALLEL LIVES (1989)
by Mo Gaffney and Kathy Najimy

KEELY AND DU (1993)
by Jane Martin

KEY EXCHANGE (1986)
by Kevin Wade

KILLER JOE (1995)
by Tracy Letts

LADY AND THE CLARINET, THE (1980)
by Michael Cristofer

LANDSCAPE OF THE BODY (1978)
by John Guare

LARGO DESOLATO (1985)
by Václav Havel (adapted by Tom Stoppard, 1986)

MOON FOR THE MISBEGOTTEN, A (1957)
by Eugene O'Neill

MRS. DALLY HAS A LOVER (1962)
by William Hanley

MRS. WARREN'S PROFESSION (1898)
by George Bernard Shaw

MURDER AT THE HOWARD JOHNSON'S (1979)
by Ron Clark and Sam Bobrick

NATURE AND PURPOSE OF THE UNIVERSE, THE (1975)
by Christopher Durang

NERD, THE (1980)
by Larry Shue

'NIGHT, MOTHER (1982)
by Marsha Norman

NIGHT OF THE IGUANA, THE (1961)
by Tennessee Williams

NORMAN CONQUESTS, THE—TABLE MANNERS (1973)
by Alan Ayckbourn

NOT ENOUGH ROPE (1962)
by Elaine May

NUMBER, A (2002)
by Caryl Churchill

NUTS (1980)
by Tom Topor

ODD COUPLE, THE (FEMALE VERSION) (1985)
by Neil Simon

ODD COUPLE, THE (ORIGINAL VERSION) (1965)
by Neil Simon

OF MICE AND MEN (1937)
by John Steinbeck

OH DAD, POOR DAD, MAMMA'S HUNG YOU IN THE CLOSET AND I'M FEELIN' SO SAD (1960)
by Arthur Kopit

OLD TIMES (1971)
by Harold Pinter

OLEANNA (1992)
by David Mamet

ON GOLDEN POND (1978)
by Ernest Thompson

ONLY GAME IN TOWN, THE (1968)
by Frank D. Gilroy

ON THE OPEN ROAD (1992)
by Steve Tesich

OPEN ADMISSIONS (1984)
by Shirley Lauro

ORPHANS (1983)
by Lyle Kessler

OTHER PEOPLE'S MONEY (1989)
by Jerry Sterner

OTHERWISE ENGAGED (1975)
by Simon Gray

OUR LADY OF THE TORTILLA (1987)
by Luis Santeiro

PAINTING CHURCHES (1983)
by Tina Howe

PHILADELPHIA STORY, THE (1939)
by Philip Barry

PIANO LESSON, THE (1989)
by August Wilson

PICNIC (1953)
by William Inge

PILLOWMAN, THE (2003)
by Martin McDonagh

PIZZA MAN (1991)
by Darlene Craviotto

PLAY MEMORY (1984)
by Joanna M. Glass

PORCH (1979)
by Jeffrey Sweet

PRELUDE TO A KISS (1988)
by Craig Lucas

PRIMARY ENGLISH CLASS, THE (1976)
by Israel Horovitz

PRISONER OF SECOND AVENUE, THE (1971)
by Neil Simon

PRIVATE LIVES (1931)
by Noel Coward

PROMISE, THE (1994)
by José Rivera

PROOF (1998)
by David Auburn

TAKE ME OUT (2002)
by Richard Greenberg

TAKEN IN MARRIAGE (1979)
by Thomas Babe

TALKING WITH... (1982)
by Jane Martin

TAPE (1993)
by José Rivera

TASTE OF HONEY, A (1958)
by Shelagh Delaney

TENTH MAN, THE (1959)
by Paddy Chayefsky

THAT CHAMPIONSHIP SEASON (1972)
by Jason Miller

TIME OF YOUR LIFE, THE (1939)
by William Saroyan

TOPDOG/UNDERDOG (2001)
by Suzan-Lori Parks

TOP GIRLS (1982)
by Caryl Churchill

TOUCH OF THE POET, A (written 1942; produced 1958)
by Eugene O'Neill

TOYER (1994)
by Gardner McKay

TOYS IN THE ATTIC (1960)
by Lillian Hellman

TRIBUTE (1978)
by Bernard Slade

TRIP BACK DOWN, THE (1975)
by John Bishop

TRUE WEST (1980)
by Sam Shepard

TWENTY-SEVEN WAGONS FULL OF COTTON (1945)
by Tennessee Williams

TWICE AROUND THE PARK (1982)
by Murray Schisgal

TWO ROOMS (1988)
by Lee Blessing

TWO SMALL BODIES (1977)
by Neal Bell

VALUE OF NAMES, THE (1982)
by Jeffrey Sweet

VIEUX CARRÉ (1977)
by Tennessee Williams

VIEW FROM THE BRIDGE, A (1955)
by Arthur Miller

VISIT, THE: A TRAGI-COMEDY (1956)
by Friedrich Durrenmatt

VITAL SIGNS (1990)
by Jane Martin

WAITING FOR LEFTY (1935)
by Clifford Odets

WAITING FOR THE PARADE (1977)
by John Murrell

WASH, THE (1985)
by Philip Kan Gotanda

WHAT I DID LAST SUMMER (1975; published 1983)
by A. R. Gurney, Jr.

WHO'S AFRAID OF VIRGINIA WOOLF? (1962)
by Edward Albee

WHOSE LIFE IS IT ANYWAY? (1978)
by Brian Clark

WILD HONEY (1984)
by Michael Frayn

WIT (1998)
by Margaret Edson

WOMEN, THE (1937)
by Clare Boothe Luce

WOOLGATHERER, THE (1979)
by William Mastrosimone

ZOOMAN AND THE SIGN (1979)
by Charles Fuller

ZOO STORY, THE (1958; produced 1960)
by Edward Albee

BOOKSELLERS SPECIALIZING IN PLAYS

While using this book, hopefully some of the plays will spark your interest and you will want to go out and get the full-length versions. My suggestion is to get the "acting edition" instead of the "library edition," if possible. In addition to the text of the play, acting editions also have the blocking that was used in the original production, and may also have other helpful production notes. In this book, I have referenced acting editions wherever possible.

Your local library may have a well-stocked theater/drama section. Just watch out for condensed compilation versions of the plays rather than full-length texts. Library editions of plays are often laid out differently than acting editions. So even if you are using a public library, do your best to get hold of an acting edition of the play rather than a library edition.

If you can't find the plays I've recommended at your local library, local bookstore, or at Amazon.com, you'll be sure to find them at the places listed below:

The Drama Book Shop, Inc.
250 West 40th St.
New York, NY 10018
Tel: 212-944-0595
http://www.dramabookshop.com
The Drama Book Shop specializes in the acting edition of plays.

Samuel French Theater & Film
7623 W. Sunset Blvd.
Los Angeles, CA 90046
Tel: 323-876-0570
http://www.samuelfrench.com
Similar to The Drama Book Shop, Samuel French specializes in the
    acting edition of plays.

The Internet Theatre Bookshop
http://www.stageplays.com/
(trades in U.S. dollars)

http://www.stageplays.co.uk/
(trades in British pounds)
This online company is set up to find plays in both the United States
    and the United Kingdom.

INDEX

Male Monologues

COMEDY

COMEDY-DRAMA

DRAMA

Female Monologues

COMEDY

COMEDY-DRAMA

DRAMA

Male/Male Scenes

COMEDY

COMEDY-DRAMA

DRAMA

Female/Female Scenes

Male/Female Scenes

COMEDY